THE BHAGAVAD GITA

THE BHAGAVAD GITA

WITH THE COMMENTARY OF *SHRI SANKARACHARYA*

TRANSLATOR: ALLADI MAHADEVA SASTRY

Published by

FacsiMile Publisher
12 Pragati Market
Ashok Vihar, Ph-2
Delhi - 110052, India
Phone: 011-47034999
Email: www.facsimilepublishers.com
info@facsimilepublishers.com

Distribution Network
gyanbooks.com
India, USA, Canada, UK, Australia

ISBN: 978-93-6168-490-6 (HB)
First Published, 1897

2nd Impression 2025

Printed at: Gyan Press, Delhi.

THE BHAGAVAD GITA
Author: TRANSLATOR: ALLADI MAHADEVA SASTRY

THE BHAGAVAD GITA

WITH THE COMMENTARY OF

SRI SANKARACHARYA

Translated from
the original Sanskrit into English
By

ALLADI MAHADEVA SASTRY

समत्वं योग उच्यते

SAMATA BOOKS
MADRAS

First Published 1897. Successive editions 1901, 1918, 1947, 1961, 1972. 7th edition 1977 with the kind co-operation of Sri S. T. Ramalingam, Official Trustee administering the Vavilla Venkateswara Sastrulu Trust.

Published by V. Sadanand
The Personal Bookshop
10, Kamaraj Bhavan, 111, Mount Road
Madras 600 006 India

Printed at All India Press
Pondicherry India

PUBLISHER'S NOTE

Sri Sankaracharya's is the earliest extant commentary on the Bhagavad Gita. He explained the need for his commentary thus:-

> "This famous Gita-Sastra is an epitome of the essentials of the whole Vedic teaching; and its meaning is very difficult to understand. Though, to afford a clear view of its teaching, it has been explained word by word and sentence by sentence, and its import critically examined by several commentators, still I have found that to the laity it appears to teach diverse and quite contradictory doctrines. I propose, therefore, to write a brief commentary with a view to determine its precise meaning."

The text of the Gita as cited by Sankara has come down the centuries as the authentic text and this commentary of his has proved to be of seminal value ever since.

Its translation into English by Sri Alladi Mahadeva Sastri has stood the test of time since its first publication in 1897, being the only English translation of Sankara's Gita Bhashya available for 80 years. The late Pandit Mahadeva Sastri was Director, Oriental Section Adyar Library, Curator, Government Oriental Library, Mysore and Fellow of the Theosophical Society. He has also translated Sankara's commentary on Taittiriya Upanishad and Amritabindu, Dakshinamurti Stotra, Pranava Vartika and Dakshinamurti Upanishad besides editing 4 out of 5 volumes of Minor Upanishads for the Adyar Library.

We consider it a privilege and a Blessing to issue this famous book as our first publication.

CONTENTS

INTRODUCTION.

First Discourse.

THE DESPONDENCY OF ARJUNA.

Second Discourse.

SANKHYA-YOGA.

Fourth Discourse.

JNANA-YOGA.

Fifth Discourse.

SAMNYASA-YOGA.

Sixth Discourse.

DHYANA-YOGA.

Seventh Discourse.

VIJNANA-YOGA.

Eighth Discourse.

ABHYASA-YOGA.

Ninth Discourse.

SOVEREIGN WISDOM AND SECRET.

Twelfth Discourse.

BHAKTI-YOGA.

Thirteenth Discourse.

MATTER AND SPIRIT.

Fourteenth Discourse.

THE THREE GUNAS.

Fifteenth Discourse.

THE SUPREME SPIRIT.

Sixteenth Discourse.

SPIRITUALITY AND MATERIALISM.

Seventeenth Discourse.

THE THREEFOLD FAITH.

Eighteenth Discourse.

CONCLUSION.

अथ श्रीमद्भगवद्गीता ।

अथ गीतामाहात्म्यम् ।

श्रीगणेशाय नमः । श्रीराधारमणाय नमः ।

धरा उवाच–

भगवन् परमेशान भक्तिरव्यभिचारिणी ।
प्रारब्धं भुज्यमानस्य, कथं भवति, हे प्रभो । १ ।

विष्णुः उवाच—

प्रारब्धं भुज्यमानो हि गीताभ्यासरतः सदा ।
स मुक्तः, स सुखी, लोके, कर्मणा नोपलिप्यते । २ ।
महापापादिपापानि गीताध्यानं करोति चेत् ।
क्वचित् स्पर्शं न कुर्वन्ति नलिनीदलमम्बुवत् । ३ ।
गीतायाः पुस्तकं यत्र, यत्र पाठः प्रवर्तते ।
तत्र सर्वाणि तीर्थानि प्रयागादीनि, तत्र वै ।
सर्वे देवाश्च, ऋषयः, योगिनः, पन्नगाश्च ये ।
गोपालाः गोपिकाः वापि, नारदोद्धवपार्षदैः (सह) । ४-५ ।
सहायो जायते शीघ्रं यत्र गीता प्रवर्तते ।
यत्र गीताविचारश्च, पठनं, पाठनं, श्रुतम् ।
तत्राहं निश्चितं, पृथ्वि, निवसामि सदैव हि । ६ ।
गीताश्रयेऽहं तिष्ठामि, गीता मे चोत्तमं गृहम् ।
गीताज्ञानमुपाश्रित्य, त्रीन् लोकान् पालयाम्यहम् । ७ ।
गीता मे परमा विद्या ब्रह्मरूपा, न संशयः ।
अर्धमात्राक्षरा नित्या, स्वनिर्वाच्यपदात्मिका । ८ ।
चिदानन्देन कृष्णेन प्रोक्ता स्वमुखतोऽर्जुनम् ।
वेदत्रयी, परानन्दा, तत्त्वार्थज्ञानसंयुता । ९ ।
योऽष्टादश (अध्यायान्) जपेन्नित्यं नरो निश्चलमानसः ।
ज्ञानसिद्धिं स लभते, ततो याति परं पदम् । १० ।

पाठे समग्रेऽसंपूर्णे ततोऽर्धं पाठमाचरेत्।
तदा गोदानजं पुण्यं लभते नात्र संशयः। ११।
त्रिभागं पठमानः तु गङ्गास्नानफलं लभेत्।
षडंशं जपमानः तु सोमयागफलं लभेत्। १२।
एकाध्यायं तु यो नित्यं पठते भक्तिसंयुतः।
रुद्रलोकमवाप्नोति, गणो भूत्वा वसेत् चिरम्। १३।
अध्यायं, श्लोकपादं वा, नित्यं यः पठते नरः।
स याति नरतां, यावत् मन्वन्तरं, वसुंधरे। १४।
गीतायाः श्लोकदशकं, सप्त, पञ्च, चतुष्टयम्।
द्वौ, त्रीनेकं, तदर्धं वा श्लोकानां, यः पठेत् नरः। १५।
चन्द्रलोकमवाप्नोति वर्षाणामयुतं ध्रुवम्।
गीतापाठसमायुक्तः मृतो, मानुषतां व्रजेत्। १६।
गीताभ्यासं पुनः कृत्वा, लभते मुक्तिमुत्तमाम्।
गीतेत्युच्चारसंयुक्तो म्रियमाणो गतिं लभेत्। १७।
गीतार्थश्रवणासक्तो, महापापयुतोऽपि वा।
वैकुण्ठं समवाप्नोति, विष्णुना सह मोदते। १८।
गीतार्थं ध्यायते नित्यं, कृत्वा कर्माणि भूरिशः।
जीवन्मुक्तः स विज्ञेयः, देहान्ते परमं पदम्। १९।
गीतामाश्रित्य बहवः भूभुजो जनकादयः।
निर्धूतकल्मषा लोके गीता याताः परं पदम्। २०।
गीतायाः पठनं कृत्वा, माहात्म्यं नैव यः पठेत्।
वृथा पाठो भवेत् तस्य, श्रमः एव ह्युदाहृतः। २१।
एतन्माहात्म्यसंयुक्तं गीताभ्यासं करोति यः।
सः तत्फलमवाप्नोति, दुर्लभां गतिमाप्नुयात्। २२।

सूत उवाच–

माहात्म्यमेतद्गीतायाः, मया प्रोक्तं सनातनम्।
गीतान्ते च पठेद् यस्तु, यदुक्तं तत् फलं लभेत्। २३।

इति श्रीवाराहपुराणे श्रीगीतामाहात्म्यं संपूर्णम्।

अथ गीताध्यानम् ।

ॐ पार्थाय प्रतिबोधितां भगवता नारायणेन स्वयं,

व्यासेन ग्रथितां पुराणमुनिना मध्ये महाभारतम् ।

अद्वैतामृतवर्षिणीं भगवतीमष्टादशाध्यायिनीम्,

अम्ब, त्वामनुसंदधामि, भगवद्गीते, भवद्वेषिणीम् । १ ।

नमोऽस्तु ते, व्यास, विशालबुद्धे, फुल्लारविन्दायतपत्रनेत्र ।

येन त्वया भारततैलपूर्णः प्रज्वालितो ज्ञानमयः प्रदीपः । २ ।

प्रपन्नपारिजाताय तोत्रवेत्रैकपाणये ।

ज्ञानमुद्राय कृष्णाय गीतामृतदुहे नमः । ३ ।

सर्वोपनिषदो गावो, दोग्धा गोपालनन्दनः ।

पार्थो वत्सः, सुधीर्भोक्ता, दुग्धं गीतामृतं महत् । ४ ।

वसुदेवसुतं देवं, कंसचाणूरमर्दनम् ।

देवकीपरमानन्दं कृष्णं वन्दे जगद्गुरुम् । ५ ।

भीष्मद्रोणतटा, जयद्रथजला, गांधारनीलोपला,

शल्यग्राहवती, कृपेण वहनी; कर्णेन वेलाकुला ।

अश्वत्थामविकर्णघोरमकरा, दुर्योधनावर्तिनी,

सोत्तीर्णा खलु पाण्डवै रणनदी, कैवर्तकै केशवे । ६ ।

पाराशर्यवचःसरोजममलं, गीतार्थगन्धोत्कटं,

नानाख्यानककेसरं, हरिकथासंबोधनाबोधितम् ।

लोके सज्जनषट्पदैरहरहः पेपीयमानं मुदा,

भूयाद् भारतपङ्कजं कलिमलप्रध्वंसि नः श्रेयसे । ७ ।

मूकं करोति वाचालं, पङ्गुं लङ्घयते गिरिम् ।

यत्कृपा, तमहं वन्दे परमानन्दमाधवम् । ८ ।

यं ब्रह्मावरुणेन्द्ररुद्रमरुतः स्तुन्वन्ति दिव्यैः स्तवैः,

वेदैः साङ्गपदक्रमोपनिषदैर्गायन्ति यं सामगाः ।

ध्यानावस्थिततद्गतेन मनसा पश्यन्ति यं योगिनो,

यस्यान्तं न विदुः सुरासुरगणा देवाय तस्मै नमः । ९ ।

इति ध्यानम् ।

THE BHAGAVAD-GITA

WITH

SRI SANKARACHARYA'S COMMENTARY

INTRODUCTION

Nârâyana is beyond the Avyakta ;
From the Avyakta the Mundane Egg is born ;
Within the Mundane Egg, verily, are these worlds
And the Earth made up of the seven Dvîpas.

[This is a paurânic verse speaking of the Antaryâmin, the Inner Guide and Regulator of all souls. It is quoted here by the commentator in order that he may begin his important work, after the orthodox fashion, with the contemplation of his favourite God (Ishta-Devatâ), namely, Nârâyana, and further with a view to shew that the Purâna (archaic history), the Itihâsa (ancient tradition) and the Gîtâ teach one and the same doctrine. Nârâyana is, in the popular conception, the Creator who was brooding over the waters just before the beginning of Creation. Cf. Manu I. 10. According to a subtler conception, Nârâyana is the Antaryâmin, the Divine Being in whom all embodied souls have their being. He is not a creature of the Avyakta, but far transcends it. It is the Avyakta,—the Avyâkrita, Mâyâ, the undifferentiated matter,—out of which, when in apparent union with Isvara, is evolved the principle of Hiranyagarbha, here spoken of as Anda or the Mundane Egg, which is composed of the five simple rudimental elements of matter. An intermingling of the five rudimental elements of matter gives rise to the principle of the Virâj, of which are formed the Earth and all the other *lokas* or inhabited regions—(*Anandagiri*). The seven Dvîpas or insular continents are Jambû, Plaksha, Kusa. Krauncha, Sâka, Sâlmala and Pushkara. For further particulars regarding these, see Wilson's Vishnupurâna, *Vol.* 1, *p. 109* ff.]

The twofold Vedic Religion

The Lord created the universe, and wishing to secure order therein He first created the Prajâpatis* (Lords of creatures) such as Marîchi and caused them to adopt the Pravritti-Dharma, the Religion of Works. He then created others such as Sanaka and Sanandana † and caused them to adopt the Nivritti-Dharma, the Religion of Renunciation, characterised by knowledge and indifference to worldly objects. It is the twofold Vedic Religion of Works and Renunciation that maintains order in the universe. This Religion which directly leads to liberation and worldly prosperity has long ‡ been practised by all castes and religious orders (varna-âsrama) —from the brâhmanas downwards,—who sought welfare.

The purpose of the Divine Incarnation

When, owing to the ascendancy of lust in its votaries, religion was overpowered by irreligion caused by the vanishing faculty of discrimination, and irreligion was advancing,—it was

* They are ten in number, *Cf. Manu III, 34, 35*. Authorities differ as to their names and number. See Wilson's Vishnupurâna, Vol. I pp. 100—102.

† They were ' without desire or passion, inspired with holy wisdom, estranged from the universe and undesirous of progeny.' See Vishnupurâna, Part I, Ch. VII. The authorities differ as to their names and number ; see Wilson's V. P., Vol. I. pp. 77—78. These, declining to create progeny, remained—as the name of the first, Sanatkumâra, implies—*ever boys, Kumâras*, that is, ever pure and innocent.

‡ The words ' dirghena kâlena ' (meaning a long time) in the Com. are also construed, as an alternative interpretation, wiih the next following sentence. Then it means ' a long time after, ' *i.e.*, when the Krita and the Tretâ Yugas had been over and the Dvâpara-Yuga was approaching its end.—(A).

then that the original Creator (Adi-kartri), Vishnu, known as Nârâya*n*a, wishing to maintain order in the universe, incarnated* Himself as Krish*n*a, begotten in Devaki by Vasudeva, for the preservation of the 'earthly Brahman' † of spiritual life (Brahmanatva) on the earth. For it was by the preservation of spiritual life that the Vedic Religion could be preserved, since thereon depend all distinctions ‡ of caste and religious order. The Lord, always possessed as He is of (infinite) knowledge, supremacy, power, strength, might and vigour, controls the Maya,—belonging to Him as Vish*n*u,—the Mûla-prak*r*iti, the First Cause, composed of three Gu*n*as § or energies, and He appears to the world as though He is born and embodied and helping the world at large; whereas really He is unborn and indestructible, is the Lord of creatures, and is by nature Eternal, Pure, Intelligent and Free

[The special stress laid here on Maya as belonging to and being under the control of the I*s*vara is chiefly intended

---

* The words in the Com. corresponding to this are 'a*m*sena sambabhûva,' As a*m*sa means a part, it would mean that K*r*ish*n*a was a partial incarnation of God Vish*n*u. But of the several forms of the incarnation of God, K*r*ish*n*a is on all hands recognised as a *full* incarnation of Vish*n*u. Accordingly, *A*nandagiri explains 'a*m*sena' to mean 'svechchhânirmitena-mâyâmayena svarûpe*n*a,' that is, 'in an illusory form created by His own will.

† The Commentator here refers to the following passage:

यं देवं देवकीदेवी वसुदेवादजीजनत् ।
भौमस्य ब्रह्मणो गुप्त्यै दीप्तमग्निमिवारणिः ॥

"That God whom Lady Devaki begot by Vasudeva for the preservation of the earthly Brahman................................" (Sânti-parva, 47th Adhyâya.) "*Earthly Brahman*" is explained by Nilaka*n*tha to mean 'the Vedas, the brâhma*n*as, and yag*n*as or sacrifices.

‡ Kshatriyas and others require the help of the brâhma*n*as, the spiritual class, in the performance of sacred rites and in the study of Scriptures.—(A.)

§ For a full description of the Gu*n*as see xiv. 5 *et. seq*.

to impress the idea that Maya does not exist or act independently of Brahman, the Isvara. He is quite independent of Maya, unlike the individual souls who are subject to its influence. The followers of the historical school of the Sankhya-darsana hold, on the other hand, that Matter and Spirit, Prak*r*iti and Purusha, are two distinct principles, the former being as real as the latter and acting in unison with it.—(A.]

Without any interest of His own, but with the sole intention of helping His creatures, He taught to Arjuna, who was deeply plunged in the ocean of grief and delusion. the towfold Vedic Religion, evidently thinking that the Religion would widely spread when accepted and practised by men of high character.

The Gita and the Commentary

It is this Religion, which was taught by the Lord, that the omniscient and adorable Veda-Vyasa (the arranger of the Vedas) embodied in the seven hundred verses called Gitas.

This famous Gîta-*S*astra is an epitome of the essentials of the whole Vedic teaching; and its meaning is very difficult to understand. Though, to afford a clear view of its teaching, it has been explained word by word and sentence by sentence, and its import critically examined by several commentators, still I have found that to the laity it appears to teach diverse and quite contradictory doctrines. I propose, therefore, to write a brief commentary with a view to determine its precise meaning.

Jnana-Yoga is the means to the Supreme Bliss

The aim of this famous Gîta-*S*astra is, briefly, the Supreme Bliss, a complete cessation of sa*m*sara or transmigratory life and of its cause. This accrues from that Religion (Dharma) which consists in a steady devotion to the knowledge of the Self, preceded by the renunciation of all works. So with reference to this Religion, the doctrine of the Gita, the Lord says in the Anu-Gita* as follows:

> "That religion, indeed, is quite sufficient for the realisation of the state of Brahman, the Absolute." (Asv. Parva xvi. 12.)

In the same place it is also said:

> "He is without merit and without sin, without weal and woe,—he who is absorbed in the One Seat, silent and thinking nothing."

And He also says:

> "Knowledge is characterised by renunciation." (*I bid* xliii. 26.)

Here also at the end Arjuna is thus exhorted:

> "Abandoning all dharmas, come to Me alone for shelter." (xviii. 66.)

How Karma-Yoga is a means to the Supreme Bliss

Though the Religion of Works,—which, as a means of attaining worldly prosperity, is enjoined on the several castes and religious orders,– leads the devotee to the region of the Devas and the like, still, when practised in a spirit of complete devotion to the Lord and without regard to the (immediate) results, it conduces to the purity of the mind (sattva-suddhi). The man whose mind is pure is competent to tread the path of knowledge, and to him comes knowledge; and thus (indirectly)

* This forms part of the Asvamedhaparva and is contained in chapters 16-51 of that parva or section. It professes to be a sort of recapitulation of the teaching of the Bhagavad-Gîtâ. Sometime after the fratricidal war was over, Arjuna requested K*r*ish*n*a "to repeat the instruction which had been conveyed to him on the holy field of Kurukshetra, but which had gone out of his degenerate mind. K*r*ish*n*a thereupon protested that He was not equal to a verbatim recapitulation of the Bhagavad-gîtâ, but agreed, in lieu of that, to impart to Arjuna the same instruction in other words through the medium of a certain ancient story."—See *Sacred Books of the East*, Vol. VIII, pp. 197—198.

the Religion of Works forms also a means to the Supreme Bliss. Accordingly, with this very idea in mind, the Lord says:

> " He who does actions, placing them in Brahman," ......" Yogins perform actions, without attachment, for the purification of the self." (v. 10, 11).

The specific subject and object of the Gita-Sastra

The Gita Sastra expounds this twofold Religion, whose aim is the Supreme Bliss. It expounds specially the nature of the Supreme Being and Reality known as Vasudeva, the Parabrahman, who forms the subject of the discourse. Thus* the Gita-Sastra treats of a specific subject with a specific object and bears a specific relation (to the subject and object). A knowledge of its teaching leads to the realisation of all human aspirations. Hence my attempt to explain it.

---

* It is considered incumbent on a commentator to state, before commenting on a work, the subject and the object, as well as the class of persons for whom it is intended, and the relation in which it stands to the three severally. Here the subject is the Para-Brahman; the object is Salvation, Moksha. It is intended for those who seek deliverance from the turmoil of sa*m*sâra. It is related to the subject as an exposition thereof, and to the object as a means of attaining it.

ॐ

FIRST DISCOURSE

THE DESPONDENCY OF ARJUNA

Samjaya narrates the course of the war

धृतराष्ट्र उवाच :—

धर्मक्षेत्रे कुरुक्षेत्रे समवेता युयुत्सवः ।

मामकाः पाण्डवाश्चैव किमकुर्वत सञ्जय ॥ १ ॥

Dh*r*itarāsh*t*ra said :

1. What did Pâ*nd*u's sons and mine do when they assembled together on the sacred plain of Kurukshetra, eager for battle, O Sa*m*jaya ?

सञ्जय उवाच :—

दृष्ट्वा तु पाण्डवानीकं व्यूढं दुर्योधनस्तदा ।

आचार्यमुपसंगम्य राजा वचनमब्रवीत् ॥ २ ॥

Sa*m*jaya said :

2. Having seen the army of the Pâ*nd*avas drawn up in battle-array, prince Duryodhana then approached his teacher and spoke (these) words :

Duryodhana addresses Drona

पश्यैतां पाण्डुपुत्राणामाचार्य महतीं चमूम् ।

व्यूढां द्रुपदपुत्रेण तव शिष्येण धीमता ॥ ३ ॥

3. "O teacher, look at this grand army of the sons of Pâ*nd*u, marshalled by thy talented pupil, the son of Drupada.

अत्र शूरा महेष्वासा भीमार्जुनसमा युधि ।
युयुधानो विराटश्च द्रुपदश्च महारथः ॥ ४ ॥

4. "Here are heroes, mighty archers, equal in battle to Bhîma and Arjuna,—Yuyudhâna, Virâta, and Drupada, the master of a great car (mahāratha).*

धृष्टकेतुश्चेकितानः काशिराजश्च वीर्यवान् ।
पुरुजित्कुन्तिभोजश्च शैब्यश्च नरपुङ्गवः ॥ ५ ॥

5. "Dhrishtaketu, Chekitâna, and the valiant king of Kâsi, Purujit and Kunti-Bhoja and that eminent man Saibya;

युधामन्युश्च विक्रान्त उत्तमौजाश्च वीर्यवान् ।
सौभद्रो द्रौपदेयाश्च सर्व एव महारथाः ॥ ६ ॥

6. "The heroic Yudhâmanyu and the brave Uttamaujas; the son of Subhadrâ and the sons of Draupadî, all masters of great cars (mahârathas).

अस्माकं तु विशिष्टा ये तान्निबोध द्विजोत्तम ।
नायका मम सैन्यस्य संज्ञार्थं तान्ब्रवीमि ते ॥ ७ ॥

7. "But know, O best of the twice-born, who are the most distinguished among us, the leaders of my army; these I name to thee by way of example.

* Technically, mahâratha means a 'warrior proficient in military science who single-handed can fight a thousand archers.'

भवान्भीष्मश्च कर्णश्च कृपश्च समितिञ्जयः ।
अश्वत्थामा विकर्णश्च सौमदत्तिस्तथैव च ॥ ८ ॥

8. "Thyself and Bhîshma, and Karna, and also Kripa, the victor in war, Asvatthâman and Vikarna, and also Jayadratha, the son of Somadatta;

अन्ये च बहवः शूरा मदर्थे त्यक्तजीविताः ।
नानाशस्त्रप्रहरणाः सर्वे युद्धविशारदाः ॥ ९ ॥

9. "And many other heroes who have given up their lives for my sake, fighting with various weapons, all well-skilled in battle.

अपर्याप्तं तदस्माकं बलं भीष्माभिरक्षितम् ।
पर्याप्तं त्विदमेतेषाम् बलं भीमाभिरक्षितम् ॥ १० ॥

10. "This army of ours protected by Bhîshma is inadequate, whereas that army of theirs which is under the protection of Bhîma is adequate.*

अयनेषु च सर्वेषु यथाभागमवस्थिताः ।
भीष्ममेवाभिरक्षन्तु भवन्तः सर्व एव हि ॥ ११ ॥

11. "And therefore do ye all, occupying your respective positions in the several divisions of the army, support Bhîshma only."

* This sloka is differently interpreted by different commentators. Anandagiri's gloss suggests various interpretations which all go to make Duryodhana mean that his army, larger and led by an abler leader than the enemy's, is more likely to win the battle.

Both armies ready for battle.

तस्य सञ्जनयन्हर्षं कुरुवृद्धः पितामहः ।
सिंहनादं विनद्योच्चैः शङ्खं दध्मौ प्रतापवान् ॥ १२ ॥

12. His mighty grandsire, (Bhîshma), the oldest of the Kauravas, in order to cheer him, sounded on high a lion's roar and blew his conch.

ततः शङ्खाश्च भेर्यश्च पणवानकगोमुखाः ।
सहसैवाभ्यहन्यन्त स शब्दस्तुमुलोऽभवत् ॥ १३ ॥

13. Then, all at once, conches and kettle-drums, cymbols, drums and horns were played upon, and the sound was a tumultuous uproar.

ततः श्वेतैर्हयैर्युक्ते महति स्यन्दने स्थितौ ।
माधवः पाण्डवश्चैव दिव्यौ शङ्खौ प्रदध्मतुः ॥ १४ ॥

14. Then, too, Màdhava and the son of Pâ*nd*u, seated in a grand chariot yoked to white horses, blew their celestial conches.

पाञ्चजन्यं हृषीकेशो देवदत्तं धनञ्जयः ।
पौण्ड्रं दध्मौ महाशङ्खं भीमकर्मा वृकोदरः ॥ १५ ॥

15. H*r*ishîkes*a* blew the Pànchajanya, and Arjuna blew the Devadatta. Bhîma, (the doer) of terrible deeds, blew his great conch Pau*nd*ra.

अनन्तविजयं राजा कुन्तीपुत्रो युधिष्ठिरः ।
नकुलः सहदेवश्च सुघोषमणिपुष्पकौ ॥ १६ ॥

16. Prince Yudhish*t*hira, the son of Kunti, blew the Anantavijaya, while Nakula and Sahadeva blew the Sughosha and the Ma*n*ipushpaka.

काश्यश्च परमेष्वासः शिखण्डी च महारथः ।
धृष्टद्युम्नो विराटश्च सात्यकिश्चापराजितः ॥ १७ ॥

17. The king of Kâsî, an excellent archer, Sikha*nd*in, the master of a great car, Dh*r*ish*t*a-dyumna and Virâ*t*a, and the unconquered Sâtyaki;

द्रुपदो द्रौपदेयाश्च सर्वशः पृथिवीपते ।
सौभद्रश्च महाबाहुः शङ्खान्दध्मुः पृथक्पृथक् ॥ १८ ॥

18. Drupada and the sons of Draupadî, O lord of earth, and the son of Subhadrâ, of mighty arms, all together blew their respective conches.

स घोषो धार्तराष्ट्राणां हृदयानि व्यदारयत् ।
नभश्च पृथिवीं चैव तुमुलो व्यनुनादयन् ॥ १९ ॥

19. That tumultuous sound rent the hearts of (the people) of Dh*r*itarâsh*t*ra's party, making both heaven and earth resound.

Arjuna's *survey* of the enemy

अथ व्यवस्थितान्दृष्ट्वा धार्तराष्ट्रान्कपिध्वजः ।
प्रवृत्ते शस्त्रसम्पाते धनुरुद्यम्य पाण्डवः ॥ २० ॥
हृषीकेशं तदा वाक्यमिदमाह महीपते ।

अर्जुन उवाच :—

सेनयोरुभयोर्मध्ये रथं स्थापय मेऽच्युत ॥ २१ ॥
यावदेतान्निरीक्षेऽहं योद्धुकामानवस्थितान् ।
कैर्मया सह योद्धव्यमस्मिन्रणसमुद्यमे ॥ २२ ॥

20-22. Then seeing the people of Dh*r*itarâsh*t*ra's party regularly marshalled, while the discharge of weapons began, Arjuna, the son of Pâ*nd*u, whose ensign was a monkey, O King of earth, took up his bow and said thus to K*r*ish*n*a :

" O Achyuta (Immortal), place my chariot between the two armies, that I may just see those who stand here desirous to fight, and know with whom I must fight in this strife of battle.

योत्स्यमानानवेक्षेऽहं य एतेऽत्र समागताः ।
धार्तराष्ट्रस्य दुर्बुद्धेर्युद्धे प्रियचिकीर्षवः ॥ २३ ॥

23. " I will observe those who are assembled here and are about to engage in battle desirous to do service in war to the evil-minded son of Dh*r*itarâsh*t*ra."

सञ्जय उवाच :—

एवमुक्तो हृषीकेशो गुडाकेशेन भारत ।
सेनयोरुभयोर्मध्ये स्थापयित्वा रथोत्तमम् ॥ २४ ॥

भीष्मद्रोणप्रमुखतः सर्वेषां च महीक्षिताम् ।
उवाच पार्थ पश्यैतान्समवेतान्कुरूनिति ॥ २५ ॥

Sa*m*jaya said :

24-25. O descendant of Bharata, H*r*ishîkes*a* (K*r*ish*n*a) thus addressed by Gu*d*âkes*a* (Arjuna) stationed that excellent car between the two armies in front of Bhishma and Dro*n*a and all the rulers of earth, and said : " O son of P*r*ithà, look at these assembled Kauravas."

तत्रापश्यत्स्थितान्पार्थः पितॄनथ पितामहान् ।
आचार्यान्मातुलान्भ्रातॄन्पुत्रान्पौत्रान्सखींस्तथा ॥ २६ ॥
श्वशुरान्सुहृदश्चैव सेनयोरुभयोरपि ।

26-27. Then the son of Pṛithā saw arrayed there in both the armies fathers and grandfathers, teachers, maternal uncles, brothers, sons, grandsons and comrades, fathers-in-law and friends.

तान्समीक्ष्य स कौन्तेयः सर्वान्बन्धूनवस्थितान् ॥ २७ ॥
कृपया परयाऽऽविष्टो विषीदन्निदमब्रवीत् ।

27-28. When the son of Kunti saw all the kinsmen standing, he was overcome with deepest pity and said thus in sorrow :

Arjuna's words of despondency

अर्जुन उवाच :—

दृष्ट्वेमं स्वजनं कृष्ण युयुत्सुं समुपस्थितम् ॥ २८ ॥
सीदन्ति मम गात्राणि मुखं च परिशुष्यति ।
वेपथुश्च शरीरे मे रोमहर्षश्च जायते ॥ २९ ॥

Arjuna said :

28-29. Seeing these kinsmen, O Kṛishṇa, arrayed and desirous to fight, my limbs droop down, and my mouth is dried up. A tremor comes on my body and my hairs stand on end.

गाण्डीवं स्रंसते हस्तात्त्वक्चैव परिदह्यते ।
न च शक्नोम्यवस्थातुं भ्रमतीव च मे मनः ॥ ३० ॥

30. The Gā*nd*īva slips from my hand, and my skin is intensely burning. I am also unable to stand and my mind is whirling round, as it were.

निमित्तानि च पश्यामि विपरीतानि केशव ।
न च श्रेयोऽनुपश्यामि हत्वा स्वजनमाहवे ॥ ३१ ॥

31. And, O Kesava, I see omens foreboding evil. Nor do I see any good from killing my kinsmen in battle.

न काङ्क्षे विजयं कृष्ण न च राज्यं सुखानि च ।
किं नो राज्येन गोविन्द किं भोगैर्जीवितेन वा ॥ ३२ ॥

32. I desire not victory, O K*r*is*n*a, nor kingdom, nor pleasures. Of what avail is dominion to us, O Govinda? Of what avail are pleasures and even life?

येषामर्थे काङ्क्षितं नो राज्यं भोगाः सुखानि च ।
त इमेऽवस्थिता युद्धे प्राणांस्त्यक्त्वा धनानि च ॥ ३३ ॥
आचार्याः पितरः पुत्रास्तथैव च पितामहाः ।
मातुलाः श्वशुराः पौत्राः स्यालाः सम्बन्धिनस्तथा ॥ ३४ ॥

33-34. They for whose sake dominion, enjoyments and pleasures are sought by us are here standing, having staked their life and wealth: teachers, fathers, sons as well as grandfathers; maternal uncles, fathers-in-law, grandsons, brothers-in-law as also (other) relatives.

एतान्न हन्तुमिच्छामि घ्नतोऽपि मधुसूदन ।
अपि त्रैलोक्यराज्यस्य हेतोः किं नु महीकृते ॥ ३५ ॥

35. These, O slayer of Madhu, I do not wish to kill, though they kill me, even for the sake of dominion over the three worlds; how much less, for the sake of the earth!

निहत्य धार्तराष्ट्रान्नः का प्रीतिः स्याज्जनार्दन ।
पापमेवाश्रयेदस्मान्हत्वैतानाततायिनः ॥ ३६ ॥

36 O Janārdana, what delight shall be ours after killing the sons of Dhritasāshtra? On killing these felons, sin only will take hold of us.

तस्मान्नार्हा वयं हन्तुं धार्तराष्ट्रान्स्वबान्धवान् ।
स्वजनं हि कथं हत्वा सुखिनः स्याम माधव ॥ ३७ ॥

37. We had then better not slay our own kinsmen, the sons of Dhritarāshtra; for, how can we be happy, O Màdhava, after slaying our own people?

Arjuna's grief at the evils of war

यद्यप्येते न पश्यन्ति लोभोपहतचेतसः ।
कुलक्षयकृतं दोषं मित्रद्रोहे च पातकम् ॥ ३८ ॥
कथं न ज्ञेयमस्माभिः पापादस्मान्निवर्तितुम् ।
कुलक्षयकृतं दोषं प्रपश्यद्भिर्जनार्दन ॥ ३९ ॥

38-39. Though these, whose intelligence is stricken by greed, perceive no evil in the extinction of families and no sin in treachery to friends, yet,

O Janārdana, should not we, who clearly see evil in the extinction of a family, learn to refrain from this sinful deed?

कुलक्षये प्रणश्यन्ति कुलधर्माः सनातनाः ।
धर्मे नष्टे कुलं कृत्स्नमधर्मोऽभिभवत्युत ॥ ४० ॥

40. On the extinction of a family, the immemorial dharmas * of that family disappear. When the dharmas disappear, impiety (adharma) overtakes the whole family. †

अधर्माभिभवात्कृष्ण प्रदुष्यन्ति कुलस्त्रियः ।
स्त्रीषु दुष्टासु वार्ष्णेय जायते वर्णसङ्करः ॥ ४१ ॥

41. By the prevalence of impiety, O K*r*ish*n*a, the women of the family become corrupt. Women corrupted, there will be intermingling of castes (var*n*a-sa*m*kara), O descendant of V*r*ish*n*is.

सङ्करो नरकायैव कुलघ्नानां कुलस्य च ।
पतन्ति पितरो ह्येषां लुप्तपिण्डोदकक्रियाः ॥ ४२ ॥

42. Confusion of castes leads the family of these destroyers of families also to hell; for, their forefathers fall (down to hell), deprived of the offerings of pi*n*da (rice-ball) and water.

---

* The duties and ceremonies practised by the family in accordance with the scriptural command.

† Of the destroyed (according to some), of the destroyer (according to some others).

दोषैरेतैः कुलघ्नानां वर्णसङ्करकारकैः ।
उत्साद्यन्ते जातिधर्माः कुलधर्माश्च शाश्वताः ॥ ४३ ॥

43. By these evil deeds of the destroyers of families which cause the intermingling of castes, the eternal dharmas of castes and families are subverted.

उत्सन्नकुलधर्माणां मनुष्याणां जनार्दन ।
नरके नियतं वासो भवतीत्यनुशुश्रुम ॥ ४४ ॥

44. We have heard, O Janârdana, that necessary is the dwelling in hell of the men whose family dharmas are subverted.

अहो बत महत्पापं कर्तुं व्यवसिता वयम् ।
यद्राज्यसुखलोभेन हन्तुं स्वजनमुद्यताः ॥ ४५ ॥

45. Alas! we have resolved to commit a great sin, inasmuch as we are endeavouring to slay our kinsmen out of a craving for the pleasures of dominion.

यदि मामप्रतीकारमशस्त्रं शस्त्रपाणयः ।
धार्तराष्ट्रा रणे हन्युस्तन्मे क्षेमतरं भवेत् ॥ ४६ ॥

46. It would be better for me, if the sons of Dh*r*itarâsh*t*ra, with arms in hand, should slay me unarmed and unresisting in the battle.

सञ्जय उवाच—

एवमुक्त्वाऽर्जुनः सङ्ख्ये रथोपस्थ उपाविशत् ।
विसृज्य सशरं चापं शोकसंविग्नमानसः ॥ ४७ ॥

Sa*m*jaya said:

47. Having said thus, Arjuna, sorrow-stricken in mind, cast aside his bow and arrows in the midst of the battle and sat down in the chariot.

इति श्रीमद्भगवद्गीतासूपनिषत्सु ब्रह्मविद्यायां योगशास्त्रे
श्रीकृष्णार्जुनसंवादेऽर्जुनविषादयोगो नाम
प्रथमोऽध्यायः ।

SECOND DISCOURSE.

SANKHYA YOGA.

Arjuna's weakness condemned by the Lord.

सञ्जय उवाच —

तं तथा कृपयाऽऽविष्टमश्रुपूर्णाकुलेक्षणम् ।
विषीदन्तमिदं वाक्यमुवाच मधुसूदनः ॥ १ ॥

Sa*m*jaya said :

1. To him who was thus overcome with pity and afflicted, and whose eyes were full of tears and agitated, the destroyer of Madhu spoke as follows:

श्रीभगवानुवाच —

कुतस्त्वा कश्मलमिदं विषमे समुपस्थितम् ।
अनार्यजुष्टमस्वर्ग्यमकीर्तिकरमर्जुन ॥ २ ॥

The Lord said :

2. Whence in (this) perilous strait has come upon thee this weakness cherished by the unworthy, debarring from heaven and causing disgrace, O Arjuna?

क्लैब्यं मा स्म गमः पार्थ नैतत्त्वय्युपपद्यते ।
क्षुद्रं हृदयदौर्बल्यं त्यक्त्वोत्तिष्ठ परन्तप ॥ ३ ॥

3. Yield not to unmanliness, O son of P*ri*thâ. It does not become thee. Cast off this base weakness of heart and arise, O tormentor of foes

Arjuna seeks instruction from the Lord.

अर्जुन उवाच—

कथं भीष्ममहं सङ्ख्ये द्रोणं च मधुसूदन ।
इषुभिः प्रतियोत्स्यामि पूजार्हावरिसूदन ॥ ४ ॥

Arjuna said :

4. O slayer of Madhu, how shall I assail in battle with arrows Bhishma and Droṇa, who are worthy of worship, O slayer of enemies.

गुरूनहत्वा हि महानुभावान्
श्रेयो भोक्तुं भैक्ष्यमपीह लोके ।
हत्वाऽर्थकामांस्तु गुरूनिहैव
भुञ्जीय भोगान्रुधिरप्रदिग्धान् ॥ ५ ॥

5. Better indeed in this world to live even upon alms than to slay the teachers of high honor. But, were I to slay these teachers, I should only in this world enjoy the pleasures of wealth, delights stained with blood.

न चैतद्विद्मः कतरन्नो गरीयो
यद्वा जयेम यदि वा नो जयेयुः ।
यानेव हत्वा न जिजीविषामः
तेऽवस्थिताः प्रमुखे धार्तराष्ट्राः ॥ ६ ॥

6. And we know not which* is the better

* Which of the two—living upon alms without slaying others, or fighting the enemy which is our duty.—(*A*)

alternative for us; nor do we know whether we shall conquer them or they will conquer us. Even the sons of Dhritarâshtra, after killing whom we do not wish to live, stand arrayed against us.

कार्पण्यदोषोपहतस्वभावः
पृच्छामि त्वां धर्मसम्मूढचेताः ।
यच्छ्रेयः स्यान्निश्चितं ब्रूहि तन्मे
शिष्यस्तेऽहं शाधि मां त्वां प्रपन्नम् ॥ ७ ॥

7. My heart contaminated by the taint of helplessness, my mind confounded about Dharma,* I ask Thee: Tell me what is absolutely good. I am Thy pupil. Instruct me, who have sought Thy grace.

न हि प्रपश्यामि ममापनुद्याद्-
यच्छोकमुच्छोषणमिन्द्रियाणाम् ।
अवाप्य भूमावसपत्नमृद्धं
राज्यं सुराणामपि चाधिपत्यम् ॥ ८ ॥

8. I do not indeed see what can dispel the grief which burns up my senses, even after attaining unrivalled and prosperous dominion on earth or even lordship over gods.

सञ्जय उवाच —

एवमुक्त्वा हृषीकेशं गुडाकेशः परन्तपः ।
न योत्स्य इति गोविन्दमुक्त्वा तूष्णीं बभूव ह ॥ ९ ॥

* Dharma' here means 'Brahman' who supports all—(

Sa*m*jaya Said:

9. Having spoken thus to H*r*ishikesa, Gudàke*s*a, the tormenter of foes, said to Govinda, 'I will not fight,' and verily remained silent.

तमुवाच हृषीकेशः प्रहसन्निव भारत ।
सेनयोरुभयोर्मध्ये विषीदन्तमिदं वचः ॥ १० ॥

10. To him who was grieving in the midst of the two armies, O descendant of Bharata, H*r*ishikesa as if smiling, spoke these words :

Self-knowledge alone eradicates misery

Now the portion from i. 2 to ii. 9 should be interpreted as showing whence arise those evils of grief, delusion, etc., which in sentient creatures cause the misery of samsara.—To explain: In ii. 4 *et seq.* Arjuna displayed grief and delusion caused by his attachment for, and the sense of separation from, dominion, the elders, sons, friends, well-wishers, kinsmen, near and remote relations,—all this arising from his notion that "I am theirs and they are mine." It was when discrimination was overpowered by grief and delusion that Arjuna, who had of himself been engaged in battle as the duty of the warrior caste, abstained from fighting and proposed to lead a mendicant's life, which was the duty of a different caste*. Accordingly, all creatures whose intelligence is swayed by grief and delusion and other evil influences naturally abandon their proper duties and resort to those which are prohibited. Even if they are engaged in their duties, their conduct in speech, thought and deed is egoistic and is prompted

* The brahma*n*as alone are allowed to enter the fourth *As*rama of sa*m*nyâsa, which consists in the renunciation of all formal religion and worldly possessions.

by a longing for reward. In their case, then owing to an accumulation of merit and demerit, of dharma and adharma, the samsâra, which consists in passing through good and bad births, happiness and misery, becomes incessant. Grief and delusion are thus the cause of samsâra. And seeing that their cessation could not be brought about except by Self-knowledge added to renunciation of all works, Lord Vasudeva wished to teach that knowledge for the benefit of the whole world through Arjuna and began His teaching with ii. 11.

The doctrine that knowledge should be conjoined with works

Against the foregoing view some* say:—Moksha cannot at all be attained by mere A'tmajnâna-nishthâ by mere devotion of Self-knowledge preceded by the renunciation of all works.—By what then?—Absolute freedom can be attained by knowledge conjoined with works, such as the Agnihôtra prescribed in the Sruti and the Smriti. This is the conclusive teaching of the whole Gita. As supporting this view may be cited—they say—the verses ii. 33, ii. 47, iv. 15, etc. It should not be supposed that the Vedic ritual is sinful because it involves cruelty, etc.†—Why?—For, our Lord says that, since fighting which is the profession of the warrior caste is

* According to A'nandagiri the Vrittikâra is the commentator here referred to. A Vrittikâra's interpretation of the Brahma-sûtras I. i. 11—19 is also referred to by Sankaracharya in his commentary on that section. It is very probable that one and the same person was the author of the two Vrittis or commentaries. The Vritti on the Gita was evidently very voluminous, inasmuch as Sri Sankaracharya's bhashya is professedly very short in comparison with it. It is, therefore, not unlikely that the author of the Vritti on the Gita was no other than Bodhayana who is said to have written a voluminous commentary on the Brahma-sûtras, nearly a million slokas in extent, and of which the Sri-bhashya of Sri Ramanujacharya is said to be a mere abstract.

† Such as the eating of uchchishta or what remains of the food, of which another has already eaten—(A).

a proper duty (of the caste), it is not sinful though it involves cruelty to elders, brother's sons and the like and is therefore very horrible; and He further says that, in the case of a neglect of this duty, "abandoning thy duty and fame thou shalt incur sin." (ii. 33). This is clearly tantamount to asserting that those rites which are enjoined as life-long duties by the Vedas are sinless though they involve cruelty to animals.

Sankhya and Yoga distinguished

This is (wrong, since the Lord has made a distinction between J*n*âna-nish*th*â and Karma-nish*th*â, between the devotion of knowledge and the devotion of works, as based respectively upon two distinct standpoints—The real nature of the Self as expounded here in ii. 11—30 by the Lord is called Sánkhya and intellectual conviction of the truth produced by a study of that section,—that the Self is no doer, owing to the absence in Him of such changes as birth—forms the Sánkhya standpoint (Sánkhya-buddhi); and the enlightened who hold this view are called Sánkhyas. Yoga consists in the performance—before the rise of the foregoing conviction—of works as a means to moksha, requiring a knowledge of virtue and sin, and presupposing that the Self is distinct from the body and is the doer and the enjoyer. Such conviction forms the Yoga standpoint (Yoga-buddhi), and the performers of works who hold this view are Yogins. Accordingly two distinct standpoints are referred to by the Lord in ii. 39. Of these, He will assign to the Sânkhyas the J â na-yoga, or devotion to knowledge, based upon the Sankhya standpoint; and so also He will assign to the Yogins the path of Karma-yoga, or devotion to works, based upon the Yoga standpoint (iii. 3). Thus with reference to the Sankhya and the Yoga standpoints two distinct paths have been shown by the Lord, seeing the impossibility of J*n*ana and Karma being conjoined in one and the same person simultaneously, the one being based upon the idea of *non-agency and unity*, and the other on the idea of *agency and multiplicity*. The distinction made here is also referred to in the Satapatha-Brâhmana.—Having enjoined renunciation of all works in the words, "The brâhma*n*as who, having no worldly attachments, wish only for this region of the Self, should give up all worldly concerns," the Brâhma*n*a continues thus in explanation of the said injunction:

> "What have we to do with progeny,—we who live in this region, this Self?" (B*r*ihadara*n*yaka-Upanishad, iv. 4, 22).

In the same Brahma*n*a (*ibid*, i. 4, 17) we are told that, before marriage and after completing the investigation into the nature of the Dharma and Vedic injunction, the man of the world 'desired' to acquire the means of attaining to the three regions (of man, of Pitris, and of Devas), namely, a son and the twofold wealth,—the one kind of wealth being called 'human (manusha),' consisting of *works* and leading to the region of Pit*r*is, and the other kind of wealth being called 'godly (daiva),' consisting in *wisdom* (vidya, upasana) and leading to the region of Devas. Thus the Vedic rites are intended for him only who has desires and has no knowledge of the Self. The renunciation of these is enjoined on him who seeks only the region of the Self and is free from desire. This assigning of the two paths to two distinct classes of people would be unjustifiable if the Lord had intended a simultaneeus conjunction of knowledge and Vedic rites.

Conjunction inconsistent with the sequel

Neither could Arjuna's question with which the Third Discourse opens be satisfactorily explained (on that theory). How might Arjuna falsely impute to the Lord—as he did in iii. I—that which is alleged (by the opponent) to have been taught before by the Lord and to have not been heard by Arjuna,—namely, the impossibility of both knowledge and works being followed by one and the same person, as well as the superiority of knowledge to works ?

Moreover, if conjunction of knowledge and works be intended for all, it must have been intended for Arjuna as well. In that ase how might Arjuna ask about only one of the two.

'Tell me conclusively that which is the better of the two' (v. 1) ?

If a physician has prescribed a mixture composed of both sweet and cooling articles for a man who wishes to reduce bilious heat (in the system), there cannot arise the question 'which one alone of the two ingredients can alleviate bilious heat' ?

Arjuna's question, it might be alleged on the other side, was due to his not having understood aright the teaching of the Lord. Even then, the reply of the Lord should have been given in accordance with the question and in the following form : "I meant a conjunction of knowledge and works ; why are you thus mistaken ?" It would not, on the other hand, be proper to answer in the words "A twofold path was taught by Me" (iii. 3),—an answer which is not in accordance with the question and is altogether beside it.

If it be held that knowledge is to be conjoined with such works only as are enjoined in the smriti, even then the assigning of the two paths to two distinct classes of people respectively and other statements in that connection would be equally inexplicable. Moreover, Arjuna's blame of the Lord as conveyed by his words "why dost Thou command me to do this horrible deed ?" (iii. 1) would be inexplicable, since he knew that figting was enjoined in the smriti as a Kshatriya's duty.

It is not, therefore, possible for anybody to show that the Gita-Sastra teaches a conjunction of knowledge with any work whatever, enjoined in the sruti or in the smriti.

Some cases of apparent conjunction explained.

Now a person who, having been first engaged in works owing to ignorance and worldly attachment and other evil tendencies, and having since attained purity of mind by sacrificial rites, gifts, austerity, etc., arrives at the knowledge of the grand truth that "all this is one, the Brahman, the Absolute, the non-agent," may continue performing works in the same manner as before with a view to set an example to the masses, though neither works nor their results attract him any longer. This semblance of active life on his part cannot constitute that course of action with which knowledge is sought to be conjoined as a means of attaining moksha, any more than Lord Vasudeva's activity in His disharge of the duty of the military caste can constitute the action that is to be conjoined with His knowledge as a means to moksha, or that conduces to the attainment of any specific end of His; egotism and hope of reward being absent in both alike. He who knows the truth does not think 'I act,' nor does he long for the results.

Or to take another example: suppose a man seeking svarga or other such objects of desire goes through the ceremony of the Agni-âdhana as a preliminary to the performance of sacrificial rites such as the Agnihotra whereby to attain his desire, and then commences the Agnihotra, which has thus become a kamya (interested) rite; and suppose further that the desire vanishes when the sacrifice is half completed, but that the man goes on with it all the same: the Agnihotra can no longer be regarded as an interested rite. Accordingly our Lord says "though doing, he is not tainted," (v. 7), and "The Self neither acts nor is tainted." (xiii. 31).

Now as regards the passages, "Do thou also perform action as did the ancients in the olden time" (iv. 15), and "By action alone, indeed, did Janaka and others aim at perfection" (iii. 20), we must distinguish two cases and interpret the passages thus:

First, suppose that Janaka and the rest were engaged in works though they knew the truth. Then, they did so lest people at large might go astray; whereas they were sincerely convinced that 'the senses'—but not the Self—were engaged in the objects (iii. 28). Thus they reached perfection by knowledge alone. Though the stage of renunciation had been reached, they attained perfection without abandoning works; that is to say, they did not formally renounce works.

Secondly, suppose that they had not known the truth. Then the passages should be interpreted thus;—By means of work dedicated to Isvara, Janaka and the rest attained perfection,—'perfection' meaning here either 'purity of mind' or 'the dawn of true knowledge.' It is to this doctrine, that the Lord refers when he says "The Yogin performs action for the purification of the self." (v. 11) Elsewhere, after having said that 'man attains perfection by worshipping Him with his own duty' (xviii. 46), the Lord again recommends the path of knowledge, to him who has attained perfection, in the following words: "How he who has attained perfection reaches Brahman, that do thou learn from Me." (xviii. 50).

The conclusion, therefore, of the Bhagavad-gita is that salvation is attained by knowledge alone, not by knowledge conjoined with works. That such is the teaching of the Gita. we shall shew here and there in the following sections according to the context.

The Self is immortal.

Now finding no means other than Self-knowledge for the deliverance of Arjuna who was thus confounded as to his duty and was deeply plunged in the mighty ocean of grief, Lord Vasudeva who wished to help him out of it introduced him to Self-knowledge in the following words:—

श्रीभगवानुवाच —

अशोच्यानन्वशोचस्त्वं प्रज्ञावादांश्च भाषसे ।
गतासूनगतासूंश्च नानुशोचन्ति पण्डिताः ॥ ११ ॥

The Lord said:

11. For those who deserve no grief thou hast grieved, and words of wisdom thou speakest. For the living and for the dead the wise grieve not.*

Such people as Bhishma and Drona deserve no grief †, for they are men of good conduct and are eternal in their real nature. You have grieved for them saying "I am the cause of their death; of what avail are pleasures of dominion and other things to me left alone without them?" And you also

* He who knows not the Self is subject to illusion. He who is subject to illusion will obtain right knowledge by devoutly listening to the words of the Scripture and the spiritual teacher, and by investigating into the nature of things as they are with a view to clearly understand such teachings. This shews to what class of persons this teaching is addressed.—(A.)

† Whether you regard their present personalities or their real nature. Personally they are men of good conduct; in their real nature (as identical with the Absolute) they are eternal.

speak the words of wise men. Thus you exhibit inconsistency in yourself,—foolishness and wisdom,—like a maniac. For †, the wise (*pandita*h)—those who know the Self—grieve neither for the living nor for the dead. They alone are wise who know the Self. For, the *s*ruti says:

> "Having obtained wisdom (p*an*ditya, *i. e.*, knowledge of the Self) in its entirety..." (B*r*i. Up. III. 5, 1.)

That is, you grieve those who are really eternal and who really deserve no grief; wherefore you are foolish.

(*Question*):—Why do they deserve no grief?

(*Answer*):—For, they are eternal.

(*Question*):—How?

(*Answer*):—The Lord says:

न त्वेवाहं जातु नासं न त्वं नेमे जनाधिपाः ।
न चैव न भविष्यामः सर्वे वयमतः परम् ॥ १२ ॥

12. **Never did I not exist, nor thou, nor these rulers of men; and no one of us will ever hereafter cease to exist.**

Never did I cease to exist; on the other hand, I always did exist; that is, through the past bodily births and deaths, I always existed. So always, never did you cease to exist; on the other hand, you always did exist. So, never did these rulers of men cease to exist; on the other hand, they always did exist. So, neither shall we ever cease to exist; on the other hand, we shall all certainly continue to exist even after

---

* Referring to what Arjuna said in i. 43 *et seq.*—(A.)

† The second half of the verse is intended to show that Arjuna's delusion was due to his ignorance of the true nature of the Self.—(A.)

the death of these bodies. As the Self, the Atman, we are eternal in all the three periods of time (past, present and future.)

The plural 'us' is used with reference to the bodies that are different; it does not mean that there are more than one Self.

(*Question*) :—Now, how is the Self eternal ?

(*Answer*) :—Here follows an illustration :

देहिनोऽस्मिन्यथा देहे कौमारं यौवनं जरा ।
तथा देहान्तरप्राप्तिर्धीरस्तत्र न मुह्यति ॥ १३ ॥

13. Just as in this body the embodied (Self) passes into childhood and youth and old age, so does He pass into another body. There the wise man is not distressed.

We see how the embodied Self passes unchanged in the present body into the three stages (avasthas) of childhood, youth or the middle age, and old age or the age of decay, all distinct from one another. At the close of the first of these stages the Self is not dead, nor is He born again at the commencement of the second; on the other hand, we see the Self passing unchanged into the second and third stages. Just so does the Self pass unchanged into another body. Such being the case the wise man is not troubled (in mind) about it.

Endurance is a condition of wisdom.

Now Arjuna might argue as follows : It is true that when one knows the Self to be eternal there is no room for the distressful delusion that the Self will die. But quite common among people, as we see, is the distressful delusion that the Self is subject to heat and cold, pleasure and pain, as also to grief due to the loss of pleasure or to the suffering of pain.

As against the foregoing, the Lord says:

मात्रास्पर्शास्तु कौन्तेय शीतोष्णसुखदुःखदाः ।
आगमापायिनोऽनित्यास्तांस्तितिक्षस्व भारत ॥ १४ ॥

14. The sense-contacts it is, O son of Kunti, which cause heat and cold; pleasure and pain; they come and go, they are impermanent. Them endure bravely, O descendant of Bharata.

The senses are those of hearing and the like, by which sound and other things are perceived. It is the contacts of the senses with their objects such as sound—or, according to another interpretation, it is the senses and the contacts—i. e., the sense-objects, such as sound, which are contacted by the senses,—which produce heat and cold, pleasure and pain. Cold is pleasant at one time and painful at another. So also heat is of an inconstant nature. † But pleasure and pain are constant in their respective natures as pleasure and pain. Wherefore heat and cold are mentioned separately

* Here Arjuna is addressed as the 'son of Kunti' and again as the 'descendant of Bharata,' to show that he alone is fit to receive the teaching who is well descended on the father's as well as on the mother's side.—(A.)

† The separate mention of heat and cold which should properly be included under the category of objects (vishayas) implies that the subjective feelings of harmony and discord are the immediate antecedents of pleasure and pain. The external objects first produce subjective changes, such as the sensations of heat and cold or the feelings of harmony and discord, and then produce pleasure and pain.—(A.)

from pleasure and pain. Because * these sense-contacts, etc., have, by nature, a beginning and an end, therefore they are not permanent. Wherefore do thou bravely endure † them, heat and cold &c.; *i.e.*, give not thyself up to joy or grief on their account.

(*Question*) :—What good will accrue to him who bears heat and cold and the like?

(*Answer*) :—Listen.

यं हि न व्यथयन्त्येते पुरुषं पुरुषर्षभ ।
समदुःखसुखं धीरं सोऽमृतत्वाय कल्पते ॥ १५ ॥

15. That wise man whom, verily, these afflict not, O chief of men, to whom pleasure and pain are same, he for immortality is fit.

That person to whom pleasure and pain are alike,—who neither exults in pleasure nor feels dejected in pain,—who is a man of wisdom, whom heat and cold and other things such as those mentioned above do not affect in virtue of his vision of the eternal Self,—that man, firm in his vision of the eternal Self and bearing calmly the pairs of opposites (such as heat and cold), is able to attain immortality (moksha). ‡

---

* Some MSS. of the Bhashya here add . " It may be objected that if the objects of the senses or their contacts give pleasure and pain, the wheel of mundane existence will be endless, since those objects and their contacts with the senses are endless. This objection does not apply here, for these..."

† Here is laid down a second condition of right knowledge, *viz.*, calm endurance in pleasure and pain —(A).

‡ Though by endurance alone one may not be able to secure the highest human end, still, when coupled with discrimination and indifference to worldly objects and pleasures, it becomes a means to the right knowledge, which leads to deliverance. He who has satisfied all the conditions laid down can realize the nature of his own eternal Self, and then only is he fit for the final teaching that leads to deliverance.—(A).

The Real and the Unreal.

For the following reason also it is proper that thou shouldst abandon grief and distressful delusion and calmly endure heat and cold, etc. For,

नासतो विद्यते भावो नाभावो विद्यते सतः ।
उभयोरपि दृष्टोऽन्तस्त्वनयोस्तत्त्वदर्शिभिः ॥ १६ ॥

16. Of the unreal no being there is; there is no non being of the real. Of both these is the truth seen by the seers of the Essence.

There is no bhâva—no being, no existence—of the unreal (asat) such as heat and cold as well as their causes. Heat cold, etc., and the causes thereof, which are (no doubt) perceived through the organs of perception, are not absolutely real (vastu-sat); for they are effects or changes (vikâra), and every change is temporary. For instance, no objective form, such as an earthen pot, presented to consciousness by the eye, proves to be real, because it is not perceived apart from clay. Thus every effect is unreal, because it is not perceived as distinct from its cause. Every effect, such as a pot, is unreal, also because it is not perceived before its production and after its destruction.* And likewise the cause, such as clay, is unreal because it is not perceived apart from its cause.†

(*Objection*):—Then it comes to this: nothing at all exists.‡

---

* Cp. 'Whatever exists not in the beginning or in the end exists not really in the present.' (Gaudapadakarikas on the Mandukya-upanishad. IV, 31).—(A).

† This implies that the Absolute Reality is not conditioned by causality; and therefore the perception of the series of causes and effects must be illusory.—(A).

‡ The objector evidently thinks that there cannot be a thing which is neither a cause nor an effect.

(*Answer*) :—No (such objection applies here). For, every fact of experience involves twofold consciousness (buddhi), the consciousness of the real (sat) and the consciousness of the unreal (asat). Now that is (said to be) *real*, of which our consciousness fails; and that to be *unreal*, of which our consciousness fails.* Thus the distinction of reality and unreality depends on our consciouness. Now, in all our experience, twofold consciousness arises with reference to one and the same substratum (samânâdhikara*n*a), as 'a cloth existent,' 'a pot existent,' 'an elephant existent'—not as in the expression a blue lotus' †—and so on everywhere. Of the two, the consciousness of pot, etc., is temporary as was already pointed out, but not the consciousness of existence. Thus, the object corresponding to our consciousness of pot, etc., is unreal, because the consciousness is temporary; but what corresponds to our

---

* There must be an Absolute Reality which is neither a cause nor an effect. For, what is fleeting must be unreal, and what is constant must be real. In the case of our illusory perception of a rope mistaken for a snake, we hold that the snake is unreal because our consciousness of it fails, whereas what corresponds to "*this*" in the perception "this is a snake,"—*viz.*, the rope,—is real, because our consciousness of it is constant through all its illusory manifestations. The reality and the unreality of things are thus to be inferred from our own experience.

† *Blue* and *lotus* being two realities. Existence and the pot refer—as in the sentence 'this is the man we saw'—to only one thing really existing. They are not two distinct realities, related to each other as the universal and the particulars, or as a substance and its attribute. If the pot, etc., were as real as existence we should be at a loss to explain why, with reference to one and the same substratum, the two—existence and the pot or the like—should always present themselves together to our consciousness any more than a pot and a cloth. Illusion, on the other hand, can account for the twofold consciousness of existence and the pot and so on, arising with reference to one and the same substratum, there being only one Reality—namely, that which corresponds to existence—and all the rest being unreal, as in the case of a rope mistaken for various other things which are unreal.—(A).

consciousness of existence is not unreal, because the consciousness is unfailing.

(*Objection*) :—When the pot is absent and the consciousness of it fails, the consciousness of existence also fails.

(*Answer*) :—No * (such objection applies here). For the consciousness of existence still arises with reference to other objects such as cloth. The consciousness of existence corresponds indeed only to the attributive (viseshana).

(*Objection*) :—Like the consciousness of existence, the consciousness of the pot also arises with reference to another pot (present).

(*Answer*) :—You cannot say so, for the consciousness of the pot does not arisewith reference to a cloth.

(*Objection*) :—Neither does the consciousness of existence arise in the case of the pot that has disappeared.

(*Answer*) :—You cannot say so, for there is no substantive (viseshya) present. The consciousness of existence corresponds to the attributive; and as there can be no consciousness of the attributive without that of the corresponding substantive, how can the consciousness of the attributive arise in the absence of the substantive?—Not that there is no objective reality present, corresponding to the consciousness of existence.

(*Objection*) :—If the substantive such as the pot be unreal, the twofold consciousness arising with reference to one and the same substratum is inexplicable.†

---

* The consciousness of existence still arises in conjunction with the absence of the pot. When we say 'here is no pot,' existence is signified by reference to the place where the pot is said to be absent.

† The objector means this: In all our experience, we find both substantive and the attributive to be real. So, here, the pot must be as real as existence.—(A)

(*Answer*):—No; for, we find the twofold consciousness arising with reference to one and the same substratum, even though one of the two objects corresponding to the twofold consciousness is unreal, as for instance in the case of a mirage, where our consciousness takes the form "this is water." Therefore, there is no existence of the unreal, the fictitious—such as the body and the pairs of opposites—or of their causes. Neither does the real—the Self (Atman)—ever cease to exist; for, as already pointed out, our consciousness of the Self never fails.

This conclusion—that the real is ever existent and the unreal is never existent—regarding the two, the Self and the non-Self, the real and the unreal, is always present before the minds of those who attend only to truth, to the real nature of the Brahman, the Absolute, the All, 'That.' Thou hadst therefore better follow the view of such truth-seers, shake off grief and delusion, and, being assured that all phenomena (vikâras) are really non-existent and are, like the mirage, mere false appearances, do thou calmly bear heat and cold and other pairs of opposites, of which some are constant and others inconstant in their nature as productive of pleasure or pain.

What, then, is that which is ever real? Listen :—

अविनाशि तु तद्विद्धि येन सर्वमिदं ततम् ।
विनाशमव्ययस्यास्य न कश्चित्कर्तुमर्हति ॥ १७ ॥

17. But know that to be imperishable by which all this is pervaded. None can cause the destruction of That, the Inexhaustible.

Uulike the uureal, That—you must understand—does not vanish; That, the Brahman, the 'Sat', the Real, by which all this world, including the akasa, is pervaded, just as pots and other objects are pervaded by the akasa or space. Brahman does not undergo increase or diminution and is therefore inexhaustable. This Brahman, the 'Sat', is not exhausted in Itself; for, unlike the body It has no parts. Nor does It diminish by (loss of) anything belonging to It; for, nothing belongs to the Self. Devadatta, for instance, is ruined by loss of wealth; but Brahman does not suffer loss in that way. Wherefore, nobody can bring about the disappearance or destruction of the inexhaustible Brahman. Nobody—not even the Isvara, the Supreme Lord—can destroy the Self. For, the Self is Brahman Itself and one cannot act upon oneself.

What, then, is the unreal (asat), whose existence is not constant? Listen:

अन्तवन्त इमे देहा नित्यस्योक्ताः शरीरिणः ।
अनाशिनोऽप्रमेयस्य तस्माद्युध्यस्व भारत ॥ १८ ॥

18. These bodies of the embodied (Self) who is eternal, indestructible and unknowable, are said to have an end. Do fight, therefore, O descendant of Bharata.

It is said by the enlightened that these bodies of the Self, who is eternal, indestructible and unknowable, have an end, like those seen in dreams or produced by a juggler.—The end of such objects as the mirage consists in the cessation—as the result of investigation into their nature by proper tests of truth—of the idea of reality which has been associated with them. So also these bodies have an end.

[No tautology is involved in the use of both 'eternal' and 'indestructible;' for, two kinds of eternality and of destruction are met with in our experience. The physical body, for instance, entirely disappearing when reduced to ashes, is said to have been destroyed. The physical body, while existing as such, may be transformed owing to sickness or such other causes, and it is then said to have ceased to be (something) and to have become (something else). "Eternal" and 'indestructible' here imply that the Self is subject to neither sort of destruction. Otherwise, the eternality of Atman, the Self, might perhaps be understood to be like that of clay or other material objects. It is the denial of this which is conveyed by the two epithets.]

The Self is unknowable,—not determinable by the senses (pratyaksha) or any other means of knowledge.

(*Objection*) :—The Self is determined by the Agama or Revelation, and by perception, etc., prior to Revelation.

(*Answer*) :—The objection is untenable, for the Self is self-determined (svatas-siddha). When the Self, the knower (pramât*r*i), has been determined, then only is possible a search for proper authorities on the part of the knower with a view to obtain right knowledge. In fact, without determining the Self—'I am I'—none seeks to determine the knowable objects. Indeed the Self is unknown (aprasiddha) to nobody. And the Scripture (Sâstra) which is the final * authority obtains its authoritativeness regarding the Self, as serving only to eliminate the adhyâropa*n*a or superimposition (on the Self) of the attributes † alien to Him, but not as revealing what has been altogether unknown. The sruti also describes the Self thus:—

"That which is the Immediate, the Unremote, the Brahman, which is the Self, which is within all." (B*r*i. Up. ii. 4. I.).

---

* *i. e.*, the last. The Sruti teaches that the Self is the only real thing and that all others are illusory and non-existent. No prama*n*a or authority can survive the realisation of this truth taught by the sruti.—(A)

† Such as humanity and agency.

Because the Self is thus eternal (nitya) and immutable (avikriya), therefore, do thou fight,—do not abstain from fighting.

Here the duty of fighting is not enjoined. Arjuna had already been engaged in fighting. But overpowered by grief and delusion he abstained from fighting. It is only the removal of obstructive causes (pratibandha, *viz.*, grief and delusion) that is here attempted by the Lord. Wherefore in the words 'do thou fight' the Lord issues here no new command (vidhi); He only refers to what is commonly known already.*

The Self is unconcerned in action.

The Lord now quotes two Vedic verses to confirm the view that the Gita-sastra is intended to remove the cause of sa*m*sara, such as grief and delusion, but not to enjoin works.

It is only a false notion of yours, says the Lord, that you think thus: "Bhishma and others will be killed by me in the battle; I will be their slayer."—How?—

य एनं वेत्ति हन्तारं यश्चैनं मन्यते हतम् ।
उभौ तौ न विजानीतो नायं हन्ति न हन्यते ॥ १९ ॥

19. Whoever looks upon Him as the slayer, and whoever looks upon Him as the slain, both these know not aright. He slays not, nor is He slain.

He who understands the Self—of whom we are speaking—as the agent in the act of slaying, and he who regards Him as the sufferer in the act of slaying when the body

---

* That is to say, the Lord does not here mean that fighting is absolutely necessary. He has simply shewn that Arjuna had no reason to desist from the fighting in which he had engaged of himself.

is slain, neither of these two has understood the Self aright, for want of discrimination. Those who think 'I slay' or 'I am slain' when the body is slain, and thus identify the Self with the object of the consciousness of 'I,' the ego (aham),—they do not understand the real nature of the Self. Being immutable (avikriya). the Self is neither the agent nor the object of the action of slaying.

The Self is immutable

How is the Self immutable?—This is answered by the next verse.

न जायते म्रियते वा कदाचि-
न्नायं भूत्वा भविता वा न भूयः ।
अजो नित्यः शाश्वतोऽयं पुराणो
न हन्यते हन्यमाने शरीरे ॥ २० ॥

20. He is not born, nor does He ever die; after having been, He again ceases not to be; nor the reverse. Unborn, eternal, unchangeable and primeval, He is not slain when the body is slain.

He is not born; no such change of condition as birth takes place in the Self. Nor does He die; this denies the last change of condition called death.—'Ever' should be construed with the denial of every change, thus: He is never born, never dies, and so on.—For, the Self, having once existed does not afterwards cease to be any more. In ordinary parlance he is said to die who, having once existed, afterwards ceases to be. Neither does the Self come into existence, like the body, having not existed before. Wherefore He is unborn. For, he is said to be born who, having not existed, comes into existence. Not so is the Self.

Wherefore He is unborn. And because He does not die, He is eternal. [Though, by the denial of the first and the last changes, all changes have been denied, yet it is thought necessary to directly deny the intermediate changes, in the words 'unchangeable,' etc., so as to imply the absence of all such changes of condition as motion, though not specified here.] He is unchangeable: He is constant, not subject to the changes of condition known as decline (apakshaya.) Having no parts, He does not diminish in His own substance. As devoid of qualities, He does not diminish by loss of a quality. He is primeval. not subject to the change known as growth (vriddhi) as opposed to decline. For, that which increases in size by the accretion of parts is said to grow and to be renewed. As devoid of parts, the Self was as fresh in the past (as He is now or will be in future; *i.e.*, He is ever the same); He never grows. And He is not slain when the body is slain: He is not transformed when the body is transformed. To avoid tautology, slaying is interpreted to mean transformation: the Self is not subject to transformation.

This verse teaches the absence in the Self of the six* bhava-vikaras,—of the six *vikaras* or changes of condition to which all *bhavas* or beings in the world are subject. The passage, on the whole, means that the Self is devoid of all sorts of change. Hence the words in the previous verse, "both these know not aright."

The enlightened man has to renounce works

Having started (in ii. 19) the proposition that the Self is neither the agent nor the object of the action of slaying, and having stated in the next verse the immutability of the Self

---

* Such as birth, existence, growth, transformation, decline, and destruction.

as the reason for that statement, the Lord concludes the proposition as follows :—

वेदाविनाशिनं नित्यं य एतमजमव्ययम् ।
कथं स पुरुषः पार्थ कं घातयति हन्ति कम् ॥ २१ ॥

21. Whoso knows Him as indestructible, eternal, unborn and inexhaustible,—How, O son of Prithâ, and whom does such a man cause to slay, and whom does he slay ?

He who knows the Self (described in the last verse) as indestructible, *i.e.*, devoid of the final change called death, as eternal, *i.e.*, devoid of change called transformation, as unborn and inexhaustible, *i.e.*, devoid of birth and decline,—how does an enlightened man of this description do the act of slaying, or how does he cause another to slay ? He slays nobody at all, nor does he at all cause another to slay.—In both the places, denial is meant, since no question can have been asked.* The reason ‡ for the denial of slaying applying to all actions alike, what the Lord means to teach in this section appears to be the denial of all action whatsoever in the case of the enlightened; the denial, however, of the specific act of slaying being only meant as an example.

(*Objection*) :—What special reason for the absence of action in the case of an enlightened man does the Lord see when denying actions in the words "how does such a man slay ?"

(*Answer*) :—The immutability of the Self has already been given as the reason for the absence of all actions.

---

* Because no reply follows.

‡ Viz., the immutability of the Self.

(*Objection*):—True, it has been given; but that cannot be a sufficient reason, since the enlightened man is distinct from the immutable Self. We cannot indeed say that a man who has known an immovable pillar can have no action to do.

(*Answer*):—This objection does not apply. For, the enlightened man is identical with the Self. Enlightenment (vidvatta) does not pertain to the aggregate of the body, etc. Therefore, as the only other alternative, the enlightened man should be identical with the Self, who is not included in the aggregate and is immutable. No action being possible in the case of an enlightened man, it is but just to deny all action in the words "how does such a man slay?" Now, for instance, the Self, while remaining immutable, is, by reason of His not being distinguished from intellectual states (buddhi-vrittis), imagined, through ignorance, to be the percipient of objects, such as sound, perceived by the intellect and other means. Similarly, the Self is imagined to be enlightened, merely because of avidya associating Him with that intellectual perception—which is unreal—which takes the form of discrimination between the Self and the not-Self, while in reality the Self has undergone no change whatever. From this assertion of impossibility of action in the case of an enlightened man, the conclusion of the Lord is evident, that those acts which are enjoined by the scripture are intended for the unenlightened.

Works are meant for the unenlightened.

(*Objection*):—Even knowledge is intended for the unenlightened only, as it would be useless—like grinding the flour over again—to impart knowledge to those who already possess it. Wherefore, it is hard to explain the distinction that works are meant for the unenlightened, and not for the enlightened.

(*Answer*) :—This objection does not apply. For, the distinction can be explained by the existence or non-existence of something to be performed in the two cases respectively. (To explain) : There remains something for the unenlightened man to do, on understanding the meaning of the injunctions regarding the Agnihotra etc. He thinks that the Agnihotra and other sacrificial rites are to be performed, and that the many necessary accessories thereto should be acquired. He thinks further, "I am the agent, this is my duty." Nothing, on the contrary, remains to be performed subsequent to the realization of the truth of such teachings as are contained in ii. 20 etc., regarding the real nature of the Self. No other conviction arises except that the Self is one and non-agent. Wherefore, the distinction referred to can be accounted for.

In the case of him who thinks that the Self is the doer of actions, there will necessarily arise the idea that he has this or that thing to do. A man who possesses this sort of knowledge is qualified for actions, and on him actions are enjoined. Such a man is unenlightened, for it is said that "both these know not aright" (ii. 19). In ii. 21, the enlightened man is specified, and with reference to him actions are denied in the words "how does such a man slay?" Therefore the enlightened man who has seen the immutable Self and the man who is eager for emancipation have only to renounce all works.* Hence it is that Lord Narayana distinguishes the enlightened Sankhyas from the unenlightened followers of works, and teaches to them respectively two distinct paths (iii. 3). Accordingly Vyasa said to his son, "Now there are two paths." (Mokshadharma, xxiv. 6). In the same connection, Vyasa said that the path of works

* The latter, *i.e.*, he who is eager for Moksha, but who does not yet possess Self-knowledge, has no doubt to perform the acts enjoined on him, these acts being not prejudicial to his devotion to knowledge.

is the first, and that renunciation comes next. Our Lord will refer to this distinction again and again in this work. (*vide* iii. 27, 28 ; v. 13, etc.)

Knowledge of the Immutable Self is possible.

(*Objection*) :—In this connection some conceited pedants say : To no man can arise the conviction 'I am the immutable Self, the One, the non-agent, devoid of the six changes, such as birth, to which all things in the world are subject ;' which conviction arising, renunciation of all works is enjoined.

(*Answer*) :—This objection does not apply here. For, in vain then would be the Scriptural teaching, such as "the Self is not born," etc. (ii. 20). They (the objectors) may be asked why knowledge of the immutablity, non-agency, unity, etc., of the Self cannot be produced by the Scripture in the same way as knowledge of the existence of *dharma* and *a-dharma* and of the doer passing through other births is produced by the teaching of the Scripture ?

(*Opponent*) ;—Because the Self is inaccessible to any of the senses.

(*Answer*) :—Not so. For, the Scripture says "It can be seen by the mind alone." (Bri. Up. iv. 19). The mind, refined by *Sama* and *Dama*—*i.e.*, by the subjugation of the body, the mind and the senses—and equipped with the teachings of the Scripture and the teacher, constitutes the sense by which the Self may be seen. Thus, while the Scripture and inference * (anumana) teach the immutability of the Self, it is mere temerity to hold that no such knowledge can arise.

---

* The inference may be thus stated : such changes as birth, death, agency and the like are not inherent in the Self, any more than infancy, youth and old age are inherent in Him.

The enlightened should resort to Jnana-Yoga.

It must be granted that the knowledge which thus arises necessarily dispels ignorance, its opposite. This ignorance has been already indicated in ii. 19. It is there taught that the notion that the Self is the agent or the object of the action of slaying is a product of ignorance. That the agency, etc., of the self is a product of ignorance holds good in the case of all actions alike, since the Self is immutable. It is only the agent, subject to variations of conditions, that causes another person, who can be acted on by him, to do an action. This agency—direct and causative with respect to all actions alike—the Lord Vasudeva denies in ii. 21 in the case of an enlightened man, with a view to show that the enlightened man has nothing to do with any action whatsoever.

(Question) :—What, then, has he to do?

(Answer) :—This has been already answered in iii. 3, that the Sankhyas should resort to J*n*âna-Yoga or devotion to knowledge. So also, the Lord will teach renunciation of all works in the words, "Renouncing all actions by thought, the self-controlled man rests happily in the nine-gated city,—in the body—neither acting nor causing to act." (v. 13).

(Objection) :—Here the word 'thought' implies that there is no renunciation of the acts of speech and body.

(Answer) :—No, for there is the qualification, 'all actions.'

(Objection) :—The renunciation of all *mental* acts only is meant.

(Answer) :—No. Since all acts of speech and body are preceded by mental activity, they cannot exist when the mind is inactive.

(*Objection*) :—Then, let him renounce all other acts of mind except such as are necessary for those acts of speech and body which are enjoined by the Scripture.

(*Answer*) :—No, for, there is the qualification, "neither acting nor causing to act."

(*Objection*) :—Then, the renunciation of all actions, here taught by the Lord, may be meant for the dying man, not for the living man.

(*Answer*) :—No; for then, the qualification 'rests in the nine-gated city—in the body' would have no meaning. No man who is dying can by giving up all activity be said to rest in the body.

(*Objection*) :—Let us then construe the passage thus: Neither acting nor causing another to act, he, the disembodied soul of the enlightened man, deposits (sa*m*+nyas) all activity in the body (*i. e.*, knows that all activity belongs to the body, not to the Self) and rests happily. Let us not, on the contrary, construe, as you have done, 'he rests in the body,' etc.

(*Answer*) :—No; Everywhere (in the *s*ruti and in the sm*r*iti) it is emphatically asserted that the Self is immutable.* Moreover, the act of resting presupposes a place to rest in, whereas the act of renunciation does not presuppose it. And the Sanskrit verb sa*m*+nyas' means 'to renounce,' not 'to deposit.'

Therefore, the Gîtâ-Sâstra teaches that he who has acquired a knowledge of the Self should resort to renunciation only, not toworks. This we shall show here and there in the following sections, wherever they treat of the Self.

---

* Wherefore the Self cannot be the agent of an action.

How the Self is immutable.

To return to the immediate subject. It has been stated that the Self is indestructible. Like what is He indestructible? Here follows the answer:

वासांसि जीर्णानि यथा विहाय
नवानि गृह्णाति नरोऽपराणि ।
तथा शरीराणि विहाय जीर्णा-
न्यन्यानि संयाति नवानि देही ॥ २२ ॥

22. Just as a man casts off worn-out clothes and puts on others which are new, so the embodied (Self) casts off worn-out bodies and enters others which are new.

Just as, in this world, a man casts off the clothes that have been worn-out and puts on others which are new, in the same manner, like the man (of the world), the embodied Self abandons old bodies, and, without undergoing any change, enters others which are new.

Why is the Self quite changeless? The Lord says:

नैनं छिन्दन्ति शस्त्राणि नैनं दहति पावकः ।
न चैनं क्लेदयन्त्यापो न शोषयति मारुतः ॥ २३ ॥

23. Him weapons cut not, Him fire burns not, and Him water wets not; Him wind dries not.

Him, *i.e.*, the embodied Self of whom we are speaking, weapons, such as swords, do not cut. As he has no parts, they can effect no division of Him into parts. So, fire does not burn Him: even fire cannot reduce Him to ashes.

Neither does water wet Him; for, the power of water lies in disjoining the parts of a thing which is made up of parts, by wetting it; and this cannot take place in the partless Self. So, wind destroys an object containing moisture, by drying it up; but even wind cannot dry up the Self.

Wherefore,

अच्छेद्योऽयमदाह्योऽयमक्लेद्योऽशोष्य एव च ।
नित्यः सर्वगतः स्थाणुरचलोऽयं सनातनः ॥ २४ ॥

24. He cannot be cut, nor burnt, nor wetted, nor dried up. He is everlasting, all-pervading stable, firm, and eternal.

Because the mutually destructive objects—namely, swords and the like—cannot destroy the Self, therefore He is overlasting. Because everlasting, He is all-pervading. Because all-pervading, He is stable like a pillar. Because stable, the Self is firm. Wherefore He is eternal, not produced out of any cause, not new.

No charge of tautology can be brought against the verses (ii. 21-24) on the ground that in (ii. 20) the eternality and the immutability of the Self have been taught and that what has been said regarding the Self in these verses (ii. 21-24) adds nothing to what was taught in that one verse,—something being repeated verbatim, and something more being repeated in idea. Since the Self is a thing very difficult to understand, the Lord Vasudeva again and again introduces the subject and describes the same thing in other words, so that in some way or other the truth may be grasped by the intellect of the mortals (samsârins) and thus the cessation of their samsâra may be brought about.

No room for grief.

Moreover,

अव्यक्तोऽयमचिन्त्योऽयमविकार्योऽयमुच्यते ।
तस्मादेवं विदित्वैनं नानुशोचितुमर्हसि ॥ २५ ॥

25. He, it is said, is unmanifest, unthinkable and unchangeable. Wherefore, knowing Him to be such, thou hadst better grieve not.

As the Self is inaccessible to any of the senses, He is not manifest. Wherefore, He is unthinkable. For, that alone which is perceived by the senses becomes an object of thought. Verily, the Self is unthinkable, because He is inaccessible to the senses. He is unchangeable. The Self is quite unlike milk, which, mixed with butter-milk, can be made to change its form. He is changeless, also because He has no parts; for, whatever has no parts is never found to undergo change. Because the Self is changeless, He is unchangeable. Therefore, thus understanding the Self, thou hadst better not grieve, nor think that thou art their slayer and that they are slain by thee.

Granting that the Self is not everlasting, the Lord proceeds:

अथ चैनं नित्यजातं नित्यं वा मन्यसे मृतम् ।
तथापि त्वं महाबाहो नैनं शोचितुमर्हसि ॥ २६ ॥

26. But even if thou thinkest of Him as ever being born and ever dying, even then, O mighty-armed, thou oughtst not to grieve thus.

Granting that the Self—of whom we are speaking—is, according to the popular view, again and again born whenever a body comes into existence, and again and again dead whenever the body dies,—even if the Self were so, as you think,

O mighty-armed, you ought not to grieve thus; for, death is inevitable to what is born; and birth is inevitable to what is dead.

Accordingly,

जातस्य हि ध्रुवो मृत्युर्ध्रुवं जन्म मृतस्य च ।
तस्मादपरिहार्येऽर्थे न त्वं शोचितुमर्हसि ॥ २७ ॥

27. To that which is born, death is indeed certain; and to that which is dead, birth is certain. Wherefore, about the unavoidable thing, thou oughtst not to grieve.

To that which has had birth, death happens without failure, and birth is sure to happen to that which is dead. Since birth and death are unavoidable, therefore you ought not to grieve regarding such an unavoidable thing. If death is natural to that which has had birth, and if birth is natural to that which has had death, the thing is unavoidable. Regarding such an unavoidable thing you ought not to grieve.

Neither is it proper to grieve regarding beings which are mere combinations of (material) causes and effects; for,

अव्यक्तादीनि भूतानि व्यक्तमध्यानि भारत ।
अव्यक्तनिधनान्येव तत्र का परिदेवना ॥ २८ ॥

28. Beings have their beginning unseen, their middle seen, and their end unseen again. Why any lamentation regarding them?

The origin—prior to manifestation—of beings such as sons and friends, who are mere combinations of material elements correlated as causes and effects, is non-perception (avyakta). And having come into existence, their middle state—previous to death—is perceived. Again their end is non-perception: after death, they become unperceived again. Thus it is said:

> "He has come from non-perception (the unseen) and has gone back to non-perception (the unseen). He is not thine, nor thou his. What is this vain lamentation for?" (Mahâbh. Striparva, 2-13)

About these mere illusions—first unseen, then seen, and again unseen—what occasion is there for any lamentation?

The Self just spoken of is very difficult to realise. Why am I to blame you alone while the cause, *viz.*, illusion, is common to all? One may ask: how is it that the Self is difficult to realise? The Lord says:

आश्चर्यवत्पश्यति कश्चिदेन-
माश्चर्यवद्वदति तथैव चान्यः ।
आश्चर्यवच्चैनमन्यः शृणोति
श्रुत्वाऽप्येनं वेद न चैव कश्चित् ॥ २९ ॥

29. One sees Him as a wonder; and so also another speaks of him as a wonder; and as a wonder another hears of Him; and though hearing, none understands Him at all.

One sees the Self as a wonder, as a thing unseen, as something strange, as seen all on a sudden. And so, another speaks of Him as a wonder; and another hears of Him as a wonder. Though seeing Him, hearing and speaking of Him, none realises Him at all.

Or (as otherwise interpreted): He that sees the Self is something like a wonder. He that speaks and he that hears of Him is only one among many thousands. Thus the Self is hard to understand.

Now the Lord concludes the subject of this section thus:

देही नित्यमवध्योऽयं देहे सर्वस्य भारत ।
तस्मात्सर्वाणि भूतानि न त्वं शोचितुमर्हसि ॥ ३० ॥

30. He, the embodied (Self) in every one's body, can never be killed, O descendant of Bharata. Wherefore thou oughtst not to grieve about any creature.

Though the body of any creature whatever is killed, the Self cannot be killed; wherefore, you ought not to grieve regarding any creature whatever, Bhishma or anybody else.

A warrior should fight.

Here (in ii. 30) it has been shown that from the standpoint of absolute truth there is no occasion for grief and attachment. Not only from the standpoint of absolute truth, but also,

स्वधर्ममपि चावेक्ष्य न विकम्पितुमर्हसि ।
धर्म्याद्धि युद्धाच्छ्रेयोऽन्यत्क्षत्रियस्य न विद्यते ॥ ३१ ॥

31. Having regard to thine own duty also, thou oughtst not to waver. For, to a Kshatriya, there is nothing more wholesome than a lawful battle.

Having regard also to the fact that fighting is a Kshatriya's duty, you ought not to swerve from that duty, which is natural to a Kshatriya,—from that which is natural to you (*i.e.*, becoming the caste and the order to which you belong). This fighting is a supreme duty, not opposed to Law, since it is conducive, through conquest of dominion, to the interests of Law and popular well-being; and to a Kshatriya nothing else is more wholesome than such a lawful battle.

And why also should the battle be fought? The Lord says:

यदृच्छया चोपपन्नं स्वर्गद्वारमपावृतम् ।
सुखिनः क्षत्रियाः पार्थ लभन्ते युद्धमीदृशम् ॥ ३२ ॥

32. Happy Kshatriya, O son of Prithâ, find such a battle as this, come of itself, an open door to heaven.

Are not those Kshatriyas happy who find a battle like this presenting itself unsought, an open door to heaven?

Though found to be your duty,

अथ चेत्त्वमिमं धर्म्यं सङ्ग्रामं न करिष्यसि ।
ततः स्वधर्मं कीर्तिं च हित्वा पापमवाप्स्यसि ॥ ३३ ॥

33. Now if thou wouldst not fight this lawful battle, then, having abandoned thine own duty and fame, thou shalt incur sin.

If, on the other hand, you will not fight this battle which is enjoined on you as a duty, and which is not opposed to Law, you will, by neglecting this battle, have abandoned your duty and lost the fame that you acquired by your encounter with such persons as Mahadeva.* Thus you will only incur sin.

Not only will you have given up your duty and fame, but also,

---

* When Yudhishthira lost his kingdom by gambling, Arjuna went on a pilgrimage to the Himalayas to propitiate the gods and obtain from them celestial weapons. There he fought with Siva who appeared in the guise of a mountaineer (Kirata), and having found the true character of his adversary, he worshipped Him and obtained the Pasupata-astra, a celestial missile.

अकीर्तिं चापि भूतानि कथयिष्यन्ति तेऽव्ययाम् ।
सम्भावितस्य चाकीर्तिर्मरणादतिरिच्यते ॥ ३४ ॥

34. People, too, will recount thy everlasting infamy; and, to one who has been esteemed, infamy is more than death.

People, too, will recount your infamy, which will survive you long. To him who has been esteemed as a hero and as a righteous man and as one possessing other such noble qualities, death is preferable to infamy.

Moreover,

भयाद्रणादुपरतं मंस्यन्ते त्वां महारथाः।
येषां च त्वं बहुमतो भूत्वा यास्यसि लाघवम् ॥ ३५ ॥

35. The great car-warriors will think thou hast withdrawn from the battle through fear; and, having been (hitherto) highly esteemed by them, thou wilt incur their contempt.

Duryodhana and others—warriors fighting in great cars—will think that you have withdrawn from the battle through fear of Karma and others, but not through compassion. —Who are they that will think so?—The very persons, Duryodhana and others, by whom you have been esteemed as possessed of many noble qualities. Having been thus esteemed, you will again grow very small (in their estimation).

Moreover,

अवाच्यवादांश्च बहून्वदिष्यन्ति तवाहिताः ।
निन्दन्तस्तव सामर्थ्यं ततो दुःखतरं नु किम् ॥ ३६ ॥

36. Thy enemies, too, scorning thy power, will take many abusive words. What is more painful than that?

There is no pain more unbearable than that of scorn thus incurred.

Now, when you fight with Karna and others,

हतो वा प्राप्स्यसि स्वर्गं जित्वा वा भोक्ष्यसे महीम् ।
तस्मादुत्तिष्ठ कौन्तेय युद्धाय कृतनिश्चयः ॥ ३७ ॥

37. Killed, thou wilt reach heaven; victorious, thou wilt enjoy the earth. Wherefore, O son of Kunti, arise, resolved to fight.

Victorious: that is, having defeated Karna and other heroes. In either case you will have an advantage only. Wherefore rise, with the resolution. "I will conquer the enemy or die."

Now listen to the advice I offer to you, while you fight the battle regarding it as a duty:

सुखदुःखे समे कृत्वा लाभालाभौ जयाजयौ ।
ततो युद्धाय युज्यस्व नैवं पापमवाप्स्यसि ॥ ३८ ॥

38. Then, treating alike pleasure and pain, gain and loss, success and defeat, prepare for the battle, and thus wilt thou not incur sin.

Treating alike pleasure and pain: i.e., without liking the one and disliking the other. Thus fighting, you will not incur sin. [This injunction as to fighting is only incidental.]

Yoga.

Worldly considerations have been adduced (ii. 31—38) to dispel grief and attachment; but they do not form the main subject of teaching. On the other hand, it is the realisation of the Supreme Reality that forms the main subject of this portion (ii. 12, &c.) of the discourse; and this, which has been treated of already (ii. 20 *et seq* , is concluded in (ii. 39) with a view to exhibit the division of the whole subject of the sàstra. For, by making such a division of the whole subject of the sàstra as has been shewn here, that portion of the work which will treat of the two paths later on (iii. 3) will proceed the more smoothly; and the hearers also will understand it the more easily for this division of the whole subject. Hence says the Lord:

एषा तेऽभिहिता साङ्ख्ये बुद्धिर्योगे त्विमां शृणु ।
बुद्ध्या युक्तो यया पार्थ कर्मबन्धं प्रहास्यसि ॥ ३९ ॥

39. This, which has been taught to thee is wisdom concerning Sankhya. Now listen to wisdom concerning Yoga, which possessing thou shalt cast off the bond of action.

This, which has been taught to you, constitutes wisdom (buddhi) concerning Sànkhya or the true nature of the Absolute Reality,—that wisdom by which may be brought about the cessation of the evil* which is the cause of samsâra, —of grief, attachment, and the like. Now, listen to the teaching (which follows presently) concerning Yoga, which is the means of attaining wisdom concerning Sãnkhya. This Yoga, which constitutes the worship of Isvara consists in practising samâdhi or in performing works without attachment, after killing all pairs of opposites (such as heat and cold).

Now He extols the wisdom concerning Yoga, in order to create an interest in it. When possessed of wisdom concerning Yoga, O son of Pritha, you will cast off the bond of action (karma), of *dharma* and *a-dharma*, of virtue and sin, of merit and demerit, this severance of the bond being effected only on attaining to a knowledge of the Self through Divine Grace (Isvara-prasàda).

* The ignorance of the true nature of the Self.

Yoga, a safe course.

Moreover,

नेहाभिक्रमनाशोऽस्ति प्रत्यवायो न विद्यते ।
स्वल्पमप्यस्य धर्मस्य त्रायते महतो भयात् ॥ ४० ॥

40. There is no loss of effort here, there is no harm. Even a little of this devotion delivers one from great fear.

Unlike agriculture, nothing that is attempted here—in this path to môksha, in this devotion by works—is entirely lost. That is, there is no uncertainty regarding the result of any effort in the path of Yoga. Neither is there any chance of harm resulting from it, as it may sometimes result from medical treatment.—What is the result ?—Anything done, however little it be, in this Path of Yoga, saves one from great fear, from the fear of sa*m*sàra, of birth and death.

Wisdom is one.

The wisdom concerning Sànkhya and Yoga thus far described is of the following nature :

व्यवसायात्मिका बुद्धिरेकेह कुरुनन्दन ।
बहुशाखा ह्यनन्ताश्च बुद्धयोऽव्यवसायिनाम् ॥ ४१ ॥

41. Here, O son of Kuru, there is one thought of a resolute nature. Many-branched and endless are the thoughts of the irresolute.

Here, O son of Kuru, in this path to Bliss, there is only one thought of a resolute nature, and it is subversive of all other many-branched thoughts opposed to it—that thought having sprung from the right source of knowledge. Those other thoughts which are opposed to it are various. By acting up to these many-branched thoughts, sa*m*sära becomes endless and ever-spreading. But when, owing to discrimination produced by the right source of knowledge, these thoughts of endless variety cease, saṁsāra also ceases. Owing to variety in each of their branches, the thoughts of the irresolute—of those who are not possessed of the discrimination produced by the right source of knowledge—are endless.

No Wisdom possible for the worldly-minded.

As regards those who have no conviction of a resolute nature,

यामिमां पुष्पितां वाचं प्रवदन्त्यविपश्चितः ।
वेदवादरताः पार्थ नान्यदस्तीति वादिनः ॥ ४२ ॥
कामात्मानः स्वर्गपरा जन्मकर्मफलप्रदाम् ।
क्रियाविशेषबहुलां भोगैश्वर्यगतिं प्रति ॥ ४३ ॥
भोगैश्वर्यप्रसक्तानां तयाऽपहृतचेतसाम् ।
व्यवसायात्मिका बुद्धिः समाधौ न विधीयते ॥ ४४ ॥

42-44. No conviction of a resolute nature is formed in the mind of those who are attached to pleasures and power, and whose minds are drawn away by that flowery speech which the unwise—enamoured of Vedic utterances, declaring there is nothing else, full of desire, having svarga as their goal—utter, (a speech) which promises birth as the reward of actions and which abounds in specific acts for the attainment of pleasure and power, O son of Pṛithâ.

They are unwise; they are wanting in discrimination. They are enamoured of the Vedic passages composed of many a praise (to gods) and unfolding various ends and means. They say that there is nothing else besides words which are the means of attaining svarga, cattle, and other such objects of desire. They are full of desires and are ever in pursuit of them. Their chief and final goal is svarga. They talk words, fine like a flowery tree, very pleasant to hear. Their speech holds out birth as the reward of works and treats of specific acts wherewith to secure svarga, cattle, progeny and the like, and wherewith to attain pleasures and power. Thus talking, these foolish people wander in the sa*m*sâra. They regard pleasure and power as necessary; they are in love with them and have identified themselves with them. Their intelligence and wisdom are blinded (as it were) by this speech abounding in specific acts. In their mind—*samadhi*, the *budhi*, the *antah-karana*, in which are gathered together all objects of enjoyment for the *purusha*, the individual soul—no conviction of a resolute nature, no wisdom concerning Sankhya or Yoga will arise.

Advice to the Yogin.

The Lord now speaks of the result accrui to those lustful persons who are thus wanting in discrimination:

त्रैगुण्यविषया वेदा निस्त्रैगुण्यो भवार्जुन ।
निर्द्वन्द्वो नित्यसत्त्वस्थो निर्योगक्षेम आत्मवान् ॥ ४५ ॥

45. The Vedas treat of the triad of the gu*n*as. Be, O Arjuna, free from the triad of the gu*n*as, free from pairs, free from acquisition and preservation, ever remaining in the Sattva (Goodness), and self-possessed.

The Vedas * treat of the triad of the gu*n*as; sa*m*sâra †

* *i e.*, the Karmaka*n*da, the rituatstic portion of the Vedas.

† Which is made up of virtuous, sinful, and mixed deeds and their results, all brought about by the interaction of the gu*n*as.

is their subject. You, on the other hand, had better be free from the triad of the gu*n*as, *i.e*, be without desires. Be free from pairs (dvandvas), from all mutually opposed objects which are the causes of pleasure and pain. Take your stand ever in the Sattva: practise purity. To him who is anxious to acquire what has not been acquired and to preserve what has been already acquired, practice of virtue is impossible; wherefore be not anxious about new acquisitions or about the preservation of the old ones. Be also self-possessed: be guarded.* This is the advice you have to follow when engaged in the performance of duty.

Karma-Yoga.

Question:—If all those endless advantage which are said to result from the Vedic rituals are not to be sought after, to what end are they to be performed and dedicated to the Isvara?

(*Answer*):—Listen to what follows:

यावानर्थ उदपाने सर्वतः सम्प्लुतोदके ।
तावान्सर्वेषु वेदेषु ब्राह्मणस्य विजानतः ॥ ४६ ॥

46. What utility there is in a reservoir by the side of an all-spreading flood of water, the same (utility) there is in all Vedas for an enlightened Brahma*n*a.

Whatever utility—of bathing, drinking, and the like—is served by a well, a tank, and many other small reservoirs of water &c.. all that utility is only as much as the utility which is served by an all-spreading flood of water; that is the former utility is comprehended in the later. So also, whatever utility there is in all the Vedic ritual, all that is comprehended in the utility of the right knowledge possessed by a Brahma*n*a who has renounced the world and has

* Do not yield to the objects of the senses.

completely realised the truth concerning the Absolute Reality; this knowledge corresponding to the all-spreading flood of water.* The *sruti* says:—"Whatever good thing is done by people, all that is possessed by him who knows what he (Raikva) knew." (Chh. Up 4. 1-4). The same thing will also be said here (iv. 33). Wherefore †, for a man who is qualified for works it is necessary to perform works (which stand in the place of wells and tanks) before he becomes fit for the path of knowledge.

And as for you,

कर्मण्येवाधिकारस्ते मा फलेषु कदाचन ।
मा कर्मफलहेतुर्भूर्मा ते सङ्गोऽस्त्वकर्मणि ॥ ४७ ॥

47. Thy concern is with action alone, never with results. Let not the fruit of action be thy motive, nor let thy attachment be for inaction.

You are qualified for works alone, not for the path of knowledge. And then, while doing works, let there be no desire for the results of works under any circumstances whatever. If you should have a thirst for the results of works, you will have to reap those fruits. Therefore let not your motive be the fruits of your action. When a person performs work thirsting for the results of those works, then he will be subject to rebirth as the result of action. Neither may you be attached to inaction, thinking "Of what

* That is to say, all the pleasure which results from the performance of all works enjoined in the Vedas is comprehended in the bliss which the man who has realised the Self finds as the essence of his own Self; and every one must admit that all kinds of limited bliss are comprehended in the Infinite Bliss. Thus the Path of Karma-Yoga, which in the end leads to the attainment of the infinite bliss of the Self, cannot be futile, as the questioner has been led to suppose.—(A)

† Because the Path of Karma-Yoga is not futile.—(A).

avail are these painful works if their fruits should not be deisred?"

If a man should not perform works urged by a desire for their results, how then are they to be performed? The reply follows:

योगस्थः कुरु कर्माणि सङ्गं त्यक्त्वा धनञ्जय ।
सिद्ध्यसिध्द्योः समो भूत्वा समत्वं योग उच्यते ॥ ४८ ॥

48. Steadfast in devotion do thy works, O Dhanamjaya, casting off attachment, being the same in success and failure. Evenness is called Yoga.

Steadfast in devotion (Yoga) perform works merely for God's sake, casting off even such attachment as this, "May God be pleased," and being equanimous in success and failure. Success (siddhi) consists in the attainment of knowledge (jnàna) as the result of the mind (Sattva attaining purity when works are done by one without longing for their fruits; and failure results from the opposite course.

What is that devotion (Yoga) to which Arjuna has been exhorted to resort in performing works? The reply is this:— Evenness of mind in success and failure is called devotion (Yoga).

In comparison with action thus performed in the service of the Isvara with evenness of mind,

दूरेण ह्यवरं कर्म बुद्धियोगाद्धनञ्जय ।
बुद्धौ शरणमन्विच्छ कृपणाः फलहेतवः ॥ ४९ ॥

49. Verily action is far inferior to devotion in wisdom (buddhi-yoga), O Dhanamjaya. In wisdom (buddhi) seek thou shelter. Wretched are they whose motive is the fruit.

Action done by a seeker of its reward is far inferior to devotion in wisdom, *i.e.*, to action performed with evenness of mind; for, the former is the cause of birth and death, O Dhana*m*jaya. Wherefore seek shelter in the wisdom of Yoga, or rather in the wisdom of Sánkhya, which latter arises when Yoga attains maturity. That is, seek refuge in the knowledge of the supreme Reality. For, wretched are they who resort to inferior action, who are incited to action by thirst for its fruit. The *s*ruti says:

"O Gargi, wretched is he who departs from this world without knowing the Akshara, the Imperishable." (B*r*i. Up. 3-8-13).

The merit of Wisdom.

Now, learn as to what result he attains who performs his own duty with evenness of mind:

बुद्धियुक्तो जहातीह उभे सुकृतदुष्कृते ।
तस्माद्योगाय युज्यस्व योगः कर्मसु कौशलम् ॥ ५० ॥

50. He who is endued with wisdom casts off here both good deeds and bad deeds. Wherefore apply thyself to devotion. In regard to actions devotion is a power.

The man that has evenness of mind casts off in this world both merit and sin (suk*r*ita and dushk*r*ita, pu*n*ya and pâpa) through attaining mental purity and knowledge. Wherefore apply yourseslf to devotion with equanimity. For devotion is a power,—devotion being the equanimity of mind in success and failure on the part of him who is engaged in the performance of his own duties, his mind resting on the I*s*vara all the while. It is indeed a power, because works which are of a binding nature lose that nature when done with evenness of mind. Wherefore be equanimous.

Results of Karma-Yoga.

कर्मजं बुद्धियुक्ता हि फलं त्यक्त्वा मनीषिणः ।
जन्मबन्धविनिर्मुक्ताः पदं गच्छन्त्यनामयम् ॥ ५१ ॥

51. For, men of wisdom cast off the fruit of action; possessed of knowledge (and) released from the bond of birth, they go to the place where there is no evil.

For, men of wisdom, possessing evenness of mind, cast off the fruit of works *i.e.*, escape from good and bad births. They then attain knowledge. While still alive, they are released from the bond of birth, and attain the supreme abode of Vishnu—the state of moksha or liberation...which is free from all turmoils.

Or, the wisdom (buddhi) referred to in the three verses (ii. 49—51) may be the Sankhya-(not the Yoga-) wisdom, the knowledge of the Absolute Reality, (corresponding to the wide-spread expanse of water), which arises when the mind is purified by Karma-Yoga; for, it is said in ii. 50 that wisdom directly brings about the destruction of good and bad deeds.

When is that conviction attained which (it is said) arises as soon as the mind is purified by Karma-Yoga or devotion through works? The answer follows:

यदा ते मोहकलिलं बुद्धिर्व्यतितरिष्यति ।
तदा गन्तासि निर्वेदं श्रोतव्यस्य श्रुतस्य च ॥ ५२ ॥

52. When thy mind shall cross beyond the mire of delusion, then wilt thou attain to a disgust of what is yet to be heard and what has been heard.

When your intuition (buddhi) shall cross beyond the mire of delusion, by which the sense of discrimination between the Self and the not-Self is confounded and the mind (anta*h*-kara*n*a) is turned towards the objects of the senses—*i. e.*, when your reason attains purity—then will you attain to a disgust of what is yet to be heard and what has already been heard *: they will appear to you to be of no use.

You may now ask: "When shall I attain the true Yoga or conviction of the Supreme Truth, by crossing beyond the mire of delusion and obtaining wisdom by discrimination of the Self?" Listen:

श्रुतिविप्रतिपन्ना ते यदा स्थास्यति निश्चला ।
समाधावचला बुद्धिस्तदा योगमवाप्स्यसि ॥ ५३ ॥

53. When thy mind, perplexed by what thou hast heard, shall stand firm and steady in the Self, then wilt thou attain Yoga.

When your intuition (buddhi= anta*h*-kara*n*a) which has been perplexed by what you have heard about the multifarious ends and means in all their relations—concerning the life of activity and the life of retirement—shall stand firm, without distraction (vikshepa=viparyaya) and doubt (vikalpa= sa*m*saya), in the Self (Sam*a*dhi, *i.e.*, the objective point of your meditation), then you will attain Yoga, samadhi, *i.e.*, the knowledge which arises from discrimination.

The characteristic attributes of a perfect Sage.

Having found an occasion for interrogation, Arjuna asks with a desire to know the characteristic marks of one who has attained wisdom in steady contemplation (sam*a*dhipraj*n*a):

---

* Except, of course, the teaching of the scripture regarding the *A*tman, the Self.—(A)

अर्जुन उवाच :—

स्थितप्रज्ञस्य का भाषा समाधिस्थस्य केशव ।
स्थितधीः किं प्रभाषेत किमासीत व्रजेत किम् ॥ ५४ ॥

Arjuna said:

54. What, O Kesava! , is the description of one of steady knowledge, who is constant in contemplation? How does one of steady knowledge speak, how sit, how move?

How is a man who has a firm conviction that he is the Supreme Brahman, and who is intent on contemplation (samadhi).—how is such a man spoken of by others? How does the man of steady knowledge himself speak? How does he sit? How does he move?—In this verse Arjuna asks in order to know what the characteristic attributes of a man of steady knowledge (sthitaprajna) are.

From ii. 55 to the end of the Discourse (adhyaya), the characteristic attributes of a man of steady knowledge as well as the means of obtaining that knowledge are taught to him who, having from the very commencement renounced all works, has entered upon a course of Devotion to knowledge (jnana-yoga-nishtha), as well as to him who has reached that stage by means of Devotion to works (Karma-yoga.) For, everywhere in spiritual science (adhyatma-sastra), the very characteristic attributes of the successful Yogin are taught as the means (of attaining that stage), since they are to be attained by effort. The Lord now points out those characteristic attributes which, as attainable by effort, constitute the means as well.

श्रीभगवानुवाच :—

प्रजहाति यदा कामान्सर्वान्पार्थ मनोगतान् ।
आत्मन्येवात्मना तुष्टः स्थितप्रज्ञस्तदोच्यते ॥ ५५ ॥

(1) Satisfaction in the Self.

The Lord said:

55. When a man, satisfied in the Self alone by himself, completely casts off all the desires of the mind, then is he said to be one of steady knowledge.

When a man completely abandons all the various desires that enter the heart and is satisfied with the True Innermost Self (Pratyagatman) in himself, without longing for external possessions, averse to everything else because of his acquisition of the immortal nectar,—*i.e.*, his realisation of the Supreme Truth,—then he is said to be a wise man (vidvan), one whose knowledge arising from the discrimination of the Self and the not-Self has been steadied. [If, on his abandoning of all desires, nothing should be found to cause satisfaction while the cause of the embodied state still operates, it would follow that his behaviour would be like that of a mad man or a maniac. Hence the words 'satisfied in the Self' etc.] That is to say, he who has abandoned all desires connected with progeny, possessions and the world, who has renounced (all works), who delights in the Self and plays with the Self,—he is the man whose knowledge is steady.

(2) Equanimity in pleasure and pain.

Moreover,

दुःखेष्वनुद्विग्नमनाः सुखेषु विगतस्पृहः ।
वीतरागभयक्रोधः स्थितधीर्मुनिरुच्यते ॥ ५६ ॥

56. He whose heart is not distressed in calamities, from whom all longing for pleasures has departed, who is free from attachment, fear and wrath, he is called a sage, a man of steady knowledge.

His heart if not distressed in calamities such as may arise from disorder in the body *, (adhyatmika), etc. Unlike fire, which increases as fuel is added, his longing for pleasures does not increase as more pleasures are attained. He is said to be a man of steady knowledge. He is called a sage, a Sannyasin, one who has renounced works.

(3) Absence of attachment, delight and aversion.

Moreover:

यः सर्वत्रानभिस्नेहस्तत्तत्प्राप्य शुभाशुभम् ।
नाभिनन्दति न द्वेष्टि तस्य प्रज्ञा प्रतिष्ठिता ॥ ५७ ॥

57. Whoso, without attachment anywhere, on meeting with anything good or bad, neither exults nor hates, his knowledge becomes steady.

The sage has no attachment even for the life of the body. He does not exult in pleasure, nor is he averse to pain that may befall him. When he is thus free from delight and distress, his knowledge arising from discrimination becomes steady.

---

* Calamities are divided into the three following classes according to their sources:

Adhyâtmika, arising from disorder in one's own body;

Adhibhautika, arising from external object such as a tiger;

Adhidaivika, arising from the action of great, intelligent, cosmic forces such as those which cause rain and storm or such beings as Yakshas, Râkshasas and Pisâchas.

Pleasures also are divided into the same three classes.

(4) Complete withdrawal of senses from objects.

Moreover,

यदा संहरते चायं कूर्मोऽङ्गानीव सर्वशः ।
इन्द्रियाणीन्द्रियार्थेभ्यस्तस्य प्रज्ञा प्रतिष्ठिता ॥ ५८ ॥

58. When he completely withdraws the senses from sense-objects, as the tortoise (withdraws) its limbs from all sides, his knowledge is steady.

He, *i.e.*, the devotee who strives in the path of knowledge (j*n*ana-nish*t*ha), withdraws his senses from all objects as the tortoise withdraws its limbs from all sides out of fear.

(*Question*) :—Now, even the senses of a diseased man who is not able to partake of sensuous objects withdraw from sense-objects, but the taste for them ceases not. How does that cease ?

(*Answer*) :—Listen :

विषया विनिवर्तन्ते निराहारस्य देहिनः ।
रसवर्जं रसोऽप्यस्य परं दृष्ट्वा निवर्तते ॥ ५९ ॥

59. Objects withdraw from an abstinent man, but not the taste. On seeing the Supreme, his taste, too, ceases.

The senses,—'vishaya*h*,' meaning literally *sense-objects*, here stands for the *senses*,—it is true, withdraw from objects even in the case of an ignorant person who, practising extremest austerity, abstains from all sensuous objects ; but the taste or inclination (rasa) for those objects ceases not. (*Rasa* is used in the sense of taste or inclination in such expressions as 'svarasena prav*r*itta*h*,' 'rasika*h*,' and 'rasaj*n*a*h*.) Even that taste, that subtle attachment, vanishes in the case of the devotee who, having seen the Supreme Reality, the Brahman, thinks 'I am myself That'; that is to say, his perception of sensuous objects becomes seedless (nir-bîja), has lost all germ of evil. The meaning is this: In the absence of right knowledge, there can be no annihilation * of taste for sensuous objects; wherefore, steadiness of right knowledge (prajñá) should be acquired.

Unrestrained senses work mischief.

He who would acquire steadiness of right knowledge (prajñá) should first bring the senses under control. For, if not controlled, they will do harm. So, the Lord says:

यततो ह्यपि कौन्तेय पुरुषस्य विपश्चितः ।
इन्द्रियानि प्रमाथीनि हरन्ति प्रसभं मनः ॥ ६० ॥

60. The dangerous senses, O son of Kunti, forcibly carry away the mind of a wise man, even while striving (to control them).

The senses are dangerous. They agitate the mind of the man who is inclined to sensuous objects. Having thus agitated the mind, they carry it away by force, while the man is wide awake † though the mind is possessed of discriminative knowledge.

(5) Devotion to the Lord

Wherefore,

तानि सर्वाणि संयम्य युक्त आसीत मत्परः ।
वशे हि यस्येन्द्रियाणि तस्य प्रज्ञा प्रतिष्ठिता ॥ ६१ ॥

* It is no fallacy of mutual dependance (anyonyâsraya) to say that knowledge arises on the killing of desires and that desires vanish when knowledge arises. For, desire in its grossest form disappears at the first dawn of knowledge, and as knowledge is steadied and perfected, even he subtlest desires are killed out.

† i.e. while repeatedly thinking of the evil nature of sensuous objects

61. Restraining them all, a man should remain steadfast, intent on Me. His knowledge is steady whose senses are under control.

He should bring the senses under control and sit calm and intent on Me, Vasudeva, the Innermost Self of all; *i.e.*, he should sit thinking 'I am no other than He.' The knowledge of that devotee is steady who, thus seated, has by practice brought the senses under his own control.

Thought of sense-objects is the source of evil.

Now the Lord proceeds to point out the source of all evil in the case of the unsuccessful:

ध्यायतो विषयान्पुंसः सङ्गस्तेषूपजायते ।
सङ्गात्सञ्जायते कामः कामात्क्रोधोऽभिजायते ॥ ६२ ॥

62. When a man thinks of objects, attachment for them arises. From attachment arises desire; from desire arises wrath.

Attachment for objects arises when a man thinks of them specifically*—Wrath arises when desire is frustrated by some cause or other.

क्रोधाद्भवति सम्मोहः सम्मोहात्स्मृतिविभ्रमः ।
स्मृतिभ्रंशाद्बुद्धिनाशो बुद्धिनाशात्प्रणश्यति ॥ ६३ ॥

63. From wrath arises delusion; from delusion, failure of memory; from failure of memory, loss of conscience; from loss of conscience he is utterly ruined.

From wrath arises delusion, a lack of discrimination between right and wrong. Verily, when a wrathful man gets

---

* *i.e.*, thinks of their beauty etc.

infatuated, he is led to insult even the Guru. From infatuation follows failure of memory. Despite the presence of favourable conditions, no reminiscences arise of things already impressed upon the mind by the teachings of the *s*astras and of the teacher (acharya). From failure of memory follows loss of conscience (buddhi)—the inability of the inner sense (anta*h*-kara*n*a) to discriminate between right and wrong (karya and a-karya). By loss of conscience he is utterly ruined. Man is man only so long as his anta*h*-kara*n*a is competent to discriminate between right and wrong. When it is unable to do so, the man is utterly ruined. Thus, by loss of conscience (anta*h*-kara*n*a, buddhi) he is ruined, he is debarred from attaining human aspirations.

Sense-control leads to peace and happiness.

The contemplation of sense-objects has been described as the source of all evil. Now the means of deliverance (moksha) is described as follows :

रागद्वेषवियुक्तैस्तु विषयानिन्द्रियैश्चरन् ।
आत्मवश्यैर्विधेयात्मा प्रसादमधिगच्छति ॥ ६४ ॥

64. He attains peace, who, self-controlled, approaches objects with the senses devoid of love and hatred and brought under his own-control.

The natural activity of the senses is characterised by love and hatred. He who longs for deliverance resorts only to unavoidable objects with the senses—hearing, etc.,—devoid of love and hatred and brought under his own control, his inner-sense (atman—anta*h*-kara*n*a) being made obedient to his own will. Such a man attains peace, tranquillity, self-possession.

(*Question*) :—What will happen when peace is attained ?

Answer :—Listen :

प्रसादे सर्वदुःखानां हानिरस्योपजायते ।
प्रसन्नचेतसो ह्याशु बुद्धिः पर्यवतिष्ठते ॥ ६५ ॥

65. In peace there is an end of all his miseries; for, the reason of the tranquil-minded soon becomes steady.

On the attainment of peace there is an end of all the devotee's miseries such as pertain to the body and the mind. For, the reason (buddhi) of the pure-minded man soon becomes steady, pervading on all sides like the akasa; *i.e.*, it remains steadfast, in the form of the Self.

The sense of the passage is this:—The man whose heart is pure and whose mind is steady has achieved his object Wherefore the devout man should resort only to those sense-objects which are indispensable and not forbidden by the sastras, with the senses devoid of love and hatred.

Tranquillity is thus extolled:

नास्ति बुद्धिरयुक्तस्य न चायुक्तस्य भावना ।
न चाभावयतः शान्तिरशान्तस्य कुतः सुखम् ॥ ६६ ॥

66. There is no wisdom to the unsteady, and no meditation to the unsteady, and to the unmeditative no peace; to the peaceless, how can there be happiness?

To the unsteady (ayukta = asamáhita), to the man who cannot fix the mind in contemplation, there can be no wisdom (buddhi), no knowledge of the true nature of the Self. To the unsteady, there can be no meditation, no intense devotion to Self-knowledge. So, to him who is not devoted to Self-knowledge there can be no peace, no tranquillity. To the peaceless man, how can there be happiness? Verily, happiness consists in the freedom of the senses from thirst of sensual enjoyment, not in the thirst (*trishna*) for objects. This last is mere misery indeed. While there is thirst, there can be no trace of happiness; we cannot so much as smell it.

Sense-restraint conduces to steady knowledge.

(*Question*) :—Why is there no knowledge for the unsteady?

(*Answer*) :—Listen :

इन्द्रियाणां हि चरतां यन्मनोऽनु विधीयते ।
तदस्य हरति प्रज्ञां वायुर्नावमिवाम्भसि ॥ ६७ ॥

67. For, the mind which yields to the roving senses carries away his knowledge, as the wind (carries away) a ship on water.

For, the mind which yields to the senses engaged in their respective objects, *i.e.*, the mind which is altogether engrossed in the thought of the various objects of the senses, destroys the devotee's discriminative knowledge of the Self and the not-Self.—How?—As the wind carries away a ship from the intended course of the sailors and drives her astray, so the mind carries away the devotee's consciousness from the Self and turns it towards sense-objects.

Having explained in several ways the proposition enunciated in ii. 60—61, the Lord concludes by reaffirming the same proposition :

तस्माद्यस्य महाबाहो निगृहीतानि सर्वशः ।
इन्द्रियाणीन्द्रियार्थेभ्यस्तस्य प्रज्ञा प्रतिष्ठिता ॥ ६८ ॥

68. Therefore, O mighty-armed, his knowledge is steady whose senses have been entirely restrained from sense-objects.

It has been shown that evil arises from the senses pursuing sense-objects. Wherefore, that devotee's knowledge is steady whose senses have been restrained from sense-objects (such as sound) in all forms, subjective and objective.

(6) The Universe, a mere dream to the Sage.

In the case of the man who possesses discriminative knowledge and whose knowledge has become steady, his experience of all matters, temporal and spiritual (laukika and vaidika, sensuous and supersensuous), ceases on the cessation of nescience (avidya); for, it is the effect of nescience: and nescience ceases because it is opposed to knowledge. To make this clear, the Lord proceeds:

या निशा सर्वभूतानां तस्यां जागर्ति संयमी ।
यस्यां जाग्रति भूतानि सा निशा पश्यतो मुनेः ॥ ६९ ॥

69. What is night to all beings, therein the self controlled one is awake. Where all beings are awake, that is the night of the sage who sees.

To all beings the Supreme Reality is night. Night is by nature tamasic, and, as such, causes confusion of things. The Reality is accessible only to a man of steady knowledge. Just as what is day to others becomes night to night-wanderers, so, to all beings who are ignorant and who correspond to the night- wanderers, the Supreme Reality is dark, is like night; for it is not accessible to those whose minds are not in It. With reference to that Supreme Reality, the self-restrained Yogin who has subdued the senses, and who has shaken off the sleep of Avidya (nescience), is fully awake. When all beings are said to be awake, *i.e.*, when all beings, who in reality sleep in the night of ignorance, imbued with the distinct notions of perceiver and things perceived, are as it were mere dreamers in sleep at night,—that state is night in the eye of the sage who knows the Supreme Reality; for, it is nescience itself.

Works are not meant of the Sage.

Wherefore works are enjoined on the ignorant, not on the wise. Wisdom (Vidya) arising, nescience (Avidya) disappears as does the darkness of the night at sunrise. Before the dawn of wisdom, nescience presents itself in various forms—as actions, means and results,—is regarded as authoritative, and becomes the source of all action. When it is regarded as of no authority, it cannot induce action. A man engages in action regarding it as his duty—regarding that action is enjoined by such an authority as the Veda, but not looking upon all this duality as mere illusion, as though it were night. When he has learnt to look upon all this dual world as a mere illusion, as though it were night, when he has realised the Self, his duty consists not in the performance of action, but in the renunciation of all action. Our Lord will accordingly show (v. 17 *et seq.*) that such a man's duty consists in devotion to wisdom, in j*n*ana-nish*t*ha.

(*Objection*):—In the absence of an injunction (Pravartaka prama*n*a = vidhi) one cannot have recourse to that course either.

(*Answer*):—This objection does not apply; for the knowledge of Atman means the knowledge of one's own Self. There is indeed no need of an injunction impelling one to devote oneself to one's Atman, for the very reason that Atman is one's own very Self. And all organs of knowledge (prama*n*as) are so called because they ultimately lead to a knowledge of the Self. When the knowledge of the true nature of the Self has been attained, neither organs of knowledge nor objects of knowledge present themselves to consciousness any longer. For, the final authority, (*viz.*, the Veda), teaches that the Self is in reality no percipient of objects, and while so denying, (*i.e.*, as a result of that teaching), the Veda itself ceases to be an authority, just as the dream-perception (ceases to be an authority) in the waking state. In ordinary experience, too, we do not find any organ of knowledge necessitating further operation (on the part of the knower) when once the thing to be percived by that organ has been perceived.

(7) Subjugation of desire and personal self.

The Lord proceeds to teach, by an illustration, that that devotee only who is wise, who has abandoned desires, and whose wisdom is steady, can attain moksha, but not he who, without renouncing, cherishes a desire for objects of pleasure.

आपूर्यमाणमचलप्रतिष्ठं
समुद्रमापः प्रविशन्ति यद्वत् ।
तद्वत्कामा यं प्रविशन्ति सर्वे
स शान्तिमाप्नोति न कामकामी ॥ ७० ॥

70. He attains peace, into whom all desires enter as waters enter the ocean, which, filled from all sides, remains unaltered ; but not he who desires objects.

The ocean is filled with waters flowing from all sides. Its state is unaltered, though waters flow into it from all sides; it remains all the while within its bounds without change. That sage into whom in this manner desires of all sorts enter from all sides without affecting him—as waters enter into the ocean—even in the presence of objects; in whose Self they are absorbed, and whom they do not enslave ;

that sage attains peace (moksha), but not the other who has a longing for external objects.

Because it is so, therefore,

विहाय कामान्यः सर्वान्पुमांश्चरति निःस्पृहः ।
निर्ममो निरहङ्कारः स शान्तिमधिगच्छति ॥ ७१ ॥

71. That man attains peace, who, abandoning all desires, moves about without attachment, without selfishness, without vanity.

That man of renunciation, who, entirely abandoning all desires, goes through life content with the bare necessities of life, who has no attachment even for those bare necessities of life, who regards not as his even those things which are needed for the mere bodily existence, who is not vain of his knowledge,—such a man of steady knowledge, that man who knows Brahman, attains peace (nirva*n*a), the end of all the misery of sa*m*sara (mundane existence). In short, becomes the very Brahman.

Knowledge leads to Divine Felicity

This devotion to knowledge is extolled as follows:

एषा ब्राह्मी स्थितिः पार्थ नैनां प्राप्य विमुह्यति ।
स्थित्वाऽस्यामन्तकालेऽपि ब्रह्म निर्वाणमृच्छति ॥ ७२ ॥

72. This is the Brahmic state, O son of P*r*itha. Attaining to this, none is deluded. Remaining in this state even at the last period of life, one attains to the felicity of Brahman.

इति श्रीमद्भगवद्गीतासूपनिषत्सु ब्रह्मविद्यायां योगशास्त्रे
श्रीकृष्णार्जुनसंवादे साङ्ख्ययोगो नाम
द्वितीयोऽध्यायः ।

This foregoing state—to renounce all and to dwell in Brahman—is the Divine state, the state of Brahman. It pertains to and has its being in Brahman. On reaching this state, one is no longer deluded. Remaining in this state even at the last period of life, one attains moksha, the felicity of Brahman. And it needs no saying that he who renounces while yet a student and dwells in Brahman throughout life attains the Felicity of Brahman, the Brahma-Nirva*n*a.

THIRD DISCOURSE.

KARMA-YOGA.

Arjuna's perplexity.

The two aspects of wisdom—relating respectively to Pravritti and Nivritti, *i.e.*, to the Path of Works and the Path of Renunciation—with which the Gita-Sastra is concerned have been pointed out by the Lord in the Second Discourse. He has recommended renunciation of action to those who hold to the Sankhya-buddhi (Sankhya aspect of wisdom) and has added in ii. 72 that their end can be achieved by being devoted to that alone. And as to Arjuna, He has declared in ii. 47 that he should resort to works (karma) alone as based on Yoga-buddhi (the Yoga aspect of wisdom), while it has not been said that the Highest Good can be attained by that alone.* Seeing this, Arjuna is troubled in mind and therefore puts a question to the Lord. (III. 1, 2).

This perplexity in Arjuna's mind is quite explicable. He thinks, "how might the Lord first describe to me—a devout seeker of Bliss—the direct means of attaining Bliss, namely adherence to the Sankhya aspect of wisdom, and then command me to do action which is fraught with many a tangible evil and which is but an indirect and uncertain means of attaining Bliss? Arjuna's question, too, points to this state of mind; and the Lord's words in reply to the question are explicable only when the sastra makes such a distinction (between Sankhya and Yoga) as has been described above.

---

* *Vide* ii 49—(A)

No conjunction of Knowledge and Action.

A certain commentator * interprets the meaning of Arjuna's question differently and explains the Lord's reply as opposed (to the question) in meaning. So also, he sums up the teaching of the Gita-*s*astra in one way in the introductory portion of his commentary, while he interprets the question and answer in this connection in a different way—How?—It is stated in the introduction that a simultaneous conjunction of knowledge and action for men in all stages of religious life is inculcated in the Gita-*s*astra; and moreover a specific statement is made amounting to an emphatic denial of the doctrine that moksha can be attained by knowledge alone, *i.e.*, without those works which are enjoined by the scriptures as obligatory throughout life. But here, in the Third Discourse, he makes out that devotion to only one of the two paths is taught. This is tantamount to saying that the very works which are enjoined by the scriptures as obligatory throughout life have to be renounced. How is it possible either for the Lord to teach such contradictions or for the disciple to accept them?

That commentator may perhaps explain away the contradiction thus:—It is only to the g*r*ihasthas (to the order of married house-holders)—but not to other orders—that salvation by mere knowledge, preceded by the renunciation of works enjoined in the *s*ruti and in the sm*r*iti, is denied.†

This, too, involves a self-contradiction. For after declaring (in the introduction) that a simultaneous conjunction of knowledge and action is meant for *all* religious orders by the Gita-*s*astra, how could he, in contradiction thereto, say here (in iii. Discourse) that salvation by mere knowledge is meant for *some* religious orders?

---

* The V*r*ittikara is here referred to. *Vide ante* note on p. 16.

† In the iii. Discourse salvation by mere knowledge is said to be possible in the case of *other* orders. Thus, they hold, there is no contradiction.

Then the commentator may explain away the contradiction thus: It is with reference to the *srauta-karma* (action enjoined in the *sruti*) that the assertion is made that salvation by mere—*i.e.*, unconjoined with the *srauta-karma*—knowledge is denied to the *gri*hastha. The smarta-karma (action enjoined in the smriti) that is meant for a *gri*hastha is ignored as if it were absent.* It is in this sense that salvation by mere knowledge is denied in the case of *gri*hasthas.†

This also involves an absurdity. For, how is it possible for any intelligent man to believe that salvation by knowledge conjoined only with the smarta-karma is denied to a *gri*hastha alone, but not to other orders? On the other hand, if, as a means of obtaining salvation, the smarta-karma should be conjoined with knowledge in the case of the sa*m*nyasins—the fourth religious order,—then it follows that, for the *gri*hasthas also, knowledge should be conjoined only with the smarta-karma, not with the srauta-karma.

Then, he may explain away the contradiction thus: it is only in the case of a *gri*hastha that a conjunction (of knowledge) with both the *srauta-karma* and the smarta-karma—both being of equal importance to him—is necessary for

* Because it is of secondary importance to him.

† It may be further explained thus:

The sa*m*nyasins have renounced only the *srauta-karma*, but they have still to do certain acts and be bound by certain restrictions as enjoined in the sm*ri*ti. Thus a conjunction of knowledge with action as a means of obtaining salvation holds good in the case of sa*m*nyasins. On the other hand, the *srauta-karma* is binding on a *gri*hastha; that is to say, he cannot attain salvation by knowledge unconjoined with the *srauta-karma*. The smarta-karma, which he is bound to do is only of secondary importance to him; and in the absence of the *srauta-karma*, which is of primary importance to him, the existence of the smarta-karma may be ignored in his case. Thus, while a sa*m*nyasin can attain salvation by knowledge conjoined with the smarta-karma, a *gri*hastha can obtain it by knowledge conjoined with the *srauta-karma*.

salvation, whereas the samnyasins can attain moksha by knowledge conjoined with the smarta-karma only.

If so, too much exertion in the shape of both the *srauta*-karma and the smarta-karma, very painful in themselves, falls to the lot of the grihastha.

Renunciation enjoined in the scriptures.

The commentator in question may now say: Because of this multiplicity of exertion, salvation is attained only by a grihastha, but not by other religious orders who have not to do the *nitya* or obligatory *s*rauta-karma.*

This, too, is wrong; for, in all the Upanishads, in the Itihasas, in the Purana, and in the Yoga-*s*astra, renunciation of all karma is enjoined on the seeker of moksha as an accessory † to knowledge. Both in the *s*ruti ‡ and in the smriti, a gradual passage (through the three orders to the fourth order) is enjoined, as well as a sudden jump (from any one of the three to the fourth order).

---

* According to a certain ritualistic school of Mimamsakas, renunciation of the *s*rauta-karma is intended for those who are afflicted with physical disabilities —for the lame and the blind who cannot perform the complicated Vedic sacrifices according to prescribed rules. According to this view, the samnyasins cannot attain moksha, as they have not performed the *s*rauta karma.

† If samnyasa were meant for the lame and the blind only, it could not have been meant as an accessory to knowledge. Hence that view is wrong.

‡ "On the completion of the student-life one should become an house-holder; then, leaving home he should become a forest-dweller and then retire from the world. Or he may retire from the world when he is yet a student, or retire from house or from the forest, whether he is engaged in austerities or not, whether he has completed or not the student's career, whether he has quenched the sacrificial fires or not. In short the very day on which he may get disgusted with the world, the same day he should retire from it." *Jabala-Upanihad*, 4.

If so—the commentator in question may retort—it follows that a conjunction of knowledge with action is necessary for all religious orders.*

No, (we reply). For, renunciation of all action is enjoined on the seeker of moksha, as the following passages from the sruti show:

"Having given up all desire for progeny, for wealth and for the world, they lead a mendicant life."—(Bri. Up. 3-5-1),

"Wherefore, of these austerities, renunciation, they say, is excellent." "Renunciation alone excelled." (Taittiriya-Up. 4-78, 79).

"Not by action, not by progeny, not by wealth, but by renunciation, some attained immortality." (*Ibid.* 4-12).

"One may renounce the world when yet a student." (Jabala-Upanishad, 4).

The following passages from the smriti may also be quoted:—

"Give up religion, give up irreligion. Give up truth, give up untruth. Having given up both truth and untruth, give up that † by which you give them up."

"Finding the samsara (mundane existence) worthless and wishing to get at the essence, the unmarried grow quite weary of life and renounce the world."—(Brihaspati).

Suka's teaching runs as follows:

---

* When it is said that all the religious orders are sanctioned by the sruti, the duties also that are assigned to them respectively are binding on them. A conjunction of knowledge with action is thus proved to be necessary in the case of all asramas or religious orders.

† Even that idea of personality which is implied in the thought, 'I have abandoned these.'

"By action a person is bound, and by wisdom he is released. Therefore, the sages who see the goal do no action." (Santiparva, Mokshadharma, 241-7).

Here (in the Bhagavad-gita) also we have, "Renouncing all actions by thought," &. (v. 12).

Moksha cannot be the effect of an action

Moksha, too, being no effect of an act, no action will be of any avail to a *mumukshu*, a seeker of moksha.

(*Objection*) :—The performance of obligatory duties is intended for the mere avoidance of the sin (of their omission).

(*Answer*) :—No. For, the sin arises only in the case of one who has not formally entered the fourth order, the order of sa*m*nyasins. It is certainly (as the opponent must admit) not possible to imagine that a sa*m*nyasin will incur sin by omitting the *agni-karya*—worship of the sacred fire—as students (Brahmacharins) do thereby incur when they are not yet sa*m*nyasins, *i.e.*, when they have not formally renounced works.*

Neither is it, indeed, possible to imagine the generation of sin—which is a *bhava* or positive effect—out of the omission of the obligatory duties,—which is an *abhava* or mere negation; for, that the generation of existence out of non-existence is impossible is taught by the sruti in the words "How can existence arise out of non-existence?" (*Chhandogya-Upanishad*, 6-2). If the Veda should teach what is inconceivable to us, *viz.*, that evil arises from the omission of prescribed duties, it is tantamount to saying that the Veda conduces to no good and is therefore no authority;

---

* It is admitted by all that a Brahmacharin alone incurs sin by omitting *agnikarya* (throwing fuel into the sacred fire) and the Vedic study, which are both enjoined only on the first order (asrama). No sin in fact is incurred by any religious order of men neglecting the duties not enjoined on that order.

for, performance and non-performance alike would only produce pain. This would further lead to the absurd * conclusion that *sastra* or revelation is *creative*, not *indicative*, a conclusion which is acceptable to none. Hence no karma for samnyasins ; and hence also the absurdity of a conjunction of knowledge and action.

Conjunction is inconsistent with Arjuna's question.

Arjuna's question (in iii) would also be inexplicable. If, in the Second Discourse, it was said by the Lord that both knowledge and action should be simultaneously conjoined in Arjuna himself, then his question (in iii. 1) cannot be explained. If it was taught to Arjuna that both knowledge and action should be conjoined in him, knowledge which is superior to action must certainly have been meant for him. Then there could be no occasion for the question, or for the blame, which is implied in Arjuna's words. "Then why dost Thou, O Kesava, direct me to this terrible action ?" (iii. 1.) It can by no means be supposed that knowledge, the superior of the two, was forbidden to Arjuna alone by the Lord in His previous teaching,—in which case the question on the part of Arjuna distinguishing (one path from the other) might arise. If, on the other hand, it has been previously taught by the Lord that knowledge and action are intended for two distinct classes of men respectively, on the ground that a simultaneous devotion—on the part of one man—to knowledge and action was impossible owing to their mutual opposition, then the question (in iii. 1.) becomes explicable. Even supposing that the question was asked from ignorance, the Lord's answer that devotion to knowledge and devotion to action are assigned to two distinct class of men cannot be explained. Neither can

* For, it is tantamouut to saying that an *abhava* which in itself cannot produce anything, is invested with a power to do so by the *sastra* which is of absolute authority.

the reply of the Lord be attributed to His ignorance. From this very answer of the Lord—that devotion to knowledge and devotion to action are assigned to distinct classes of persons—follows the impossibility of a conjunction of knowledge and action.

Wherefore the conclusion of the Gita and all the Upanishads is this, that moksha can be obtained by knowledge alone, unaided (by action).

If a conjunction of the two were possible (for one man,) Arjuna's request to the Lord to teach him only one of the two, j*n*ana or karma, would be unaccountable. The Lord, moreover, emphatically teaches the impossibility of devotion to j*n*ana in the case of Arjuna, in the words "do thou therefore perform action only." (iv, 15).

Which is better, Knowledge or Action?

अर्जुन उवाच—

ज्यायसी चेत्कर्मणस्ते मता बुद्धिर्जनार्दन ।
तत्किं कर्मणि घोरे मां नियोजयसि केशव ॥ १ ॥

Arjuna said:

1. If it be thought by Thee that knowledge is superior to action, O Janardana, why then dost Thou, O Ke*s*ava, direct me to this terrible action?

If it had been meant that knowledge and action should be conjoined, then the means of salvation would be one only; and, in that case, a groundless separation of knowledge from action would have been made by Arjuna declaring knowiedge to be superior to action. If the two be regarded as constituting together a single means to a single end, they cannot at the same time be regarded to be distinct as producing distinct effects.* Neither could we account for what Arjuna said—" Why then dost Thou direct me to this terrible action?"—as if meaning to censure the Lord, on finding that He—for what reason Arjuna could not see clearly—had exhorted him to follow the unwholesome course of action after declaring that knowledge was superior to action.

Now, if a conjunction of knowledge with the smarta-karma only were intended for all by the Lord and understood by Arjuna as so intended, how could we then justify the words of Arjuna † "why dost Thou direct me to this terrible action?"

Moreover,

व्यामिश्रेणेव वाक्येन बुद्धिं मोहयसीव मे ।
तदेकं वद निश्चित्य येन श्रेयोऽहमाप्नुयाम् ॥ २ ॥

2. With an apparently perplexing speech, Thou confusest as it were my understanding. Tell me with certainty that one (way) by which I may attain bliss.

---

* This may be explained with reference to the present case thus :—When knowledge and action are held to form together but one means to moksha, they cannot at the same time be supposed to become distinct as producing distinct effects. If this were possible, Arjuna's considering of the two as distinct from each other might find some justification.

† For, then, the Lord who had taught a conjunction of knowledge and action could not have enjoined mere action on Arjuna, and so there would be no occasion for Arjuna's complaint.

No doubt the Lord speaks clearly; still, to me of dull understanding the speech of the Lord appears to be perplexing. Thereby "Thou confusest as it were my understanding." Arjuna means—"It is not possible That thou wouldst confuse me, Thou who hast undertaken to remove my confusion? Hence I say 'Thou confusest *as it were* my understanding," He goes on:—If Thou thinkest that knowledge and action, which are intended for two distinct classes of aspirants, cannot both be followed by one and the same person, then teach me one of the two, knowledge or action, after determining (within Thyself) that "this one alone is suited to Arjuna, and is in accordance with the state and powers of his understanding;" teach me that one of the two knowledge or action, by which I may attain bliss.

If knowledge had been intended by the Lord to be at least an accessory to devotion to action, why then should Arjuna wish to know about only one of them. It had not indeed been said by the Lord that He would teach him one only of the two, knowledge or action, but not both,—in which case alone Arjuna might ask for one only, seeing that *both* would not be taught to him.

The Paths of Knowledge and Action.

The Blessed Lord gives the following reply, which is in conformity with the question:

श्रीभगवानुवाच —

लोकेऽस्मिन्द्विविधा निष्ठा पुरा प्रोक्ता मयाऽनघ ।
ज्ञानयोगेन साङ्ख्यानां कर्मयोगेन योगिनाम् ॥ ३ ॥

The Blessed Lord said:

3. In this world a twofold path was taught by Me at first, O sinless one: that of Sankhyas by

devotion to knowledge, and that of Yogins by devotion to action.

In this world—with reference to the people of the three castes, for whom alone are intended the teachings of the sastra (Scripture),—a twofold nishtha or path of devotion was taught by Me, the Omniscient Lord, when at first, at the beginning of creation, I created people and revived the tradition of the Vedic doctrine for teaching them the means of attaining worldly prosperity and Bliss.—What was that twofold path of devotion?—One of them was jnana-yoga, the devotion of knowledge—knowledge itself being yoga—suited to the Sankhyas, to those who possessed a clear knowledge of the Self and the not-Self, who renounced the world from the Brahmacharya (the first holy order or asrama), who determined the nature of things in the light of the Vedantic wisdom, who belonged to the highest class of samnyasins known as the Paramahamsas, whose thoughts ever dwelt on Brahman only. The other was karma-yoga, the devotion of action,—action itself being Yoga or devotion,—suited to Yogins, to karmins, to those who were inclined to action.

If it had already been taught or is going to be taught by the Lord in the Gita—and if it had been taught in the Vedas as well—that both knowledge and action should be conjoined in one and the same person as a means to one and the same end, how might the Lord teach Arjuna, who approached Him as a beloved pupil, that the two paths of knowledge and action were respectively intended for two distinct classes of aspirants? If, on the other hand, we suppose, that the Lord meant that Arjuna, after hearing Him teach knowledge and action, would devote himself, of his own accord, to both of them simultaneously conjoined, but that to others He would teach that the two paths were intended for two distinct classes of aspirants, then it would be tantmount to saying that the Lord is subject to love and hatred and that therefore He is no authority (in such matters): which is absurd. Wherefore by no argument can a conjunction of knowledge and action be proved.

Karma-Yoga leads to freedom from action.

The superiority of knowledge to action, referred to by Arjuna (iii. 1), must be true, because there is no denial of it. And it must also be true that the path of knowledge is intended for *sam*nyasins only. Since it has been stated that the two paths are intended for two distinct classes of aspirants, such is evidently the opinion of the Lord. Now seeing that Arjuna, afflicted as he was at heart on the ground that the Lord had urged him to action which caused bondage, was resolved not to perform action, the Lord proceeds with iii. 4.

Or, the connection of what has gone before with the sequel may be thus stated: As devotion to knowledge and devotion to action are mutually opposed, it is impossible for one man to resort to both of them at one and the same time. From this it may follow that each leads to the goal quite independently of the other. But the truth is this: Devotion to action is a means to the end, not directly, but only as leading to devotion to knowledge; whereas the latter, which is attained by means of devotion to action, leads to the goal directly, without extraneous help. To show this, the Lord says:

न कर्मणामनारम्भान्नैष्कर्म्यं पुरुषोऽश्नुते ।
न च संन्यसनादेव सिद्धिं समधिगच्छति ॥ ४ ॥

4. Not by abstaining from action does man win actionlessness, nor by mere renunciation does he attain perfection.

'Action' refers to the acts of worship (Yaj*n*a) which, performed in this or a previous birth, conduce to the destruction of sins committed in the past and cause purity of mind (sattva, antah-karana); and by thus purifying mind, they cause knowledge to spring up and lead to the path of devotion to knowledge. It is said in the Mahabharata:

> "Knowledge springs in men on the destruction of sinful karma, when the Self is seen in self as in a clean mirror." (Santiparva, 204-8.)

By abstaining from action man cannot attain to actionlessness (naishkarmya), freedom from activity, *i.e.*, devotion in the path of knowledge, the condition of the actionless Self. From the statement that man wins not freedom from activity by abstaining from action, it is understood that by the opposite course, *i.e.*, by performing action, man attains freedom from activity. For what reason, then, does he not attain freedom from activity by abstaining from action? The answer follows:—For, performance of action is a means of attaining freedom from activity. Certainly there is no attaining of an end except by proper means. Devotion to action is the means of attaining freedom from activity, *i.e.*, devotion to knowledge,—as taught in the sruti, as well as here. In the sruti, for instance, karma-yoga is declared to be a means to jnana-yoga in the following passage:

> "The Brahmanas seek to know this (the Self) by the study of the Vedas, by yajna or worship." (Bri. Up. 4-4-22).

In this passage, karma-yoga is pointed out as a means of realising the Self that is sought after. Here (in the Bhagavad-Gita) the following passages point to the same view:

"But without Yoga, O mighty-armed, renunciation is hard to attain." (v. 6.)

> "Having abandoned attachment, Yogins perform action for the purification of the Self." (v. 11.)

"Sacrifice, gift and also austerity are the purifiers of he wise." (xviii. 5.)

Now the following objection may be raised:—A passage in the smriti,—"Having promised* immunity from fear to all beings, one should resort to freedom from activity (naishkarmya),"—shows that actionlessness can be attained by renouncing the prescribed duties. Our experience also favours the idea that freedom from activity can be attained by abstaining from action. Of what use then is the performance of action to one who seeks for freedom from action?

In reply the Lord says: Nobody can attain perfection,—*i.e.*, freedom from activity, or devotion in the path of knowledge—by mere renunciation, by merely abandoning action, without possessing knowledge.

The ignorant are swayed by Nature.

For what reason, then, does a person not attain perfection, *i.e.*, freedom from activity, by mere renunciation unaccompanied with knowledge?—The reason thus asked for is given as follows:

न हि कश्चित्क्षणमपि जातु तिष्ठत्यकर्मकृत् ।
कार्यते ह्यवशः कर्म सर्वः प्रकृतिजैर्गुणैः ॥ ५ ॥

5. None, verily, even for an instant, ever remains doing no action; for every one is driven helpless to action by the energies born of Nature.

The energies (gunas) are three, Sattva, Rajas and Tamas.† 'Every one' means every living being that is ignorant, (ajna), who knows not (the Self); for, it is said of a

* Having promised that he would sacrifice no animal, that he would do no harm to any being as he used to do when he was grihastha *i.e.*, having renounced all the sacrificial rites enjoined on a grihastha.

† For a description of these *vide* Discourse xiv.

wise man* (that he is one) "who is unshaken by the energies" (xiv 23)

Since the Sankhyas have been distinguished from the Yogins (iii. 3), the Karma-yoga, devotion to action, is indeed meant for the ignorant only, not for the wise. As for the wise who are unshaken by the gu*n*as, and who in themselves are devoid of any change whatever, the Karma-yoga is out of place. And this was explained at length in our comments on (ii. 21.)

The unenlightened should not give up Karma-Yoga.

Now, for him who knows not the Self, it is not right to neglect the duty enjoined on him. So, the Lord says:

कर्मेन्द्रियाणि संयम्य य आस्ते मनसा स्मरन् ।
इन्द्रियार्थान्विमूढात्मा मिथ्याचारः स उच्यते ॥ ६ ॥

6. He who, restraining the organs of action, sits thinking in his mind of the objects of the senses, self-deluded, he is said to be one of false conduct.

The organs of action are the hand, etc. The self-deluded man, the man whose anta*h*-kara*n*a is thus deluded, is called a hypocrite, a man of sinful conduct.

यस्त्विन्द्रियाणि मनसा नियम्यारभतेऽर्जुन ।
कर्मेन्द्रियैः कर्मयोगमसक्तः स विशिष्यते ॥ ७ ॥

7. But whoso, restraining the senses by mind O Arjuna, engages in Karma-Yoga, unattached, with organs of action, he is esteemed.

---

* He who knows the Self is immoveable by the gu*n*as, and is therefore said to have crossed over them. The man who knows not the Self and who has not completely controlled the body and the senses—he alone is driven to action by the gunas;—(A)

If the ignorant man, who is only qualified for action, performs action with the hand, with the organ of speech, etc., restraining the organs of knowledge by mind and unmindful of the result, he is more worthy than the other, who is a hypocrite.

Wherefore,

नियतं कुरु कर्म त्वं कर्म ज्यायो ह्यकर्मणः ।
शरीरयात्राऽपि च ते न प्रसिध्येदकर्मणः ॥ ८ ॥

8. Do thou perform (thy) bounden duty; for action is superior to inaction. And even the maintenance of the body would not be possible for thee by inaction.

Thy bounden duty is the obligatory (nitya) act, that which one is bound to perform, and which is not prescribed (in the scriptures) as a means to a specific end. Action is superior to inaction in point of result. By inaction you cannot attain success in the life's journey. The distinction between action and inaction is thus seen in our own experience.

It is also wrong to suppose that actions lead to bondage and that they should not therefore be performed.—Why?

यज्ञार्थात्कर्मणोऽन्यत्र लोकोऽयं कर्मबन्धनः ।
तदर्थं कर्म कौन्तेय मुक्तसङ्गः समाचर ॥ ९ ॥

9. Except in the case of action for Sacrifice's sake, this world is action-bound. Action for the sake Thereof, do thou, O son of Kunti, perform, free from attachment.

Sacrifice (Yajna) here means Isvara, the Supreme Lord So, the sruti* says 'Yajna, verily, is Vishnu.' 'This world' means those persons who, as qualified for action only, are bound to do it and who accordingly perform it. The world is not bound by action done for the Lord's sake. Perform action without attachment.

For the following reason also, action should be done by him who is qualified for it:

सहयज्ञाः प्रजाः सृष्ट्वा पुरोवाच प्रजापतिः ।
अनेन प्रसविष्यध्वमेष वोऽस्त्विष्टकामधुक् ॥ १० ॥

10. Having first created mankind together with sacrifices, the Prajapati said, "By this shall ye propagate; let this be to you the cow of plenty.

Mankind: composed of the three castes. *First*: at the beginning of creation. *The cow of plenty*: the cow which yields all desires.

How can this be achieved by sacrifice?

देवान्भावयतानेन ते देवा भावयन्तु वः ।
परस्परं भावयन्तः श्रेयः परमवाप्स्यथ ॥ ११ ॥

11. With this do ye nourish the Gods, and the Gods shall nourish you; thus nourishing one another, ye shall attain the supreme good.

"By this sacrifice ye nourish the Gods such as Indra. The Gods shall nourish you with rain, etc." 'The supreme

---

* Taittiriya-Samhita, 1-7-4.

good' is the attainment of the knowledge of Brahman in due course. Or, the 'supreme good' may mean 'svarga.' *

Moreover,

इष्टान्भोगान्हि वो देवो दास्यन्ते यज्ञभाविताः ।
तैर्दत्तानप्रदायैभ्यो यो भुङ्क्ते स्तेन एव सः ॥ १२ ॥

12. "Nourished by the sacrifice, the Gods shall indeed bestow on you the enjoyments ye desire." Whoso enjoys—without offering to Them—Their gifts, he is verily a thief.

Pleased with your sacrifices, the Gods shall bestow on you all enjoyments, including women, cattle, children, etc. He who enjoys what is given by Gods, *i.e.*, he who gratifies the cravings of his own body and senses † without discharging the debt due to the Gods, is a thief indeed, a robber of the property of the Gods, etc.

On the other hand,

यज्ञशिष्टाशिनः सन्तो मुच्यन्ते सर्वकिल्बिषैः ।
भुञ्जते ते त्वघं पापा ये पचन्त्यात्मकारणात् ॥ १३ ॥

13 The righteous, who eat the remnant of the sacrifice, are freed from all sins; but sin do the impious eat who cook for their own sakes.

---

* The 'supreme good' here spoken of may be either the knowledge of Brahman or svarga. The result depends upon the motive of the aspirant, according as he desires salvation or worldly enjoyment. In the former case, the sacrifice leads to purity of heart in this or a subsequent birth and ultimately leads to knowledge, whereas in the latter case it eads directly to svarga.

† *i. e.*, he who is bent upon feeding his own body and senses without satisfying the Gods, the *R*ishis and the Pit*r*is, respectively, by sacrifice by study of the sacred scriptures, and by offspring.

Those who, after performing sacrifices to the Gods, etc., eat the remains of the food—which is called amrita, ambrosia—are freed from all sins committed at the five* places of animal-slaughter (such as the fire place), as well as from those sins which result from involuntary acts of injury and other causes. But as to the others, who are selfish and cook food for their own sakes, what they eat is sin itself, while they themselves are sinners.

The wheel of the world should be set going.

For the following reason also should action be performed by him who is qualified for action. For, it is action that sets the wheel of the world going.—How?—The answer follows.

अन्नाद्भवन्ति भूतानि पर्जन्यादन्नसम्भवः ।
यज्ञाद्भवति पर्जन्यो यज्ञः कर्मसमुद्भवः ॥ १४ ॥
कर्म ब्रह्मोद्भवं विद्धि ब्रह्माक्षरसमुद्भवम् ।
तस्मात्सर्वगतं ब्रह्म नित्यं यज्ञे प्रतिष्ठितम् ॥ १५ ॥

14-15. From food creatures come forth; the production of food is from rain; rain comes forth from sacrifice; sacrifice is born of action; know thou that action comes from Brahman, and that Brahman comes from the Imperishable. Therefore, the all-pervading Brahman ever rests in sacrifice.

---

* The five places referred to are the fire-place, the water-pot, the cutting, grinding and sweeping apparatus. These are the five-places where injury to life is daily committed. The sins committed here are said to be washed away by the five maha-yajnas or great sacrifices, which every dvija ought to perform, and which are intended to satisfy the Bhutas, the Rishis, men, the Gods, and the Pitris. *Vide* Manu, ii. 67—73.

All living creatures, it is evident, are born from food, which, when eaten, is converted into blood and semen. Rain proceeds from sacrifice as taught in the following text from the smriti:

> "The offering thrown into the fire reaches the sun; from the sun comes rain; from rain food; and from this (food) all creatures." (*Manu*, iii. 76).

Yajna or sacrifice here spoken of refers to what is called apûrva;* and this apûrva is the result of the activities of the sacrificer and his priests (ritviks) engaged in a sacrifice. These activities are enjoined in the Veda (Brahman), and the Veda comes from the Imperishable, the Paramâtman, the Highest Self. Because the Veda has arisen from the Highest Self—the Akshara, the Imperishable,—as the breath comes out of a man, therefore, the Veda, though all-comprehending as revealing all things, ever rests in sacrifice, *i.e.*, it treats mainly of sacrifices and the mode of their performance.

एवं प्रवर्तितं चक्रं नानुवर्तयतीह यः ।
अघायुरिन्द्रियारामो मोघं पार्थ स जीवति ॥ १६ ॥

16. He who follows not here the wheel thus set in motion, who is of sinful life, indulging in senses, he lives in vain, O son of Pritha.

He who ought to perform action, but who, indulging in sensual pleasures, does not follow the wheel of the world thus

* The unseen from which a sacrifice is said to assume between the time of its performance and the time when its results become manifested; it being, in short, the connecting link between the two, the cause and the effect.

set revolving by Isvara on the basis of the Veda and sacrifices, * he lives in vain.

The main drift, therefore, of this section (iii. 4. 16) is that action should be performed by the ignorant man, for whom it is intended. In iii. 4-8, it was taught that till he attains the qualification for Devotion to the knowledge of the Self, the man who knows not the Self and is therefore qualified (for action only) should resort to Devotion to action as a means of attaining Devotion to knowledge; and, further, there were incidentally propounded (in iii. 9-16) many reasons why the man who knows not the Self and is (therefore) qualified for action should perform it. Mention, too, has been made of evils arising from a neglect of action.

Karma-Yoga is not meant for the Self-knower.

Now, the Lord Himself supposes Arjuna to ask the following question: Is the wheel, thus set in motion, to be followed by all, or by him only who has not yet attained to devotion in the path of knowledge which the Sankhyas or Self-knowers tread and which is attainable by the ignorant by means of devotion in the path of action already described? In answer to this question, or with a view to afford, of his own accord, a clear understanding of the teaching of the sastra, He proceeds to show that what is intended to be taught in the Gita-sastra is the same truth that is embodied in the following passage of the sruti:

"The Brâhmanas (the devotees of the Brahman, the Self), knowing this, the Self, and free from illusory knowledge, shake off all desires of progeny, etc., cherished, of necessity, by those who are still subject to illusion; and they lead a mendicant life for the barest necessaries of

---

* *i.e.*, he who does not follow the wheel by studying the Vedas and performing the sacrifices therein enjoined, as commanded by *Isvara*.

life. They have nothing else to do than resort to devotion to Self-knowledge." (Bri. Up. 3-5-1).

यस्त्वात्मरतिरेव स्यादात्मतृप्तश्च मानवः ।
आत्मन्येव च सन्तुष्टस्तस्य कार्यं न विद्यते ॥ १७ ॥

17. That man, verily, who rejoices only in the Self, who is satisfied with the Self, who is content in the Self alone,—for him there is nothing to do.

But that man—a samnyasin, the Sankhya, one devoted to Self-knowledge—whose joy is in the Self, not in the objects of the senses; who is satisfied only with the Self, not with food-essence, etc.; who is contented in the Self;—all others derive contentment from possession of external things, whereas, disregarding these, he is content in the Self only and has no desire for anything;—for such a man, for the man who knows the Self, there is nothing to do.

Moreover,

नैव तस्य कृतेनार्थो नाकृतेनेह कश्चन ।
न चास्य सर्वभूतेषु कश्चिदर्थव्यपाश्रयः ॥ १८ ॥

18. For him, there is here no interest whatever in what is done or what is not done. Nor is there in all beings any one he should resort to for any object.

For the man thus rejoicing in the Self, no purpose is served by action.—Does, then, any evil called sin (pratyavâya) arise from inaction?—No evil whatever, either by way of incurring sin, or by way of losing the Self, arises in this world from inaction. Nor is there, in all beings from Brahma (Prajâpati) down to the sthâvara or immovable objects, any whose support he has to gain by action. He has no object whatever to gain, for which he has to depend upon any particular being: if he were to have any object in view, then he would have to exert himself to gain that object.

Arjuna qualified for Karma-yoga.

You have not attained to the right knowledge, which corresponds to the all-spreading flood of water (*vide* ii. 46). Wherefore:

तस्मादसक्तः सततं कार्यं कर्म समाचर ।
असक्तो ह्याचरन्कर्म परमाप्नोति पूरुषः ॥ १९ ॥

19. Therefore, without attachment, constantly perform the action which should be done; for, performing action without attachment, man reaches the Supreme.

Performing action, without attachment, for the sake of the Isvara, man attains moksha, through attaining purity of mind (sattva-suddhi).

The wise should set an example to the masses.

For the following reason also (shouldst thou perform action):

कर्मणैव हि संसिद्धिमास्थिता जनकादयः ।
लोकसंग्रहमेवापि सम्पश्यन्कर्तुमर्हसि ॥ २० ॥

20. By action only, indeed, did Janaka and others try to attain perfection. Even with a view to the protection of the masses thou shouldst perform (action).

The wise kshatriyas of old, such as Janaka and Asvapati * tried by action alone to attain moksha (samsiddhi). If they were persons possessed of right knowledge, then we should understand that, since they had been engaged in works, they tried to reach moksha with action, *i.e.*, without abandoning action, † with a view to set an example to the world. If, on the other hand, such men as Janaka were persons who had not attained right knowledge, then, (we should understand), they tried to attain moksha through action which is the means of attaining purity of mind (sattva-suddhi).

If you think that obligatory works were performed by the ancients such as Janaka because they were ignorant, and that it does not follow from that fact alone that action should be performed by another who possesses right knowledge and has done all his duties,—even then, as subject to your prârabdha-karma (the karma which has led you to this birth as a kshatriya), and having regard also to the purpose of preventing the masses from resorting to a wrong path, you ought to perform action.

Who should secure the welfare of the world? And how? The answer follows:

---

* *Vide* Chhandogya-Upanishad v. 11. 4, *et. seq.*

† Though such persons as Janaka were men of right knowledge, they had no right to enter the fourth order of samnyâsa, as they were kshatriyas. In obedience therefore to their prârabdha-karma (*i.e.*, the karma which led them to that birth and which had to be worked out in that birth) which caused them to be born as kshatriyas, they went on in their spiritual career without renouncing works, lest, otherwise, the masses would follow their example. It is, however, proper that they should attain moksha in virtue of their right knowledge.

यद्यदाचरति श्रेष्ठस्तत्तदेवेतरो जनः ।
स यत्प्रमाणं कुरुते लोकस्तदनुवर्तते ॥ २१ ॥

21. Whatsoever a great man does, that alone the other men do; whatever he sets up as the standard, that the world follows.

Whatever authority the chief among men follows, whether in relation to the spiritual or temporal matters, the same is regarded as the authority by his followers.

If you have a doubt even as regards the necessity there is for the protection of the masses, why do you not observe Me*?

न मे पार्थास्ति कर्तव्यं त्रिषु लोकेषु किञ्चन ।
नानवाप्तमवाप्तव्यं वर्त एव च कर्मणि ॥ २२ ॥

22. I have nothing whatsoever to achieve in the three worlds, O son of Pritha, nor is there anything unattained that should be attained; yet I engage in action.

I have nothing to achieve, for, there is nothing unattained.

यदि ह्यहं न वर्तेयं जातु कर्मण्यतन्द्रितः ।
मम वर्त्मानुवर्तन्ते मनुष्याः पार्थ सर्वशः ॥ २३ ॥

23. For, should I not ever engage in action, unwearied, men would in all matters follow My path, O son of Pritha.

My: I being the chief among men.

---

* *i.e.*, why do you not follow My example and try to prevent the masses from going astray by setting an example yourself.

And what harm is there in that?—The Lord says:

उत्सीदेयुरिमे लोका न कुर्यां कर्म चेदहम् ।
सङ्करस्य च कर्ता स्यामुपहन्यामिमाः प्रजाः ॥ २४ ॥

24. These worlds would be ruined if I should not perform action; I should be the cause of confusion of castes, and should destroy these creatures.

If I should not perform action, then there would be no action conducive to the continuance of the universe, and all these worlds would fall into ruin. Moreover, I would be the author of confusion of castes, and thereby destroy these creatures. Thus, though working for the welfare of the creatures, I would bring about their ruin,—which would be unbecoming of ME, their lord.

The wise man's action as contrasted with that of the ignorant.

Suppose, on the other hand, you—or suppose (for that matter) any other man thinks that he has achieved his ends and has realised the Self, even he should work* for the welfare of others, though for himself he may have nothing to do.

सक्ताः कर्मण्यविद्वांसो यथा कुर्वन्ति भारत ।
कुर्याद्विद्वांस्तथाऽसक्तश्चिकीर्षुर्लोकसङ्ग्रहम् ॥ २५ ॥

25. As ignorant men act attached to work, O Bhârata, so should the wise man act, unattached from a wish to protect the masses.

The ignorant expect the result of their action thus: "The result of this action shall accrue to me." *The wise man*: he who knows the Self.

* Even he should perform action in view of the welfare of others.

For Me, or for any other person who, knowing the Self, thus seeks the welfare of the world, there is nothing to do except it be with a view to that welfare of the world at large. To such a man who knows the Self, the following advice is offered:

न बुद्धिभेदं जनयेदज्ञानां कर्मसङ्गिनाम् ।
जोषयेत्सर्वकर्माणि विद्वान्युक्तः समाचरन् ॥ २६ ॥

26. Let no wise man cause unsettlement in the minds of the ignorant who are attached to action; he should make them do all actions, himself fulfilling them with devotion.

An ignorant man who is attached to action believes "I should do this action and enjoy its result." No wise man should unsettle that firm belief.—What then should he do?—Himself doing diligently and well the actions which the ignorant have to do, he should make them do those actions.

In what way is an ignorant man attached to actions?

प्रकृतेः क्रियमाणानि गुणैः कर्माणि सर्वशः ।
अहङ्कारविमूढात्मा कर्ताऽहमिति मन्यते ॥ २७ ॥

27. Actions are wrought in all cases by the energies of Nature. He whose mind is deluded by egoism thinks 'I am the doer.'

Nature (Prak*r*iti, Pradhâna) is the equipoised state of the three gu*n*as or energies, viz., *sattva* (goodness), *rajas* (activity), *tamas* (darkness). It is by the gu*n*as or the modifications of Nature, manifesting themselves as the body and the senses, that all our actions, conducive to temporal and spiritual ends, are done. The man whose mind (anta*h*kara*n*a) is variously deluded by aha*m*kara, by egoism identifying the aggregate of the body and the senses with the Self, *i. e.*, who ascribes to himself all the attributes of the body and the senses and thus thoroughly identifies himself with them—he, by nescience, sees actions in himself: as regards every action, he thinks "I am the doer."

But as regards the wise man:

तत्त्ववित्तु महाबाहो गुणकर्मविभागयोः ।
गुणा गुणेषु वर्तन्त इति मत्वा न सज्जते ॥ २८ ॥

28. But he who knows the truth, O mighty-armed, about the divisions of the energies and (their) functions, is not attached, thinking that the energies act upon the energies.

He who is versed in the classification of the energies (gu*n*as) and their respective functions holds that the energies as sense-organs move amid the energies as sense-objects, but not the Self. Thus holding, he forms no attachment (for actions).

Now,

प्रकृतेर्गुणसम्मूढाः सज्जन्ते गुणकर्मसु ।
तानकृत्स्नविदो मन्दान्कृत्स्नविन्न विचालयेत् ॥ २९ ॥

29. Those deluded by the energies of Nature are attached to the functions of the energies. He who knows the All should not unsettle the unwise who know not the All.

The foolish believe "we do action for the sake of its result." These men who are attached to action look only to the result of their actions. The man who knows the

All—the man who knows the Self—should not of himself unsettle such men, *i.e.*, he should not disturb their conviction.

How an aspirant for Moksha should do actions.

How then should action be performed by the ignorant man who seeks moksha and who is qualified for action only? The answer follows:

मयि सर्वाणि कर्माणि संन्यस्याध्यात्मचेतसा ।
निराशीर्निर्ममो भूत्वा युध्यस्व विगतज्वरः ॥ ३० ॥

30 Renouncing all action in Me, with thy thought resting on the Self, being free from hope, free from selfishness, devoid of fever, do thou fight.

To Me, Vâsudeva, the Divine Being, the Supreme Lord, the Omniscient, the Self of all, surrender all actions, with the wise thought that "I, the agent, do this for the Isvara's sake as His liege." *Fever*: anguish, grief.

ये मे मतमिदं नित्यमनुतिष्ठन्ति मानवाः ।
श्रद्धावन्तोऽनसूयन्तो मुच्यन्ते तेऽपि कर्मभिः ॥ ३१ ॥

31. Men who constantly practise this teaching of Mine with faith and without cavilling, they too are liberated from actions.

Men who always follow this teaching of Mine without cavilling, *i.e.*, without cherishing any feeling of envy towards Me, Vasudeva, the Supreme Master (Parama-Guru)—they too are released from actions, *i.e.*, from dharma and a-dharma, from the merit and demerit of actions.

ये त्वेतदभ्यसूयन्तो नानुतिष्ठन्ति मे मतम् ।
सर्वज्ञानविमूढांस्तान्विद्धि नष्टानचेतसः ॥ ३२ ॥

32. But those who, carping at this, My teaching, practise it not,—know them as deluded in all knowledge, as senseless men doomed to destruction.

Influence of man's nature on his conduct.

Then, why do they, not following Thy doctrine, perform others' duties and neglect their own? Thus opposed to Thee, why are they not afraid of the sin of transgressing Thy command?

सदृशं चेष्टते स्वस्याः प्रकृतेर्ज्ञानवानपि ।
प्रकृतिं यान्ति भूतानि निग्रहः किं करिष्यति ॥ ३३ ॥

33. Even the man of knowledge acts in conformity with his own nature; (all) beings follow (their) nature; what shall coercion avail?

Nature (prak*r*iti) is the sa*m*skara (the latent self-reproductive impression of the past acts of dharma and a-dharma) manifesting itself at the commencement of the present birth. Even the man of knowledge acts according to his own nature; it needs no saying that an ignorant man acts according to his own nature. Thus all living beings follow their own nature. What shall coercion in the shape of prohibition avail? That is to say, to Me or to anybody else, nature is irresistible.

Scope for man's personal exertion.

(Objection):—If every being acts according to its own nature only,—and there is none that has no nature of its own,—then, there being possibly no scope for personal exertion

(purushakâra), the Teaching (sastra) would be quite purposeless.

(*Answer*) :—The Lord replies as follows :

इन्द्रियस्येन्द्रियस्यार्थे रागद्वेषौ व्यवस्थितौ ।
तयोर्न वशमागच्छेत्तौ ह्यस्य परिपन्थिनौ ॥ ३४ ॥

34. Love and hate lie towards the object of each sense; let none become subject to these two; for, they are his enemies.

As regards all sense-objects, such as sounds, there necessarily arises in each sense love for an agreeable object, and aversion for a disagreeable object. Now I shall tell you where lies the scope for personal exertion and for the Teaching (sastra). He who would follow the Teaching should at the very commencement rise above the sway of affection and aversion. For, what we speak of as the nature (prakriti) of a person draws him to its course only through love and aversion. He then neglects his own duties and sets about doing those of others. When, on the other hand, a person restrains these feelings by means of their enemy*, then he will become mindful of the Teaching only, no longer subject to his own nature. Wherefore, let none come under the sway of these two; for, they are his adversaries, obstacles to his progress in the right path, like thieves on the road.

Now, the man who is led by love and aversion may misunderstand the Teaching; he may think that one man may follow the duty (dharma) of another because the latter is also a duty. But it is not right to think so :

---

* Viveka-jnâna or Right knowledge is the enemy ; for, it is inimical to *mithya-jnana* or illusory knowledge, the source of affection and aversion.

श्रेयान्स्वधर्मो विगुणः परधर्मात्स्वनुष्ठितात् ।
स्वधर्मे निधनं श्रेयः परधर्मो भयावहः ॥ ३५ ॥

35. Better one's own duty, though devoid of merit, than the duty of another well discharged. Better is death in one's own duty; the duty of another is productive of danger.

For a man to die doing his own duty though devoid of merit is better than for him to live doing the duty of another though perfectly performed. For, the duty of another leads to danger, such as hell (naraka).

Desire is the Enemy of Man.

Though the source of evil has been pointed out in ii. 62, etc., and in iii. 34, yet with a view to eliciting a concise and clear statement of what was but desultorily and vaguely expressed,—for, the exact cause being known, he might exert himself to exterminate it,—Arjuna asks :

अर्जुन उवाच—

अथ केन प्रयुक्तोऽयं पापं चरति पूरुषः ।
अनिच्छन्नपि वार्ष्णेय बलादिव नियोजितः ॥ ३६ ॥

Arjuna said :

36. But by what dragged on, O Varshneya, does a man, though reluctant, commit sin, as if constrained by force?

Dragged on and constrained : as a servant by the king. *Varshneya* : one born in the family of the Vrishnis.

The Lord says : Listen, I shall tell you who that enemy is, of whom you ask, who the source of all evil is :

[Vasudeva is here called the Lord (Bhagavat), because He is one in whom the six attributes of unimpeded dominion etc., ever abide collectively and in perfection, and who possesses a complete knowledge of the origin of the universe etc. Says the Vishnu-Purana:

> "'Bhaga' means the six attributes—perfect dominion, might, glory, splendour, dispassion and salvation," (vi. 5-74).
>
> "He is called the Lord (Bhagavat), who knows the origin and the end, the coming and the going of beings, what is wisdom and what is ignorance." (vi. 5-78.)]

श्रीभगवानुवाच—

काम एष क्रोध एष रजोगुणसमुद्भवः ।
महाशनो महापाप्मा विद्ध्येनमिह वैरिणम् ॥ ३७ ॥

The Blessed Lord said :

37. It is desire, it is wrath, born of the energy of Rajas, all-devouring, all sinful ; that, know thou, is the foe here.

The enemy of the whole world is desire, from which all the evil comes to living beings. When obstructed by some cause, desire is transformed into wrath. Whence wrath is desire itself. It is born of the energy of Rajas.—Or, desire itself is the cause of the energy of Rajas ; for, when desire arises, it rouses the Rajas and urges the person to action. We often hear the cry of miserable persons—who are engaged in servitude, etc., under the impulse of the Rajas,—saying 'I have been led to act so by desire.' It is very sinful ; for it is only when urged by desire that a man commits sin. Wherefore, know that this desire is man's foe here in samsara.

Desire Enshrouds Wisdom.

He now illustrates how it is our foe :

धूमेनाव्रियते वह्निर्यथाऽऽदर्शो मलेन च ।
यथोल्बेनावृतो गर्भस्तथा तेनेदमावृतम् ॥ ३८ ॥

38. As fire is surrounded by smoke, as a mirror by rust, as the foetus is enclosed in the womb, so is this covered by it.

As a bright fire is surrounded by dark smoke co-existent with it...so this is covered with desire.

What is the thing referred to by 'this' and which is covered with desire ?—The answer follows :

आवृतं ज्ञानमेतेन ज्ञानिनो नित्यवैरिणा ।
कामरूपेण कौन्तेय दुष्पूरेणानलेन च ॥ ३९ ॥

39. Covered, O son of Kunti, is wisdom by this constant enemy of the wise, in the form of desire, which is greedy and insatiable.

The wise man knows, even before suffering the consequence, that he has been led by desire to evil ways, and therefore he feels ever miserable. Whence desire is a constant enemy of the wise, not of the ignorant. For, the latter regards desire as a friend at the time he thirsts for objects, and it is only when suffering results from it,—but not before,—that he learns the truth that he has been rendered miserable by desire. Wherefore it is a constant enemy of the wise alone.........It is insatiable and greedy; it never has enough, *i.e.*, it finds nothing enough for itself, *i. e.*, there is no limit to its consuming power.

The Seat of Desire.

He now tells us where is seated desire which by enveloping wisdom, forms the enemy of the whole world. The seat of the enemy being known, it is easy to kill it.

इन्द्रियाणि मनो बुद्धिरस्याधिष्ठानमुच्यते ।
एतैर्विमोहयत्येष ज्ञानमावृत्य देहिनम् ॥ ४० ॥

40. The senses, mind, and reason are said to be its seat; veiling wisdom through these, it deludes the embodied.

Its seat : the seat of desire. ***These*** : the senses mind (manas), and reason (buddhi).

How to Kill out Desire.

Wherefore,

तस्मात्त्वमिन्द्रियाण्यादौ नियम्य भरतर्षभ ।
पाप्मानं प्रजहि ह्येनं ज्ञानविज्ञाननाशनम् ॥ ४१ ॥

41. Therefore, O lord of the Bharatas, restrain the senses first, do thou cast off this sinful thing which is destructive of knowledge and wisdom.

Jnana is the knowledge of the Self and other things acquired from the *sastra* (scripture) and from a teacher (acharya). *Vi-jnana* is the personal experience of the things so taught. Do thou cast off from you the destroyer of jnana and vijnana which lead to the highest good

It has been taught, "first master the senses, and cast off desire, thy enemy." Now it may be asked,—Where should one take one's stand and cast off desire? The answer follows:

इन्द्रियाणि पराण्याहुरिन्द्रियेभ्यः परं मनः ।
मनसस्तु परा बुद्धिर्यो बुद्धेः परतस्तु सः ॥ ४२ ॥

42. They say that the senses are superior; superior to the senses is mind; superior to mind is reason; one who is even superior to reason is He.

The senses are five, the sense of hearing, etc. When compared with the physical body, which is gross, external, and limited, the senses are superior as they are comparatively more subtle and internal, and have a more extensive sphere of action. So say the wise. Superior to the senses is mind (manas, the impulsive nature) which is composed of thoughts and desires, of errors and doubts, (sankalpa and vikalpa), Superior to mind is reason (buddhi) characterized by determination (nischaya). So, He who is behind all things visible. inclusive of reason, the Dweller in the body, whom—it has been said—desire, seated in the senses and other quarters, bewilders by enveloping wisdom,—He, the Self, the witness of reason, is superior to reason.

एवं बुद्धेः परं बुद्ध्वा संस्तभ्यात्मानमात्मना ।
जहि शत्रुं महाबाहो कामरूपं दुरासदम् ॥ ४३ ॥

43. Then knowing Him who is superior to reason, subduing the self by the self, slay thou, O mighty-armed, the enemy in the form of desire, hard to conquer.

Thus understanding the Self who is superior to reason, and subduing the self by the elf, *i.e.*, steadily composing the self by means of the self.* do thou slay desire. It is difficult to conquer desire, on account of its complex and incomprehensible nature.

इति श्रीमद्भगवद्गीतासूपनिषत्सु ब्रह्मविद्यायां योगशास्त्रे
श्री कृष्णार्जुनसंवादे कर्मयोगो नाम
तृतीयोऽध्यायः ॥

* The regenerated or purified mind (self, manas) is the means of attaining self-composure (manas-samâdhâna)—(A).

FOURTH DISCOURSE.

JNANA-YOGA.

Tradition of Jnana-Yoga.

This Yoga of Devotion to knowledge taught in the last two Discourses, accompanied with renunciation and attained by means of Karma-Yoga,—this Yoga in which the Vedic teaching regarding the life of activity and retirement (Pravritti and Nivritti) is comprehended,—it is this Yoga which forms the subject of the Lord's teaching throughout the Gita. Thinking, therefore, that the Vedic Doctrine has been concluded, He extols it by relating its pedigree.

श्रीभगवानुवाच—

इमं विवस्वते योगं प्रोक्तवानहमव्ययम् ।
विवस्वान्मनवे प्राह मनुरिक्ष्वाकवेऽब्रवीत् ॥ १ ॥

The Blessed Lord said:

1. I taught this imperishable Yoga to Vivasvat; Vivasvat taught it to Manu; Manu taught to Ikshvâku.

This Yoga, treated of in the two preceding Discourses, I taught to the Sun (Vivasvat) at the commencement of Evolution in order to infuse strength into the Kshatriyas, the rulers of the world. It is only when possessed of the strength of this Yoga that they can protect the Brahmanas, the spiritual class. And when the spiritual and ruling classes are well maintained, it is possible to maintain the world. That Yoga is imperishable, because of its imperishable results. Indeed, Moksha, the fruit of this Yoga of complete devotion to right knowledge, never perishes. Vivasvat taught it to Manu; and Manu taught it to his son Ikshvaku the first ruler.

एवं परम्पराप्राप्तमिमं राजर्षयो विदुः ।
स कालेनेह महता योगो नष्टः परन्तप ॥ २ ॥

2. This, handed down thus in succession, the King-sages learnt, This Yoga, by long lapse of time, has been lost here, O harasser of foes.

This Yoga, thus handed down in regular succession among the Kshatriyas, the king-sages—men who were at once kings and sages — learnt. The tradition of this Yoga has now for a long time been broken here, O Arjuna, who harassest thy foes, like the sun, by the heat of thy prowess.

Seeing that the Yoga has been lost by falling into the hands of the weak who could not control their senses, and seeing also that the people have not been able to attain the object of life.

स एवाऽयं मया तेऽद्य योगः प्रोक्तः पुरातनः ।
भक्तोऽसि मे सखा चेति रहस्यं ह्येतदुत्तमम् ॥ ३ ॥

3. That same ancient Yoga has been to-day taught to thee by Me, seeing that thou art My devotee and friend; for, this is the Supreme Secret.

This knowledge, this Yoga, is the Supreme Secret.

Divine Incarnations.

In order not to leave in anybody's mind an impression that an inconsistent statement has been made by the Lord.

and with a view to avoiding that impression, Arjuna asks as though he were to raise an objection :

अर्जुन उवाच—

अपरं भवतो जन्म परं जन्म विवस्वतः ।
कथमेतद्विजानीयां त्वमादौ प्रोक्तवानिति ॥ ४ ॥

Arjuna said ;

4. Later is Thy birth, and prior the birth of Vivasvat; how am I to understand that Thou taughtest this Yoga in the beginning ?

Thy birth is later, in the house of Vasudeva: Vivasvat's (Aditya's) birth is prior, in the beginning of evolution; how then, am I to reconcile the statement that Thou taughtest this Yoga in the begioning (to Vivasvat), and that Thou, the self-same person, has now taught it to me?

To remove—as was the aim of Arjuna's question—from the ignorant the impression that Vasudeva was not the Omnipotent and the Omniscient, the Blessed Lord says :

श्रीभगवानुवाच :—

बहूनि मे व्यतीतानि जन्मानि तव चार्जुन ।
तान्यहं वेद सर्वाणि न त्वं वेत्थ परन्तप ॥ ५ ॥

The Blessed Lord said :

5. Many births of Mine have passed, as well as of thine, O Arjuna ; all these I know, thou knowes not, O harasser of foes.

Thou knowest not, because the power of vision is obstructed by thy past action, good and bad (dharma and adharma). I, on the other hand, know them, because I am by nature eternal, pure, wise, unbound, and My power of vision is unobstructed.

How, then, canst Thou, the eternal Lord, have a birth, in the absence of dharma and a-dharma ?—Listen :

अजोऽपि सन्नव्ययात्मा भूतानामीश्वरोऽपि सन् ।
प्रकृतिं स्वामधिष्ठाय सम्भवाम्यात्ममायया ॥ ६ ॥

6. Though I am unborn, of imperishable nature, and though I am the Lord of all beings, yet ruling over My own nature, I am born by My own Mâyâ.

Though I am unborn, though by nature my power of vision (jnana-sakti) is undecaying, though I am by nature the Lord of all creatures from Brahma down to grass, yet ruling over by nature—the Prakriti, the Maya of Vishnu, which is made up of the three energies of Sattva, Rajas and Tamas, to which this whole universe is subject, and by which deluded the whole world knows not Vasudeva, its own Self,—I appear to be born and embodied, through my own Maya, but not in reality, unlike others.

THE PURPOSE OF DIVINE INCARNATION.

When and for what purpose is He so born ?—The answer follows :

यदा यदा हि धर्मस्य ग्लानिर्भवति भारत ।
अभ्युत्थानमधर्मस्य तदाऽऽत्मानं सृजाम्यहम् ॥ ७ ॥

7. Whenever there is a decay of religion, O Bharata, and an ascendency of irreligion, then I manifest Myself.

Religion: Dharma as embodied in the institution of castes (varna) and religious orders (asrama) which are the means of attaining worldly prosperity and salvation. Whenever there is a decay of religion (Dharma),.........I manifest Myself through Maya.

For what purpose ?

परित्राणाय साधूनां विनाशाय च दुष्कृताम् ।
धर्मसंस्थापनार्थाय सम्भवामि युगे युगे ॥ ८ ॥

8. For the protection of the good, for the destruction of evil-doers, for the firm establishment of religion, I am born in every age.

The Good : those who are in the right path.

जन्म कर्म च मे दिव्यमेवं यो वेत्ति तत्त्वतः ।
त्यक्त्वा देहं पुनर्जन्म नैति मामेति सोऽर्जुन ॥ ९ ॥

9. Whoso knows thus My divine birth and action in truth is not born again on leaving this body; he comes to Me, O Arjuna.

My birth is an illusion (Maya). It is Divine, peculiar to Isvara, not of ordinary nature (aprakrita). *He comes to me*: He is liberated.

JNANA-YOGA IS THE SOLE MEANS TO MOKSHA.

This path of salvation is not recent, but it was in vogue, even in ancient times:

वीतरागभयक्रोधा मन्मया मामुपाश्रिताः ।
बहवो ज्ञानतपसा पूता मद्भावमागताः ॥ १० ॥

10. Free from passion, fear and anger, absorbed in Me, taking refuge in Me, purified by the fire (tapas) of wisdom, many have reached My being.

Absorbed in Me: knowing Brahman, *i. e.*, seeing their identity with Isvara. *Taking refuge in Me*, Paramesvara, the Supreme Lord, *i. e.*, firmly devoted to wisdom only. *Jnana-tapas*: religious austerity (tapas) in the form of j*n*ana or knowledge of the Highest Self. Paramatman.—This compound indicates that Devotion to knowledge is quite independent of all other austerities (tapases). Having attained to highest purity by means of this fire of austerity (*tapas*), many have attained moksha.

DIVINE DISPENSATION OF WORLDLY BENEFITS AND SALVATION.

Then, Thou cherishest the feelings of affection and aversion, since Thou awardest moksha, Thy Being (identity with Thy Self), to a few only, not to all ?—The answer follows :

ये यथा मां प्रपद्यन्ते तांस्तथैव भजाम्यहम् ।
मम वर्त्मानुवर्तन्ते मनुष्याः पार्थ सर्वशः ॥ ११ ॥

11. Howsoever men approach Me, even so do I reward them ; My path do men follow in all things O son of P*r*itha.

I reward men by granting them the things they desire just in accordance with the way in which they seek Me and the motive with which they seek Me ; for they do not seek for moksha. One cannot indeed pursue pleasure and at the same time seek for moksha. Wherefore, I reward seekers of fruits by securing to them their selfish ends ; I reward the unselfish, who do their prescribed duties and seek for moksha, by granting them knowledge ; I reward men of knowledge who have renounced the world and seek for moksha, by granting them moksha ; similarly, I reward men in distress by relieving them from distress. Thus do I reward all, just in the way they seek Me. But never do I reward any from affection or aversion, or from delusion. In all things, men follow My path, the path of the Isvara who exists in all forms.* [Here 'men' stands for all those † who are engaged in works prescribed according to their respective ends.]

(*Question*) :—If Thou, Isvara, art free from affection and other evil passions, then, since Thou art gracious to all creatures alike and able to grant every desire, why do they not all desire moksha and seek Thee, with the knowledge that Vasudeva is all?

(*Answer*) :—Listen why it is so :

काङ्क्षन्तः कर्मणां सिद्धिं यजन्त इह देवताः ।
क्षिप्रं हि मानुषे लोके सिद्धिर्भवति कर्मजा ॥ १२ ॥

12. They who long after success in actions sacrifice here to the Gods : for, soon in this world of man accrues success from action.

They who long after success in action sacrifice to the Gods, such as Indra and Agni. The sruti says :

> " He who, on the other hand, worships a separate God, thinking, ' He is separate from me and I am separate from Him '—he knows not. He is to the Devas as cattle (to men)" (Bri. Up. 1·4·10).

For, quickly is the fruit of action reaped in this world of men by those who, with selfish ends in view, sacrifice to external Gods, performing the works enjoined on them according to their caste (varna) and order (asrama). It is for this world of men that Vedic injunctions are meant.—By

---

i.e., whether it be for a selfish end or for moksha, every one should follow the Lord, in the path of works or of knowledge. It is the Supreme Lord Himself that abides as the Self in every form.—(A)

† Not men only, but other beings as well.—(A)

the expression "soon in this world of man" the Lord implies that even in other worlds actions produce results: the only difference being that it is only to this world of men that injunctions based upon castes and religious orders apply:

Caste, A Divinely ordered human institution

What is the foundation of the law that the respective duties of the several castes and religious orders obtain only is world of men, but not in other worlds?—Or the ques- may be put thus: It has been said that men, split up into :ommunities of several castes and orders (varnas and nas), should follow Thy path in all things. Why should necessarily follow Thy path only, but not that of any ?—The answer follows:

चातुर्वर्ण्यं मया सृष्टं गुणकर्मविभागशः ।
तस्य कर्तारमपि मां विद्ध्यकर्तारमव्ययम् ॥ १३ ॥

13. The fourfold caste has been created by according to the distribution of energies and)ns; though I am the author thereof, know Me on-agent and immutable.

The four castes (varnas, *lit.*, colours) have been created [e, Isvara, according to the distribution of energies (gunas) of actions. The energies are Sattva (goodness), Rajas ness, activity,) and Tamas (darkness). The actions of a nana (priest), in whom Sattva predominates, are serenity 'estraint, austerity &c., (xviii 42). The actions of a riya (warrior), in whom Rajas predominates and Sattva)ordinate to Rajas, are prowess, daring, &c., (xviii 43). actions of a vaisya (merchant), in whom Rajas pre- nates and Tamas is subordinate to Rajas, are agriculture, (xviii. 44). The action of a sudra (servant) in whom

Tamas predominates and Rajas is subordinate to Tamas, is only servitude. Thus have been created the four castes according to the distribution of energies and actions. This fourfold caste does not exist in other worlds. Hence the limitation "in this world of man." (iv. 12).

(*Objection*) :—Oh ! then Thou art the author of the act of creating the four castes, and as such Thou art bound by its effect; wherefore Thou art not the eternal Lord nor the eternally unbound

Answer :—Though I am the author of this act when viewed from the standpoint of Maya, still know thou that I am in reality no agent and therefore not subject to sa*m*sara.

Action without attachment does not bind the soul.

Since I am not in reality the author of those actions, of which you think Me to be the author,

न मां कर्माणि लिम्पन्ति न मे कर्मफले स्पृहा ।
इति मां योऽभिजानाति कर्मभिर्न स बध्यते ॥ १४ ॥

14. Actions pollute Me not, nor have I a desire for the fruit of actions. He who knows Me thus is not bound by actions.

For want of egoism (aha*m*kara), these actions do not pollute Me by necessitating incarnation; nor have I a desire for the fruit of thess actions. On the other hand, it is but right that actions should pollute those men of the world (sa*m*sara) who are attached to their actions, thinking themselves to be the authors thereof, and longing for the fruits of such actions. As I have none of these, (*viz.*, desire and attachment), action cannot pollute Me. Any other person, too, who knows Me to be his Self, who thinks "I am no agent. I have no longing for the fruits of actions,"—his action too will not necessitate incarnation.

Knowing that 'I am no agent. I have no longing for the fruits of actions.'

एवं ज्ञात्वा कृतं कर्म पूर्वैरपि मुमुक्षुभिः ।
कुरु कर्मैव तस्मात्त्वं पूर्वैः पूर्वतरं कृतम् ॥ १५ ॥

15. Thus knowing, men of old performed action in the hope of liberation : therefore do thou also perform action as did the ancients in the olden time.

As the ancients performed action, do thou also perform action ; do not sit quiet, nor renounce action. if thou art ignorant, do thou perform action to purify the self. If thou art wise and knowest the truth, do thou perform action for the protection of the masses. It was performed by the ancients such as Janaka in the olden time : it is not a recent instruction.

The real nature of action and inaction.

If action should be performed here (in this world of man) I shall perform it on the authority of Thy word. Why shouldst thou add that it was performed by the ancients in the olden time ?—In reply the Lord says : (Listen). For there is a great difficulty in (understanding) action.—How ?

किं कर्म किमकर्मेति कवयोऽप्यत्र मोहिताः ।
तत्ते कर्म प्रवक्ष्यामि यज्ज्ञात्वा मोक्ष्यसेऽशुभात् ॥ १६ ॥

16. What is action ? What is inaction—As to this, even the wise are deluded I shall teach thee such action, by knowing which thou shalt be liberated from evil.

Even the wise are deluded as to what is action and what is inaction. Wherefore I will explain to you the nature of action and of inaction, knowing which thou shalt be released from the evil of sa*m*sara.

Neither shouldst thou think thus; "It is familiar to all that action means movement of the body, and inaction means absence of it, to sit quiet. What is there to be learnt about them?"

Wherefore?

The answer follows:

कर्मणो ह्यपि बोद्धव्यं बोद्धव्यं च विकर्मणः ।
अकर्मणश्च बोद्धव्यं गहना कर्मणो गतिः ॥ १७ ॥

17. For, thou hast to know something even of action, something to know of unlawful action, and something to know of inaction; hard to understand is the nature of action.

For there is much to be learnt about the action which is enjoined by the scripture, about the action which is unlawful, and about inaction. In fact, it is hard to understand the true nature of action (enjoined), of inaction, and of unlawful action.

What, then, is the true nature of action and inaction about which much has to be learnt, and which you have promised to teach?—Listen:

कर्मण्यकर्म यः पश्येदकर्मणि च कर्म यः ।
स बुद्धिमान्मनुष्येषु स युक्तः कृत्स्नकर्मकृत् ॥ १८ ॥

18. He who can see inaction in action, who can also see action in inaction, he is wise among men, he is devout, he is the performer of all action.

'Action' means what is done, an act in general. Inaction can be seen in action, and action in inaction, since both inaction (nivritti) and action (pravritti) presuppose an agent.* In fact all our experience of such things as action and agent is possible only in a state of avidya, only when we have not yet attained to the Real (vastu). He who sees inaction in action and who sees action in inaction,—he is wise among men, he is devout (yukta, yogin), he has done all action—Thus is he extolled who sees action in inaction and *vice versa*.

(Objection) :—What means this incongruity, "who can see inaction in action and action in inaction"? Surely action can never realize such an incongruity?

(Answer) :—This objection does not apply to our interpretation. To an ignorant man of the world, what in reality is inaction appears as action, and what in reality is action appears as inaction. With a view to teach what their real nature is, the Lord says "He who can see inaction in action," &c. Hence no incongruity. It must be a bare truth that the Lord means to teach here, inasmuch as He has said that he who realizes this view of action and inaction is *wise*, and has introduced the subject by saying that there is much to be *learnt* about action and inaction, (iv. 17). It has also been said that 'by knowing which thou shalt be liberated from evil' (iv. 16); and certainly freedom from evil cannot be achieved by means of *false* knowledge. Wherfore, we should understand that action and inaction are misunderstood by all living

* It has been said that action should be seen in inaction and *vice versa* because in both an agent is presupposed. This cannot be objected to on the ground that nivritti or inaction is resorted to only when the One real Self is known, and that therefore it presuppose no agency of the Self. For action or inaction, Pravitti or Nivritti, is resorted to only *before* obtaining a knowledge of the Real Self, as a means of attaining —(A.)

beings and that the Lord, wishing to remove this false view of them, teaches " He who can see inaction in action " &c. Moreover, inaction cannot be said to be *located in* action or contained in it, as jujube (badara) fruits in a vessel, nor can action be said to be located in inaction: for, inaction is but the absence of action. Wherefore (the meaning of the Lord must be that) action and inaction are not rightly understood by people and that the one is mistaken for the other, as the mirage is mistaken for water, or as the mother-of-pearl is mistaken for silver.

(*Objection*) :—Action is ever action to all; it never appears to be anything else ?

(*Answer*) :—Not so. When a ship is in motion, the motionless trees on the shore appear, to a man on board the ship, to move in the opposite direction; distant and moving bodies which are far away from our eye appear to be motionless. Similarly, here, (in the case of the Self) inaction is mistaken for action, and action for inaction. Wherefore, to remove this false impression, the Lord says " He who can see inaction in action " &c.

Though such an objection has been more than once answered, people who have long been subject to great misconceptions are deluded often and often, forget the truth though often and often taught, and often and often raise objections based on false premises. Wherefore, seeing how difficult the Real is for us to know, the Lord often answers such objections.

The truth that the Self is actionless, so clearly taught by sruti, smriti, and reason, has been taught here also in ii. 20-24; and it will also be taught hereafter. It is, however a deep-rooted habit of the mind to connect action with the actionless Self, though it is contrary to His real nature wherefore, "even the wise are deluded as to what is action and what is inaction" (v. 16). Action pertains to the physical body (deha) etc., but man falsely attributes action to the Self and imagines "I am the agent, mine is action, by me shall the fruit of action to reaped." Similarly, he falsely imputes to the Self the cessation (of activity) which really pertains to the body and the senses, as also the happiness which results from that cessation (of activity): he imagines 'I shall be quiet, so that I may be happy, without worry and without action; and I do nothing now, I am quiet and happy.' To remove this false impression, the Lord says "He who can see inaction in action," &c.

Now, action which belongs to the body and the senses, while yet retaining its own nature as action, is falsely imputed by all to the Self who is actionless and immutable; whence even a learned man thinks "I act." Hence the passage means:—He who sees inaction in action, *i.e.*, he who has the right knowledge that action which is commonly supposed by all to pertain to the Self, does not really belong to the Self, just as motion does not really pertain to the trees (on the shore of the river) which appear (to a man on board the ship) to move in the opposite direction; and he who sees action in inaction, *i.e.*, he who knows that even inaction is action,—for, inaction is but a cessation of bodily and mental activities, and like *action* it is falsely attributed to the Self and causes the feeling of egoism as expressed in the words "quiet and doing nothing, I sit happy;"—he who can realize the nature of action and inaction as now explained is wise among men; he is devout (Yogin), he is the performer of all actions. He is released from evil; he has achieved all.

This verse has been interpreted in a different way by some commentators.—How?—The obligatory duties (nitya-karma), performed for the sake of Isvara, do not produce any effect and may therefore, be figuratively termed inaction *i.e.*, they are equivalent to inaction; and neglect of those duties produces evil and may therefore, only figuratively, be termed action *i.e.*, it is equivalent to action. Accordingly, they have interpreted the verse thus:—He who regards the obligatory duties (nityakarma) as inaction, since they do not produce any effect—just as a cow may be said to be no cow when she does not serve the purpose of yielding milk,—and he who regards the neglect of obligatory duties as an action, since it produces evil such has hell (naraka), he is wise among men. &c.

This interpretation cannot hold good. As such knowledge cannot lead to liberation from evil, the Lord's statement that "by knowing which thou shalt be liberated from evil" (iv. 16) would prove false. Even though it be granted (for mere argument's sake) that liberation from evil accrues from the *performance* of obligatory duties (nitya-karma) it can never be granted that it will accrue from the mere *knowledge* that they do not produce any effect. Certainly it is nowhere taught (in sruti) that liberation from evil accrues from the knowledge that obligatory duties do not produce effects or from a knowledge of those obligatory duties themselves. It cannot be urged that it has been taught here by the Lord.* The same argument holds good also against their view as to seeing action in inaction. Indeed, this precept enjoins, (they hold). not that neglect of obligatory duties (nitya-karma) should be regarded as action, but only that obligatory duties should be performed. Moreover, no good can result from the knowledge that non-performance of obligatory duties leads to evil. Neither

* For in the words "by knowing which thou shalt be liberated from vil," (v. 16) the Lord refers to knowledge of the things there spoken of, ut not to the particular knowledge that obligatory duties produce no effects.

can non-performance (which is non-existent in itself) of obligatory duties be enjoined as an object on which to fix our thought. Nor by a false knowledge which regards inaction as action can a man be released from evil, or said to be wise and devout and to have performed all actions: and such a knowledge deserves no praise. False knowledge is itself *the* evil; how can it release us from another evil? Darkness does not expel darkness.

(*Objection*):—The knowledge that inaction is action or that action is inaction is not an illusion, but a figurative idea based upon the fact of productiveness or unproductiveness of effects.

(*Answer*):—No. For, nowhere is it taught that even such a figurative idea regarding action and inaction is of any good. Neither is any purpose served by thus ignoring the immediate subject of discourse and speaking of something else. It is, moreover, possible to express more directly the fact that obligatory duties do not produce effects and that their omission leads to hell. What, then, might be the purpose served by such an ambiguous circumlocution as "he who can see inaction in action" &c.? Such an explanation is tantamount to saying that the Lord wanted to confound others by these utterances. It is not necessary to mistify the doctrine (of obligatory duties) by means of symbolic language, nor is it possible to maintain that it can be easily understood if expressed often and often and in more ways than one.* For, the same doctrine is more clearly expressed in ii. 47, and needs no reiteration. It is only what is high and worthy of our effort that is worth knowing, but not the worthless. No false knowledge is worth acquiring: nor is its

* Just as we are to fix our idea of Vishnu on a symbol such as an idol. The symbol alleged to be presented here to fix our thought upon, is an abhava or nonentity.

object*—which is unreal—worth knowing. No evil can arise from non-performance; no existence can arise from non-existence. It has been said here, "Of the unreal no being there is," (ii. 16), and in the sruti "How can the existent arise from the non-existent?" (Chha. Up. 6-2-2). To say that an existent object arises from the non-existent is tantamount to saying that non-existence itself becomes existence and *vice versa*, which cannot be maintained as it is against all evidence. The scripture (*sastra*) cannot enjoin an act which is productive of no good; for, such an act is painful in its performance, and no pain would ever be deliberately incurred. Since it is admitted that omission of such duties leads to hell, it would simply amount to this, that Revelation (*sastra*) is of no good, since performance as well as omission of duties therein enjoined alike result in pain. Moreover, he who admits that obligatory duties produce no effects and at the same time holds that they lead to salvation, lands himself in a self-contradiction.

Wherefore, this verse admits only of a literal interpretation, and we have interpreted it accordingly.

Who is a Sage?

The realization of inaction in action and *vice versa* is extolled as follows:

यस्य सर्वे समारम्भाः कामसङ्कल्पवर्जिताः ।
ज्ञानाग्निदग्धकर्माणं तमाहुः पण्डितं बुधाः ॥ १९ ॥

19. He whose engagements are all devoid of desires and purposes, and whose actions have been burnt by the fire of wisdom, him the wise call a sage.

* The object of illusory knowledge, such as action (karma.)

The man who has realized the truth described above, whose works are all free from desires and from purposes (sankalpa) which cause those desires, who performs mere deeds without any immediate purpose,—if he be engaged in wordly action, he does so with a view to set an example to the masses; if he has renounced wordly life, he performs deeds only for bodily maintenance,—whose actions, good and bad, are consumed in the fire of wisdom which consists in the realization of inaction and *vice versa* : him the wise who know Brahman call a real sage (pandita).

The Sage's Worldly Action as an Example to the Masses.

He who can see action in inaction and *vice versa*, (*i.e.*, who has realized the true nature of action and inaction), is, by virtue of that very realization, free from action; he renounces (the world) and engages in no action,—only doing what is required for the bare existence of his body,—even though he had been engaged in action before realizing the truth. On the other hand, there may be a person who, having started with action and having since obtained the right knowledge of the Self, really abandons action with all its accessories, as he finds action of no use; but who, finding that for some reason he cannot abandon action, may continue doing action as before, with a view to set an example to the world at large, devoid of attachment to action and its result, and therefore having no selfish end in view; such a man really does nothing. His action is equivalent to inaction, since all his actions are consumed in the fire of knowledge. To teach this, the Lord says :

त्यक्त्वा कर्मफलासङ्गं नित्यतृप्तो निराश्रयः ।
कर्मण्यभिप्रवृत्तोऽपि नैव किञ्चित्करोति सः ॥ २० ॥

20. Having abandoned attachment for the fruits of action, ever content, dependent on none, though engaged in actions, nothing at all does he do.

He who has abandoned all concern for action and all attachment for its results in virtue of the knowledge of the truth explained above, who is always content, longing for no objects of senses: who seeks nothing whereby to achieve any end of his (*i.e.*, to secure enjoyments in this birth or the next); who, for want of any selfish end in view, might give up action with its accessories; but who finding it impracticable to get away from action, engages in action as before with a view to set an example to the world or to avoid the displeasure of the orthodox,—such a man, though engaged in actions, really does nothing at all, since he is endued with knowledge of the actionless Self.

The Sage's Action For Bodily Maintenance.

He who, unlike the one just spoken of, has, even before engaging in action, realized his indentity with Brahman (the absolute) abiding within all as the innermost actionless Self (the Pratyagatman); who is free from desire for objects of pleasure seen or unseen: and who, therefore, finding no use in action which is intended to secure such objects of pleasure, renounces all action with accessories, except what is necessary for the bare bodily maintenance; such a devotee, steady in his devotion to knowledge, is liberated. To teach this, the Lord ssys:

निराशीर्यतचित्तात्मा त्यक्तसर्वपरिग्रहः ।
शारीरं केवलं कर्म कुर्वन्नाप्नोति किल्बिषम् ॥ २१ ॥

21. Free from desire, with the mind and the self controlled, having relinquished all possessions doing mere bodily action, he incurs no sin.

He from whom all desires have departed, by whom the mind and the body (the self, the external aggregate of causes and effects) have been controlled, by whom all property has been disowned, who does mere bodily action (action necessary for the bare existence of the body), without attachment even for that action,—he incurs no sin which will produce evil effects. Even dharma is a sin,—in the case of him who seeks liberation,—inasmuch as it causes bondage. He is liberated from both (dharma and a-dharma), *i.e*, he is liberated from sa*m*sâra.

Now, what does the phrase 'mere bodily action', (sârîra-karma) mean? Does it mean action which can be performed by means of the body only? Or does it mean action required for the bare existence of the body?

One may ask: What is the good of this enquiry? What if 'bodily action' means 'action done by means of the body, or 'action necessary for the bare existence of the body'?

We reply as follows:

Firstly:—If 'mere bodily action' means 'action which can be performed by means of the body only', the words would imply that even he who, by means of the body, does an unlawful action productive of some visible or invisible results, incurs no sin. Then this teaching would contradict the teaching of the sâstra. And to say that he who does by means of the body a lawful action productive of some visible or invisible results incurs no sin is to deny something which even the opponent would never advance. Moreover, the qualifications 'doing bodily action' and 'mere' would imply that sin accrues to him who in speech or thought performs actions enjoined or prohibited by the sâstra, respectively called dharma and a-dharma. To say, then, that he who does a lawful act in speech or thought incurs sin would be to contradict the scripture ; and to say that he who does an unlawful act in speech or thought incurs sin is a useless reiteration of what is known.

Secondly: If, on the other hand, "bodily action" be interpreted to mean 'action required for the bare existence of the body,' then the teaching amounts to this: He who in deed, speech and thought does no other action, lawful or unlawful, productive of results here or hereafter; who, in deed, speech or thought, performs in the eye of the world just those acts which are required for the bare existence of the body without even such attachment to those acts as is implied in the words "I do," he does not incur sin. Since it cannot even be imagined that such a man can do any wrong which may be called sin, he is not subject to rebirth ; he is liberated without any let or hindrance, since all his actions have been consumed in the fire of knowledge.—Thus, there is here only a reiteration of the results of the right knowledge, which have been described already (in iv. 18). The phrase 'mere bodily action' thus understood gives no room to objection.

Since an ascetic who has disowned all property does not own even the articles of food and other things required for the maintenance of the body, it would follow that the body should be maintained by begging or such other means. Now the Lord points out such means of obtaining food and other things required for the maintenance of the body as are sanctioned by the texts like the following:

> "What is not begged for, not previously arrranged for, what has been brought to him without his effort..." (*Baudhayana-Dharmasutra* 2-8-12).

यदृच्छालाभसन्तुष्टो द्वन्द्वातीतो विमत्सरः ।
समः सिद्धावसिद्धौ च कृत्वाऽपि न निबध्यते ॥ २२ ॥

22. Satisfied with what comes to him by chance, rising above the pairs of opposites, free from envy, equanimous in success and failure, though acting he is not bound.

He who is satisfied with whatever he may obtain by chance, without his effort or request, who his not affected in mind by the attack of such pairs of opposite (dvandva) as heat and cold, who cherishes no feelings of envy and jealousy, who is calm whether he obtains or not such things as might come to him without effort,—such a devotee, feeling no pleasure or pain whether he obtains or not food and other things required for the maintenance of the body, seeing action in inaction and *vice versa*, ever steady in his knowledge of the true nature of the Self, always disowning agency—"I do nothing at all, energies act upon energies,"—in all acts of the body, etc., while begging or doing anything else for the bare existence of the body,—thus realizing the non-agency of the Self, he really does no act at all, not even the act of begging. But as he appears to act like the generality of mankind, agency is imputed to him by people, and so far he is the agent in the act of begging and the like. From his own point of view, however, as based on the teaching of the scriptures which are the source of right knowledge, he is no agent at all. Thus, though he performs the act of begging and the like required for the bare existence of the body, and though with reference to these acts agency is imputed to him by others, he is not bound, since action and its cause, which are the source of bondage, have been burnt in the fire of wisdom. This is only a reiteration of what has been already said (iv. 19, 21).

The sage's worldly action does not bind him.

It has been shown in iv. 20 that that man does no action who, having started in life with action, has since realized the actionless Self as one with Brahman and has seen the non-existence of the agent, action and results, but who, though competent to renounce action, yet, on account of something preventing him from doing so, has continued in action as before. Of him who, as thus shown, does no action, the Lord says:

गतसङ्गस्य मुक्तस्य ज्ञानावस्थितचेतसः ।
यज्ञायाचरतः कर्म समग्रं प्रविलीयते ॥ २३ ॥

23. Of the man whose attachment is gone, who is liberated, whose mind is established in knowledge, who acts for the sake of sacrifice,—his whole action melts away.

That man from whom all attachment is gone, from whom all cause of bondage, dharma and a-dharma, has fled away, whose mind is ever fixed in wisdom alone, who acts with a view, to the performance of a sacrifice —his action with its result is dissolved away, is reduced to nothing.

Wisdom-sacrifice.

For what reason, then, is all action which he does, entirely dissolved, without producing its natural result?— Listen why.

ब्रह्मार्पणं ब्रह्महविर्ब्रह्माग्नौ ब्रह्मणा हुतम् ।
ब्रह्मैव तेन गन्तव्यं ब्रह्मकर्मसमाधिना ॥ २४ ॥

24. Brahman is the offering, Brahman the oblation; by Brahman is the oblation poured into the fire of Brahman; Brahman verily shall be reached by him who always sees Brahman in action.

* With a view to please the Lord, Narâyana (Yajna—Sacrifice, Vishnu).—(A).

The man who has realized Brahman sees that the instrument by which the oblation is poured in the fire is nothing but Brahman: that it has no existence apart from that of the Self, just as silver has no existence apart from that of the mother-of-pearl (mistaken for silver). What (in the illustration) appears as silver is nothing but the mother-of-pearl. What people look upon as the instrument of offering is, to one who has realized Brahman, nothing but Brahman. Brahman is the oblation; *i.e.*, what is regarded as oblation is to him nothing but Brahman; and it is by Brahman that the offering is made, *i.e.*, the agent is none other than Brahman. The act of offering is nothing but Brahman; and the result, the goal to be reached by him who always sees Brahman in action is nothing but Brahman.

Thus, the action performed by him who wishes to set an example to the world is in reality no action, as it has been destroyed by the realization of Brahman in action. This representation as a sacrifice (Yaj*n*a) of the right knowledge possessed by him who has given up all rites and has renounced all action is quite in its place, as serving to extol that right knowledge. For him who has realised the supereme Reality, the instrument of offering and other accessories connected with the actual sacrifice are nothing but Brahman, who is one with his own Self. Else, it would be to no purpose to speak specifically of the instrument and other accessories of a sacrificial rite as Brahman, when everything is Brahman. Wherefore, to one who realises that all is Brahman, there is no action. Moreover, all idea of the accessories of action is absent; and indeed, no act of sacrifice is ever possible in the absence of such an idea. Every sacrificial rite, such as agnihotra, is associated with an idea (derived from the revealed texts) of the accessories of action, such as a particular God or Gods to whom the oblation should be offered, and with egoism on the part of the agent and his attachment for the results. No sacrificial rite is ever found unassociated with the idea of the accessories of action and results, unaccompanied with the egoism and a longing for the results. But this (wisdom-sacrifice) is an action wherein all idea of the instrument and other various accessories of action, all idea of action itself and of its results, has been replaced by the one idea of Brahman. Whence it is no action at all. This is shewn in iv 18. 20; iii. 28; v. 8 Thus teaching, our Lord here and there tries also to remove all idea of duality, *i.e.*, of action, its result and its accessories. It is admitted in the case of the Kâmya-Agnihotra—the sacrifice of Agnihotra performed for some selfish purpose—that it ceases to be a Kâmya-Agnihotra in the absence of that purpose. So also we are given to know that actions produce different results according as they are performed deliberately or otherwise. Accordingly, here too, in the case of the wise man in whom the idea of Brahman has replaced all idea of duality—such as, the instrument and other accessories of the act of offering, the act itself and its results—his action, though appearing as such externally, ceases to be action. Whence it is said "the whole action melts away". (iv. 23).

In interpreting this passage, some say:—What we call Brahman is the instrument of action and so on. And in fact it is Brahman that manifests Himself in the five forms—such as action and its accessories,—and does the action. In this case, the idea of the instrument and other accessories of action does not cease to exist. On the other hand, it is taught that the idea of Brahman should be fixed upon action and its accessories in the same way that the idea of Vishṇu is fixed upon an idol or the idea of Brahman is fixed upon 'name' (*Vide* Chh. Upanishad, 7-1-5).

Indeed, even this view would be possible if this particular section of the discourse were not here concerned with the praise of the Wisdom-sacrifice (jnâna-yajna). On the other hand, our Lord will here speak of the several acts of worship termed yajnas (sacrifice) and then praise wisdom, the right knowledge, in these terms: "Superior is the wisdom-sacrifice to the sacrifice with objects." (iv. 33). And it has been shewn that the verse is intended to represent wisdom as a sacrifice (*vide* p. 126). But, with those who maintain that the idea of Brahman should be fixed upon the sacrificial rite and all its accessories, just as the idea of Vishnu is fixed upon an idol or the idea of Brahman on 'name'—the Brahma-vidyâ (knowledge of Brahman), which has been hitherto spoken of cannot be the aim of the teaching here; for, this verse would be mainly concerned, according to their interpretation, with the instrument, etc., connected with a sacrificial rite. Moreover, moksha cannot be obtained by that knowledge which consists in fixing the idea of Brahman on a symbol (such as a sacrificial rite). It has been here said that Brahman is the goal to be reached. It is indeed opposed to truth to maintain that moksha can be obtained without knowledge.

Such interpretation is also opposed to the context. Right knowledge is the subject of which this Discourse treats (*vide* iv. 18), and the concluding portion of the Discourse treats of the same subject as shewn by the closing verses. The Discourse indeed concludes by extolling right knowledge (iv. 33, 39). Accordingly it is not right to maintain that, all on a sudden, and without reference to the present topic, it is here taught that the idea of Brahman should be fixed on an idol.

Wherefore this verse should be interpreted as has been done by us.

Sacrifices Effected By Action.

After representing the right knowledge as a sacrifice, the Lord proceeds to enumerate other kinds of sacrifice, with a view to extol right knowledge:

दैवमेवापरे यज्ञं योगिनः पर्युपासते ।
ब्रह्माग्नावपरे यज्ञं यज्ञेनैवोपजुह्वति ॥ २५ ॥

25. Other yogins resort to sacrifices to Gods; in the fire of Brahman others offer the Self by the Self.

Some yogins, devotees to action, perform only sacrificial rites in devotion to the Gods, while others who know Brahman, the Absolute, sacrifice the Self by the Self in the fire of Brahman. The oblation (ahuti) in his latter sacrifice is yajna, the Self,—for 'yajna,' is enumerated among the terms synonymous with 'atman'—who is in reality one with Brahman, but who is conditioned by the upadhis (such as buddhi) with all their attributes superimposed upon Him. This oblation of the Self is poured by the Self into Brahman, —here termed fire, the place into which that oblation is poured.—as described in the following texts:

"Brahman is the Real, Consciousness, the Infinite." (Tait. Up 2-1).

"Brahman who is Consciousness and Bliss." (B*ri*. Up. 5-9-28).

"Brahman who is immediately cognised by all, and who is the innermost Self of all" (B*ri*. Up. 3-2-1)

Brahman is devoid of all characteristics of mundane existence (sa*m*sara) such as hunger and thirst, inconceivable in any particular form of aspect, as taught by the Scripture in the terms "It is not thus, it is not thus." (B*ri*. Up. 4-4-27).

To know the conditioned Self as identical with the unconditioned Brahman is to sacrifice the Self in Brahman. This is the sacrifice which is performed by those who, having renounced all action, areever steady in their knowledge of the identity of the Self with Brahman.

This Wisdom-Sacrifice (described in iv. 24) is here enumerated along with the Gods-Sacrifice (Daiva-yajna) and others, with a view to extol it (iv. 33).

श्रोत्रादीनीन्द्रियाण्यन्ये संयमाग्निषु जुह्वति ।
शब्दादीन्विषयानन्य इन्द्रियाग्निषु जुह्वति ॥ २६ ॥

26. Others offer hearing and other senses in the fires of restraint; others offer sound and other objects in the fires of the senses.

Some yogins offer hearing and other senses in the fires of restraint (sa*m*yama);—the plural 'fires' is used because the restraint differs with each sense;—they are ever engrossed in restraining their senses; while others sacrifice the objects of senses in the fires of the several senses, *i.e.*, they regard it as a sacrifice to direct their senses only to the unforbidden objects of senses.

सर्वाणीन्द्रियकर्माणि प्राणकर्माणि चापरे ।
आत्मसंयमयोगाग्नौ जुह्वति ज्ञानदीपिते ॥ २७ ॥

27. And others sacrifice all the functions of the senses and the functions of the vitality in the wisdom-kindled fire of the Yoga of Self-restraint.

Wisdom-kindled: kindled by discriminative wisdom, as a lamp is kindled by oil. The functions of prâ*n*a, the vital air in the individual's body, are expansion, contraction, etc. The functions of the senses and of the vital air are completely dissolved while the yogin concentrates the mind on the Self.

द्रव्ययज्ञास्तपोयज्ञा योगयज्ञास्तथाऽपरे ।
स्वाध्यायज्ञानयज्ञाश्च यतयः संशितव्रताः ॥ २८ ॥

28. Others are sacrificers by their wealth, sacrificers by austerity, sacrificers by Yogas, sacrificers by reading and knowledge, ascetics of rigid vows.

Of others, some sacrifice by way of giving away their wealth to the deserving; some by austerity; some by Yoga, comprising such parctices as Prâ*n*âyâma (restraint of vital airs) and Pratyâhâra (withdrawal of the mind from external objects); some by way of repeating Vedic texts such as the Rig-Veda according to prescribed rules; some by way of studying the contents of the Scriptures (*s*âstra).

अपाने जुह्वति प्राणं प्राणेऽपानं तथाऽपरे ।
प्राणापानगती रुद्ध्वा प्राणायामपरायणाः ॥ २९ ॥

29. Others offer prâ*n*a (outgoing breath) in apâna (incoming breath), and apâna in prâ*n*a, restraining the passages of prâ*n*a and apâna, absorbed in prâ*n*âyâma (restraint of breath).

Some practise the kind of prâ*n*âyâma called Pûraka (filling in); some practise the kind of Prâ*n*âyama called Rechaka (emptying); some are engaged in the practise of Prâ*n*âyâma called Kumbhaka by impeding the outward passage of the air through nostrils and the mouth, and by impeding the inward passage of the air in the opposite direction.

Moreover.

अपरे नियताहाराः प्राणान्प्राणेषु जुह्वति ।
सर्वेऽप्येते यज्ञविदो यज्ञक्षपितकल्मषाः ॥ ३० ॥

30. Others, with regulated food, offer life-breaths in life-breaths. All these are knowers of sacrifice, whose sins are destroyed by sacrifice.

Regulated: limited. Whatever life-breath has been controlled, into it they sacrifice all other life-breaths; these latter become, as it were, merged in the former.

यज्ञशिष्टामृतभुजो यान्ति ब्रह्म सनातनम् ।
नायं लोकोऽस्त्ययज्ञस्य कुतोऽन्यः कुरुसत्तम ॥ ३१ ॥

34. Eating of ambrosia, the remnant of the sacrifice, they go to Eternal Brahman. This world is not for the non-sacrificer; whence the other?—O best of Kurus.

Performing the sacrifices mentioned above, they eat, at intervals, of prescribed food in a prescribed manner. Food so eaten is called ambrosia, am*r*ita (immortal). If they wish for moksha, they go to Brahman in course of time, not at once, as we should understand for consistency's sake. Even this world, which is common to all beings, is not for one who performs none of the sacrifices mentioned above. How can there be to him another world which can be secured only by superior means?

एवं बहुविधा यज्ञा वितता ब्रह्मणो मुखे ।
कर्मजान्विद्धि तान्सर्वानेवं ज्ञात्वा विमोक्ष्यसे ॥ ३२ ॥

32. Thus manifold sacrifices are spread at the mouth of Brahman. Know them all as born of action. Thus knowing, thou shalt be liberated.

Thus various sacrifices, such as those mentioned above, are spread at the mouth of Brahman, *i.e*, are known from the Vedas through such passages as the following: "We sacrifice prâna in speech." Know that they are all born of the not-Self,—of action in deed, speech and thought,—for the Self is actionless. If you realise that "these are not my actions, I am actionless, I am unconcerned," you will be released, by this right knowledge, from evil, from the bond of sa*m*sara.

Wisdom-sacrifice is superior to other sacrifices.

Right knowledge was represented as a sacrifice in iv. 24. Then several sacrifices have been taught. Knowledge is now extolled as compared with these latter kinds of sacrifices which are all means of attaining the several objects of human pursuit.

श्रेयान्द्रव्यमयाद्यज्ञाज्ज्ञानयज्ञः परन्तप ।
सर्वं कर्माखिलं पार्थ ज्ञाने परिसमाप्यते ॥ ३३ ॥

33. Superior is wisdom-sacrifice to the sacrifice with objects, O harasser of thy foes. All action, without exception, O son of Prithâ, is comprehended in wisdom.

The sacrifice performed with material objects produces material effects, whereas wisdom-sacrifice does not. Wherefore wisdom-sacrifice is superior to the sacrifice performed with material objects. For, wisdom, which is the means to moksha, comprehends all action. So says the sruti :

> " Just as (in the game of four dice) the three dice are comprehended in the fourth termed krita, so whatever good people do, all that reaches him. Any other man who knows that which he knew (obtains the same result).—(Chha. Up. 4-1-4).

How and where one should seek wisdom.

By what means is this grand wisdom to be obtained ?

तद्विद्धि प्रणिपातेन परिप्रश्नेन सेवया ।
उपदेक्ष्यन्ति ते ज्ञानं ज्ञानिनस्तत्त्वदर्शिनः ॥ ३४ ॥

34. Know this : by long prostration, by enquiry, by service, those men of wisdom who have realised the truth will teach thee wisdom.

Know thou by what process it is obtained. Go to the teachers (Acharyas) and humbly prostrate thyself before them. Ask them what is the cause of bondage (bandha) and what the means of deliverance; what is wisdom (vidya) and what nescience (avidya). Do service to the Guru. Won over by these and other marks of respect, the teachers who, knowing the truth as well as realising it themselves, will impart to thee their wisdom,—that wisdom which has been described above. Some only, but not all, know as well as realise the truth.—By this the Lord means to say that that knowledge alone which is imparted by those who have realised the truth—and no other knowledge—can prove effective.

Then alone the following statement will hold good:

यज्ज्ञात्वा न पुनर्मोहमेवं यास्यसि पाण्डव ।
येन भूतान्यशेषेण द्रक्ष्यस्यात्मन्यथो मयि ॥ ३५ ॥

35. Knowing which, thou shalt not again thus fall into error, O Pa*nd*ava; and by which, thou wilt see all beings in thy Self and also in Me.

Having obtained the wisdom imparted by them, you will not be again subject to confusion as you now are. By this wisdom you will also immediately perceive all beings, from Brahma (the Creator) down to grass, in your own Self. You will then realise that "these beings exist in Me." You will also see them all in Me, Vasudeva, thus: "And these beings exist in the Supreme Lord;" *i.e.*, you will realise that unity of the individual Soul (Kshetraj*n*a) and the Isvara which is so clearly taught in all the Upanishads.

Wisdom, a consumer of all sins and actions.

Moreover, see how excellent knowledge is:

अपि चेदसि पापेभ्यः सर्वेभ्यः पापकृत्तमः ।
सर्वं ज्ञानप्लवेनैव वृजिनं सन्तरिष्यसि ॥ ३६ ॥

36. Even shouldst thou be the most sinful of all the sinful, thou shalt verily cross all sin by the bark of wisdom.

With the boat of this knowledge, verily, you can cross the ocean of sin. For one who seeks liberation, even dharma proves to be a sin.

How does wisdom destroy sin?—Here is an example:

यथैधांसि समिद्धोऽग्निर्भस्मसात्कुरुतेऽर्जुन ।
ज्ञानाग्निः सर्वकर्माणि भस्मसात्कुरुते तथा ॥ ३७ ॥

37. As kindled fire reduces fuel to ashes, O Arjuna, so does wisdom-fire reduce all actions to ashes.

Just as a well-kindled fire reduces fuel to ashes, so does the fire of the wisdom reduce all actions to ashes, *i.e.*, it renders them important. The fire of wisdom cannot indeed literally reduce actions to ashes as fire reduces fuel to ashes. Accordingly we should understand that right knowledge is the cause which renders all actions impotent. But the actions by which this body has been brought into existence will come to an end only when their effects will have been fully worked out; for, those actions have already commenced their effects. Thus wisdom can destroy only such actions as have not yet begun to produce their effects, whether they are actions done in this birth before the rise of knowledge and along with knowledge, or those done in the many previous births.

Wherefore,

न हि ज्ञानेन सदृशं पवित्रमिह विद्यते ।
तत्स्वयं योगसंसिद्धः कालेनात्मनि विन्दति ॥ ३८ ॥

38. Verily, there exists here no purifier equal to wisdom. He who is perfected by Yoga finds it in time in himself by himself.

The seeker of moksha who has perfected and regenerated himself by Yoga—by Karma-Yoga and by Samadhi-Yoga—will after a long practice, himself find spiritual wisdom in himself.

The surest means to wisdom.

The surest means of acquiring wisdom is taught as follows :

श्रद्धावाँल्लभते ज्ञानं तत्परः संयतेन्द्रियः ।

ज्ञानं लब्ध्वा परां शान्तिमचिरेणाधिगच्छति ॥ ३९ ॥

39. He obtains wisdom who is full of faith, who is devoted to it, and who has subdued the senses. Having obtained wisdom, he ere long attains to the Supreme Peace.

A man full of faith obtains wisdom. But he may be slow; whence it is enjoined that he should ever be intently devoted to the means of obtaining wisdom, such as constant attendance on the Teachers (Gurus)*. A man of faith and devotion may not have mastery over the senses; whence it is also enjoined that he should withdraw his senses away from their engrossment in objects. Such a man of faith, devotion and self-control is sure to obtain wisdom. Mere external acts (iv. 35), such as long prostration before the Guru, may fail to produce the required effect, since they may be tinged with hypocrisy. But hypocrisy is impossible when a man is full of faith and so on. Whence these are the certain means of acquiring wisdom.—What is the result of this acquisition of wisdom?—The answer follows: Having obtained wisdom, he swiftly attains the Supreme Peace, called Moksha. That

* And listening to their teachings, etc,

the right knowledge quickly leads to moksha is an established truth clearly taught by all sastras as well as reason.

Wisdom the killer of doubt.

Thou shalt not doubt this, for doubt is most sinful.—How?—Listen:

अज्ञश्चाश्रद्दधानश्च संशयात्मा विनश्यति ।
नायं लोकोऽस्ति न परो न सुखं संशयात्मनः ॥ ४० ॥

40. The ignorant, the faithless, and one of doubting self, is ruined. There is neither this world, nor the other, nor happiness, for one of doubting self.

The man who knows not the Self is ruined, as also the man who has no faith in the teachings and the words of his Guru, and the man whose mind is full of doubts. No doubt the ignorant and the faithless are ruined, but not to the same extent as a man of doubting mind. He is the most sinful of all.—How?—Even this world which is common to all men is not won by a sceptic, nor the other world, nor happiness: for even these things come within the sweep of his doubt. Wherefore thou shalt not doubt.

Wherefore?—For,

योगसंन्यस्तकर्माणं ज्ञानसञ्छिन्नसंशयम् ।
आत्मवन्तं न कर्माणि निबध्नन्ति धनंजय ॥ ४१ ॥

41. Him who has renounced actions by Yoga, whose doubts have been cloven asunder by wisdom, who is self-possessed, actions bind not, O Dhana*m*jaya.

He who sees the Supreme Being renounces all actions—dharma and a-dharma—by virtue of Yoga or knowledge of the Supreme Being. He attains this stage when his doubt has been cloven asunder by the realisation of the oneness of the Self with the Isvara. As he traces all actions to the interactions of the energies (gu*n*as), actions do not bind him; they do not produce any effects (good or bad) in the case of him who, in virtue of his Yoga, has renounced all actions and is ever watchful over his self.

Since that man who, in virtue of the practice of karma-yoga, has all his doubts cut asunder by knowledge which arises as a result of all impurity having been washed away, is not bound by actions because they have been consumed in the fire of wisdom, and since that man is ruined who entertains doubts as to the practice of karma and knowledge.

तस्मादज्ञानसम्भूतं हृत्स्थं ज्ञानासिनाऽऽत्मनः ।
छित्त्वैनं संशयं योगमातिष्ठोत्तिष्ठ भारत ॥ ४२ ॥

42. Therefore with the sword of wisdom cleave asunder this doubt of the Self lying in the heart and born of ignorance, and resort to Yoga. Arise, O Bharata.

Doubt is most sinful. It is born of ignorance and lies in the buddhi. Kill it by wisdom, by right knowledge of the Self.

[The word "atmana*h*" means 'of the Self,' 'concerning the Self,' but not 'cherished by thyself.' Arjuna's doubt here is about the Self. If Arjuna could ever think that one man's doubt is ever to be cut by another, then the Lord might say 'kill *thy* doubt' as opposed to *another's* doubt. Even if Arjuna has been asked to kill the doubt concerning the Self, it implies also that the doubt is one cherished by Arjuna.]

Knowledge is destructive of all evil, such as grief, folly, and the like. Having thus slain doubt, the cause of thy ruin, apply thyself to Karma-Yoga, the means of acquiring right knowledge. Now arise and fight, O descendant of Bharata.

FIFTH DISCOURSE.

SAMNYASA-YOGA

Which is better for the ignorant, Karma-Yoga or Samnyasa?

In iv. 18, 19, 21, 22, 24, 32, 33, 37 and 41, the Lord has spoken of the renunciation of all actions; and in iv. 42 He has exhorted Arjuna to engage in Yoga, in performance of action. Owing to the mutual opposition between performance of action and renunciation thereof as between motion and rest, the two cannot be accomplished by an individual at one and the same time. Neither have two distinct periods of time been prescribed for their respective observance. By inference, therefore, only one of them forms Arjuna's duty; so that thinking that, of the two,—performance of action and renunciation thereof,—he should resort to the better of the two to the exclusion of the other, Arjuna asks (v. 1) of the Lord with a desire to know which is the better of the two.

(*Objection*):—As going to speak of entire devotion to J*n*anayoga on the part of him who has realised the Self, the Lord has taught, in the passages quoted above, that such a man has to renounce action, but not he who has not realised the Self. Since performance of action and renunciation of action thus pertain to two distinct classes of people respectively, Arjuna's question with a view to know which of the two is better than the other is irrelevant.

(*Answer*):—Yes; from your standpoint the question is irrelevant. But from the questioner's (Arjuna's) own standpoint, the question, we say, is quite relevant—How?—In the passages quoted above, the Lord enjoins renunciation as a duty (in the form "Let the wise man renounce"); and it cannot be enjoined as a duty unless it (the term 'renounce') is more important than the agent (*i.e.*, the term 'wise'); so that this injunction of renunciation should be extended so as to apply to that man also who has not realised the Self, because renunciation is elsewhere enjoined on him also.* It cannot be made out that renunciation of action is here intended for that man only who has realised the Self.† Thus arguing, Arjuna thinks that an ignorant man may either perform action or renounce it. But, owing to the mutual opposition of the two courses as shown above, only one of them can form the duty (of an individual at a time). And inasmuch as it is the better one of the two that should be followed, but not the other, the question with a view to know which of the two is the better is not irrelevant.

The question is not with reference to the enlightened.

That this is the meaning of Arjuna's question is also evident from an examination of the meaning of the words in reply.—How?—The reply runs as follows: "Sa*m*nyasa and Karma-Yoga both lead to the highest bliss; but Karma-Yoga is the better of the two" (v. 2). We should now ascertain: Is it in reference to the Karma-Yoga and the Karma-Sa*m*nyasa resorted to by a man who has realised the Self that it is said that they lead to the highest bliss as their result, and that the Karma-Yoga is for some reason the better of the two? Or is it in reference to those resorted to by a man who has not realised the Self that the statement is

* When he is full of vairagya or indifference to all worldly concerns —(A).

† The Mima*m*sakas hold that a single proposition can embody but a single injunction. Accordingly, if the proposition "The wise should renounce" be meant to enjoin renunciation, it cannot at the same time enjoin that renunciation should be resorted to by the wise alone. Else it would involve the fallacy of a double injunction in a single proposition.

made ?—What then ?*—Listen: As a man who has realised the Self resorts to neither Karma-Yoga nor Samnyasa, it is not right to speak of them as alike leading to the highest bliss or of the superiority of his Karma-Yoga over his Karma-Samnyasa. If for a man who has realised the Self, Karma-samnyasa and its opposite—Karma-Yoga (performance of action)—were possible, then it would have been right to speak of them as alike leading to the highest bliss or to speak of the superiority of his Karma-Yoga over his Karma-Samnyasa. Inasmuch as, however, neither Karma-Samnyasa nor Karma-Yoga is possible for a man who has realised the Self, it is not right to speak of them as alike leading to the highest bliss, or to say that Karma-Yoga is better than Karma-Samnyasa.

Karma-Yoga and Samnyasa inapplicable to the enlightened.

(*Question*):—Are both Karma-Yoga and Karma-Samnyasa impossible, or is only one of them impossible, for a man who has realised the Self? If only one of them, is it Karma-Yoga or Karma-Samnyasa? What is the reason for the impossibility?

(*Answer*):—Since the man who has realised the Self is free from illusory knowledge, Karma-Yoga which is based upon illusion must be impossible for him. Here, in the Gita-sastra, in the sections treating of the real nature of the Self, it is said that a man who knows the Self, who knows himself to be the Self that is devoid of all changes of birth, etc., and is actionless, and whose illusory knowledge has been replaced by right knowledge,—that such a man has to renounce all actions, ever dwelling in the true actionless Self; and it is further said that, owing to the opposition between right

* How is the former supposition liable to objection? or how is the latter reasonable?—(*Anandagiri*) [Here the two suppositions are repeated in the Bhashya, but they have been omitted in the translation].

knowledge and illusory knowledge as well as between their effects, he has nothing to do with Karma-Yoga, the reverse of Karma-Sa*m*nyasa, presupposing an active Self and based on the idea of agency caused by illusory knowledge. Wherefore it is but right to say that, for him who has realised the Self and who is free from illusory knowledge, Karma-Yoga which is based upon the illusory knowledge is impossible.

(*Question*) :—What then, are the sections treating of the real nature of the Self in which the man who knows the Self is said to have no action to do?

(*Answer*) :—In ii. 17, in ii. 19 and ii. 21, and in other places here and there, the man who has realised the Self is said to have no action to do.

(*Objection*) :—Karma-Yoga is also taught here and there in the sections treating of the real nature of the Self, *e.g.*, in ii. 18, 31, 47, etc. How, then, can Karma-Yoga be said to be impossible for a man who has realised the Self?

(*Answer*) :—It is so, because there is an opposition between right knowledge and illusory knowledge as well as between their effects. In iii. 3 it is said that the Sankhyas who have realised the true nature of the Self apply themselves to devotion in the path of wisdom—ever dwelling in the actionless Self—as distinguished from devotion in the path of action which is intended for those who have not realised the Self. The man who has realised the Self has no longer any object to gain, since he has achieved all. In iii. 17 it is said that he has no more duties to perform. In such passages as iii. 4 and v. 6 Karma-Yoga is enjoined as an accessory to the acquisition of the knowledge of the Self, while in vi. 3 it is said that the man who has obtained right knowledge has no longer anything to do with Karma-Yoga. Further, in iv. 21 all action is denied to him except that which is required for bodily maintenance; and even with reference to such acts of hearing and seeing as may be required for mere bodily maintenance, the man who knows the true nature of the Self is directed in v. 8 always to meditate with a concentrated mind on the idea that 'it is not I that do it.' It is not possible to imagine even in a dream that the man who knows the Self can have anything to do with Karma-Yoga, so opposed to right knowledge and entirely based upon illusory knowledge. Wherefore it is the Sa*m*nyasa and the Karma-Yoga of the man who has not realised the Self that are spoken of (in this connection) as leading alike to moksha. This Sa*m*nyasa, which consists in renouncing a few actions only while yet there is an idea of agency,* is different from the one already spoken of, from the renunciation of all actions,—which is resorted to by the man who has realised the Self. The former becomes very difficult of performance as it is further associated with 'yama' and 'ni-yama' and the like (which are the various forms of self-control). Karma-Yoga is comparatively easier of performance and is therefore spoken of as the better of the two. Thus an examination of the meaning of the words in reply leads also to the same conclusion as has been arrived at before as regards the meaning of Arjuna's question.

At the beginning of the third Discourse, Arjuna, seeing that knowledge and action could not coexist in one man, asked the Lord "tell me that which is the better of the two;" and in reply the Lord declared decisively that devotion in the path of knowledge was meant for the Sankhyas—the renouncers, the Sa*m*nyasins.—and that devotion in the path of action was meant for the Yogins. And from the statement "nor by *mere*

* He thinks that he has yet to learn what the Vedanias or the Upanishads teach, to reason about it and to meditate upon it. He has renounced only those actions which are specially enjoined on the g*r*ihasthas or the second religious order (asrama) This sort of renunciation is thus partial and is meant to afford to the aspirant greater leisure to apply himself to the acquisition of spiritual wisdom.

renunciation does he attain perfection" (iii. 4) it is clear that, in the view of the Lord, renunciation with knowledge is a means of attaining perfection. And Karma-Yoga, too, must lead to perfection, inasmuch as it has been enjoined (iv. 42). Arjuna now asks with a view to know as to which one of them, Karm-Yoga or Sa*m*nyasa, is better for a man who has no knowledge.

अर्जुन उवाच :—

संन्यासं कर्मणां कृष्ण पुनर्योगं च शंससि ।
यच्छ्रेय एतयोरेकं तन्मे ब्रूहि सुनिश्चितम् ॥ १ ॥

Arjuna said:

1. Renunciation of actions, O K*r*ish*n*a, Thou praisest, and again Yoga. Tell me conclusively that which is the better of the two.

Thou teachest renunciation of those actions which are enjoined in the *s*astras, and Thou teachest also that performance of those very actions is necessary. I have, therefore, a doubt as to which of them is better, performance of (prescribed) actions or renunciation of those actions. It is the better course which must be followed. Wherefore tell me conclusively that one,—it being impossible for one man to resort to both at the same time,—be it performance of actions or renunciation of actions, by which you think I may attain to perfection.

Karma-Yoga suits the ignorant better than Samnyasa.

To state His own opinion with a view to clear the doubt, the Lord says:

श्रीभगवानुवाच :—

संन्यासः कर्मयोगश्च निःश्रेयसकरावुभौ ।
तयोस्तु कर्मसंन्यासात्कर्मयोगो विशिष्यते ॥ २ ॥

The Blessed Lord said:

2. Renunciation and Yoga through action both lead to the highest bliss: but, of the two, Yoga through action is esteemed more than renunciation of action.

Sa*m*nyasa and Karma-yoga, renunciation of actions and performance of actions, both lead to moksha, as giving rise to (spiritual) knowledge. Though both lead to moksha, yet, of the two means of attaining moksha, Karma-Yoga is better than mere—*i.e.*, unaccompanied with knowledge—Karma-sa*m*nyasa. Thus the Lord has praised Karma-Yoga.*

Wherefore?—The answer follows:

ज्ञेयः स नित्यसंन्यासी यो न द्वेष्टि न काङ्क्षति ।
निर्द्वन्द्वो हि महाबाहो सुखं बन्धात्प्रमुच्यते ॥ ३ ॥

3. He should be known as a perpetual renouncer who neither hates nor desires: for, free from the pairs of opposites, O mighty-armed, he is easily set free from bondage.

The Karma-Yogin who neither hates pain and the objects causing pain, nor desires pleasure and the objects causing pleasure, should be known as a perpetual renouncer (sa*m*-nyasin), though he is engaged in action.

Sankhya and Yoga lead to the same goal.

(*Objection*):—Sa*m*nyasa and Karma-Yoga, which are meant for two distinct classes of people and are opposed to each other, should, properly speaking, be mutually opposed in

* The Lord does not of course mean that Karma-Yoga is superior to true Karma-sa*m*nyasa. True Karma-sa*m*nyasa, that which is accompanied with knowledge, is a far higher path than Karma-Yoga, though the latter is easier than, and therefore preferable to, that Karma-sa*m*nyasa which is unaccompanied with knowledge.

their results also. They should not, on the other hand, both lead to moksha alike.

(*Answer*) :—The Lord says :

साङ्ख्ययोगौ पृथग्बालाः प्रवदन्ति न पण्डिताः ।
एकमप्यास्थितः सम्यगुभयोर्विन्दते फलम् ॥ ४ ॥

4. Children, not the wise, speak of Sankhya and Yoga as distinct. He who is rightly devoted to even one obtains the fruits of both.

It is children who speak of Sankhya and Yoga as producing distinct and opposite results. But the wise, men of knowledge, believe that they produce but one harmonious result. He who rightly observes even one of them, Sankhya or Yoga, obtains the fruits of both. Both lead to the same result, *viz.*, moksha. Wherefore, there is no diversity in the result.

(*Objection*) :—Having started with the words 'Samnyasa' and 'Karma-Yoga', how is it that He speaks of Sankhya and Yoga—with which we are not at present concerned—as producing the same results ?

(*Answer*) :—There is no fault here. Arjuna indeed asked the Question with reference to simple Sa*m*nyasa and simple Karma-Yoga. But the Lord, without leaving these, has added to them some additional conceptions of His own and has answered the question, speaking of them under other names, Sankhya and Yoga. In the opinion of the Lord, Sa*m*nyasa and Karma-Yoga are themselves termed Sankhya and Yoga when knowledge of the Self (j*n*ana) and equanimity (sama-buddhitva) are added to them respectively. Hence no irrelevant topic.

How can a man obtain the results of both by the right observance of only one ?—The answer follows :

यत्साङ्ख्यैः प्राप्यते स्थानं तद्योगैरपि गम्यते ।
एकं साङ्ख्यं च योगं च यः पश्यति स पश्यति ॥ ५ ॥

5 That state which is reached by Sankhyas is reached by Yogins also. He sees, who sees Sankhya and Yoga as one.

Sankhyas are those who are devoted to knowledge and have renounced the world. They reach the state called moksha. The same state is reached by Yogins also,—but indirectly through, the attainment of true knowledge and renunciation,—by those who perform their duties as a means of attaining knowledge, dedicating them to the Isvara, and having no selfish end in view. That man sees rightly who sees that Sankhya and Yoga are one, as leading to an identical result.

(*Question*) :—If so Sa*m*nyasa must be superior to Yoga. How then is it that it has been declared that Karma-Yoga is better than Karma-sa*m*nyasa?

(*Answer*) :—Listen why it is so. It is the simple Karma-sa*m*nyasa and the simple Karma-Yoga with reference to which you have asked me "which one is the better of the two?". In accordance with the question, My answer has been given—without having regard to knowledge—that Karma-Yoga is superior to Karma-sa*m*nyasa. But that Sa*m*nyasa which is based upon knowledge is regarded by Me as Sankhya, and Sankhya itself is the true (paramartha) Yoga. It is only by a figure that the Yoga through Vedic rites is called Yoga or Sa*m*nyasa, inasmuch as it conduces to that (true Yoga or Sa*m*nyasa).

Karma-Yoga is a means to Samnyasa.

How is it that the aim of the Karma-Yoga is that (true Yoga or Sa*m*nyasa)?—Listen:

संन्यासस्तु महाबाहो दुःखमाप्तुमयोगतः ।
योगयुक्तो मुनिर्ब्रह्म न चिरेणाधिगच्छति ॥ ६ ॥

6. But renunciation, O mighty-armed, is hard to attain except by Yoga; a sage equipped with Yoga ere long reaches Brahman.

Renunciation (Samnyasa) here spoken of is the true (paramarthika) Samnyasa; and Yoga is the Vedic Karma-Yoga (performance of Vedic ritual) dedicated to the Isvara and entirely free from motives. A sage (muni) is so called because of his meditation (manana) on the form of the Isvara. 'Brahman' here means renunciation (samnyasa, which is now being spoken of), because renunciation consists in the knowledge of the Highest Self (Paramatman); and the sruti says:

"What is called Nyasa is Brahman; and Brahman is verily the Great." (*Tait. Up.* 4-78).

A sage equipped with Yoga soon reaches Brahman, the true renunciation, which consists in steady devotion to right knowledge. Wherefore, I have said that Karma-Yoga is better.

A sage's actions do not affect him.

When the devotee resorts to Yoga, as a means of attaining right knowledge:

योगयुक्तो विशुद्धात्मा विजितात्मा जितेन्द्रियः ।
सर्वभूतात्मभूतात्मा कुर्वन्नपि न लिप्यते ॥ ७ ॥

7. He who is equipped with Yoga, whose mind is quite pure, by whom the self has been conquered, whose senses have been subdued, whose Self has become the Self of all beings,—though doing, he is not tainted.

He who is equipped with Yoga, whose mind (atman, sattva) has been purified, who has conquered the body (atman, the self) and the senses, who sees rightly, whose Inner Concsiousness, the Self, has formed the Self of all beings from Brahma down to a clump of grass,—he will not be tainted, *i.e.*, he will not be bouud by actions, though he may continue to perform them for the protection of the masses, *i.e.*, with a view to set an example to the masses.

A sage's actions are really no actions.

Neither does he really do anything. Wherefore,

नैव किञ्चित्करोमीति युक्तो मन्येत तत्त्ववित् ।
पश्यन्शृण्वन्स्पृशञ्जिघ्रन्नश्नन्गच्छन्स्वपन्श्वसन् ॥ ८ ॥
प्रलपन्विसृजन्गृह्णन्नुन्मिषन्निमिषन्नपि ।
इन्द्रियाणीन्द्रियार्थेषु वर्तन्त इति धारयन् ॥ ९ ॥

8—9. 'I do nothing at all'; thus would the truth-knower think, steadfast,—though seeing, hearing, touching, smelling, eating, going, sleeping, breathing, speaking, letting go, seizing, opening and closing the eyes,—remembering that the senses move among sense-objects.

The truth-knower is he who knows the true nature of the Self, who sees the Supreme Reality.—When and how would he think so ever intent on the truth?—The answer is given thus: 'though seeing, etc.'

The duty of the man who, thus knowing the truth and thinking rightly, sees only inaction in actions—in all the movements of the body and the senses—consists in renouncing all actions; for, he sees the absence of action. The man, for instance, who thinks of quenching his thirst in a mirage, mistaking it for water, will not, even after knowing that it is no water, resort to the same place for the purpose of quenching his thirst.

Karma-Yogin is untainted by the results of his action.

But as to the man who is not a truth-knower and is engaged in action:

ब्रह्मण्याधाय कर्माणि सङ्गं त्यक्त्वा करोति यः ।
लिप्यते न स पापेन पद्मपत्रमिवाम्भसा ॥ १० ॥

10. He who does actions, offering them to Brahman, abandoning attachment, is not tainted by sin, as a lotus leaf by water.

He offers all actions to the Isvara, in the faith that 'I act for His sake', as a servant acts for the sake of the master. He has no attachment for the result, even for moksha. The result of actions so done is only purity of the mind, and nothing else.

Because,

कायेन मनसा बुद्ध्या केवलैरिन्द्रियैरपि ।
योगिनः कर्म कुर्वन्ति सङ्गं त्यक्त्वाऽऽत्मशुद्धये ॥ ११ ॥

11. By the body, by the mind, by the intellect, by mere senses also, Yogins perform action, without attachment, for the purification of the self.

Mere: free from egotism, resolute in the faith that 'I act only for the sake of the Lord, not for my benefit.' 'Mere' should be construed along with 'body' &c,, with each one of them separately, Yogins are those who are devoted to works, free from egotism in all their acts, without attachment for their results. They act only for the purification of the mind (sattva). Wherefore, as thy duty lies only there, do thou only perform action.

Also because,

युक्तः कर्मफलं त्यक्त्वा शान्तिमाप्नोति नैष्ठिकीम् ।
अयुक्तः कामकारेण फले सक्तो निबध्यते ॥ १२ ॥

12. The steady-minded one, abandoning the fruit of action, attains the peace born of devotion. The unsteady one, attached to the fruit through the action of desire, is firmly bound.

The steady-minded man who, resolved that "I do actions for the sake of the Lord, not for my benefit," abandons the fruit of action attains the peace called moksha, as the result of devotion, through the following stages: first, purity of the mind; then, attainment of knowledge; then, renunciation of all actions; and lastly, devotion to knowledge. But he who is unsteady is led by desire and is attached to the fruit, thinking 'I do this act for my benefit.' He is firmly bound. Wherefore, be thou steady-minded.

The blissful embodied life of a sage.

But as to the man who sees the Supreme Being.

सर्वकर्माणि मनसा संन्यस्यास्ते सुखं वशी ।
नवद्वारे पुरे देही नैव कुर्वन्न कारयन् ॥ १३ ॥

13. Renouncing all actions by thought, and Self-controlled, the embodied one rests happily in the nine-gated city, neither at all acting nor causing to act.

Actions are either the obligatory duties (nitya-karma*n*i), or those arising on the occurrence of some special events (naimittika-karma*n*i), or those intended for securing some special ends, and which are only optional (kamya-karma*n*i), of those which are forbidden (pratishiddha-karma*n*i). The man who has subdued the senses, renounces all actions in speech, thought, and deed, by discrimination, by seeing inaction in action, and rests happily. He rests happily because he has given up all action in speech, thought and deed, because he is without worry, because his mind is calm, because, excepting the Self, all interests (foreign to the Self) have departed from his mind,—Where and how does he rest?—In the body which has nine openings; seven in the head, being the organs of sensation; two nether ones for the passage of the urine and the dung. As having these nine openings, the body is said to be a nine-gated city. It is like a city, with the Self for its monarch, inhabited by the citizens of the senses, mind, inlellect, as well as their objects,—all working for the sole benefit of their Lord and producing consciousness of various objects. In such a nine-gated city the embodied one rests, having renounced all action.

(*Objection*) :—Of what use is the qualification "he rests in the body"? Every man, be he a sa*m*nyasin or not, rests in the body only. So, the qualification is meaningless.

(*Answer*) :—He that is ignorant identifies himself with the mere aggregate of the body and the senses, and thinks: "I rest in a house, on the ground, on a seat." Such a man regarding the mere body as himself, cannot indeed cherish the idea that he rests in the body as in a house. But in the case of a man who regards the Self as distinct from the aggregate of the body, &c., the idea that he rests in the body is quite possible. And it is also right that he should renouce by thought—by knowledge, by discriminative wisdom—the action attributed to the Self through ignorance, but which really pertains to the not Self. Though a man has attained discriminative wisdom (*i.e.*, has realised his true Self as distinguished from the not-Self) and has renounced all concern with action, still, it may be said that he rests in the nine-gated city of the body as in a house, inasmuch as his personal consciousness (of resting arises only with reference to the body in virtue of the traces of the unspent portion of the prarabdha-karma—the karma which brought the present body into existence—still continuing to be felt. Thus the qualification 'he rests in the body' has a meaning, as pointing to a distinction between the respective standpoints of the wise and the ignorant.

(Objection) :—It is true that he renounces the actions of the body and of the senses attributed falsely to the Self through ignorance; still, the power of acting and of causing to act may be inherent in the Self and may remain in him who has renounced actions.

(Answer) :—The Lord says: He neither acts himself, nor causes the body and the senses to act.

(Question) :—Do you mean that the power of acting and of causing to act is inherent in the Self and that it ceases by renunciation, like the motion of a moving person: or that the power is not inherent in the Self?

(Answer) :—The power of acting or of causing to act is not inherent in the Self; for, the Lord has taught that the Self is unchangeable (ii. 25), and "though seated in the body, he acts not, nor is he tainted" (xiii. 31). The sruti says, "It thinks as it were and moves as it were." (Bri. Up. 4-3-7).

Nature is the source of activity.

Moreover,

न कर्तृत्वं न कर्माणि लोकस्य सृजति प्रभुः ।
न कर्मफलसंयोगं स्वभावस्तु प्रवर्तते ॥ १४ ॥

14. Neither agency nor objects does the Lord create for the world, nor union with the fruits of actions. But it is the nature that acts.

The Self, the Lord (of the body), does not create agency *i.e.*, does not of Himself urge any one to action, 'do this.' Neither does the Self create cars, jars, mansions, and other objects of desire. Nor does the Self unite him who makes a car or the like with the fruit of the act.

(*Question*):—If the Self in the body does not Himself act nor cause others to act, what then is it that acts and causes others to act?

(*Answer*):—Listen. It is Nature, Svabhava, Prak*r*iti, Maya, 'the Divine Maya made up of gu*n*as' * (vii. 14).

Wisdom and Unwisdom.

In reality,

नादत्ते कस्यचित्पापं न चैव सुकृतं विभुः ।
अज्ञानेनावृतं ज्ञानं तेन मुह्यन्ति जन्तवः ॥ १५ ॥

15. The Lord takes neither the evil nor even the good deed of any; wisdom is enveloped by unwisdom; thereby mortals are deluded.

Of any: even of His devotees.

(*Question*):—With what object then is done by devotees any meritorious act,—an act of worship, sacrifice, or charity, the offering of an oblation into the fire, or the like?

(*Answer*):—The Lord says in reply; Discriminative knowledge is enveloped by ignorance. mortal creatures in sa*m*sara are deluded and think, "I act, I cause to act, I shall enjoy, I cause to enjoy," and so on.

---

* That is to say, *A*tman forms the agent, the enjoyer, and the Lord of Creation, through avidya—(A).

ज्ञानेन तु तदज्ञानं येषां नाशितमात्मनः ।
तेषामादित्यवज्ज्ञानं प्रकाशयति तत्परम् ॥ १६ ॥

16. But to those whose unwisdom is destroyed by wisdom of the Self, like the sun wisdom illuminates that Supreme.

When that unwisdom by which the mortals are enveloped and deluded is destroyed by wisdom or discriminative knowledge of the Self, then, as the sun illuminates all objects, so wisdom illuminates the whole of the Knowable, the Supreme Reality.

The sage has no more births.

The Supreme Reality having been illuminated by wisdom.

तद्बुद्धयस्तदात्मानस्तन्निष्ठास्तत्परायणाः ।
गच्छन्त्यपुनरावृत्तिं ज्ञाननिर्धूतकल्मषाः ॥ १७ ॥

17. With their consciousness in That, their Self being That, intent on That, with That for their supreme goal, they go never again to return, their sins shaken off by means of wisdom.

Fixing their consciousness in Brahman and realising that the very Supreme Brahman is their Self, they renounce all actions and dwell in Brahman alone,—the Supreme Brahman being their highest goal, their delight being solely in the unconditioned Self. In the case of such men, all sins and other causes of mundane existence (sa*m*sara) are destroyed by wisdom described above, and they depart from here, never returning to embodied life.

The sage sees the One in all beings.

How do those wise men see truth whose ignorance of the Self has been removed by knowledge?—Listen:

विद्याविनयसम्पन्ने ब्राह्मणे गवि हस्तिनि ।
शुनि चैव श्वपाके च पण्डिताः समदर्शिनः ॥ १८ ॥

18. In a Brahma*n*a endued with wisdom and humility, in a cow, in an elephant, as also in a dog and in a dog-eater,* the wise see the same.

Humility is tranquillity, the condition of a well-disciplined soul. Of the creatures mentioned, the highest is the brahma*n*a who is spiritually regenerated, and highly Sattvic (*i.e.*, in whom the energy of *Sattva* predominates). Next comes the cow, not spiritually regenerated, and Rajasic (*i. e.*, in which the energy of *Rajas* predominates) Last come the elephant, &c., which are purely Tamasic (the energy of *Tamas* predominating). In all of them the sages see the same, the One who is immutable in Himself and quite untouched by Sattva and other energies, or by the tendencies born of those energies, whether Sattvic, Rajasic or Tamasic.

The sage is liberated while still on earth.

(*Objection*):—They (the sages just spoken of) are sinful persons, whose food should not be eaten by others. For, the Law says:

> "Where one's equals are honored in a different manner, and where persons who are not one's equals are honored in the same manner as oneself, a dinner must not be eaten." (Gautama's Institutes, xvii. 20.)

(*Answer*):—They are not sinful; for,

---

* A cha*nd*ala, an outcaste.

इहैव तैर्जितः सर्गो येषां साम्ये स्थितं मनः ।
निर्दोषं हि समं ब्रह्म तस्माद्ब्रह्मणि ते स्थिताः ॥ १९ ॥

19. Even here birth is overcome by them whose mind rests on equality. Spotless, indeed, and equal is Brahman; wherefore in Brahman they rest.

Even while living here on earth, birth has been brought under control by those sages who see the One, and whose intuition (anta*h*-kara*n*a) rests unwavering on the equality (*i. e.*, homogeneity) of Brahman in all creatures. Though, to the ignorant, Brahman in such impure bodies as those of dog-eaters and the like appears to be contaminated by their impurities, yet He is unaffected by them and is therefore spotless. Further, He is not heterogeneous either, owing to any heterogeneous attributes inherent in Himself; for, consciousness (chaitanya) has no attributes. And the Lord speaks of desire and the like as the attributes of the Kshetra—of the body, of the not-Self (xiii. 6),—and He speaks also of the Self as beginningless and without attributes (xiii. 31). Nor are there what are called 'ultimate particulars (antyaviseshas)' as the basis of individual distinctions in the Self, since no evidence can be adduced to prove their existence in relation to the several bodies.* Hence Brahman is homogeneous

* According to the Vaiseshika system of philosophy '*antya-visesha* is that indefinable peculiar attribute inherent in an eternal substance which distinguishes it from another eternal substance. It is that in an eternal substance which marks its individual identity. The existence of such an attribute is only inferred in order to account for a distinction which is otherwise perceived. The eternal substances are thus enumerated :—The atoms of Earth, of Water, of Light, and of Air; *A*kasa (ether), Time, Space, *A*tman (soul) and Manas (mind). The *antya viseshas* in the *A*tman is only inferable from a distinction in the Self, for which Vedanta sees no evidence. Distinctions in the body cannot certainly point to distinctions in the Self since a yogin can simultaneously assume various bodies.

and one. Wherefore they (the sages) rest in Brahman only. Not in the slightest can blemishes of bodies affect them, since they have no egotism and do not identify themselves with the aggregate of the body and the like. It is only to those who are egotistic and who identify the Self with the aggregate of the body and the like, that the institute quoted above is applicable, since it refers to persons who are the objects of honor. In honoring and giving gifts, some special qualifications are taken into account, such as a knowledge of Brahman, knowledge of the six auxiliary sciences (a*n*gas), a knowledge of the four Vedas and the like. But Brahman is free from all attributes, good and bad. Hence the statement 'they rest in Brahman.' Moreover, the institute quoted above is taken from a section which is concerned with works (Karma), whereas this portion of the Gita (from v. 13 to the end of the adhyaya) is a section treating of renunciation of all works.

The sage is free from grief and rejoicing.

Because Brahman, the Self, is blemishless and homogeneous, therefore,

न प्रहृष्येत्प्रियं प्राप्य नोद्विजेत्प्राप्य चाप्रियम् ।
स्थिरबुद्धिरसम्मूढो ब्रह्मविद्ब्रह्मणि स्थितः ॥ २० ॥

20. He who knows Brahman can neither rejoice on obtaining the pleasant, nor grieve on obtaining the unpleasant,—steady-minded, undeluded, resting in Brahman.

Pleasant and unpleasant objects can cause pleasure and pain to them only who regard the body as the Self, not to him who sees the pure Self, since the latter never comes by pleasant and unpleasant objects. He is undoubtingly conscious that the Self is free from delusion. He rests in Brahman described above; that is, he does no action, he has renounced all action.

The sage's infinite joy.

Moreover, resting in Brahman,

बाह्यस्पर्शेष्वसक्तात्मा विन्दत्यात्मनि यत्सुखम् ।
स ब्रह्मयोगयुक्तात्मा सुखमक्षय्यमश्नुते ॥ २१ ॥

21. With the self unattached to external contacts, he finds the joy which is in the Self; with the Self engaged in the contemplation of Brahman he attains the endless joy.

When his intuition (anta*h*-kara*n*a) is uncontaminated by attachment to things contacted by the senses, to the sound and other sense-objects which are all external (to the Self), the sage realises the joy which there is in the Self. When his intuition (anta*h*-kara*n*a) is engaged in Yoga, in Samadhi, in a deep and steady contemplation of Brahman, then the sage attains the imperishable bliss. Therefore, he who seeks for the endless joy of the Self should withdraw the senses from the momentary pleasure of external objects.

For the following reason also he should withdraw (the senses from external objects):—

ये हि संस्पर्शजा भोगा दुःखयोनय एव ते ।
आद्यन्तवन्तः कौन्तेय न तेषु रमते बुधः ॥ २२ ॥

22. For, those delights which are born of contacts are only generators of pain, having a beginning and an end, O son of Kunti; a wise man rejoices not in them.

The pleasures that are caused by contacts of the senses with sense-objects are only generators of pain, since those delights are caused by nescience (avidya). We do find that all troubles arising in the body (adhyatmika). etc., are traceable to them (delights) only. As in this world, so in the other,—as the word 'only' indicates. Seeing that there is no trace of joy in the samsara, the devotee should withdraw the senses from the mirage of sense-objects. Not only do the delights cause pain, but also they have a beginning and an end, The contact of a sense with its object marks the beginning of a pleasure, and their separation its end. Delights are temporary, occurring in the moment of interval (between the origin and the end.) A man who possesses discrimination and who has realised the Supeme Reality does not rejoice in them. It is only quite ignorant persons that are, like cattle and the like, found to rejoice in the sense-objects.

The path of Nirvana.

And there is also a a wicked thing, an enemy on the path to Bliss, a most difficult thing to deal with, the source of all evil, very difficult to ward off, so that, very mighty efforts should be made, says the Lord, to repel the enemy :

शक्नोतीहैव यः सोढुं प्राक् शरीरविमोक्षणात् ।
कामक्रोधोद्भवं वेगं स युक्तः स सुखी नरः ॥ २३ ॥

23. He that is able, while still here, to withstand, before liberation from the body, the impulse of desire and anger, he is a Yogin, he is a happy man.

While still here: while yet living. *Before liberation from the body* : up to the point of death. By thus marking death as the limit, the Lord teaches that the impulse of desire and anger is unavoidable during life, since its causes are innumerable, and that till the very moment of death it should not be trusted. Desire (Kama) is the longing for a pleasure-giving agreeable object of our experience when coming within the ken of our senses, heard of, or remembered; and anger (krodha) is the aversion for the disagreeable, for the cause of pain, when being seen, heard of, or remembered. The impulse of desire (kama) is the agitation of the mind (anta*h*kara*n*a) as indicated by hairs standing on end and by a joyful countenance; and the impulse of anger is the mental agitation indicated by the trembling of the body, by perspiration, lip-biting, fiery eyes, and the like. He who can withstand the impulses of desire and anger is a Yogin, and he is a happy man here on earth.

What sort of a man resting in Brahman attains Brahman?—The Lord says:

योऽन्तःसुखोऽन्तरारामस्तथान्तर्ज्योतिरेव यः ।
स योगी ब्रह्मनिर्वाणं ब्रह्मभूतोऽधिगच्छति ॥ २४ ॥

24. Whoso has his joy within and his pastime within, and whoso has his light within only, that Yogin attains Brahman's bliss, himself becoming Brahman.

Within: in the Self. He attains the bliss (nirva*n*a) in Brahman,—*i e.*, he attains moksha,—while still living here on earth.

Moreover,

लभन्ते ब्रह्मनिर्वाणमृषयः क्षीणकल्मषाः ।
छिन्नद्वैधा यतात्मानः सर्वभूतहिते रताः ॥ २५ ॥

25. The sages attain Brahman's bliss,—they whose sins have been destroyed and doubts removed, who are self-controlled and intent on the welfare of all beings.

Sages (*Rishis*) : men of right knowledge and renunciation. *Intent*, etc. : injuring none.

Moreover,

कामक्रोधवियुक्तानां यतीनां यतचेतसाम् ।
अभितो ब्रह्मनिर्वाणं वर्तते विदितात्मनाम् ॥ २६ ॥

26. To the devotees who are free from desire and anger, who have controlled their thought, and who have known the Self, Brahman's bliss exists everywhere.

Those who have renounced all actions and attained right knowledge are liberated, whether living or dead.

Realisation of the Lord by Dhyana-Yoga.

It has been said that those who, renouncing all actions, remain steady in right knowledge obtain instant liberation. It has often been and will be declared by the Lord that Karma-Yoga, which is performed in complete devotion to the Lord and dedicated to Him, leads to moksha step by step: *first* the purification of the mind, *then* knowledge, *then* renunciation of all actions, and *lastly* moksha. And now, with a view to propound at length the Dhyana-Yoga, the proximate means to right knowledge, the Lord teaches the Dhyana-Yoga in the following few aphoristic verses:

स्पर्शान्कृत्वा बहिर्बाह्यांश्चक्षुश्चैवान्तरे भ्रुवोः ।
प्राणापानौ समौ कृत्वा नासाभ्यन्तरचारिणौ ॥ २७ ॥
यतेन्द्रियमनोबुद्धिर्मुनिर्मोक्षपरायणः ।
विगतेच्छाभयक्रोधो यः सदा मुक्त एव सः ॥ २८ ॥

27-28. Shutting out all external contracts and fixing the sight between the eye-brows, equalising the out-going and the in-going breaths which pass through the nostrils, controlling the senses, mind and intellect, having moksha as his highest goal, free from desire, fear and anger,—the sage who ever (remains thus) is verily liberated.

The sound and other sense-objects enter the mind within through the respective organs. These objects which are external are kept outside when a man does not think of them. A sage (muni) is one who is given to contemplation (manana) and who renounces all actions. Keeping the body in the posture described, he should always look up to moksha as his supreme goal. When the sage leads constantly this kind of life, renouncing all, he is no doubt liberated: he has nothing else to do for liberation.

What has he—he whose mind is thus steadily balanced—to know and meditate upon in the Dhyana-Yoga?

भोक्तारं यज्ञतपसां सर्वलोकमहेश्वरम् ।
सुहृदं सर्वभूतानां ज्ञात्वा मां शान्तिमृच्छति ॥ २९ ॥

29. On knowing Me,—the Lord of all sacrifices and austerities, the Great Lord of all Worlds, the Friend of all beings,—he goes to Peace.

I am Narayana, the Lord of all sacrifices and austerities, both as their author and as their Devata (*i.e.*, as the God whose grace is sought by their means). I am the Friend of all, doing good to them without expecting any return for it. Lying in the heart of all beings I am the dispenser of the fruits of all actions and the witness of all cognitions. On knowing Me, they attain peace, the cessation of all samsara.

SIXTH DISCOURSE.

DHYANA-YOGA.

Dhyana-yoga is incompatible with works.

At the close of the next preceding Discourse, Dhyana-Yoga—Yoga by meditation,—which is the proximate means to right knowledge has been taught in a few aphoristic verses (v. 27-29). Here commences the Sixth Discourse which occupies the position of a commentary thereon. Now, action (karma) is an external aid to Dhyana-Yoga; and a gṛihastha (householder), on whom action is enjoined, should perform it till he is able to attain to Dhyana-Yoga; and bearing this in mind, the Lord extols action in vi. 1.

(Objection):—* Now, since action which is enjoined should be performed throughout life, what is the meaning of the limitation, 'till he is able to attain to Dhyana-Yoga'?

(Answer):—This objection does not apply here because of the specification that, 'for the sage who wishes to attain to Yoga, action is the means' (vi. 3); and because it is also said that he who has attained Yoga has only to resort to renunciation (*sama*). If it were meant that each of them—he who wishes to attain to Yoga as well as he who has attained to Yoga—should resort to both action and renunciation, then it would be useless to specify that action and renunciation are respectively intended for him who wishes to attain Yoga and for him who has attained Yoga, or to divide them into two distinct classes.

* The Samuchchaya-Vadin maintains that knowledge should be conjoined with action if it should produce the intended result.

(*The opponent*) :—Among religious devotees (asramins= grihasthas), one class comprises persons who wish to attain Yoga, another class comprises persons who have already attained Yoga, while the rest are those who neither wish to attain Yoga nor have attained Yoga; and it is but right that the first two classes should be specified and shown separately as distinguished from the third*

(*Answer*) :—No ; the words 'for the same devotee' (in vi. 3) and the repetition of 'yoga' in the clause 'when he has attained to Yoga' imply this, that the same person who at first wished to attain to Yoga has only to renounce action when he has attained Yoga, this renunciation leading to the fruition of Yoga. Thus, no action forms a necessary duty throughout life.

Failures in Yoga are also spoken of here (vi. 37, 38). If in the Sixth Discourse Yoga were meant for a grihastha, then there could be no occasion for the supposition of his ruin, inasmuch as he, though a failure in Yoga, may obtain the fruit of Karma. An action done, whether interested (*kamya*) or obligatory and disinterested (*nitya*), must produce its effect;—(it cannot of course produce) moksha, which, being eternal, cannot be produced by an action. We have also said † that the obligatory duty (nitya-karma), as taught by so great an authority as the Veda, must produce a result of its own, since, otherwise, the Veda would serve no purpose. Neither would it be proper to speak of a grihastha as a failure in both ways; for he would still perform Karma and there would therefore be no occasion for a failure therein.

* The opponent drives at this conclusion, that while the first and third classes of aspirants are bound to perform Karma, those who have attained Yoga should not, as belonging to the order of grihasthas, renounce Karma, though they may practise Yoga with a view to realise the true nature of the Self.

† *Vide* commentary on iv. 18.

(*The opponent*) :—The Karma which has been done has been offered to the Lord: wherefore, such Karma can bring in no result to the author.

(*Answer*) :—No; for, the offering of Karma to the Lord must lead to still greater results.

(*The opponent*) :—It leads only to moksha.—The offering of all actions to the Lord, when conjoined with Yoga, leads to moksha and to no other result; but, since he has failed in Yoga, it is but right to suppose that such a man will be ruined.

(*Answer*) :—No; for, the verses vi. 10, 14, enjoin renunciation of action. It is not possible to think of any kind of wife's aid at the time of Dhyana; if it were possible, then it might be argued that loneliness is enjoined (vi. 10) with a view to prohibit that aid*. And what is taught in vi. 10—"without desire, without property"—is not compatible with the life of a grihastha. The question (vi. 38), too, regarding him who may prove a failure in both ways would not arise.

(*The opponent*) :—In vi. 1, a man of action (Karmin) is said to be both a Samnyasin and a Yogin, and it is further said that he who does no action or keeps no fire cannot be a Yogin or a Samnyasin.

(*Answer*) :—No; vi. 1, merely extols the abandonment of attachment for results of actions, performance of which forms an external aid (bahiranga) to Dhyana-Yoga, (*i.e.*, which leads one to Dhyana-Yoga in due course).—It is not he alone who is without fire and without action that is both a Samnyasin and a Yogin, but also one devoted to action, who abandoning attachment for the results of actions, performs them for the purification of the mind (sattva suddhi). Thus

* That is to say, Dhayana-Yoga as taught in the sequel is not meant for a grihastha who is engaged in works; for he cannot fulfil the conditions laid down in vi. 10, 14, etc.

by way of praise the latter is said to be a Samnyasin and a Yogin. It is, moreover, not proper to hold that one and the same proposition,* both praises the abandonment of attachment for results of actions and forbids the fourth order. Further, the Lord cannot contradict the *S*ruti, Sm*r*iti, the Puranas, the Itihasa and the Yoga-sastras, which clearly teach that a man who is without fire and without action—*i.e.*, who is literally a samnyasin—is a Samnyasin and a Yogin. To forbid the fourth order would contradict what the Lord Himself teaches in iv. 13, xii. 16, 19, ii. 71.

Therefore, for the sage who wishes to attain Yoga and has already entered on the career of a g*r*ihastha, action (such as the Agnihotra) performed without a desire for its fruit becomes, by way of purifying the mind, a means to Dhyana-Yoga. On this ground he is said to be a Samnyasin and a Yogin by way of praise.

Renunciation in action.

The Blessed Lord said:

अनाश्रितः कर्मफलं कार्यं कर्म करोति यः ।
स संन्यासी च योगी च न निरग्निर्न चाक्रियः ॥ १ ॥

1. He who, without depending on the fruits of action, performs his bounden duty, he is a Samnyasin and a Yogin : not he who is without fire and without action.

He who desires the fruits of actions is dependent thereon; but different from him is the man in question; he is not dependent on the fruits of actions.

He who is thus free from a desire for the fruits of actions and performs action, such as the Agnihotra or fire-sacrifice as a bounden duty (nitya-karma),—not as a kamya-karma or

* *Vide* note † P 155.

action done with a motive, as a means of attaining some immediate specific end in view,—he who performs actions thus is superior to those who perform actions in a different spirit. Wtth a view to impress this truth, the Lord says that he is Samnyasin and a Yogin. He should be regarded as possessing both the attributes, the attributes of renunciation (samnyasa) and steadfastness of mind (Yoga). Not he alone should be regarded as a Samnyasin and a Yogin who is without fire and without action, who neither lights sacrificial fires nor engages in other actions, such as austerities and the like which require no help of sacrificial fires.

(Objection) :—In the sruti, in the smriti, and in the yoga-sastras, it is plainly taught that a Samnyasin or a Yogin is one who is without fire and without action. How is it that the Lord teaches here a strange doctrine that he who lights fire and performs actions is a Samnyasin and a Yogin?

(Answer) :—This is not to be regarded as a fault; for, it is intended to represent a devotee to action as a Samnyasin and a Yogin in a secondary sense of the two terms. He is regarded as a Samnyasin because of his renunciation of the thoughts concerning the fruits of action; and he is regarded as a Yogin because he performs action as a means of attaining to Yoga or because he abandons thoughts concerning the fruits of actions as causing unsteadiness of mind. Thus, it is only in a secondary sense that the two terms are applied to him. It is not, on the other hand, meant that he is in reality a Samnyasin and a Yogin. The Lord, accordingly, says:

यं संन्यासमिति प्राहुर्योगं तं विद्धि पाण्डव ।
न ह्यसंन्यस्तसङ्कल्पो योगी भवति कश्चन ॥ २ ॥

2. Do thou, O Pandava, know Yoga to be that which they call renunciation; no one, verily, becomes a Yogin who has not renounced thoughts

Do thou understand that the Yoga, which consists in performance of action, is that which those who are versed in the sruti and the smriti declare to be samnyasa, the true renunciation which consists in the abandonment of all action as well as its fruit.

(*Question*):—On what point of similarity between Karma-Yoga which consists in the performance of action (pravritti) and the pure Samnyasa which consists in abstaining from action (nivritti) is the representation of identity of the former with the latter based?

(*Answer*):—There is of course a certain amount of similarity between Karma-Yoga and pure samnyasa so far as the agent is concerned. For, he who is a pure Samnyasin, who has renounced all actions as well as their accessories, abandons thoughts (samkalpa) concerning all actions and their fruits,—those thoughts causing the desires which impel one to action. A follower of Karma-Yoga, too, renounces thoughts of results, while he performs actions. This the Lord teaches in the following words: No devotee to action who has not given up the thought of reward can be a Yogin, a man of steadfastness; for the thought of reward causes unsteadiness of mind. That is to say, that devotee to action who has given up all thoughts of reward will become a Yogin, a man of steadfastness, a steady-minded man, inasmuch as all thought of reward which is the cause of unsteadiness has been given up.

Action is a stepping-stone to Dhyana-Yoga

Thus, having regard to the likeness between pure Samnyasa and Karma-Yoga in so far as the devotee in either case renounces (the thoughts concerning the fruit of action), Karma-Yoga has been represented in vi. 2. as Samnyasa with a view to extol it. And the Lord extols it because the Karma-Yoga, practised without regard to the fruit of action, forms an external aid (bahiranga) to Dhyana-Yoga, *i.e.*, leads the devotee to Dhyana-Yoga (in due course). He now proceeds to show how Karma-Yoga is a means to Dhyana-Yoga.

आरुरुक्षोर्मुनेर्योगं कर्म कारणमुच्यते ।
योगारूढस्य तस्यैव शमः कारणमुच्यते ॥ ३ ॥

3. For a devotee who wishes to attain to Yoga, action is said to be the means. For the same (devotee), when he has attained to Yoga, quiescence (*s*ama) is said to be the means.

For a devotee (muni) who has given up the fruit of action, and who wishes to attain to Yoga,—*i.e.*, who has not already risen to it, who is unable to remain steady in Dhyana-Yoga,—action (karma) is said to be the means* of attaining his end. For the same devotee, on the other hand, when he has attained to Yoga, quiescence—*i.e.*, the abstaining from all action—is said to be the means (of attaining his end). The more thoroughly he abstains from action, the more free he is from trouble, the more the senses are controlled, and the more steadfast his mind remains. Then he becomes a Yogârû*d*ha, one who has attained to Yoga. Accordingly it is said in the Mahabharata:

"For a Brahma*n*a there is no wealth equal to this, *viz.*, (knowledge of) oneness and homogeneity (of Brahman in all creatures), truthfulness, character, steadiness, harmlessness, straightforwardness, and renunciation of the several actions." —(Santiparva, 175-38).

Who is a Yogin?

When is a man said to be a Yogârû*d*ha, to have attained to Yoga?—The answer follows:

---

* His end is Dhyana-Yoga, and this he attains by action which first purifies the mind and then creates desire and capacity for Dhyana-Yoga.

यदा हि चेन्द्रियार्थेषु न कर्मस्वनुषज्जते ।
सर्वसङ्कल्पसंन्यासी योगारूढस्तदोच्यते ॥ ४ ॥

4. When a man, renouncing all thoughts, is not attached to sense-objects and actions, then he is said to have attained to Yoga.

When a Yogin, keeping the mind steadfast, feels no attachment for the objects of the senses such as sound, nor thinks that he has to do any action,—whether *nitya* (obligatory) or *naimittika* (obligatory and incidental) or *kamya* (done with a motive) or *pratishiddha* (forbidden by law),—regarding it has of no use to him; and when he has learned to habitually renounce all thoughts which give rise to desires for objects of this world and of the next, then he is said to have become a Yogaru*d*ha, to be one who has attained to Yoga.—The words "renouncing all thoughts" imply that all desires as well as all actions should be renounced. For, all desires spring from thoughts, as the sm*r*iti says:

"Verily desire springs from thought (sa*m*kalpa), and of thought yaj*n*as are born."—*Manu* ii. 2).

"O Desire, I know where thy root lies. Thou art born of thought. I shall not think of thee, and thou shalt cease to exist as well as thy root."—(Mahabharata, Santiparva, 177-25).

On the abandonment of all desires, the abandonment of all actions necessarily follows, as passages in the sruti like the following show:

"Whatever forms the object of desire, that he wills; and whatever he wills, that he acts."—(B*r*i. Up. 4-4-5).

Reasoning also leads to the same conclusion. For, on surrendering all thoughts, one cannot move at all. Wherefore, by saying that the aspirant should renounce all thoughts, the Lord implies that he should abandon all desires and all actions as well.

When a man has attained to Yoga, then the self is raised by the self from out of the numerous evils of samsara. Therefore,

उद्धरेदात्मनाऽऽत्मानं नात्मानमवसादयेत् ।
आत्मैव ह्यात्मनो बन्धुरात्मैव रिपुरात्मनः ॥ ५ ॥

5. Let a man raise himself by himself, let him not lower himself; for, he alone is the friend of himself, he alone is the enemy of himself.

Let a man lift up himself who is drowned in the ocean of samsara, *i.e.*, let him so train himself as to become a Yogarudha, let him practise and attain to Yoga. Let him not lower himself; for, he alone is the friend of himself. There is indeed no other friend that can lead to liberation from samsara; nay, the so-called friend is only inimical to him who seeks liberation, as the former forms an object of affection, which is the cause of bondage Hence the emphasis 'he alone is the friend of himself.' And he alone is the enemy of himself. The other enemy who is outside is made an enemy only by himself. Hence the emphasis 'he alone is the enemy of himself.'

It has been said that "he alone is the friend of himself, he alone is the enemy of himself." Now it may be asked, what sort of a man is the friend of himself and what sort of a man is the enemy of himself?—The answer follows:

बन्धुरात्माऽऽत्मनस्तस्य येनात्मैवात्मना जितः ।
अनात्मनस्तु शत्रुत्वे वर्तेतात्मैव शत्रुवत् ॥ ६ ॥

6. To him who has conquered himself by himself, his own self is the friend of himself, but

to him who has not (conquered) himself, his own self stands in the place of an enemy like the (external) foe.

His self is the friend of himself who is self-controlled, who has brought under control the aggregate of the body and the senses. But in the case of a man who is not self-controlled, his own self does injury to himself, just as any external foe may do injury to him.

जितात्मनः प्रशान्तस्य परमात्मा समाहितः ।
शीतोष्णसुखदुःखेषु तथा मानावमानयोः ॥ ७ ॥

7. The self-controlled and serene man's Supreme Self is steadfast in cold and heat, in pleasure and pain, as also in honour and disgrace.

When a man has subdued the aggregate of the body and the senses, when his mind (anta*h*-kara*n*a) is tranquil, when he has renounced all actions, then the Supreme Self actually becomes his own Self.

ज्ञानविज्ञानतृप्तात्मा कूटस्थो विजितेन्द्रियः ।
युक्त इत्युच्यते योगी समलोष्टाश्मकाञ्चनः ॥ ८ ॥

8. The Yogin whose self is satisfied with knowledge and wisdom, who remains unshaken, who has conquered the senses, he is said to be a saint,—for whom a lump of earth, a stone and gold are equal.

When the Yogin is satisfied with knowledge (j*n*ana) of things as taught in the scriptures, and with wisdom (vij*n*ana), *i.e.*, with the realisation (in his own experience) of the things so taught—then he is said to be a saint (yukta), he is said to have attained samadhi or steadfastness of mind.

Moreover,

सुहृन्मित्रार्युदासीनमध्यस्थद्वेष्यबन्धुषु ।
साधुष्वपि च पापेषु समबुद्धिर्विशिष्यते ॥ ९ ॥

9. He is esteemed, who is of the same mind to the good-hearted, friends, foes, the indifferent, the neutral, the hateful, relatives, the righteous, and the unrighteous.

He is esteemed: He is the best among the Yogarudhas, among those who have attained to Yoga. [There is also another reading which means 'he is liberated.'] *Who is of the same mind*: who thinks not of a man as to what he is or what he does. A '*good-hearted*' man does good to another without expecting any service in return; an '*indifferent*' man is one who is partial to neither of two contending sides; a '*neutral*' man is one who means well by both the contending sides. The *righteous* are those who follow the Sastras, and the *unrighteous* are those who resort to forbidden acts.

Directions for the practice of Yoga.

Wherefore, to attain the highest results,

योगी युञ्जीत सततमात्मानं रहसि स्थितः ।
एकाकी यतचित्तात्मा निराशीरपरिग्रहः ॥ १० ॥

10. Let the Yogin try constantly to keep the mind steady, remaining in seclusion, alone, with the mind and body controlled, free from desire, and having no possessions.

Yogin: he who meditates. *In seclusion*; in a mountain-cave, or the like. The words 'in seclusion' and 'alone' evidently show that he should resort to renunciation (sa*m*nyasa). Not only should he renounce the world when he practises Yoga, but he should also abandon all possessions.

Now, in the sequel, the Lord proceeds to prescribe for him who practises Yoga particular modes of sitting, eating, recreation and the like as aids to Yoga, as also to define the characteristic marks of the man who has attained Yoga, and to describe the effects of Yoga and other particulars in connection with it. First of all, He prescribes a particular mode of sitting as follows:

शुचौ देशे प्रतिष्ठाप्य स्थिरमासनमात्मनः ।
नात्युच्छ्रितं नातिनीचं चेलाजिनकुशोत्तरम् ॥ ११ ॥

11. Having in a cleanly spot established a firm seat, neither too high nor too low, with cloth, skin, and kusa grass thereon;

Cleanly: either naturally so, or made so by artificial improvements. Cloth, &c., should be spread on the seat in the reverse order of their enumeration here.

What should be done after establishing the seat?

तत्रैकाग्रं मनः कृत्वा यतचित्तेन्द्रियक्रियः ।
उपविश्यासने युञ्ज्याद्योगमात्मविशुद्धये ॥ १२ ॥

12. Making the mind one-pointed, with the actions of the mind and the senses controlled, let him, seated there on the seat, practise Yoga for the purification of the self.

He should withdraw the mind from all sense-objects before concentrating it. *The self*: the antah-karana, the inner sense, the mind.

The external seat has been described. Now, what should be the posture of the body?—Listen:

समं कायशिरोग्रीवं धारयन्नचलं स्थिरः ।
सम्प्रेक्ष्य नासिकाग्रं स्वं दिशश्चानवलोकयन् ॥ १३ ॥

13 Holding erect and still the body, the head, and the neck, firm, gazing on the tip of his nose, without looking around ;

An erect body may be in motion; hence the qualification 'still.' He is to gaze *as it were* on the tip of his nose.— Here we have to understand the words 'as it were'; for, the Lord means to prescribe, not the very act of 'gazing on the tip of his nose', but the fixing of the eye-sight within (by withdrawing it from external objects); and this, of course, depends on the steadiness of mind. If, on the other hand, the very act of 'gazing on the tip of his nose' were meant here, then the mind would be fixed only there, not on the Self. As a matter of fact, the Yogin is to concentrate his mind on the Self, as will be taught in vi. 25, 'Making the mind dwell in the Self.' Wherefore the words 'as it were' being understood, 'gazing' means here 'the fixing of the eye-sight within.'

Moreover,

प्रशान्तात्मा विगतभीर्ब्रह्मचारिव्रते स्थितः ।
मनः संयम्य मच्चित्तो युक्त आसीत मत्परः ॥ १४ ॥

14. Serene-minded, fearless, firm in the vow of godly life, having restrained the mind, thinking on Me, and balanced, let him sit, looking up to Me as the Supreme.

The vow of godly life (Brahmachari-vrata) consists in doing service to the Guru, in eating of the food obtained by begging, &c. He should strictly observe the vows of godly life. He should also restrain the mind, *i.e.*, repress its modifications. He should ever think of Me, the Paramesvara, the Supreme Lord. He should also regard Me as the Supreme. A lover may always think of a woman, but he never regards her as supreme. He regards either his sovereign, or Mahadeva (the Great God), as the case may be, as the Supreme. The Yogin, on the other hand, ever thinks of Me, and also regards Me as the Supreme Being.

Now the fruit of Yoga is described as follows:

युञ्जन्नेवं सदाऽऽत्मानं योगी नियतमानसः ।
शान्तिं निर्वाणपरमां मत्संस्थामधिगच्छति ॥ १५ ॥

15. Thus always keeping the mind balanced, the Yogin, with the mind controlled, attains to the Peace abiding in Me, which culminates in Nirvana (moksha,)

Thus: in the manner prescribed above.

Here follow regulations as regards a Yogin's food, &c:

नात्यश्नतस्तु योगोऽस्ति न चैकान्तमनश्नतः ।
न चातिस्वप्नशीलस्य जाग्रतो नैव चार्जुन ॥ १६ ॥

16. Yoga is not possible for him who eats too much, nor for him who does not eat at all, nor for him who is addicted to too much sleep, nor for him who is (ever) wakeful, O Arjuna.

Eats too much: eats more food than what is suited to him. The sruti says:

"Whatever food is suited to oneself, that protects; it injures not. A greater quantity injures and a smaller quantity protects not."—(Satapatha-Brahmana).

The Yogin should therefore eat neither more nor less than what is suitable for him. Or it may mean this: Yoga is not possible for him who eats more than the quantity prescribed for a Yogin in the Yogasastra. The quantity of food is thus prescribed:

"Half (the stomach) for food and condiments, the third (quarter) for water, and the fourth should be reserved for free motion of air."

How then can Yoga be achieved?—The answer follows:

युक्ताहारविहारस्य युक्तचेष्टस्य कर्मसु ।
युक्तस्वप्नावबोधस्य योगो भवति दुःखहा ॥ १७ ॥

17. To him whose food and recreation are moderate, whose exertion in actions is moderate, whose sleep and waking are moderate, to him accrues Yoga which is destructive of pain.

To him who resorts to food and recreation (such as walking) within prescribed limits, and who sleeps and who wakes up at the prescribed hours, to him accrues Yoga which is destructive of the misery of sa*m*sara.

Consummation.

When does he become a saint (Yukta)?—The answer follows:

यदा विनियतं चित्तमात्मन्येवावतिष्ठते ।
निःस्पृहः सर्वकामेभ्यो युक्त इत्युच्यते तदा ॥ १८ ॥

18. When the well-restrained thought is established in the Self only, without longing for any of the objects of desire, then he is said to be a Saint.

Well-restrained: which attained to one-pointedness or concentration. *In the Self only*: having abandoned all thoughts of external objects, the thinking principle (chitta) remains steadily in the Self. *Objects of desire*: seen or unseen.

The simple of such a Yogin's steadfast mind is described below:

यथा दीपो निवातस्थो नेङ्गते सोपमा स्मृता ।
योगिनो यतचित्तस्य युञ्जतो योगमात्मनः ॥ १९ ॥

19. 'As a lamp in a sheltered spot does not flicker,'—this has been thought as the simile of a Yogin of subdued thought, practising Yoga in the Self.

This simile has been thought out by those versed in Yoga, by those who know the ways of the thinking principle.

Having thus, by virtue of the practice of Yoga, become one-pointed (fit for concentration), like a lamp sheltered from the wind,

यत्रोपरमते चित्तं निरुद्धं योगसेवया ।
यत्र चैवात्मनाऽऽत्मानं पश्यन्नात्मनि तुष्यति ॥ २० ॥

20. When thought is quiescent, restrained by the practice of Yoga; when, seeing the Self by the self, he is satisfied in his own Self;

When the mind is restrained from all quarters by practice of Yoga, the Yogin sees the Self—the Supreme Intelligence (chaitanya) and the All-resplendent Light—by self (the anta*h*kara*n*a, the inner sense), by the mind which has been purified by samadhi and attains satisfaction in the Self.

And:

सुखमात्यन्तिकं यत्तद् बुद्धिग्राह्यमतीन्द्रियम् ।
वेत्ति यत्र न चैवाऽयं स्थितश्चलति तत्त्वतः ॥ २१ ॥

21. When he knows that Infinite Joy which, transcending the senses, can be grasped by reason; when, steady (in the Self), he moves never from the Reality;

He: the wise man. That joy can be grasped by reason (buddhi), independently of the senses, It lies beyond the ken of the senses; it is not produced by sense-objects.

And:

यं लब्ध्वा चापरं लाभं मन्यते नाधिकं ततः ।
यस्मिन्स्थितो न दुःखेन गुरुणाऽपि विचाल्यते ॥ २२ ॥

22. When, having obtained it, he thinks no other acquisition superior to it; when, therein established, he is not moved even by a great pain;

It: the gain of the Self. *Therein*: in the real Self. *Pain*: such as may be caused by a sword-cut, etc.

This Yoga,—this peculiar state of the Self which has been described in so many of its attributes in the verses beginning with vi. 20:

तं विद्याद् दुःखसंयोगवियोगं योगसंज्ञितम् ।
स निश्चयेन योक्तव्यो योगोऽनिर्विण्णचेतसा ॥ २३ ॥

23. This severance from union with pain, be it known, is called *union* (Yoga). That Yoga must be practised with determination and with undepressed heart.

Severance from union with pain is called *Yoga* (which means *union*) by a sort of irony. Having thus concluded speaking of the effect of Yoga, the Lord again refers to the necessity of it, with a view to show that determination and non-depression (self-reliance) are necessary means to Yoga *That Yoga*: the Yoga which can produce the result described above.

Further directions concerning the practice of Yoga.

Moreover,

सङ्कल्पप्रभवान्कामांस्त्यक्त्वा सर्वानशेषतः ।
मनसैवेन्द्रियग्रामं विनियम्य समन्ततः ॥ २४ ॥

24. Abandoning without reserve all fancy-born desires, well-restraining all the senses from all quarters by the mind;

By the mind: endued with discrimination:

शनैःशनैरुपरमेद् बुद्ध्या धृतिगृहीतया ।
आत्मसंस्थं मनः कृत्वा न किञ्चिदपि चिन्तयेत् ॥ २५ ॥

25. Little by little let him withdraw, by reason (buddhi) held in firmness; keeping the mind established in the Self, let him not think of anything.

He should make the mind constantly abide in the Self, bearing in mind that the Self is all and that nothing else exists. This * is the highest form of Yoga.

Now, as to the Yogin who thus strives to make the mind abide in the Self,

* The steadinesf of mind.—(A.)

यतो यतो निश्चरति मनश्चञ्चलमस्थिरम् ।
ततस्ततो नियम्यैतदात्मन्येव वशं नयेत् ॥ २६ ॥

26. By whatever cause the wavering and unsteady mind wanders away, from that let him restrain it and bring it back direct under the control of the Self.

Sound and other objects are the causes which make the mind wander away. It is a natural weakness of the mind to be thus led away by sense-objects. By convincing oneself of the illusoriness of sense-objects through an investigation into their real nature, and by cultivating indifference to worldly objects, the mind can be restrained from sense-objects and brought back to the Self wherein to abide firmly. In virtue of this practice of Yoga, the Yogin's mind attains peace in the Self.

The effect of Dhyana-Yoga.

प्रशान्तमनसं ह्येनं योगिनं सुखमुत्तमम् ।
उपैति शान्तरजसं ब्रह्मभूतमकल्मषम् ॥ २७ ॥

27. Supreme Bliss verily comes to this Yogin, whose mind is quite tranquil, whose passion is quieted, who has become Brahman, who is blemishless.

Whose passion &c.: in whom all passion, including attachment and other causes of pain, has disappeared; who has become a *Jivan-mukta* (a man whose soul is liberated while still alive), convinced that all is Brahman; who has no blemish whatsoever, who is not affected by dharma and a-dharma.

युञ्जन्नेवं सदाऽऽत्मानं योगी विगतकल्मषः ।
सुखेन ब्रह्मसंस्पर्शमत्यन्तं सुखमश्नुते ॥ २८ ॥

28. Thus always keeping the self steadfast, the Yogin, freed from sins, attains with ease to the infinite bliss of contact with the (Supreme) Brahman.

Always: unimpeded by any of the obstacles to Yoga.

Now will be discribed the effect of Yoga, the perception of oneness with Brahman, which leads to the cessation of all sa*m*sara :

सर्वभूतस्थमात्मानं सर्वभूतानि चात्मनि ।
ईक्षते योगयुक्तात्मा सर्वत्र समदर्शनः ॥ २९ ॥

29. The Self abiding in all beings, and all beings (abiding) in the Self, sees he whose self has been made steadfast by Yoga, who everywhere sees the same.

He sees all beings—from Brahma, the Creator, down to a clump of grass—as one with the Self; and in all the different beings—from Brahma, the Creator, down to inanimate objects—he sees the same; *i.e.*, he sees that the Self and Brahman (the Absolute) are one.

Now will be discribed the effect of this perception of the unity of the Self;

यो मां पश्यति सर्वत्र सर्वं च मयि पश्यति ।
तस्याहं न प्रणश्यामि स च मे न प्रणश्यति ॥ ३० ॥

30. He who sees Me everywhere and sees everything in Me, to him I vanish not, nor to Me does he vanish.

He who sees Me, Vasudeva, the Self of all, in all beings, and who sees Brahma, the Creator, and all other beings, in Me, the Self of all ;—when he has thus seen the unity of the Self, I—who am the Isvara—never leave his presence, nor does that wise man leave My presence; for his Self and Mine are one, and one's own Self cannot but be manifest to oneself.

Now, referring to the knowledge imparted in the preceding verse—namely that 'I Myself, the Self of all, am the seer of the unity of Self',—the Lord will speak of moksha as the effect of that knowledge:

सर्वभूतस्थितं यो मां भजत्येकत्वमास्थितः ।
सर्वथा वर्तमानोऽपि स योगी मयि वर्तते ॥ ३१ ॥

31. Whoso, intent on unity, worships Me who abide in all beings, that Yogin dwells in Me, whatever his mode of life.

This man of right knowledge dwells in Me, in the supreme state, in the state of Vishnu; he is ever liberated nothing obstructs his path to moksha.

Moreover,

आत्मौपम्येन सर्वत्र समं पश्यति योऽर्जुन ।
सुखं वा यदि वा दुःखं स योगी परमो मतः ॥ ३२ ॥

32. Whoso, by comparison with himself, sees the same everywhere, O Arjuna, be it pleasure or pain, he is deemed the highest Yogin.

He sees that whatever is pleasant to himself is pleasant to all creatures, and that whatever is painful to himself is painful to all beings. Thus seeing that what is pleasure or pain to himself is alike pleasure or pain to all beings, he causes pain to no being; he is harmless. Doing no harm, and devoted to right knowledge, he is regarded as the highest among all Yogins.

Practice and Indifference are the surest means to Yoga.

Seeing that the Yoga above described, the Yoga of right knowledge, is very difficult of attainment, Arjuna wished to know the surest means of attaining it, and said:

Arjuna said:

योऽयं योगस्त्वया प्रोक्तः साम्येन मधुसूदन ।
एतस्याहं न पश्यामि चंचलत्वात् स्थितिं स्थिराम् ॥ ३३ ॥

33. This Yoga in equanimity, taught by Thee, O Destroyer of Madhu,—I see not its steady continuance, because of the restlessness (of the mind.)

This is a well-known fact:

चञ्चलं हि मनः कृष्ण प्रमाथि बलवद् दृढम् ।
तस्याऽहं निग्रहं मन्ये वायोरिव सुदुष्करम् ॥ ३४ ॥

34. The mind verily, is, O K*r*ish*n*a, restless, turbulent, strong and obstinate. Thereof the restraint I deem quite as difficult as that of the wind.

'K*r*ish*n*a' is derived from 'k*r*ish' to scrape. K*r*ish*n*a is so called because He scrapes or draws away all sins and other causes of evil from his devotees.—Not only is the mind restless, but also turbulent: it agitates the body and the senses and makes them subject to foreign influences. It is not possible to restrain it by any means, as it is quite irrepressible. It is as impossible to cut it as to cut the *tantunaga*, the *Varuna-pasa*, a kind of shark. To restrain the mind of such a nature is even more difficult than to restrain the wind.

The Lord says :—So it is, as you say :

The Blessed Lord said :

असंशयं महाबाहो मनो दुर्निग्रहं चलम् ।
अभ्यासेन तु कौन्तेय वैराग्येण च गृह्यते ॥ ३५ ॥

35. Doubtless, O mighty-armed, the mind is hard to restrain and restless; but by practice, O son of Kunti, and by indifference it may be restrained.

'Practice' consists in constantly repeating the same idea or thought regarding some one object of thought. 'Indifference' means freedom from desire for any pleasures seen or unseen, attained through a constant perception of evil in them. It is by practice and indifference that *vikshepa*, the passage of thought in the direction of external objects, can be restrained.—It is thus that the mind is restrained.

But as regards him who is not self-controlled :

असंयतात्मना योगो दुष्प्राप इति मे मतिः ।
वश्यात्मना तु यतता शक्योऽवाप्तुमुपायतः ॥ ३६ ॥

36. Yoga, methinks is hard to attain for a man of uncontrolled self; but by him who (often) strives, self-controlled, it can be acquired by (proper) means.

Uncontrolled self: the anta*h*-kara*n*a not controlled by means of constant practice and by indifference to worldly gain. *Self-controlled*: who has subdued the mind.

Failures in Yoga and the after-career.

On engaging in the practice of Yoga, all works which are the means of attaining success in this world and in the other world have been renounced, while the right knowledge, which is the result of perfection in Yoga and which is the means to moksha, has not yet been attained; and the Yogin's mind strays away from the path of Yoga at the time of death. Arjuna thought that such a man would meet destruction and therefore asked :

Arjuna said :

अयतिः श्रद्धयोपेतो योगाच्चलितमानसः ।
अप्राप्य योगसंसिद्धिं कां गतिं कृष्ण गच्छति ॥ ३७ ॥

37. He who strives not, but who is possessed of faith, whose mind wanders away from Yoga,—having failed to attain perfection in Yoga, what end, O K*r*ish*na*, does he meet?

He has faith in the efficacy of Yoga but does not strive in the path of Yoga; and during the last moments of life his mind wanders away from Yoga, with memory lost. Having failed to attain the fruition of Yoga—namely, right knowledge—what end does such a man meet?

कच्चिन्नोभयविभ्रष्टश्छिन्नाभ्रमिव नश्यति ।
अप्रतिष्ठो महाबाहो विमूढो ब्रह्मणः पथि ॥ ३८ ॥

38. Having failed in both, does he not perish like a riven cloud, supportless, O mighty-armed, and perplexed in the path to Brahman?

Both : the path of Karma and the path of Yoga. *The path to Brahman* : the path by which Brahman can be reached.

एतं मे संशयं कृष्ण छेत्तुमर्हस्यशेषतः ।
त्वदन्यः संशयस्यास्य छेत्ता नह्युपपद्यते ॥ ३९ ॥

39. This doubt of mine, O K*r*ish*n*a, do Thou dispel completely; for none other than Thyself can possibly destroy this doubt.

None other : be he a *R*ishi or Deva. Thou alone canst destroy this doubt.

The Blessed Lord said:

पार्थ नैवेह नामुत्र विनाशस्तस्य विद्यते ।
न हि कल्याणकृत्कश्चिद्दुर्गतिं तात गच्छति ॥ ४० ॥

40. O Partha, neither in this world nor in the next is there destruction for him; none, verily, who does good, My son, ever comes to grief.

He who has failed in Yoga will not be subject to a lower birth than the present one either here or hereafter. *My son :* [Sk. 'tata' is translated into 'son']. 'Tata' in Sanskrit means 'father' because the father propagates (Sk. root 'tan') himself in the form of his son. Since thus the father himself is the son, the son also is called *tata.* Even a disciple, though not a son, is addressed as son because he is like a son.

What, then will happen to him?

प्राप्य पुण्यकृतां लोकानुषित्वा शाश्वतीः समाः ।
शुचीनां श्रीमतां गेहे योगभ्रष्टोऽभिजायते ॥ ४१ ॥

41. Having attained to the worlds of the righteous and having dwelt there for eternal years, he who failed in Yoga is reborn in a house of the pure and wealthy.

This is said, as the context shows, of a samnyasin engaged in the path of (Dhyana) Yoga. *The righteous*: those who worship by the *asva-medha* or horse-sacrifice, &c. Having completely enjoyed the pleasure (he is entitled to) in such a world, he is reborn in a house of the pure and wealthy. *The pure*: acting according to the prescribed rules.

अथवा योगिनामेव कुले भवति धीमताम् ।
एतद्धि दुर्लभतरं लोके जन्म यदीदृशम् ॥ ४२ ॥

42. Else, he is born in family of wise Yogins only. This, verily, a birth like this, is very hard to obtain in this world.

Or else he is born in quite a different family, that of poor wise Yogins. A birth in a family of this sort, in a family of poor Yogins, is more difficult to obtain than the one mentioned above.

And for the following reason:

तत्र तं बुद्धिसंयोगं लभते पौर्वदेहिकम् ।
यतते च ततो भूयः संसिद्धौ कुरुनन्दन ॥ ४३ ॥

43. There he gains touch with the knowledge that was acquired in the former body and strives more than before for perfection, O son of the Kurus.

More than before: with greater vigour than that with which he strove in the former birth.

पूर्वाभ्यासेन तेनैव ह्रियते ह्यवशोऽपि सः ।
जिज्ञासुरपि योगस्य शब्दब्रह्मातिवर्तते ॥ ४४ ॥

44. By that very former practice is he borne on, though unwilling. Even he who merely wishes to know of Yoga rises superior to the Word-Brahman.

The man who failed in Yoga is borne on towards perfection by the force of the practice of the former birth. If he had done no unrighteous deed (a-dharma) which could overpower the tendency caused by the practic of Yoga, then, certainly, the tendency of Yoga prevails. If a-dharma be stronger, then, even the tendency born of Yoga is certainly overpowered by a-dharma. But on the exhaustion of a-dharma the tendency caused by Yoga begins to produce its effects: that is to say, it is not liable to destruction though it may have long been in abeyance. Thus he—*i.e.* as the context shows, a sa*m*nyasin who has failed in Yoga—who works in the path of Yoga, only wishing to know its nature, even he will free himself from the Word-Brahman (Sabda-Brahman), from the effects of the observance of Vedic Karma: what need is there to say that he who knows Yoga and practises it in steady devotion will be free from its effects?

The best of Yogins.

And why is the life of a Yogin preferable?

प्रयत्नाद्यतमानस्तु योगी संशुद्धकिल्बिषः ।
अनेकजन्मसंसिद्धस्ततो याति परां गतिम् ॥ ४५ ॥

45. Verily, a Yogin who strives with assiduity, purified from sins and perfected in the course of many births, then reaches the Supreme Goal.

In the course of many births he acquires facility in Yoga little by little, and by the aggregate facility thus acquired in many births he is perfected. Then he obtains right knowledge and reaches the Supreme Goal.

तपस्विभ्योऽधिको योगी ज्ञानिभ्योऽपि मतोऽधिकः ।
कर्मिभ्यश्चाधिको योगी तस्माद्योगी भवार्जुन ॥ ४६ ॥

46. A Yogin is deemed superior to men of austerity, and superior to even men of knowledge; he is also superior to men of action; therefore be thou a Yogin, O Arjuna.

Knowledge: of the teachings of the sastra. *Action*: such as Agnihotra. worship of the sacred fire.

योगिनामपि सर्वेषां मद्गतेनान्तरात्मना ।
श्रद्धावान्भजते यो मां स मे युक्तमो मतः ॥ ४७ ॥

47. Of all Yogins, whoso, full of faith, worships Me with his inner self abiding in Me, he is deemed by Me as most devout.

Yogins: those who meditate upon Rudra, Aditya, etc. *The inner self abiding in Me*: The antah-karana kept steadfast in Me, Vasudeva.

इति श्रीमद्भगवद्गीतासूपनिषत्सु ब्रह्मविद्यायां योगशास्त्रे
श्रीकृष्णार्जुनसंवादे आत्मसंयमयोगो नाम
षष्ठोऽध्यायः ।

SEVENTH DISCOURSE.

VIJNANA-YOGA.

Realisation of the Lord by meditation.

Having given in vi. 47 an occasion for further interrogation, and wishing to teach, without being asked, that "so and so is My Real Being, and such and such is the one whose inner self abides in Me," the Lord said:

The Blessed Lord said:

मय्यासक्तमनाः पार्थ योगं युञ्जन्मदाश्रयः ।
असंशयं समग्रं मां यथा ज्ञास्यसि तच्छृणु ॥ १ ॥

1. With the mind intent on Me, O Partha, practising Yoga, and finding refuge in Me, how in full without doubt thou shalt know Me, that do thou hear.

The Yogin's mind is intent on Me, the Supreme Lord, possessed of such attributes as will be mentioned below. He pratises Yoga or steadfastness of mind and finds refuge in Me alone, the Supreme Lord. He who seeks a human end resorts to some action such as Agnihotra, or to an austerity, or to a gift or the iike, as a means of attaining that end. They Yogin, on the other hand, resorts to Me alone, abandoning all other means, with his thought intent on Me alone. Now, listen to what I am going to say as to how you also, thus acting, will, without doubt, know Me in full, possessed of infinite greatness, strength, power, grace and other attributes; you will know Me undoubtingly, that "The Lord is so and so only."

ज्ञानं तेऽहं सविज्ञानमिदं वक्ष्याम्यशेषतः ।
यज्ज्ञात्वा नेह भूयोऽन्यज्ज्ञातव्यमवशिष्यते ॥ २ ॥

2. I shall fully teach thee this knowledge combined with experience, which being known, nothing more besides here remains to be known.

And this knowledge concerning Me, as born out by My own experience, I shall relate to thee in full. In the latter portion of the verse the Lord extols the knowledge which is going to be taught, with a view to prepare the hearer to follow it.—*Nothing more*; no other means to a human end. He who knows Me in truth becomes omniscient. Thus the knowledge is productive of great results and is therefore very hard to obtain.

How?—Listen:

मनुष्याणां सहस्रेषु कश्चिद्यतति सिद्धये ।
यततामपि सिद्धानां कश्चिन्मां वेत्ति तत्त्वतः ॥ ३ ॥

3. Among thousands of men, one perchance strives for perfection; even among those who strive and are perfect, only one perchance knows me in truth.

Perfect: they are indeed perfect who strive for moksha.

Evolution of the Universe out of Divine Prakriti.

Having prepared the hearer for the teaching by inducing in him a taste for it, the Lord proceeds thus:

भूमिरापोऽनलो वायुः खं मनो बुद्धिरेव च ।
अहङ्कार इतीयं मे भिन्ना प्रकृतिरष्टधा ॥ ४ ॥

+ Earth, water, fire, air, ether, thought (Manas) and reason (Buddhi), egoism (Aha*m*kara) —thus is My Prak*r*iti divided eightfold.

Earth stands for the subtile rudimental element or Tanmatra, the Prithivi-tanmatra or the subtile rudimental element of earth; and so water, fire, air and ether stand for the Tanmatras of water, etc. Thought (Manas) stands for its cause *Ahamkara* or egoism: reason (Buddhi) for the *Mahat* principle, which is the cause of Aha*m*kara; and Aha*m*kara for the Avyakta, the Uumanifested, conjoined with Avidya or nescience. Just as food which is mixed with poison is itself called poison, so the Avyakta, the First Cause, conjoined with the vasana, or latent unconscious impression, of Aha*m*kara, is itself called here Aha*m*kara inasmuch as Egoism is the impelling cause of all. As a matter of fact, we find, from our ordinary experience, that egoism is the cause of the activity of every being. Thus divided eightfold is My Prak*r*iti, the Maya belonging to the I*s*vara.

अपरेयमितस्त्वन्यां प्रकृतिं विद्धि मे पराम् ।
जीवभूतां महाबाहो ययेदं धार्यते जगत् ॥ ५ ॥

5. This is the inferior (Prak*r*iti); but as distinct from this know thou My superior Prak*r*iti, the very life, O mighty-armed, by which this universe is upheld.

This Parkriti is inferior, impure, productive of evil, itself constituting the bondage of sa*m*sara; but the superior Prak*r*iti is pure; it is My very Self, the Kshetraj*n*a, that by which life is sustained, that which enters within the whole universe and sustains it.

एतद्योनीनि भूतानि सर्वाणीत्युपधारय ।
अहं कृत्स्नस्य जगतः प्रभवः प्रलयस्तथा ॥ ६ ॥

6. Know that all beings have their birth in these. So, I am the source and dissolution of the whole universe.

These, My inferior Nature (Prakriti) and My superior Nature (Prakriti) matter (Kshetra) and spirit (Kshetrajna), are the womb of all creatures. Because my Prakriti is the womb of all beings, I am the origin and the end of the whole universe. That is to say, through this twofold Prakriti, I, the omniscient Isvara, am the cause of the universe.

Wherefore,

मत्तः परतरं नान्यत्किञ्चिदस्ति धनञ्जय ।
मयि सर्वमिदं प्रोतं सूत्रे मणिगणा इव ॥ ७ ॥

7. There is naught else higher than I, O Dhananjaya: in Me all this is woven as clusters of gems on a string.

There is no other cause besides Me, the Supreme Lord I alone am the cause of the universe. Wherefore all beings as well as the whole of this universe are woven in Me, as a cloth in the warp, clusters of beads on a string.

The Divine Principle penetrating the Universe.

What are Thy attributes showing that the whole of thi is woven in Thee?—Listen:

रसोऽहमप्सु कौन्तेय प्रभाऽस्मि शशिसूर्ययोः ।
प्रणवः सर्ववेदेषु शब्दः खे पौरुषं नृषु ॥ ८ ॥

8. I am the sapidity in water, O son of Kunti. I am the light in the moon and the sun.

I am the syllable *Om* in all the Vedas, sound in ether, humanity in men.

The essence of water is sapidity. In Me who am that sapidity waters are woven.—So in all cases.—Just as I am the sapidity in waters, so am I the light in the moon and the sun; I am the Pranava, the syllable *Om* in all the Vedas: in Me who am that Pranava all the Vedas are woven. So also, I am humanity in men, *i. e.*, I am that in a person which makes that person regarded a human being. In Me as humanity all persons are woven. Sound is the essence of akasa: in Me as sound akasa is woven.

पुण्यो गन्धः पृथिव्यां च तेजश्चास्मि विभावसौ ।

जीवनं सर्वभूतेषु तपश्चास्मि तपस्विषु ॥ ९ ॥

9. And I am the agreeable odour in the earth and the brilliance in the fire, the vitality in all beings, and I am the austerity in ascetics.

In Me as odour the earth is woven.—Odour by itself is agreeable; the disagreeableness of odour in the earth and of the like being due to the combination of one element with some other element or elements under the influence of the avidya and a-dharma of individual souls in the world. The agreeableness thus spoken of with reference to the earth applies also to the agreeableness of the sapidity in waters, and so on.—I am the vitality in all beings, that by which all beings live. In Me as austerity the ascetics are woven.

बीजं मां सर्वभूतानां विद्धि पार्थ सनातनम् ।

बुद्धिर्बुद्धिमतामस्मि तेजस्तेजस्विनामहम् ॥ १० ॥

10. Know Me, O Partha, as the eternal seed of all beings; I am the intelligence of the intelligent, the bravery of the brave.

Seed: the cause of growth. *Intelligence*: the discriminative power af the anta*h*-kara*n*a.

बलं बलवतामस्मि कामरागविवर्जितम् ।
धर्माविरुद्धो भूतेषु कामोऽस्मि भरतर्षभ ॥ ११ ॥

11. And of the energetic am I the energy devoid of passion and attachment; and in (all) beings I am the desire unopposed to dharma, O lord of the Bharatas.

Passion (Kama): thirst for objects not present to the senses. *Attachment* (raga): love for those presented to the senses. I am that energy which is necessary for the bare sustenance of the body, certainly not that which causes thirst and attachment (for sense-objects) in the case of worldly mortals. So I am the desire not opposed to the teaching of the scriptures: I am, for instance, the desire for that much of eating and drinking, *etc.*, which is necessary for the bare sustenance of the body.

Moreover,

ये चैव सात्विका भावा राजसास्तामसाश्च ये ।
मत्त एवेति तान्विद्धि न त्वहं तेषु ते मयि ॥ १२ ॥

12. And whatever beings are of Sattva or of Rajas or of Tamas, know them to proceed from Me: still, I am not in them, they are in me.

Know that all beings, whether formed of Sattva or of Rajas, or of Tamas, and which come into existence as the result of the respective karma of living beings, proceed from Me. Though they thus proceed from Me, I am not subject to them like mortal beings (sa*m*sarins). On the other hand, they are subject to Me: they are dependent on Me.

Maya : How to overcome it.

The Lord now expresses His regret that the world does not understand Him, who is thus the Supreme Lord ; who by nature is eternal, pure, intelligent and free ; who is the Self of all beings, devoid of all attributes; by knowing whom they might burn up the evil which is the seed of sa*m*sara.—What is this ignorance on the part of the world due to ?—Listen :

त्रिभिर्गुणमयैर्भावैरेभिः सर्वमिदं जगत् ।
मोहितं नाभिजानाति मामेभ्यः परमव्ययम् ॥ १३ ॥

13. Deluded by these three (sorts of) things composed of gu*n*as, all this world knows not Me as distinct from them and immutable.

All living beings are deluded by such things as love, hatred and attachment, which are all modifications of gu*n*as.

Immutable : devoid of such changes as birth and the like, which pertain to all things in the world.

How then can one surmount this Divine Illusion (Maya) of Vish*n*u made up of the three gu*n*as ?—Listen :

दैवी ह्येषा गुणमयी मम माया दुरत्यया ।
मामेव ये प्रपद्यन्ते मायामेतां तरन्ति ते ॥ १४ ॥

14. Verily this Divine Illusion of Mine, made up of gu*n*as, is hard to surmount. Whoever seek Me alone, they cross over this Illusion.

This Illusion (Maya), formed of gu*n*as, is inherent in Me, Vish*n*u, the Lord. Such being the case, whoever abandon all formal religion (Dharma) and completely devote themselves to Me, their own Self, the Lord of Illusion, they cross over the Illusion which deludes all living beings: they are liberated from the bondage of sa*m*sara.

If those who resort to Thee cross over the Illusion, why do not all resort to Thee only ?—

न मां दुष्कृतिनो मूढाः प्रपद्यन्ते नराधमाः ।
माययाऽपहृतज्ञाना आसुरं भावमाश्रिताः ॥ १५ ॥

15. Not Me do the evil-doers seek, the deluded, the vilest of men, deprived of wisdom by Illusion, following the ways of the Demons.

Me, the Supreme Lord, Narayana. *The ways of the Demons* are cruelty, untruth, and the like.

Four classes of devotees.

But as to the best of men, men of good deeds :

चतुर्विधा भजन्ते मां जनाः सुकृतिनोऽर्जुन ।
आर्तो जिज्ञासुरर्थार्थी ज्ञानी च भरतर्षभ ॥ १६ ॥

16. Four kinds of virtuous men worship Me, O Arjuna—the distressed, the seeker of knowledge, the seeker of wealth, and the wise man, O lord of the Bharatas.

The distressed : he who is in distress, overpowered by a robber, a tiger, illness or the like. *Knowledge* : of the real nature of the Lord. *The wise man* : he who knows the real nature of Vishnu.

तेषां ज्ञानी नित्ययुक्त एकभक्तिर्विशिष्यते ।
प्रियो हि ज्ञानिनोऽत्यर्थमहं स च मम प्रियः ॥ १७ ॥

17. Of them the wise man, ever steadfast and devoted to the One, excels ; for, excessively dear am I to the wise, and he is dear to Me.

Of the four, the wise man, as knowing the truth, is ever steadfast, and devoted to the One, finding no other object of worship. Thus, he who is devoted to the One is superior to all others. Since I am his very Self, I am excessively dear to the wise man.—It is well-known to all in this world that the Self is dear to every one. Therefore Vasudeva, as the Self of the wise man, is dear to him.—And the wise man is My very Self and is therefore very dear to Me.

Then the three others, the distressed and the rest, are not dear to Vasudeva ?—Not so.—What then ?

उदाराः सर्व एवैते ज्ञानी त्वात्मैव मे मतम् ।
आस्थितः स हि युक्तात्मा मामेवानुत्तमां गतिम् ॥ १८ ॥

18. Noble indeed are all these ; but the wise man, I deem, is the very Self ; for, steadfast in mind, he resorts to Me alone as the unsurpassed goal.

These are all noble indeed ; *i.e.*, those three also are dear to Me. There is no devotee of Mine but is dear to Me, Vasudeva. There is, however, this difference : the wise man is excessively dear to Me.—Why so ?—It is my conviction that the wise man is the very Self, not different from Me. The wise man strives to reach Me, firm in the faith that he himself is the Lord Vasudeva and is no other than He. He seeks Me only, the Supreme Brahman, as the highest goal to be reached.

The wise man is again extolled :

बहूनां जन्मनामन्ते ज्ञानवान्मां प्रपद्यते ।
वासुदेवः सर्वमिति स महात्मा सुदुर्लभः ॥ १९ ॥

19. At the end of many births, the man of wisdom comes to me, (realising) that Vasudeva is

the all: he is the noble-souled (Mahatman), very hard to find.

At the end of many births occupied in spiritual regeneration as preparatory to the attainment of wisdom, the man of mature wisdom resorts to Me, Vasudeva, the innermost Self (Pratyagatman).—How?—Realising that Vasudeva is the All. He who thus comes to Me, Narayana, the Self of All, is a Mahatman, a man of high soul; there is no other either equal to him or superior to him. Therefore such a man is very hard to find; it has indeed been said that "among thousands of men, one perchance strives for perfection" (vii. 3.)

The ignorant worship inferior Gods.

Now will be shown the cause of (the people) not seeing that the Self or Vasudeva alone is the All:

कामैस्तैस्तैर्हृतज्ञानाः प्रपद्यन्तेऽन्यदेवताः ।
तं तं नियममास्थाय प्रकृत्या नियताः स्वया ॥ २० ॥

20. Those whose wisdom has been led away by this or that desire resort to other Gods, engaged in this or that rite, constrained by their own nature.

Their desires for progeny, cattle, svarga and the like deprive them of their power of discrimination, and they resort to other Gods (Devatas), other than Vasudeva, the Self. They engage in rites peculiar to the worship of these Gods; they being constrained to do so by their own nature (prakriti), by that peculiar tendency (samskara) which they acquired in the previous births.

Of these lustful men,

यो यो यां यां तनुं भक्तः श्रद्धयार्चितुमिच्छति ।
तस्य तस्याचलां श्रद्धां तामेव विदधाम्यहम् ॥ २१ ॥

21. Whatever devotee seeks to worship with faith what form soever, that same faith of his I make unflinching.

Whatever form of God (Devata) a man of desire worships in devotion and faith, I confirm his faith in the worship of that same form.

By whatever faith a man is naturally actuated and seeks to worship a particular form of Devata,

स तया श्रद्धया युक्तस्तस्याराधनमीहते ।
लभते च ततः कामान्मयैव विहितान्हितान् ॥ २२ ॥

22. Possessed of that faith he engages in the worship of that (form); thence he obtains his desires, these being indeed ordained by me.

Possessed of that faith ordained by Me, he engages in the worship of that form of God. From the God worshipped in this form he obtains the objects of his desire as ordained by Me, the Supreme Lord, the Omniscient, as I alone know the precise relation between actions and their fruits. Because their desires are all ordained by the Lord Himself, therefore the devotees are sure to obtain them.

Another interpretation is also given which would make the last part of the verse mean that desires are beneficial. But desires can be beneficial only in a secondary sense; for, strictly speaking, they are beneficial to nobody.

Because they are unwise and full of desires and resort to the means of attaining finite results, therefore,

अन्तवत्तु फलं तेषां तद्भवत्यल्पमेधसाम् ।
देवान्देवयजो यान्ति मद्भक्ता यान्ति मामपि ॥ २३ ॥

23. That result indeed is finite, (which accrues) to those men of small intellect. Worshippers of Gods (Devatas) go to Gods (Devatas); My devotees come unto Me.

Though there is the same amount of exertion (in the two kinds of worship), people do not resort to Me so that they may attain infinite results. Alas! it is very miserable.—Thus does the Lord express His regret.

Why do they not come unto Me?—it may be asked. The answer follows:

अव्यक्तं व्यक्तिमापन्नं मन्यन्ते मामबुद्धयः ।
परं भावमजानन्तो ममाव्ययमनुत्तमम् ॥ २४ ॥

24. The foolish regard Me as the unmanifested coming in manifestation, knowing not My higher, immutable, unsurpassed nature.

Not knowing my higher nature as the Supreme Self, the ignorant think that I have just now come into manifestation, having been unmanifested hitherto, though I am the ever luminous Lord.

To what is their ignorance due?—Listen:

नाहं प्रकाशः सर्वस्य योगमायासमावृतः ।
मूढोऽयं नाभिजानाति लोको मामजमव्ययम् ॥ २५ ॥

25. I am not manifest to all, veiled (as I am) by Yoga-Maya. This deluded world knows not Me, unborn and imperishable.

I am not manifest to all people; that is to say, I am manifest only to a few who are my devotees. I am veiled by Yoga-Maya.—Yoga-Maya is the Maya which is none other than the Yoga or union of the three *gunas*.—Or, Yoga is the firm will of the Lord or Isvara. The Illusion or veil thereby spread is called Yoga-Maya.—Wherefore people are deluded and know Me not as unborn and imperishable.

The Yoga-Maya by which I am veiled and on account of which people do not recognise Me, is Mine, *i. e.*, subject to My control, and as such, it cannot obstruct My knowledge—the knowledge of the Isvara, of the possessor (for wielder) of the Maya, just as the glamour (maya) caused by a juggler (mayavin) does not obstruct his own knowledge. Wherefore,

वेदाहं समतीतानि वर्तमानानि चार्जुन ।
भविष्याणि च भूतानि मां तु वेद न कश्चन ॥ २६ ॥

26. I know, O Arjuna, the past and the present and the future beings, but Me nobody knows.

Nobody knows Me, except that one man who worships Me and seeks refuge with Me. Just for want of knowledge of My real nature, nobody worships Me.

The root of ignorance

It may be asked, "What is that obstacle to their knowledge of My real nature, whereby deluded, all creatures that are born know Me not?—Listen:

इच्छाद्वेषसमुत्थेन द्वन्द्वमोहेन भारत ।
सर्वभूतानि सम्मोहं सर्गे यान्ति परन्तप ॥ २७ ॥

27. From the delusion of pairs caused by desire and aversion, O Bharata, all beings are subject to illusion at birth, O harasser of thy foes.

The very desire and aversion which are opposed to each other like heat and cold, and which, arising in connection with pleasure and pain and their causes, occur to every being in its turn, are known as pairs (dvandva). Now, when desire, and aversion arise on the occurrence of pleasure and pain or of the causes thereof they cause delusion in all beings and create obstruction to the rise of a knowledge of the Supreme Reality, the Self, by subjugation to themselves the intelligence of those beings. To one whose mnid is subject to the passions of desire and aversion, there cannot indeed arise a knowledge of things as they are, even of the external world; and it needs no saying that to a man whose intellect is overpowered by passion there cannot arise a knowledge of the Innermost Self, inasmuch as there are many obstacles in its way. All creatures into existence are born subject to this delusion. Wherefore every being has its intelligence obscured by the delusion of pairs; and thus deluded it knows not that I am the Self, and therefore worships Me not as the Self.

Divine worship leads to realisation.

Who then are free from the delusion of pairs and know Thee and worship Thee as their Self according to the Teaching (Sastra)?—In answer to this, the Lord says:

येषां त्वन्तगतं पापं जनानां पुण्यकर्मणाम् ।
ते द्वन्द्वमोहनिर्मुक्ता भजन्ते मां दृढव्रताः ॥ २८ ॥

28. Those mortals of pure deeds whose sin has come to an end, who are freed from the delusion of pairs, they worship Me with a firm resolve

Those persons of good deeds—good deeds causing purity of mind—whose sin has almost come to an end are freed from the delusion of pairs spoken of above and worship Me, their Highest Self. They resolutely abandon all else, firm in the conviction that "This is the Supreme Reality and no other."

With what object do they worship?—Listen:

जरामरणमोक्षाय मामाश्रित्य यतन्ति ये ।
ते ब्रह्म तद्विदुः कृत्स्नमध्यात्मं कर्म चाखिलम् ॥ २९ ॥

29. Whoever resorting to Me strive for liberation from decay and death, they realise in full that Brahman, the individual Self and all action.

Those who, with the mind steadfast in Me, the Supreme Lord, strive for liberation from decay and death, realise in full the Reality underlying the Innermost individual Self (adhyatma), and they know all about action (karma).

साधिभूताधिदैवं मां साधियज्ञं च ये विदुः ।
प्रयाणकालेऽपि च मां ते विदुर्युक्तचेतसः ॥ ३० ॥

30. Those who realise Me in the Adhibhuta (physical region), in the Adhidaiva (the divine region) and in the Adhiyajna (region of Sacrifice), realise Me even at the time of departure, steadfast in mind.

इति श्रीमद्भगवद्गीतासूपनिषत्सु ब्रह्मविद्यायां योगशास्त्रे
श्रीकृष्णार्जुनसंवादे विज्ञानयोगो नाम
सप्तमोऽध्यायः ।

EIGHTH DISCOURSE.

ABHYASA-YOGA.

The seven things to be realised by meditation.

In vii 29, 30 such things have been mentioned by the Lord as have given occasion to Arjuna to put a question. Accordingly Arjuna proceeds to ask thus:

अर्जुन उवाच :—

किं तद्ब्रह्म किमध्यात्मं किं कर्म पुरुषोत्तम ।
अधिभूतं च किं प्रोक्तमधिदैवं किमुच्यते ॥ १ ॥

अधियज्ञः कथं कोऽत्र देहेऽस्मिन्मधुसूदन ।
प्रयाणकाले च कथं ज्ञेयोऽसि नियतात्मभिः ॥ २ ॥

Arjuna said:

1—2. What is that Brahman? What about the Individual Self (Adhyatma)? What is action (Karma), O Purushottama? And what is declared to be the physical region (Adhibhuta)? And what is the divine region (Adhidaiva) said to be? And how and who is Adhiyaj*n*a (the Entity concerned with Sacrifice) here in this body, O Madhusudana, and how at the time of death art Thou to be known by the self-controlled?

The Lord proceeds to answer these questions in their order:

श्रीभगवानुवाच :—

अक्षरं ब्रह्म परमं स्वभावोऽध्यात्ममुच्यते ।
भूतभावोद्भवकरो विसर्गः कर्मसंज्ञितः ॥ ३ ॥

The Blessed Lord said:

3. Brahman is the Imperishable (Akshara), the Supreme. The Ego is said to be the Individual Self (Adhyatma, He who dwells in the body). The offering which causes the origin of physical beings is called action (Karma).

Brahman is the Akshara, the Imperishable, the Supreme Self (Paramatman); the sruti says "O Gargi, it is at the command of this Akshara, the imperishable Paramatman, that heaven and earth remain, held in their places." (Bri. Upanishad, 3-8-9). 'Akshara' does not here mean the syllable "Om"; for, the latter is subsequently specified thus:—"Uttering the syllable 'Om,' the Brahman" (viii. 13). And the epithet 'supreme' applies better to Brahman, the Imperishable, who transcends all, (than to the syllable 'Om').

The same Supreme Brahman existing as the Ego, as the Innermost Self, as the Pratyagatman, in every individual body, is said to be *Adhyatma*: that which first shows itself as the Innermost Self in the body and turns out in the end to be identical with the Supreme Reality, the Brahman, is known by the term 'Adhyatma'.

The sacrificial act which consists in offering cooked rice, cakes and the like to the Gods (Devatas) and which causes the origin of all creatures, is known by the term '*Karma*'; for, it forms the seed as it were of all beings; it is in virtue of this act that all beings, animate and inanimate, come into existence, after passing through rain and other regions of life

अधिभूतं क्षरो भावः पुरुषश्चाधिदैवतम् ।
अधियज्ञोऽहमेवात्र देहे देहभृतां वर ॥ ४ ॥

4. The physical region (Adhibhuta) is the perishable existence, and Purusha or the Soul is the divine region (Adhidaivata). The Adhiyaj*n*a (Entity concerned with Sacrifice) is Myself, here in the body, O best of the embodied.

The Adhibhuta is that which gathers itself round the whole animated creation and is composed of the whole perishable existence, *i.e.*, of every thing that has birth.

Purusha is, literally, that by which every thing is filled, (pri=to fill) or that which lies in the body (pur), *i.e.*, the Hira*n*yagarbha, the Universal Soul abiding in the Sun (Aditya), the Sustainer and the Stimulator of the sense-organs of all living beings.

The *Adhiyajna* is He who identifies himself with all acts of sacrifice, the Deity named Vish*n*u; the *s*ruti says: "Yaj*n*a (Sacrifice) is verily Vish*n*u" (Taittiriya-Sa*m*hita, 1-7-4). He is verily Myself. I am the Deity concerned with all acts of sacrifice in the body.—As an act of sacrifice (yaj*n*a) has to be performed by the body, it is said to be inherent in it, and as such it may be said to rest *in the body*.

अन्तकाले च मामेव स्मरन्मुक्त्वा कलेवरम् ।
यः प्रयाति स मद्भावं याति नास्त्यत्र संशयः ॥ ५ ॥

5. And whoso, at the time of death, thinking of Me alone, leaves the body and goes forth, he reaches My being; there is no doubt in this.

Me: Vish*n*u, the Supreme Lord. *My being*: My real being as Vish*n*u. *In this*: as to whether he reaches or not.

Constant meditation of the Divine is necessary.

Not to Me alone does this rule apply; but also:

यं यं वापि स्मरन्भावं त्यजत्यन्ते कलेबरम् ।
तं तमेवैति कौन्तेय सदा तद्भावभावितः ॥ ६ ॥

6. Of whatever Being thinking at the end a man leaves the body, Him alone, O son of Kunti, reaches he by whom the thought of that Being has been constantly dwelt upon.

Being: a particular Devata or Diety, *At the end*: at the time of life's departure. *Him alone*: Only the Being thought of, and no other. *Dwelt upon*: constantly meditated.

Because thus the final thought determines the character of the body to be attained next,

तस्मात्सर्वेषु कालेषु मामनुस्मर युध्य च ।
मय्यर्पितमनोबुद्धिर्मामेवैष्यस्यसंशयम् ॥ ७ ॥

7. Therefore at all times do thou mediate on Me and fight: with mind and reason fixed on Me thou shalt doubtless come to Me alone.

Meditate: According to the Teaching (sastra). *Fight*: do thou perform thy proper duty of fighting. *Me*: Vasudeva. *Come to Me*: as meditated upon by thee.

The Divine Being to be meditated upon.

Moreover,

अभ्यासयोगयुक्तेन चेतसा नान्यगामिना ।
परमं पुरुषं दिव्यं याति पार्थानुचिन्तयन् ॥ ८ ॥

8. Meditating with the mind engaged in the Yoga of constant practice, not passing over to any

thing else, one goes to the Supreme Purusha, the Resplendent, O son of Pritha.

Practice consists in the repetition of one and the same idea, uninterrupted by any other thought, with reference to Me, the sole object of your thought. Such a practice is itself said to be *Yoga*. With the mind thus solely engaged in Yoga, not passing over to any other object, the Yogin who meditates according to the teaching of the scripture and of the teacher—of the *sastra* and acharya—reaches the Purusha, the Transcendental Being in the Solar Orb.

What sort of Purusha does he reach ?—Listen :

कविं पुराणमनुशासितारमणोरणीयांसमनुस्मरेद्यः ।
सर्वस्य धातारमचिन्त्यरूपमादित्यवर्णं तमसः परस्तात् ॥

प्रयाणकाले मनसाऽचलेन भक्त्या युक्तो योगबलेन चैव ।
भ्रुवोर्मध्ये प्राणमावेश्य सम्यक् स तं परं पुरुषमुपैति दिव्यम् ॥

9—10. Whoso meditates on the Sage, the Ancient, the Ruler, smaller than an atom, the Dispenser of all, of unthinkable nature, glorious like the Sun, beyond the darkness, (whoso meditates on such a Being) at the time of death, with a steady mind endued with devotion and strength of Yoga, well fixing the life-breath betwixt the eye-brows, he reaches that Supreme Purusha Resplendent.

Sage: the Omniscient. *The Ruler*: of the whole world. *Dispenser*: who allots to all living beings actions and their results in all their variety. It is very difficult for anybody to conceive of His form though it exists. Like the Sun, He is *glorious* with the splendour of His Eternal Intelligence (Nitya-Chaitanya) which is *beyond the darkness* of delusion or nescience (Aj*n*ana). The *strength of Yoga* consists in the steadiness of mind which results from the after-effects of the (constant practice of) samadhi. At first the mind (chitta) is subdued in the lotus of the heart (hridayapu*n*darika); then, by means of the up-going na*d*i (sushumna), after gradually obtaining control over the several stages of matter (earth and the other four rudimental elements), the life-breath of the heart is drawn up and carefully fixed betwixt the eye-brows. By this means the wise man, the Yogin, reaches the Supreme Purusha, who is resplendent.

Meditation of the Divine in the Pranava.

The Lord now assigns a name to that Brahman whom the Yogin wishes to reach by means to be pointed out again in the sequel, and who will be now described in such terms as being declared by the knowers of the Veda,' &c.:

यदक्षरं वेदविदो वदन्ति विशन्ति यद्यतयो वीतरागाः ।
यदिच्छन्तो ब्रह्मचर्यं चरन्ति तत्ते पदं सङ्ग्रहेण प्रवक्ष्ये ॥

11. That Imperishable Goal which the knowers of the Veda declare, which the self-controlled and the passion-free enter, which desiring they lead the godly life,—That Goal will I declare to thee with brevity.

Those who understand the teaching of the Veda declare the Imperishable as devoid of any attribute whatsoever. The sruti says: "This verily is that (which you wished to know of), the Imperishable, O Gargi, as the brahma*n*as (the knowers of the Brahman) declare, not gross, not subtle," &c. (B*r*i-Upa. 3-8-8.) The sa*m*nyasins, ever controlling themselves, free from passion, enter the Imperishable, on attaining to right knowledge. And desiring to know the Imperishable they enter on godly life (Brahmacharya) with a Guru. Of That Goal which is called Akshara, the Imperishable, I shall tell thee with brevity.

Having started with the words "He who verily among men meditates on the syllable 'Om' till death, what region will he thereby attain to?" he (Pippalada) said to him (Satyakama): "O Satyakama, this, the Brahman, the Higher and the Lower, is the syllable 'Om'." (Prasna-Upanishad, 5—1, 2); and it was subsequently said: "He who will meditate on the Supreme Purusha by the three-lettered syllable 'Om'—he is borne up by the Sama-hymns to the Brahma-loka, to the region of Brahman." (*Ibid*, 5-5).

Again, having started with the words "Elsewhere than in dharma and elsewhere than in a-dharma, tell me that thou seest;" (Katha-Upanished, 2-13), the *sruti* says, "that goal which all the Vedas speak of (*i.e.*, are intended for), which all the austerities speak of, desiring which they lead the life of Brahmacharya (celibacy), that goal I tell thee in brevity: It is this, the syllable 'Om.'" (*Ibid* 2-14).

In such passages as these, the syllable 'Om', regarded either as an expression of the Para-Brahman or as a symbol of Him like an idol, is intended for persons of dull and middling intellects as a means of knowing the Para-Brahman; and the contemplation of the 'Om' is said to produce moksha at a subsequent period. Now, the same contemplation (conjoined with firmness in Yoga) of the syllable 'Om,' productive of mukti at a subsequent period—the 'Om' forming, as shown above, a means of knowing the Para-Brahman described here (viii. 9, 11)—has to be taught here as well as some minor matters connected with the main subject. With this view, the Lord proceeds with the sequel;

सर्वद्वाराणि संयम्य मनो हृदि निरुध्य च ।
मूर्ध्न्याधायात्मनः प्राणमास्थितो योगधारणाम् ॥ १२ ॥
ओमित्येकाक्षरं ब्रह्म व्याहरन्मामनुस्मरन् ।
यः प्रयाति त्यजन्देहं स याति परमां गतिम् ॥ १३ ॥

12-13. Having closed all the gates, having confined mind in the heart, having fixed his life-breath in the head, engaged in firm Yoga, uttering Brahman, the one-syllabled 'Om,' thinking of Me, whoso departs, leaving the body, he reaches the Supreme Goal.

Having closed all the avenues of knowledge and having concentrated thought in the lotus of the heart, and with thought thus controlled, he ascends by the Na*d*i which passes upwards from the heart, and then fixing life-breath in the head, he utters the syllable 'Om', the appellation of the Brahman, and meditates on Me.—'*Leaving the body*, shows the mode of departure. The departure takes place by the Self leaving the body, not by the Self being destroyed.

No re-birth on attaining to the Divine Being.

Moreover,

अनन्यचेताः सततं यो मां स्मरति नित्यशः ।
तस्याहं सुलभः पार्थ नित्ययुक्तस्य योगिनः ॥ १४ ॥

14. Whoso constantly thinks of me and long, to him I am easily accessible, O son of P*r*itha, to the ever-devout Yogin.

He who thinks of Me, the Supreme Lord, long—*i.e.*, not for six months or a year, but uninterruptedly throughout life,—to that Yogin who is ever steadfast in thought, I am easily accessible. This being so, therefore, without thinking of another, one should ever dwell steadfast in Me.

It may be asked, "What if Thou art easily accessible?"— Listen: I shall tell you of what use is My being thus easily accessible:

मामुपेत्य पुनर्जन्म दुःखालयमशाश्वतम् ।
नाप्नुवन्ति महात्मानः संसिद्धिं परमां गताः ॥ १५ ॥

15. Having attained to Me, they do not again attain birth, which is the seat of pain and is not eternal, they having reached highest perfection.

Having attained to Me, the Isvara, having reached My being, they are not again subject to birth. Birth here is the seat of all pain arising from the body, etc., and is of an ever-changing nature. Having reached the highest stage called moksha, they do not attain birth again. Those, on the other hand, who do not attain to Me, return again (to the earth).

Do those again return who have reached any other being than Thyself?—Listen:

आब्रह्मभुवनाल्लोकाः पुनरावर्तिनोऽर्जुन ।
मामुपेत्य तु कौन्तेय पुनर्जन्म न विद्यते ॥ १६ ॥

16. (All) worlds including the world of Brahma are subject to returning again, O Arjuna; but, on reaching Me, O son of Kunti, there is no rebirth.

The Day and the Night of Brahma.

Why are all the worlds including the world of Brahma subject to returning?—Because they are limited by time.— How?

सहस्रयुगपर्यन्तमहर्यद्ब्रह्मणो विदुः ।
रात्रिं युगसहस्रान्तां तेऽहोरात्रविदो जनाः ॥ १७ ॥

17. They—those people who know day and night—know that the day of Brahma is a thousand yugas long and the night is a thousand yugas long.

Brahma is the Prajapati, the Viraj. Those persons who know how to compute Time know that Brahma's day is a thousand yugas long, and that His night is of the same duration as His day. Because the worlds are thus limited by time, therefore they return again.

What takes place during the Prajapati's day and what takes place during His night will now be described:

अव्यक्ताद्व्यक्तयः सर्वाः प्रभवन्त्यहरागमे ।
रात्र्यागमे प्रलीयन्ते तत्रैवाव्यक्तसंज्ञके ॥ १८ ॥

18. From the Unmanifested all the manifestations proceed at the coming on of day; at the coming on of night they dissolve there only, in what is called the Unmanifested.

The Unmanifested (Avyakta) is the sleeping condition of the Prajapati who is asleep. Out of That, all manifestations (vyaktis), all creatures unmoving and moving (sthavara and jangama), are manifested at the coming on of day, *i.e.*, when Brahma awakes. So, at the coming on of night, *i.e.*, when Brahma goes to sleep, all the manifestations dissolve there only, in what is called Avyakta, the one already spoken of.

With a view to avoid the fallacious implication that a man reaps the fruits of what he has not done, or that he does not reap the fruits of what he has done, with a view to show that the teaching of the scripture concerning bondage (bandha) and liberation (moksha) has a purpose to serve, and with a view further to teach detachment from samsara by showing that, as the effect of karma caused by avidya (nescience) and other sources of evil, all creatures involuntarily come into being again and again and dissolve, the Lord says:

भूतग्रामः स एवायं भूत्वा भूत्वा प्रलीयते ।
राञ्यागमेऽवशः पार्थ प्रभवत्यहरागमे ॥ १९ ॥

19. This same multitude of beings having come into being again and again, is dissolved at the coming on of night, not of their will, O son of Pritha, and comes forth at the coming on of day.

This multitude of beings comprising those that move as well as those that do not—the same multitude that existed in the preceding kalpa or age, and no other—involuntarily comes into being at the coming on of day, and is dissolved again at the coming on of night—at the close of the day, Again at the coming on of day, it involuntarily comes into existance.

The Highest Goal—how reached.

In viii. 13, *etc.*, has been shown the way, by which to reach the Imperishable (Akshara) described above. Now, with a view to indicate the nature of the Akshara, with a view thus to specify that so and so is the thing to be reached by this path of Yoga, the Lord proceeds as follows:

परस्तस्मात्तु भावोऽन्योऽव्यक्तो ऽव्यक्तात्सनातनः ।
यः स सर्वेषु भूतेषु नश्यत्सु न विनश्यति ॥ २० ॥

20. But that other eternal Unmanifested Being, distinct from this Unmanifested (Avyakta), —He does not perish when all creatures perish.

'But' indicates that the Akshara who is to be described now is distinct from the Avyakta. *Being*: the Supreme, the Para-Brahman, called the Akshara. Though distinct from the Avyakta, one may suppose that He is of the same nature as the Avyakta. To remove this impression. the Lord qualifies Him by 'other', meaning thereby that He is of a different nature from the Avyakta. He is unmanifested, imperceptible to the senses. He is distinnct from the Avyakta mentioned above, which is Avidya itself, the seed of the whole multitude of created beings; that is to say, He is of quite a different nature from the Avyakta. He does not perish when all beings from Brahma downwards perish.

अव्यक्तोऽक्षर इत्युक्तस्तमाहुः परमां गतिम् ।
यं प्राप्य न निवर्तन्ते तद्धाम परमं मम ॥ २१ ॥

21. What is called the Unmanifested and the Imperishable, That, they say, is the highest goal; which having reached none return. That is My highest place.

That: that Avyakta which is called Akshara, the Imperishable, the Unmanifested Being. Having reached that state, none has returned to samsara, the mundane life. That is My (*i.e.*, Vishnu's) Supreme Abode.

The means of attaining to that state will now be pointed out:

पुरुषः स परः पार्थ भक्त्या लभ्यस्त्वनन्यया ।
यस्यान्तःस्थानि भूतानि येन सर्वमिदं ततम् ॥ २२ ॥

22. Now, that Highest Purusha, O son of Pritha, within Whom all beings dwell, by Whom all this is pervaded, is attainable by exclusive devotion

Purusha is so called because He rests in the body, or because He is full. Than Him none is higher. He is attained by exclusive devotion, by jnana or knowledge of the Self. All the created beings abide within the Purusha; for, every effect rests within its cause; and by that Purusha the whole world is pervaded.

The Paths of Light and Darkness.

Now it is necessary to speak of the Uttaramarga, 'the Northern Path', the Path of Light by which the Yogins just spoken of attain to Brahman,—those Yogins who meditate here on Brahman as inhering in the Pranava, in the syllable 'Om', and who attain to moksha later on.* And this will be taught in the section beginning with viii. 23. The path of return is also described, only with a view to extol the other path.

यत्र काले त्वनावृत्तिमावृत्तिं चैव योगिनः ।
प्रयाता यान्ति तं कालं वक्ष्यामि भरतर्षभ ॥ २३ ॥

23. Now, in what time departing, Yogins go to return not, as also to return, that time will I tell thee, O chief of the Bharatas.

'In what time' should be construed with 'departing,' 'To return' means to be reborn—'Yogins' stand for those who are engaged in meditation (*i.e.*, those who are properly called Yogins) as well as for Karmins, *i.e.*, those who are engaged in karma or action. The latter are spoken of as Yogins only by courtesy; and they are so spoken of in iii. 3. I shall tell you, when dying the Yogins are not born again, and when dying they will be born again.

He speaks of that time:

अग्निर्ज्योतिरहः शुक्लः षण्मासा उत्तरायणम् ।
तत्र प्रयाता गच्छन्ति ब्रह्म ब्रह्मविदो जनाः ॥ २४ ॥

---

* At the end of the kalpa.

24. Fire, light, day-time, the bright fortnight, the six months of the northern solstice,—then departing, men who know Brahman reach Brahman.

'Fire' is the deity presiding over time ; so also is 'light' a deity presiding over time.—Or, it may be that 'fire' and 'light' are the deities so called ; the reference, however, to the path as a whole by the expressions 'in what time' and 'that time' being due to the predominance of the deities presiding over 'time.'—The 'day-time' is the deity presiding over the day-time, the 'bright fortnight' is the deity presiding over the bright fortnight. *The six months of the northern solstice* : here also, it is the deity that forms the path, The principle on which this interpretation of the passage is based has been established elsewere.* Those who die, having been engaged in the contemplation of Brahman, reach Brahman by this path. The expression "in course of time" should be understood after 'reach'; for, those who are firm in devotion to right knowledge and attain to immediate liberation have no place to go to or to return from.

धूमो रात्रिस्तथा कृष्णः षण्मासा दक्षिणायनम् ।
तत्र चान्द्रमसं ज्योतिर्योगी प्राप्य निवर्तते ॥ २५ ॥

25. Smoke, night-time, and the dark fortnight, the six months of the southern solstice,—attaining by these to the lunar light, the Yogin returns.

'Smoke,' 'night time,' the 'dark fortnight,' and the 'six months of the southern solstice,' are all deities presiding over smoke and periods of time spoken of. By this path, the Yogin—the Karmin who performs sacrifices (to Gods) and other works—attains to the lunar light, and on the exhaustion thereof, returns again to earth.

* Sariraka Mimamsa, iv 3-4.

शुक्लकृष्णे गती ह्येते जगतः शाश्वते मते ।
एकया यात्यनावृत्तिमन्ययाऽऽवर्तते पुनः ॥ २६ ॥

26. These bright and dark Paths of the world are verily deemed eternal ; by the one a man goes to return not, by the other he returns again.

The one is bright* because it illumines knowledge : the other is dark* because it is wanting in that light. The two paths are open to those only in the world who are engaged in action or devoted to knowledge ; they are not open to the whole world. They are eternal, because sa*m*sara is eternal. *By the one* : by the bright one.

नैते सृती पार्थ जानन्योगी मुह्यति कश्चन ।
तस्मात्सर्वेषु कालेषु योगयुक्तो भवार्जुन ॥ २७ ॥

27. Knowing these paths, O son of P*r*itha, no Yogin is deluded : wherefore at all times be steadfast in Yoga, O Arjuna.

The Yogin who knows that one of the two foregoing paths leads to sa*m*sara and that the other leads to moksha is no longer deluded †

Excellency of Yoga

Now, hear of the greatness of that Yoga :

---

* The two paths are respectively called Devayana and Pit*r*iyana, the path to the Devas and the path to the Pit*r*is. The one is said to be bright because it illumines knowledge and is reached by knowledge, and its course is marked throughout by bright objects ; the other is said to be dark because it does not illumine knowledge, is reached by avidya or nescience, and is marked throughout by smoke and other dark things.

† As the Yogin dwells on the Path of Light in his Meditation, he will not regard the other path as the one he should resort to.—(A.)

वेदेषु यज्ञेषु तपस्सु चैव दानेषु यत्पुण्यफलं प्रदिष्टम् ।
अत्येति तत्सर्वमिदं विदित्वा योगी परं स्थानमुपैति चाद्यम् ॥

28. Whatever fruit of merit is declared to accrue from the Vedas, sacrifices, austerities and gifts,—beyond all this goes the Yogin on knowing this; and he attains to the Supreme Primeval Abode.

Whatever fruit of merit is declared by the scriptures to be attainable when the Vedas are properly studied, when the sacrifices are performed in all their parts, when austerities are well practised,—beyond all this multitude of fruits rises the Yogin who rightly understands and follows the teaching imparted (by the Lord) in His answers to the seven questions, and he then attains to the highest abode of Isvara—which existed even in the beginning;—He attains Brahman, the Cause.

इति श्रीमद्भगवद्गीतासूपनिषत्सु ब्रह्मविद्यायां योगशास्त्रे
श्रीकृष्णार्जुनसंवादे विज्ञानयोगो नाम
अष्टमोऽध्यायः ।

NINTH DISCOURSE

SOVEREIGN WISDOM AND SECRET.

Brahma-Jnana is the best Religion.

In the eighth discourse has been declared the Yoga of concentration (dhara*n*a) through na*d*i* as well as its process†, and its result has heen shown to be none other than the attainment of Brahman—at a subsequent period, through 'fire and light' and the like,—whence there is no return. Now, with a view to give no room to the supposition that the attainment of moksha is possible only by this means and by no other, the Lord proceeds as follows:

श्रीभगवानुवाच —

इदं तु ते गुह्यतमं प्रवक्ष्याम्यनसूयवे ।
ज्ञानं विज्ञानसहितं यज्ज्ञात्वा मोक्ष्यसेऽशुभात् ॥ १ ॥

The Blessed Lord said:

1. To thee who dost not cavil, I shall now declare this, the greatest secret, knowledge combined with experience,‡ which having known thou shalt be liberated from evil.

This: the Brahma-J*n*ana, the knowledge of Brahman, which is going to be declared, and which has been declared in the preceding discourses. *Now*: this word points to the superiority of knowledge (over Dhyana): this right knowledge

---

* The *Sushumna* 'the bright,' Concentration (dhara*n*a) is only an *anga* or auxiliary of Yoga.

† Such as closing all the gates (viii. 12, 13.)

‡ *Sakshatkara*, intuitive or direct perception.

alone forms the direct means of attaining moksha, as declared in the sruti and the smriti :

" Vasudeva is the All "—(*Bhagavadgita*, vii. 19.)
" All this is the Self."—(*Chhand. Upa.*, 7-25-2.)
" One only without a second "—(*Ibid*, 6-2-1.)

And nothing else is a direct means to moksha, as the passages of the sruti like the following declare :

" Now the other princes who understand otherwise than thus, * they shall attain to perishable regions."—(*Ibid*, 7-25-2.)

On attaining this knowledge you will be liberated from the bondage of samsara.

And it is

राजविद्या राजगुह्यं पवित्रमिदमुत्तमम् ।
प्रत्यक्षावगमं धर्म्यं सुसुखं कर्तुमव्ययम् ॥ २ ॥

2. The Sovereign Science, the Sovereign Secret, the Supreme Purifier is this ; immediately comprehensible, unopposed to Dharma, very easy to perform, imperishable.

Of sciences it is the king, because it is of great splendour. Indeed, the science of Brahman is the most brilliant † of all sciences. So also, it is the king of secrets. Of all the purifiers, this knowledge of Brahman is the best purifier. That it is a purifier needs no saying, since it reduces karma to ashes in an instant, root and all,—all the karma, dharma and a-dharma, which has been accumulated during many thousand births. Moreover, it ‡ can be comprehended by *pratyaksha*,

* That all this is one Brahman.

† Greater reverence is shown to those who know Brahman than to other men of learning.

‡ The Brahma-jnana or its effect. Unlike the other things which are, equally with the Brahma-jnana, revealed by the sruti and the smriti, it is not known through revelation solely, but it is known by *pratyaksha*, by immediate or intuitive perception as well.

by immediate perception, like the feeling of pleasure and so on. What is possessed of many a desirable quality may be opposed to Dharma; but not so is the knowledge of Atman opposed to Dharma; on the other hand it is not separable from Dharma, *i.e.*, not opposed to it. Even then it may be supposed that it is very difficult to attain; but it is not so, says the Lord. It is very easy to acquire, like the power of discriminating gems.* Now, of the other acts, those which involve little trouble and are easily accomplished are seen to be productive of small results, and difficult acts are found to be productive of great results. Accordingly it may be imagined that this Brahma-j*n*ana which is so easily attained perishes when its effect is exhausted: to prevent this supposition, the Lord says that it is imperishable. It does not perish like an act when the effect is exhausted. Wherefore knowledge of Atman (Self) is worth acquiring.

But,

अश्रद्दधानाः पुरुषा धर्मस्यास्य परन्तप ।
अप्राप्य मां निवर्तन्ते मृत्युसंसारवर्त्मनि ॥ ३ ॥

3. Persons having no faith in this Dharma, O harasser of thy foes, without reaching Me, remain verily in the path of the mortal world.

Those who have no faith in this Dharma (law, religion) *viz.*, knowledge of the Self, those who do not believe in its existence or in its effects, the sinful who follow the doctrine of the Demons (Asuras), regarding the physical body itself as the Self,—these greedy and sinful persons do not attain to Me the Supreme Lord—The attaining of Me is certainly out of question; wherefore, the implication is that they do not

* Verily this knowledge is easily acquired when taught by an adept; so is Brahma-j*n*ana.

attain even to devotion (Bhakti) which is one of the paths leading to Me; they are sure to remain in the path of the mortal world, in that path only which leads to hell (naraka) and to the lower kingdoms of animals, etc.

All beings rest in the Lord.

Having prepared Arjuna (to listen to the Doctrine) by extolling it, the Lord says:

मया ततमिदं सर्वं जगदव्यक्तमूर्तिना ।
मत्स्थानि सर्वभूतानि न चाहं तेष्ववस्थितः ॥ ४ ॥

4. By Me all this world is pervaded, My form unmanifested. All beings dwell in Me; and I do not dwell in them.

All this world is pervaded by My Highest Being, My form being invisible to the senses. In Me, of unmanifested form, dwell all beings from Brahma down to the plant. No being devoid of the Self can ever become an object of experience. Wherefore they dwell in Me, *i.e.*, they are self-existent (or have an individual existence) through Me, the Self, (*i e*, they are what they are in virtue of Me, the Self, underlying them all.) Since I am the Self of all those beings, it would seem to the deluded as though I dwell in them. Wherefore I say: I do not dwell in those beings, because of the absence of contact with others, unlike corporeal things. I am certainly the innermost essence even of the akasa. That which is unconnected with any object cannot indeed be contained anywhere as though in a receptacle.

Wherefore, as I am unconnected with any object,

न च मत्स्थानि भूतानि पश्य मे योगमैश्वरम् ।
भूतभृन्न च भूतस्थो ममात्मा भूतभावनः ॥ ५ ॥

5. Nor do those beings dwell in Me; behold My Divine Yoga! Sustaining all the beings, but not dwelling in them, is My Self, the cause of beings.

And yet these beings, from Brahma downwards, dwell not in Me; behold My Divine working, the Divine Mystery, the real nature of the Self. Accordingly, the sruti speaks of the unattached condition of the Self, seeing that He is unconnected with any object: "Devoid of attachment, He is never attached"—(*Brih. Up.* 3-9-26.)

Bohold, there is yet another mystery. Though unattached, My Self supports all beings, but does not dwell in them, as shown above with reasons.*—Then how to justify the Lord's words, 'My Self'?—We answer: Separating (from the Real Self) the aggregate of the physical and other material environments, and regarding that aggregate as the 'I', the Lord speaks of the Self as 'My Self,'—so far following only the popular conception; not certainly that He believes, as the masses ignorantly believe, that the Atman, the Self, is distinct from Himself.† And further it is Myself that cause all beings to come into being, that cause all beings to grow.

By way of illustrating by an example what has been taught in the two preceding verses, the Lord says:

यथाऽऽकाशस्थितो नित्यं वायुः सर्वत्रगो महान् ।
तथा सर्वाणि भूतानि मत्स्थानीत्युपधारय ॥ ६ ॥

6. As the mighty wind moving everywhere rests ever in the akasa, so, know thou, do all beings, rest in Me.

* Because the Self is unconnected with any object.—(A.)

† Because such a relation between the Self and the bodily aggregate is illusory. (A)

It is observed in our ordinary experience that the wind, moving everywhere and mighty in expanse, ever rests in the akasa; so also in Me, who am all-pervading like the akasa, do all beings rest without any contact at all.

The Lord is the source and the end of all beings.

Thus, as the wind rests in the akasa, so do all beings rest in Me as long as the world lasts.

सर्वभूतानि कौन्तेय प्रकृतिं यान्ति मामिकाम् ।
कल्पक्षये पुनस्तानि कल्पादौ विसृजाम्यहम् ॥ ७ ॥

7. All beings, O son of Kunti, go into My Prak*r*iti at the end of a kalpa. I send them forth again at the beginning of (the next) kalpa.

Prakriti: the inferior one composed of the three gu*n*as. The end of a kalpa is the time of dissolution (pralaya,) and the beginning of a kalpa is the time of production (utpatti).

Thus:

प्रकृतिं स्वामवष्टभ्य विसृजामि पुनः पुनः ।
भूतग्राममिमं कृत्स्नमवशं प्रकृतेर्वशात् ॥ ८ ॥

8. Resorting to My Prak*r*iti, I again and again send forth the whole multitude of beings, powerless under the control of the Prak*r*iti.

With the help of the Prak*r*iti, *i.e.*, of Avidya, which is subject to Me, I cause all these beings we now see to emanate again and again from the Prak*r*iti; all of them being rendered powerless by avidya and other sources of evil under the influence of the Prak*r*iti, *i.e.*, of Svabhava or Nature.

The Lord is not bound by His acts.

Then as creating this multitude of beings of unequal conditions, Thou, the Supreme Lord, shalt be subject to dharma and a-dharma arising from that act ?—In reply, the Lord says:

न च मां तानि कर्माणि निबध्नन्ति धनञ्जय ।
उदासीनवदासीनमसक्तं तेषु कर्मसु ॥ ९ ॥

9. Nor do these acts, O Dhana*n*jaya, bind Me, remaining like one unconcerned, unattached to those acts.

The acts involved in the unequal creation of the multitudinous beings do not bind Me, the I*s*wara.—Now, the Lord gives the reason why He is not affected by the acts:— I, knowing the immutability of the Self, remain like one who is unconcerned, without attachment for the fruit of the act, *i.e.*, without the egotistic feeling 'I do.' Wherefore, in the case of others also, the absence of the egotistic feeling of agency and the absence of attachment for results is the cause of freedom (from dharma and a-dharma) Otherwise, the deluded man is bound by his own acts like the silk-worm in the cocoon.

Now, the statements 'I send forth this multitude of beings' (ix. 7) and 'remaining like one unconcerned' involve a self-contradiction. In explanation thereof, the Lord says:

मयाऽध्यक्षेण प्रकृतिः सूयते सचराचरम् ।
हेतुनाऽनेन कौन्तेय जगद्विपरिवर्तते ॥ १० ॥

10. By Me presiding, Prak*r*iti produces the moving and the unmoving; because of this, O son of Kunti, the world revolves.

By Me presiding: as a mere viewer on every side and the immutable witness. My Maya *i.e.*, the Avidya, composed of the three gu*n*as, produces the universe comprising the moving and the unmoving objects. So says the chant:

'The one, the luminous, hidden in all beings, all-pervading, the Inner Self of all, the superintendent of all acts, the abode of all beings, the witness, the perceiver, alone, and free from qualities.'—(*Svetasvatara-Up.* 6-11).

Because I am the witness, because I preside, this universe comprising the moving and the unmoving objects, the manifested and the unmanifested, moves on through all stages. Indeed, all activity in the world—such as 'I shall enjoy this, 'I see this,' 'I hear this,' 'I feel pleasure,' 'I feel pain,' 'To gain this I shall do it,' 'I shall learn this '—arises by way of forming an object of consciousness; it has its being in consciousness and has its end in consciousness. Such chants as 'Who in the Supreme Heaven (of the heart) is the witness of this;' (Tai. Br. 2-8-9) point only to this view. Accordingly * as there is no conscious entity other than the One Divine Being, there cannot be a separate enjoyer; and it is therefore irrelevant to ask or to answer the question †, 'Of what purpose is this creation by the One, the Divine, the pure all-witnessing Spirit or Consciousness, having really no concern with any enjoyment whatever?' So says the *sruti*: ‡

'Who could perceive (It) directly, and who could declare whence born and why this variegated creation? '—(Tai. Br. 2-8-9.)

* The *Is*vara being the creator of the Universe is the mere witness thereof.

† It is not right to ask or answer the question 'what is the purpose of Creation?' We cannot say that it is meant for the enjoyment of the Supreme; for, the Supreme really enjoys nothing. It is pure consciousness, a mere witness. And there is no other enjoyer, for there is no other conscious entity. The *Is*vara is one only; and what is not conscious cannot enjoy. Nor is Creation intended to secure moksha, because it is opposed to moksha. Thus, neither the question nor an answer to it is possible; and there is no occasion for it, as Creation is due to the Maya of the Supreme.—(A.)

‡ This *sruti* means that it is very hard to know the Supreme Self.

The Lord has also said:

'Wisdom is enveloped by unwisdom; thereby mortals are deluded.'*—(v. 15).

The life of the impious.

Though I am thus eternal, pure, wise, and free, by nature, Omniscient, the Self of all,

अवजानन्ति मां मूढा मानुषीं तनुमाश्रितम् ।
परं भावमजानन्तो मम भूतमहेश्वरम् ॥ ११ ॥

11. Fools disregard Me clad in human form, not knowing My higher being as the Great Lord of beings.

Fools, unable to discriminate, despise Me living among them with a human body, these fools not understanding My higher being,—not knowing that I am the Supreme Self, that I am, like akasa, that I am the Great Lord, the very Self, of all beings. Then by continually despising Me, these poor creatures are ruined.

How (is their condition pitiable)?

मोघाशा मोघकर्माणो मोघज्ञाना विचेतसः ।
राक्षसीमासुरीं चैव प्रकृतिं मोहिनीं श्रिताः ॥ १२ ॥

12. Of vain hopes, of vain actions, of vain knowledge, devoid of discrimination, partaking only of the delusive nature of Rakshasas and Asuras.

They cherish vain hopes. The agnihotra and other actions performed by them are fruitless, because they insult the Lord, because they neglect their own Self. Even their

* This passage shows that creation is due to ajnana or nescience.

knowledge is fruitless. They are devoid of discrimination. They partake of the nature of Rakshasas and Asuras.* They see no self beyond the body and engage in cruel deeds, their rule of conduct being 'cut, break, drink, devour, rob others' property.'

The ways of the faithful devotees.

But, the faithful who are engaged in devotion (Bhakti) to the Lord, *i.e.*, who walk in the path of moksha,

महात्मानस्तु मां पार्थ दैवीं प्रकृतिमाश्रिताः ।

भजन्त्यनन्यमनसो ज्ञात्वा भूतादिमव्ययम् ॥ १३ ॥

13. The Mahatmans, O son of Pritha, partaking of the nature of the Devas, worship Me with mind turned to no other,† knowing (Me) as the imperishable source of all beings.

Mahatmans; the high-souled.‡ The nature of the Devas (Gods) consists in their control over the body, mind and the senses, in kindness, in faith and the like. *Beings*: bhutas, all living creatures as well as all elements of matter.

How (do they worship)?

सततं कीर्तयन्तो मां यतन्तश्च दृढव्रताः ।

नमस्यन्तश्च मां भक्त्या नित्ययुक्ता उपासते ॥ १४ ॥

14. Always talking of Me, strenuous, firm in vows, and reverent, they worship Me with love, always devout.

---

* After death such people will be born as Rakshasas or Asuras The nature of Rakshasas consists in committing deeds of cruelty, and that of Asuras in robbing another's property, in the absence of charity and of sacrifice.

† With the mind resting on Me, the Innermost Self, who am no other than their own Self.

‡ Those whose mind (sattva) has been purified by yajna or sacrifice, etc.

They always talk of Me, their Lord, the very Brahman. They ever strive by way of subjugating the senses, by way of cultivating the virtues of self-control, kindness, innocence, and the like. Firm in their vows, they worship Me in love, Me who am their very Self lying in the heart.

In what different ways do they worship?—Listen:

ज्ञानयज्ञेन चाप्यन्ये यजन्तो मामुपासते ।
एकत्वेन पृथक्त्वेन बहुधा विश्वतोमुखम् ॥ १५ ॥

15. Worshipping by the wisdom-sacrifice, others adore Me, the All-faced, in various ways, as One, as different.

Knowledge of the Lord is itself a sacrifice. Worshipping by this sacrifice of wisdom, others* adore Me, having abandoned all other forms of worship. And that knowledge varies thus;—Some worship with the knowledge of the real truth that 'One, verily, is the Para-Brahman' Some worship with the knowledge that the Lord Vishnu Himself exists as different beings, as the sun, the moon and the like. Others worship Him, who exists in all forms—as the All-faced, thinking that the one Lord exists in all the different forms, with his face on all sides.

All worship goes to the Lord.

If they worship in so many different ways, how do they (as Thou sayest) worship Thee only?—The Lord says:

अहं क्रतुरहं यज्ञः स्वधाऽहमहमौषधम् ।
मन्त्रोऽहमहमेवाज्यमहमग्निरहं हुतम् ॥ १६ ॥

16. I am kratu, I am yajna, I am svadha, I am aushadha, I am mantra, Myself the butter, I am fire, I the act of offering.

* The Brahma-nishthas, those who are devoted to Brahman.

Kratu is a class of Vedic sacrifices. *Yajna* is the worship enjoined in the smriti. *Svadha* is the food offered to ancestors (Pitris). The *aushadha* means plants in general, including rice and barley, eaten by all living beings. Or, *svadha* is food in general, and *aushadha* is the medical (food) serving to alleviate sickness.—I am the *mantra*, the chant with which the oblation is offerd to the Pitris and the Devatas. I am the fire into which the offering is poured.

And,

पिताऽहमस्य जगतो माता धाता पितामहः ।
वेद्यं पवित्रमोङ्कार ऋक् साम यजुरेव च ॥ १७ ॥

17. I am the father of this world, the mother, the dispenser, and grandsire; I am the knowable, the purifier, the syllable 'Om,' and also the *R*ik, the Saman, and the Yajus also.

The dispenser: of the fruits of action.

And,

गतिर्भर्ता प्रभुः साक्षी निवासः शरणं सुहृत् ।
प्रभवः प्रलयः स्थानं निधानं बीजमव्ययम् ॥ १८ ॥

18. I am the Goal, the Sustainer, the Lord, the Witness, the Abode, the Shelter and the Friend, the Origin, Dissolution and Stay, the Treasure-house, the Seed imperishable.

I am the goal, the fruit of action......I am the witness of what is done and what is not done by all living beings. I am the abode wherein all living beings dwell. I am the shelter for the distressed; I relieve from distress those who come to Me. I am the Friend: I do good without expecting any return. I am the source of the world. I am that in which it is dissolved, and that in which it stays. I am the treasure-house, that which living beings shall enjoy in a future period. I am the imperishable seed, that which causes the growth of all things that germinate, and which endures as long as the world (sa*m*sara) endures. Nothing indeed springs up without a seed; and since growth is constant, it is understood that continuity of the seed never fails.

And,

तपाम्यहमहं वर्षं निगृह्णाम्युत्सृजामि च ।
अमृतं चैव मृत्युश्च सदसच्चाहमर्जुन ॥ १९ ॥

19. I give heat, I hold back and send forth rain, I am the immortality as well as death, existence and non-existence, O Arjuna.

As the sun I give heat by some powerful rays; by certain rays I send forth rain; and having sent it forth I take it back by certain rays during eight months, and again send it forth in the rainy season. I am the immortality of the gods (devas) and the death of the mortals. I am existence, (the *manifested*, the effect), which *manifests itself* in *relation* (to the cause); and I am the reverse, the non-existence (the *unmanifested*, the cause).—Indeed the Lord can never be altogether non-existent; nor (can it be said) that the effect is existence and the cause is non-existence.*

* The manifested world of effects is spoken of as 'existence' and the unmanifested cause as 'non-existence.' We cannot indeed hold that the Divine essence is non-existence, for then we are driven to nihilism; nor can the cause be spoken of as non-existence, as it is impossible to conceive existence arising out of non-existence; for the sruti itself says, 'How can existence come out of non-existence?"—*Chhand. Up.* 6

The fruits of interested acts of Vedic ritual.

These men of wisdom who are devoted to Me, adoring Me by the sacrifices mentioned above, leading lives of retirement in various forms described above and regarding Me as One or as different,—they reach Myself according to their knowledge. But as regards those who are ignorant and who long for objects of desire,

त्रैविद्या मां सोमपाः पूतपापा
यज्ञैरिष्ट्वा स्वर्गतिं प्रार्थयन्ते ।
ते पुण्यमासाद्य सुरेन्द्रलोक
मश्नन्ति दिव्यान्दिवि देवभोगान् । ॥ २० ॥

20. Men of the three Vedas, the soma-drinkers, purified from sin, worshipping Me by sacrifices, pray for the goal of heaven ; they reach the holy world of the Lord of the Gods and enjoy in heaven the heavenly pleasures of the Gods.

Men who know the three Vedas, the *R*ik, the Saman and the Yajus ; who drink Soma and are thereby purified from sins ; who worship Me as the Vasus and other gods by sacrifices such as the Agnish*t*oma ; who seek for Svarga as the reward of their sacrifices ;—they go to the world of Indra who had performed a hundred sacrifices, and there enjoy supernatural (a-prak*r*ita) pleasures.

ते तं भुक्त्वा स्वर्गलोकं विशालम्
क्षीणे पुण्ये मर्त्यलोकं विशन्ति ।
एवं त्रयीधर्ममनुप्रपन्ना
गतागतं कामकामा लभन्ते ॥ २१ ॥

21. They, having enjoyed that spacious world of Svarga, their merit (pu*n*ya) exhausted, enter the world of the mortals; thus following the Dharma of the Triad, desiring (objects of) desires, they attain to the state of going and returning.

The Dharma of the Triad: mere Vedic ritual (karma), that which is enjoined by the three Vedas. They have to go and return, and never attain independence anywhere.

The Supreme watching over His devotees' interests.

Now, as regards those men of right knowledge who are free from desires,

अनन्याश्चिन्तयन्तो मां ये जनाः पर्युपासते ।
तेषां नित्याभियुक्तानां योगक्षेमं वहाम्यहम् ॥ २२ ॥

22. Those men who, meditating on Me as non-separate, worship Me all around,—to them who are ever devout, I secure gain and safety.

Those men of renunciation (sa*m*nyasins) who worship Me all around,* ever meditating on Me, regarding themselves as non-separate,—*i.e.*, looking upon the Supreme God, Naraya*n*a, as their own Self,—to these who see the Reality, who are ever devout, † I secure gain. I secure to them what is not already possessed; and I secure to them *safety*, *i.e.*, preservation of what is already possessed. As said in vii. 17 18, they form My very Self and are dear to Me.

(*Objection*):—To other devotees also the Lord secures gain and safety.

---

* *i.e.*, Who see Me all around, as infinite.—(A.)

† Constantly and earnestly engaged in dhyana.

(*Answer*):—True, He undoubtedly secures (to them gain and safety); but there is this difference: while other devotees work themselves also for their own gain and safety, those who see nothing as separate from themselves do not work for their own gain and safety. Indeed these latter never cherish a desire for life or death; the Lord alone is their refuge. Wherefore the Lord Himself secures to them gain and safety.

Other devotees do but worship the Supreme in ignorance.

(*Objection*):—If other gods (Devatas) are Thyself only, their devotees also worship Thyself.

(*Answer*):—Just so, indeed:

येऽप्यन्यदेवताभक्ता यजन्ते श्रद्धयाऽन्विताः ।
तेऽपि मामेव कौन्तेय यजन्त्यविधिपूर्वकम् ॥ २३ ॥

23. Even those who, devoted to other Gods, worship Them with faith, worship Myself, O son of Kunti, in ignorance.

With faith: believing in the efficacy (of the worship of those Gods).

Why dost Thou say that they worship in ignorance?—For,

अहं हि सर्वयज्ञानां भोक्ता च प्रभुरेव च ।
न तु मामभिजानन्ति तत्त्वेनातश्च्यवन्ति ते ॥ २४ ॥

24. I am indeed the Enjoyer, as also the Lord, of all sacrifices; but they do not know Me in truth; whence they fail.

As the Devata* (*i.e.*, as the God to whom sacrifices are offered) I am the Enjoyer and the Lord of all sacrifices enjoined in the sruti and the smriti. I am indeed the Lord of yajna or sacrifice, as said in viii, 4. So they do not know Me as I am; whence, having worshipped in ignorance, they fail to attain the fruit of the sacrifice.†

The fruit of sacrifice certainly accrues ‡ to them also who, devoted to other gods, worship Me in ignorance.—How?—

यान्ति देवव्रता देवान् पितॄन्यान्ति पितृव्रताः ।
भूतानि यान्ति भूतेज्या यान्ति मद्याजिनोऽपि माम् ॥ २५ ॥

25. Votaries of the Gods go to the Gods; to the Pitris go the votaries of the Pitris; to the Bhûtas go the worshippers of the Bhûtas; My worshippers come to Myself.

The votaries of the Gods, those whose devotion and vows are directed to the Gods, go to the Gods. The votaries of the Pitris such as the Agnishvattas, engaged in performing sraddha and other rites in devotion to the Pitris, go to the Pitris. The Bhutas are the Vinayakas, the hosts of Matris, the four *Bhaginis* and the Like. My worshippers, *i.e.*, Vishnu's votaries, come to Myself. Notwithstanding the equality of trouble, people do not worship Me alone, because of their ignorance. Wherefore they attain very small results.

* As the Vasus and other Devatas to whom the sacrifices are offered, I am the Enjoyer of all sacrifices; and as the Antaryamin, as the Inner Regulator of the Universe, I am the Lord of all sacrifices.

† Not having dedicated their actions to Me, they return to this world from the region to which they attain as the result of their sacrifice.

‡ The worship of the Gods is not quite useless. The worshippers do attain results suited to the form of worship, but they have to return to this world after a time.

Facility in Devotion to the Supreme.

Not only do My devotees attain an endless result, *i.e.*, attain a state from which there is no return to this world, but it is also easy for them to worship Me.—How ?—

पत्रं पुष्पं फलं तोयं यो मे भक्त्या प्रयच्छति ।
तदहं भक्त्युपहृतमश्नामि प्रयतात्मनः ॥ २६ ॥

26. When one offers to Me with devotion a leaf, a flower, a fruit, water,—that I eat, offered with devotion by the pure-minded.

Because it is so, therefore,

यत्करोषि यदश्नासि यज्जुहोषि ददासि यत् ।
यत्तपस्यसि कौन्तेय तत्कुरुष्व मदर्पणम् ॥ २७ ॥

27. Whatever thou doest, whatever thou eatest, whatever thou sacrificest, whatever thou givest, in whatever austerity thou engagest, do it as an offering to Me.

Whatever thou doest of thy own accord (*i.e.*, not enjoined in the *s*astra) and whatever thou offerest in sacrifice as enjoined in the *s*ruti or the sm*r*iti, whatever thou givest—such things as gold—to the brahma*n*as and others,......do all that as an offering to Me.

Now listen as to what will accrue to you doing thus:

शुभाशुभफलैरेवं मोक्ष्यसे कर्मबन्धनैः ।
संन्यासयोगयुक्तात्मा विमुक्तो मामुपैष्यसि ॥ २८ ॥

28. Thus shalt thou be liberated from the bonds of actions which are productive of good and evil results; equipped in mind with the Yoga of renunciation, and liberated, thou shalt come to Me.

Thus: when you thus offer everything to Me. This (act of offering everything to Me) constitutes the Yoga of renunciation. It is *renunciation* inasmuch as every thing is offered to Me; and it is also *Yoga* inasmuch as it is an action (karma). Thus, with mind equipped with Yoga and renunciation, thou shalt be liberated from bonds while yet living; and when this body is dead, thou shalt come to Me.

The impartiality of the Supreme.

(Objection):—Then the Lord has love and hatred, since He bestows His grace on His devotees, not on others.

(Answer):—Not so:

समोऽहं सर्वभूतेषु न मे द्वेष्योऽस्ति न प्रियः ।
ये भजन्ति तु मां भक्त्या मयि ते तेषु चाप्यहम् ॥ २९ ॥

29. The same I am to all beings; to Me there is none hateful or dear; but whoso worship Me with devotion, they are in Me, and I am also in them.

I am like fire: just as fire does not ward off cold from those who are at a distance and wards it off from those who go near it, so I bestow My grace on My devotees, not on others. Those who worship Me, the Lord, with devotion are in Me, as a matter of course, but not owing to any attachment on My part. In them also I am, only as a matter of course, not in others. By this behaviour, I cannot (be said to) hate the latter.*

* Those who are devoted to Me, performing the duties of their caste and order, become pure in mind, in virtue of that very devotion of unthinkable grandeur; and they are in Me, *i.e.*, their minds are rendered fit for My presence. And, being in their presence as a matter of course, I ever do good to them. Just as the Sun's light, though pervading everywhere, is reflected in a clean mirror, so also is the Supreme Lord present as a matter of course in those persons only from whose minds all dirt has been removed by devotion. It has been said in ix. 13 that those are devoted to the Lord, who partake of the nature of the devas.—(A).

Even the low-born attain salvation by Devotion

Now I shall tell you how excellent a thing devotion to Me is:

अपि चेत्सुदुराचारो भजते मामनन्यभाक् ।
साधुरेव स मन्तव्यः सम्यग्व्यवसितो हि सः ॥ ३० ॥

30. If one of even very evil life worships Me, resorting to none else, he must indeed be deemed righteous, for he is rightly resolved.

He is rightly resolved: he is a man of good resolution.

By abandoning evil ways in his external life, and by the power of his internal right resolution,

क्षिप्रं भवति धर्मात्मा शश्वच्छान्तिं निगच्छति ।
कौन्तेय प्रतिजानीहि न मे भक्तः प्रणश्यति ॥ ३१ ॥

31. Soon he becomes righteous and attains eternal peace; do thou, O son of Kunti, proclaim that my devotee never perishes.

Listen, this is the real truth thou mayest proclaim that He who is devoted to Me in his inner soul never perishes.

मां हि पार्थ व्यपाश्रित्य येऽपि स्युः पापयोनयः ।
स्त्रियो वैश्यास्तथा शूद्रास्तेऽपि यान्ति परां गतिम् ॥ ३२ ॥

32. For, finding refuge in Me, they also who, O son of Prithâ, may be of a sinful birth—women, vaisyas as well as sudras,—even they attain to the Supreme Goal.

The Yoga of Devotion.

किं पुनर्ब्राह्मणाः पुण्या भक्ता राजर्षयस्तथा ।
अनित्यमसुखं लोकमिमं प्राप्य भजस्व माम् ॥ ३३ ॥

33. How much more then the holy brâhma*n*as and devoted royal saints! Having reached this transient joyless world, do thou worship Me.

Holy: of pure birth. *This world*: the world of man, human birth* which is the means of attaining spiritual aspirations (purushartha), and which is very hard to attain.

Moreover,

मन्मना भव मद्भक्तो मद्याजी मां नमस्कुरु ।

मामेवैष्यसि युक्त्वैवमात्मानं मत्परायणः ॥ ३४ ॥

34. Fix thy mind on Me, be devoted to Me, sacrifice to Me, bow down to Me. Thus steadied, with Me as thy Supreme Goal, thou shalt reach Myself, the Self.

Me: Vasudeva. *Steadied*: in thought (chitta). I am the Self of all beings, and I am the Supreme goal.

इति श्रीमद्भगवद्गीतासूपनिषत्सु ब्रह्मविद्यायां योगशास्त्रे श्रीकृष्णार्जुनसंवादे राजविद्या राजगुह्ययोगो नाम नवमोऽध्यायः ।

---

* As non-human bodies such as those of animals are not fit for a life of devotion to the Lord, those who have attained to human birth hould lead a life of devotion to the lord.

TENTH DISCOURSE.

DIVINE MANIFESTATIONS.

The Lord is the source of all manifestations.

In the seventh discourse and in the ninth, the essential nature of the Lord and His manifestations have been pointed out. Now it is necessary to point out in what forms of being the Lord should be thought of: and it is also necessary to describe the essential nature of the Lord,—though it has been described already,—as it is a hard thing to understand. With this view, the Lord says:

The Blessed Lord said:

भूय एव महाबाहो शृणु मे परमं वचः ।
यत्तेऽहं प्रीयमाणाय वक्ष्यामि हितकाम्यया ॥ १ ॥

1. Again, O mighty-armed, listen to My Supreme word, which I, from a desire for thy well-being, shall speak to thee who art delighted.

Supreme: as revealing the unsurpassed Thing. *Delighted*: you are intensely delighted with My speech, as though you are drinking the immortal nectar.

Why should He speak of it?—The Lord says:

न मे विदुः सुरगणाः प्रभवं न महर्षयः ।
अहमादिर्हि देवानां महर्षीणां च सर्वशः ॥ २ ॥

2. Neither the hosts of the Gods nor the Great *R*ishis know my origin; for I am the source of all the Gods and the Great *R*ishis.

Prabhava (interpreted as *origin*) may also mean "Great Lordly Power." *Rishis*: such as Bhrigu.

Moreover,

यो मामजमनादिं च वेत्ति लोकमहेश्वरम् ।
असम्मूढः स मर्त्येषु सर्वपापैः प्रमुच्यते ॥ ३ ॥

3. He who knows Me as unborn and beginningless, as the great Lord of the worlds, he among mortals is undeluded, he is liberated from all sins.

Because I am the source of the Gods and the Great Rishis, none else exists as the source of My existence; wherefore, I am unborn and beginningless. Because I am beginningless, therefore I am unborn. *Undeluded:* devoid of delusion. *All sins:* consciously or unconsciously incurred.

For the following reason also I am the great Lord of the worlds:

बुद्धिर्ज्ञानमसम्मोहः क्षमा सत्यं दमः शमः ।
सुखं दुःखं भवोऽभावो भयं चाभयमेव च ॥ ४ ॥
अहिंसा समता तुष्टिस्तपो दानं यशोऽयशः ।
भवन्ति भावा भूतानां मत्त एव पृथग्विधाः ॥ ५ ॥

4-5. Intelligence, wisdom, non-illusion, patience, truth, self-restraint, calmness, pleasure, pain, birth, death, fear, and security; innocence, equanimity, contentment, austerity, beneficence, fame, shame, (these) different kinds of dispositions of beings arise from Me alone.

Intelligence (buddhi) is the power which the inner sense (antah-karana) has of understanding subtle objects of thought.

He, indeed, is said to be intelligent who is possessed of this power. *Wisdom* is the knowledge of the Self and other such things. *Non-illusion* consists in acting with discrimination when anything has to be done or known at the moment. *Patience:* not being agitated in mind when assaulted or abused. *Truth*: giving utterance to one's own actual experience of things, as heard or seen, with a view to impress it on the mind of another. *Self-restraint*: quieting the external senses. *Calmness*: the tranquillity of the inner sense or anta*h*-kara*n*a.........*Innocence*: not injuring living beings. *Contentment*: being satisfied with one's present acquisitions. *Austerity*: bodily torture accompanied with the restraint of the senses. *Beneficence*: sharing (one's own things with others as far as one's own means may permit. *Fame*: due to dharma. *Shame*: due to a-dharma. All these different dispositions of living beings mentioned above, such as intelligence, arise from Me alone, the Lord (Isvara), according to their respective karma.

Moreover,

महर्षयः सप्त पूर्वे चत्वारो मनवस्तथा ।
मद्भावा मानसा जाता येषां लोक इमाः प्रजाः ॥ ६ ॥

6. The seven Great *R*ishis as well as the four ancient Manus, with their being in Me, were born of mind; and theirs are these creatures in the world.

The seven great *R*ishis such as Bh*r*igu, as well as the four Manus of the past ages known as Savar*n*is, had directed their thoughts to Me exclusively and were therefore endowed with the power of Vish*n*u. They were produced by Me by mind alone. Born in the creation of these Manus and of the

Great *R*ishis are these creatures comprising the moving and the unmoving beings.*

Knowledge of the Lord's Glory conduces to Yoga.

एतां विभूतिं योगं च मम यो वेत्ति तत्त्वतः ।
सोऽविकम्पेन योगेन युज्यते नात्र संशयः ॥ ७ ॥

7. He who knows in truth this glory and power of Mine is endowed with unshaken Yoga; there is no doubt of it.

He who knows in truth this vast extent of My being † and My achievement (Yoga)—or Yoga may here stand for what is born of Yoga, *viz.*, the power of achieving and controlling mighty things as well as Omniscience‡—he is endowed with unshaken Yoga, *i.e.*, with steadiness in right knowledge. §

What is that unshaken Yoga with which they are endowed?—The answer follows:

---

* The Lord is not only the material cause (prak*r*iti) of all, but, as the Omniscient Lord of all. He is also the Ruler of all, for He produced the Great Rishis and the Manus. The Great Rishis, from Bh*r*igu to Vasish*t*ha, were omniscient and were the original teachers of the Traditional wisdom. The Manus were the *R*ulers of creatures and were themselves Lords. Both these belonged to the primeval age and were born of the mind of the Lord. The Great Rishis and Manus had their thought directed to the Omniscient Lord and were therefore endowed with the power of Vish*n*u and obtained wisdom and power. The present denizens of this world are their creatures, by birth and by knowledge.—(A.)

† He who knows Me as infinite.—(A.)

‡ *i.e.*, he who knows the fact that the Great *R*ishis and the Manus possessed their power and wisdom, as partaking of a very small portion of the Lord's power and wisdom.—(A.)

§ The knowledge of the Conditioned is the doorway leading to the knowledge of the Unconditioned.—(A.)

अहं सर्वस्य प्रभवो मत्तः सर्वं प्रवर्तते ।
इति मत्वा भजन्ते मां बुधा भावसमन्विताः ॥ ८ ॥

8. I am the source of all: from Me everything evolves; thus thinking the wise worship Me, endowed with contemplation.

I, the Supreme Brahman, termed Vasudeva, am the source of the whole world. From Me* alone evolves the whole universe in all its changes, including existence and disappearance, action, effect and enjoyment. Thus thinking, the wise who know the Superme Reality † worship Me, ardently engaged in the contemplation of the Supreme Reality.

Moreover,

मच्चित्ता मद्गतप्राणा बोधयन्तः परस्परम् ।
कथयन्तश्च मां नित्यं तुष्यन्ति च रमन्ति च ॥ ९ ॥

9. With their thought on Me, with their life absorbed in Me, instructing each other, and ever speaking of Me, they are content and delighted.

All their senses (pranas) such as the eye are absorbed in Me. Or—according to another interpretation—their very life (prana) is devoted to Me. They ever speak of Me as possessed of supreme wisdom, power, might and other qualities. They thus obtain satisfaction and are delighted as if in the company of the beloved.

---

* Controlled and impelled by Me as the Inner Regulator, every thing moves on in accordance with the Law.—(A.)

† It is only those who see the emptiness of the worldly life that are fit for a life of devotion to the Lord. When men know the Lord as the Self of all, the Cause of all, the Omniscient Lord of all, they become devoted to Me. The knowledge of the Supreme Reality leads to love, regard and earnestness, and these lead to devotion to the Lord.—(A.)

The Lord endows His devotees with wisdom.

As to those who worship Me devoutly in the ways mentioned above,

तेषां सततयुक्तानां भजतां प्रीतिपूर्वकम् ।
ददामि बुद्धियोगं तं येन मामुपयान्ति ते ॥ १० ॥

10. To these, ever devout, worshipping Me with love, I give that devotion of knowledge by which they come to Me.

To them who are ever devout, worshipping Me, not for any purpose of their own, but out of love for Me.—to them I give that devotion of right knowledge (buddhi-yoga) of My essential nature by which they* those who worship Me "with their thought on Me" (x. 9) and so on—know Me, the Supreme Lord, the Self, as their own Self.

Why dost Thou give the devotion of knowledge (buddhi-yoga) to Thy devotees?—And what is that obstacle in the path leading to Thee which the devotion of knowledge that Thou givest to Thy devotees serves to remove?—In answer to this question, the Lord says:

तेषामेवानुकम्पार्थमहमज्ञानजं तमः ।
नाशयाम्यात्मभावस्थो ज्ञानदीपेन भास्वता ॥ ११ ॥

11. Out of mere compassion for them, I, abiding in their self, destroy the darkness born of ignorance, by the luminous lamp of wisdom.

---

* Those alone who are thus devoted to the Lord can attain to Buddhi-Yoga that exteremely superior condition of the *antahkarana* produced by Dhyana, by which they reach that form of the Lord which is devoid of all limitations.—(A.)

Out of mere compassion: out of mercy, anxious as to how they may attain bliss. I dwell in their anta*h*-kara*n*a* which is engaged in thinking exclusively of the Self and destroy the darkness of ignorance,-that illusory knowledge which is caused by the absence of discrimination,—by the lamp of wisdom, by the lamp of discriminatory knowledge, fed by the oil of pure Devotion (Bhakti-prasada), fanned by the wind of earnest meditation on Me, furnished with the wick of right intuition purified by the cultivation of piety, chastity and other virtues, held in the ant*a*h-kara*n*a which is completely detached from all worldly concerns, placed in the wind-sheltered enclosure of the mind which is withdrawn from the sense-objects and untainted by attachment and aversion, and shining with the light of right knowledge generated by incessant practice of concentration and meditation.

Arjuna's question about the Lord's manifestations.

Having heard of the Lord's Glory and His mysterious power, Arjuna says:

Arjuna said:

परं ब्रह्म परं धाम पवित्रं परमं भवान् ।
पुरुषं शाश्वतं दिव्यमादिदेवमजं विभुम् ॥ १२ ॥

* *i.e.*, in the anta*h*-kara*n*a functioning on the plane of Spirit exclusively. Darkness here includes both the beginningless nescience and the illusory perception resulting from that nescience. It cannot be removed by matter or any material phenomenon, belonging as it does to the same class as darkness; therefore the Lord has said that He Himself destroys darkness. But the Spirit (Chaitanya) cannot directly remove darkness. It is only an intellectual state that is found to illumine an object unknown before. Hence it is that the Spirit removes ignorance by itself shining through a state of the intellect such as the one induced by the teaching of the *Sastra*. It is either the Spirit manifesting itself through an intellectual state, or an intellectual state pervaded by the Spirit, that can destroy nescience and illusory knowledge.

आहुस्त्वामृषयः सर्वे देवर्षिर्नारदस्तथा ।
असितो देवलो व्यासः स्वयं चैव ब्रवीषि मे ॥ १३ ॥

12-13. The Supreme Brahman, the Supreme Light, the Supreme Purifier art Thou. All the Rishis declare Thee as Eternal, Divine Purusha, the Primal God, Unborn, Omnipresent; so said the divine sage Narada, as also Asita, Devala and Vyasa; and Thou Thyself also sayest (so) to me.

The Supreme Brahman: the Highest Self. *The Primal God*: the God who existed before all other Gods. *Rishis*: such as Vasishtha.

सर्वमेतदृतं मन्ये यन्मां वदसि केशव ।
न हि ते भगवन्व्यक्तिं विदुर्देवा न दानवाः ॥ १४ ॥

14. I believe to be true all this which Thou sayest to me; for neither the Gods nor the Danavas, O Lord, know Thy manifestation.

Because Thou art the source of the Devas and others therefore,

स्वयमेवात्मनाऽऽत्मानं वेत्थ त्वं पुरुषोत्तम ।
भूतभावन भूतेश देवदेव जगत्पते ॥ १५ ॥

15. Thou Thyself knowest Thyself as the Self,* O Purusha Supreme, O Source of beings, O Lord of beings, O God of Gods, O Ruler of the world.

* *Thou Thyself*, i.e., without being taught: *knowest Thyself* i.e. the unconditioned nature of Thyself. *As the Self*: not as something external.—(A.)

Knowest Thyself: as the Lord,* as the Isvara possessed of unsurpassed wisdom, sovereignty and other powers.

वक्तुमर्हस्यशेषेण दिव्या ह्यात्मविभूतयः ।
याभिर्विभूतिभिर्लोकानिमांस्त्वं व्याप्य तिष्ठसि ॥ १६ ॥

16. Thou shouldst† indeed tell, without reserve, of Thy divine Glories, by which Glories Thou remainest pervading all these worlds.

कथं विद्यामहं योगिंस्त्वां सदा परिचिन्तयन् ।
केषु केषु च भावेषु चिन्त्योऽसि भगवन्मया ॥ १७ ॥

17. How ‡ shall I, ever meditating, know Thee, O Yogin; in what several things, O Lord, art Thou to be thought of by Me?

विस्तरेणात्मनो योगं विभूतिं च जनार्दन ।
भूयः कथय तृप्तिर्हि शृण्वतो नास्ति मेऽमृतम् ॥ १८ ॥

18. Tell me again in detail, O Janardana, of Thy power and Glory, for there is no satiety for me in hearing the immortal.

Tell me in detail of Thy mysterious power (*Yoga*) and sovereignty (aisvarya) and the various things to be meditated upon.—Janardana is so called because He sends—or *causes to go* (ardayati)—the Asuras, those *people* (janas) who are the

---

* Not even Thy conditioned nature as the Lord of the Universe, etc., can be seen by others.—(A.)

† Since Thy nature, which it is necessary to know, is invisible to others. (A.)

‡ In what manner should I, who am of dull understanding, meditate constantly on Thee, in order that my reason may thereby be purified so as to be able to know Thy unconditioned being.—(A.)

enemies of the Gods, to hell and the like; or because He is *prayed to* by all *people* for worldly success and salvation.—Tell me again of them, though described before; for, there is no satiety in hearing the immortal (ambrosia) of the speech issuing from Thy mouth.

The Lord's enumeration of His manifestations.

The Blessed Lord said:

हन्त ते कथयिष्यामि दिव्या ह्यात्मविभूतयः ।
प्राधान्यतः कुरुश्रेष्ठ नास्त्यन्तो विस्तरस्य मे ॥ १९ ॥

19. Now will I tell thee of My heavenly Glories, in their prominence, O best of the Kurus; there is no limit to My extent.

Now I will tell you of My heavenly Glories, in their prominence, *i.e.*, where they are severally the most prominent. It is not, indeed, possible even in a whole century to describe all of them, as there is no limit to the extent of My Glories.

Now, listen to this, in the first place:

अहमात्मा गुडाकेश सर्वभूताशयस्थितः ।
अहमादिश्च मध्यं च भूतानामन्त एव च ॥ २० ॥

20. I am the Self, O Gu*d*akesa, seated in the heart of all beings; I am the beginning and the middle, as also the end, of all beings.

You should think of Me as the innermost Self, seated in the heart within of all beings.—'*Gudakesa*' means either 'conqueror of sleep' or 'thick-haired'—He who is unable to think of Me as the Self should think of Me in those things which are mentioned below; for I am the source, the stay, and the end of all beings.

आदित्यानामहं विष्णुर्ज्योतिषां रविरंशुमान् ।
मरीचिर्मरुतामस्मि नक्षत्राणामहं शशी ॥ २१ ॥

21. Of the Adityas I am Vish*n*u; of the radiances, the resplendent Sun; I am Marichi of the Maruts; of the asterisms, the Moon.

Of the twelve Adityas, I am the Aditya known as Vish*n*u. Maruts are a kind of Devatas.

वेदानां सामवेदोऽस्मि देवानामस्मि वासवः ।
इन्द्रियाणां मनश्चास्मि भूतानामस्मि चेतना ॥ २२॥

22. Of the Vedas I am the Sama-Veda, I am Vasava of the Gods, and of the senses I am the mind, I am the intelligence in living beings.

Gods: such as the Rudras and the Adityas. *Vasava*: *i.e.*, Indra. Of the eleven senses I am the mind. *Chetana*, sentiency or intelligence, is that state of* the intellect (buddhi) which manifests itself in the aggregate of the body and the senses.

रुद्राणां शङ्करश्चास्मि वित्तेशो यक्षरक्षसाम् ।
वसूनां पावकश्चास्मि मेरुः शिखरिणामहम् ॥ २३ ॥

23 And of the Rudras I am *Sankara*, of the Yakshas and Rakshasas the Lord of wealth, and of the Vasus I am Agni, of the mountains I am the Meru.

The Rudras are eleven in number, and the Vasus eight. *The Lord of wealth*: Kubera.

* It exhibits itself in the aggregate body, pervading it throughout till death, and forming the medium for the manifestation of the Spirit or Consciousness (Chaitanya.).—(A.)

पुरोधसां च मुख्यं मां विद्धि पार्थ बृहस्पतिम् ।
सेनानीनामहं स्कन्दः सरसामस्मि सागरः ॥ २४ ॥

24. And of the household priests of Kings, O son of Pritha, know Me the chief one, Brihaspati; of generals I am Skanda, of lakes I am the Ocean.

Brihaspati is the chief of priests, because he is the house-hold priest of Indra. *Skanda* is the general of the Gods. Of the natural—*i.e.*, made by the Gods—reservoirs, I am the Ocean.

महर्षीणां भृगुरहं गिरामस्म्येकमक्षरम् ।
यज्ञानां जपयज्ञोऽस्मि स्थावराणां हिमालयः ॥ २५ ॥

25. Of the Great Rishis I am Bhrigu; of words I am the one syllable 'Om;' of offerings I am the offering of Japa (silent repetition), of unmoving things the Himalaya.

अश्वत्थः सर्ववृक्षाणां देवर्षीणां च नारदः ।
गन्धर्वाणां चित्ररथः सिद्धानां कपिलो मुनिः ॥ २६ ॥

26. Of all trees (I am) the Asvattha, and Narada of divine Rishis, Chitraratha of Gandharvas, the Sage Kapila of the Saints (Siddhas).

Divine Rishis: Who are Devas and are at the same time Rishis or seers of mantras. *The Saints* (Siddhas): those who at their very birth attained to a very high degree of Dharma, of knowledge, of detachment (vairagya) from worldly concerns, and of supremacy.

उच्चैःश्रवसमश्वानां विद्धि माममृतोद्भवम् ।
ऐरावतं गजेन्द्राणां नराणां च नराधिपम् ॥ २७ ॥

27. Know Me among horses as Uchchais-ravas, born of Amrita, of lordly elephants the Airavata, and of men the king.

Uchchais-sravas is the name of the kingly horse who was born in the ocean when it was churned for the amrita (ambrosia). Know Me among kingly elephants as the Airavata, the offspring of Iravat

आयुधानामहं वज्रं धेनूनामस्मि कामधुक् ।
प्रजनश्चास्मि कन्दर्पः सर्पाणामस्मि वासुकिः ॥ २८ ॥

28. Of weapons I am the thunderbolt, of cows I am the Kamadhuk, I am the progenitor Kandarpa, of serpents I am Vasuki.

The thunderbolt: the Vajra made of Dadhichi's bone. *Kamadhuk*: that cow of Vasishtha which yielded all objects desired; or any cow in general which may yield plenty of milk. *Kamadhuk*: Kama or love. *Vasuki*: the lord of serpents.

अनन्तश्चास्मि नागानां वरुणो यादसामहम् ।
पितृणामर्यमा चास्मि यमः संयमतामहम् ॥ २९ ॥

29. And Ananta of snakes I am, I am Varuna of water-being, and Aryaman of Pitris I am, I am Yama of controllers.

Ananta: the king of snakes. *Varuna*: the king of water-gods. *Water-beings*: the Devatas or Gods connected with waters. *Aryaman* is the king of Pitris.

प्रह्लादश्चास्मि दैत्यानां कालः कलयतामहम् ।
मृगाणां च मृगेन्द्रोऽहं वैनतेयश्च पक्षिणाम् ॥ ३० ॥

30. And Prahlada am I of Diti's progeny, of reckoners I am Time, and of beasts I am the lord of beasts, and Vainateya of birds.

The lord of beasts: the lion or the tiger. *Vainateya*: Vinata's son, Garutmat.

पवनः पवतामस्मि रामः शस्त्रभृतामहम् ।
झषाणां मकरश्चास्मि स्रोतसामस्मि जाह्नवी ॥ ३१ ॥

31. Of purifiers I am the wind, Rama of warriors am I, of fishes I am the shark, of streams I am the Ganges.

Of those who bear weapons I am Rama, Dasaratha's son.

सर्गाणामादिरन्तश्च मध्यं चैवाहमर्जुन ।
अध्यात्मविद्या विद्यानां वादः प्रवदतामहम् ॥ ३२ ॥

32. Of creations I am the beginning and the middle and also the end; of all knowledges I am the knowledge of the Self, and Vada of disputants

I am the source, the stay and the end of all evolution.—At the commencement (x. 20) it was said that He is the beginning, the middle, and the end of all sentient existence; but here the whole creation in general is referred to. The knowledge of the Self is the chief among all knowledges, because it leads to moksha. By 'disputants' we should here understand the several kinds of disputation,—vada, jalpa, vita*n*da,* etc. Vada is the chief of them, as it is a means of determining truth.

---

* *Vada* is that way of arguing, of which the object is to arrive at ruth regarding a certain question. '*Jalpa*' is an argument in which a disputant tries to assert his own opinion and to refute that of his adversary by an overbearing reply or a wrangling rejoinder. '*Vitanda*' consists in idly carping at the arguments or assertions of another without attempting to establish the opposite side of the question.

अक्षराणामकारोऽस्मि द्वन्द्वः सामासिकस्य च ।
अहमेवाक्षयः कालो धाताऽहं विश्वतोमुखः ॥ ३३ ॥

33. Of letters the letter 'A' am I, and *dvandva* of all compounds; I am, verily, the inexhaustible Time; I am the All-faced Dispenser.

'Time' here refers either to what is generally so called, —*viz.*, 'kshana,' a moment, the ultimate element of time,—or to the Supreme Lord who is the Time (Kala=the Measurer) even of time. I am the Dispenser of results of actions to the whole world.

मृत्युः सर्वहरश्चाहमुद्भवश्च भविष्यताम् ।
कीर्तिः श्रीर्वाक्च नारीणां स्मृतिर्मेधा धृतिः क्षमा ॥ ३४ ॥

34. And I am all-seizing Death, and the prosperity of those who are to be prosperous; of the feminine (I am) Fame, Fortune and Speech, Memory, Intelligence, Constancy, Endurance.

Death is of two sorts, he who seizes wealth, etc., and he who seizes life. Of them the seizer of life is the all-seizer, I am He. Or, I am the Supreme Lord who is the All-seizer, because of His carrying all away at the time of pralaya or dissolution. I am the prosperity—and the means of attaining it—of those who are to be prosperous in future, who are fit to attain prosperity. I am Fame, etc., the best of the feminine; and possessed of the mere semblance thereof, people regard themselves successful in life.

बृहत्साम तथा साम्नां गायत्री छन्दसामहम् ।
मासानां मार्गशीर्षोऽहमृतूनां कुसुमाकरः ॥ ३५ ॥

35. Of Samans also I am the Brihat-Saman

of metres Gayatri am I, of months I am Margasirsha, of seasons the flowery season.

'*Brihat-Saman*' is the chief of the Samans. Of the Riks, composed in Gayatri and other metres, I am the Gayatri Rik. *The flowery season* is what is called *Vasanta*, the spring.

द्यूतं छलयतामस्मि तेजस्तेजस्विनामहम् ।
जयोऽस्मि व्यवसायोऽस्मि सत्त्वं सत्त्ववतामहम् ॥ ३६ ॥

36. I am the gambling of the fraudulent, I am the splendour of the splendid, I am victory, I am effort, I am the goodness of the good.

Gambling: such as dice-play. I am the victory of the victorious; I am the effort of those who make an effort.

वृष्णीनां वासुदेवोऽस्मि पाण्डवानां धनञ्जयः ।
मुनीनामप्यहं व्यासः कवीनामुशना कविः ॥ ३७ ॥

37. Of the Vrishnis I am Vasudeva, of the Pandavas I am Dhananjaya, and of the saints I am Vyasa, of the sages I am Usanas the sage.

Vasudeva: Myself, who am your friend. *Vrishnis*: the descendants of Yadu. *The saints*: those who are engrossed in meditation and know all things. *Sages*: those of extensive knowledge, the omniscient beings.

दण्डो दमयतामस्मि नीतिरस्मि जिगीषताम् ।
मौनं चैवास्मि गुह्यानां ज्ञानं ज्ञानवतामहम् ॥ ३८ ॥

38. Of punishers I am the sceptre, of those who seek to conquer I am the polity, and of things secret I am also silence, the knowledge of knowers am I.

यच्चापि सर्वभूतानां बीजं तदहमर्जुन ।
न तदस्ति विना यत्स्यान्मया भूतं चराचरम् ॥ ३९ ॥

39. And what is the seed of all being, that also am I, O Arjuna. There is no being, whether moving or unmoving, that can exist without me.

To conclude the present section, the Lord summarises His Glory (vibhuti) as follows:—There is no being without Me; for, anything into which I have not entered would be without Self (could not exist) and would be void (*s*unya). Wherefore, everything is of My nature, *i.e.*, I am the essence of everything.

नान्तोऽस्ति मम दिव्यानां विभूतीनां परन्तप ।
एष तूद्देशतः प्रोक्तो विभूतेर्विस्तरो मया ॥ ४० ॥

40. There is no end of My heavenly Glories, O harasser of thy foes; but the details of My Glory have been declared only by way of instance.

It is indeed not possible for anybody to describe or know the exact extent of the Divine Glories of the Lord, the Self of all.

Divine Glory described in brief.

यद्यद्विभूतिमत्सत्त्वं श्रीमदूर्जितमेव वा ।
तत्तदेवावगच्छ त्वं मम तेजोंऽशसम्भवम् ॥ ४१ ॥

41. Whatever being is glorious, prosperous, or strong, that know thou to be a manifestation of a part of My Splendour.

My: the Isvara's.

अथवा बहुनैतेन किं ज्ञातेन तवार्जुन ।
विष्टभ्याहमिदं कृत्स्नमेकांशेन स्थितो जगत् ॥ ४२ ॥

42. But, of what avail to thee is this vast things being known, O Arjuna? I stand sustaining this whole world by one part (of Myself).

Of what avail to you can be this knowledge of vast but imperfect details? Listen, I will tell you completely of it. I stand sustaining firmly this whole world by one part, by one limb, by one foot; *i.e.*, one part of Myself constitutes all beings. So says the chant:

'All beings form His foot.'—(*Taittiriya Aranyaka* 3-12).

इति श्रीमद्भगवद्गीतासूपनिषत्सु ब्रह्मविद्यायां योगशास्त्रे
श्रीकृष्णार्जुनसंवादे विभूतियोगो नाम
दशमोऽध्यायः ।

ELEVENTH DISCOURSE.

THE UNIVERSAL FORM.

Arjuna's prayer for a vision of the Universal Form.

The Glories of the Lord have been described. Now, on hearing the Lord's statement that 'I stand supporting the whole world by one part of Myself,' Arjuna was desirous to see with his own eyes that Primal Form of the Lord which is manifested as the universe, and accordingly said:

अर्जुन उवाच :—

मदनुग्रहाय परमं गुह्यमध्यात्मसंज्ञितम् ।
यत्त्वयोक्तं वचस्तेन मोहोऽयं विगतो मम ॥ १ ॥

Arjuna said:

1. By that speech which has been delivered by Thee for my benefit,—that highest secret which is called Adhyatma,—this, my delusion, is gone.

Adhyatma: that which treats of the dintinction between the Self and the non-Self. *Delusion*: non-discrimination.

Moreover,

भवाप्ययौ हि भूतानां श्रुतौ विस्तरशो मया ।
त्वत्तः कमलपत्राक्ष माहात्म्यमपि चाव्ययम् ॥ २ ॥

2. The origin and the dissolution of beings, verily, have been heard by me in detail from Thee, O Lotus-eyed, as also Thy inexhaustible greatness.

In detail: not in brevity. *Lotus-eyed*: having eyes like lotus-leaves.

एवमेतद्यथाऽऽत्थ त्वमात्मानं परमेश्वर ।
द्रष्टुमिच्छामि ते रूपमैश्वरं पुरुषोत्तम ॥ ३ ॥

3. So it is, as Thou, Supreme Lord, hast declared Thyself to be. (Still) I desire to see Thy form as Isvara, O Purusha Supreme.

Form etc.; that of Vishnu, as possessed of (infinite) wisdom, sovereignty, strength, power, prowess and splendour.

मन्यसे यदि तच्छक्यं मया द्रष्टुमिति प्रभो ।
योगेश्वर ततो मे त्वं दर्शयात्मानमव्ययम् ॥ ४ ॥

4. If Thou, O Lord, thinkest it possible for me to see it, do Thou, then, O Lord of Yogins, show me Thy Eternal Self,

Then: because I am very anxious to see.

Arjuna endowed with heavenly sight wherewith to see the Universal Form.

Thus implored by Arjuna, the Lord said:

श्रीभगवानुवाच :—

पश्य मे पार्थ रूपाणि शतशोऽथ सहस्रशः ।
नानाविधानि दिव्यानि नानावर्णाकृतीनि च ॥ ५ ॥

The Blessed Lord said:

5. See, O son of Pritha, My heavenly forms, by hundreds and thousands, of different sorts, and of various colours and shapes.

Heavenly: Supernatural. *By hundreds and thousands*: innumerable. *Colours*: such as blue, green and the like. *Shapes*: arrangements of parts.

पश्यादित्यान्वसून्रुद्रानश्विनौ मरुतस्तथा ।
बहून्यदृष्टपूर्वाणि पश्याश्चर्याणि भारत ॥ ६ ॥

6. Behold the Adityas, the Vasus, the Rudras, the Asvins, and also the Maruts; behold many marvels never seen before, O Bharata.

Behold the twelve Adityas, the eight Vasus, the eleven Rudras, the two Asvins, the seven heptads of Maruts. Behold also many other marvels never seen before by you or anybody else in this world of man.

Not this alone:

इहैकस्थं जगत्कृत्स्नं पश्याद्य सचराचरम् ।
मम देहे गुडाकेश यच्चान्यद्द्रष्टुमिच्छसि ॥ ७ ॥

7. Now behold here in My body, Gudakesa, the whole world established in one,—including the moving and the unmoving—and whatever else thou desirest to see.

Whatever else: Your success or defeat, about which you have entertained a doubt (ii. 6).

But,

न तु मां शक्यसे द्रष्टुमनेनैव स्वचक्षुषा ।
दिव्यं ददामि ते चक्षुः पश्य मे योगमैश्वरम् ॥ ८ ॥

8. Thou art not indeed able to see Me with this thy eye alone; I give thee a divine eye; behold My lordly Yoga.

Me: putting on the Universal Form. *This:* Prakrita, of prakriti, natural, (fleshy, of the earth). I give thee a divine eye, by which you will be able to see Me. By that eye, behold My great miraculous power of Yoga, that which belongs to me as Isvara.

The Lord's manifestation of the Universal Form.

सञ्जय उवाच—

एवमुक्त्वा ततो राजन् महायोगेश्वरो हरिः ।
दर्शयामास पार्थाय परमं रूपमैश्वरम् ॥ ९ ॥

Sanjaya said:

9. Having thus spoken, O King, then, Hari, the great Lord of Yogins, showed to the son of Pritha the Supreme Form as Isvara.

King: Dhritarashtra. *Hari:* Narayana. *Form:* the Universal Form.

अनेकवक्त्रनयनमनेकाद्भुतदर्शनम् ।
अनेकदिव्याभरणं दिव्यानेकोद्यतायुधम् ॥ १० ॥

10. Containing many mouths and eyes, possessed of many wondrous sights, of many heavenly ornaments, of many heavenly weapons held up. Such a form He showed.

Moreover,

दिव्यमाल्याम्बरधरं दिव्यगन्धानुलेपनम् ।
सर्वाश्चर्यमयं देवमनन्तं विश्वतोमुखम् ॥ ११ ॥

11. Wearing heavenly garlands and vestures, anointed with heavenly unguents, all-wonderful, resplendent, boundless, with faces on all sides.

With faces on all sides: as He is the Self of all beings. Such a form He showed; or, such a form did Arjuna see.

Here follows an illustration, by an example, of the splendour of the Lord's Universal Form:

दिवि सूर्यसहस्रस्य भवेद्युगपदुत्थिता ।
यदि भाः सदृशी सा स्याद्भासस्तस्य महात्मनः ॥ १२ ॥

12. If the splendour of a thousand suns were ever to present itself at once in the sky, that would be like the splendour of that Mighty Being.

In the sky: in antariksha or the middle loka; or in the heavenly region, which forms the third (from here). *The Mighty Being:* the Universal Form.—If no such thing can ever exist, then the splendour of the Universal Form excels all else.

Moreover,

तत्रैकस्थं जगत्कृत्स्नं प्रविभक्तमनेकधा ।
अपश्यद्देवदेवस्य शरीरे पाण्डवस्तदा ॥ १३ ॥

13. There, in the body of the God of Gods, the son of Pa*n*du then beheld the whole world established in one, and separated into many groups.

There: in the Form. *Many groups:* Devas, Pit*r*is, men and other sorts of beings. *The son of Pandu:* Arjuna. *God of Gods:* Hari.

ततः स विस्मयाविष्टो हृष्टरोमा धनञ्जयः ।
प्रणम्य शिरसा देवं कृताञ्जलिरभाषत ॥ १४ ॥

14. Then he, Dhana*n*jaya, filled with amazement, with his hair standing on end; bowed down with his head, and, with joined palms, thus addressed the God.

Then: having seen Him. *The God:* putting on the Universal Form. *With joined palms:* in order to bow down.

How?—Arjuna declares his own experience, *viz.*, that he sees the Universal Form shewn by the Lord:

अर्जुन उवाच—

पश्यामि देवांस्तव देव देहे
सर्वांस्तथा भूतविशेषसङ्घान् ।
ब्रह्माणमीशं कमलासनस्थ-
मृषींश्च सर्वानुरगांश्च दिव्यान् ॥ १५ ॥

Arjuna said:

15. I see all the Gods, O God, in thy body, as also hosts of various classes of beings: Brahma, the Lord, seated on the lotus-seat, and all *R*ishis and heavenly serpents.

Various classes of beings: both animate and inanimate, and of various forms. *Brahma*: the Four-faced, the Lord of creatures. He is seated in the centre of the Earth-Lotus, on the Meru which forms the cup or seed-vessel as it were of the Earth-Lotus. *Rishis*: such as Vasish*t*ha. *Serpents*: such as Vasuki.

अनेकबाहूदरवक्त्रनेत्रम्
पश्यामि त्वां सर्वतोऽनन्तरूपम् ।
नान्तं न मध्यं न पुनस्तवादिम्
पश्यामि विश्वेश्वर विश्वरूप ॥ १६ ॥

16. I see Thee of boundless form on every side with multitudinous arms, stomachs, mouths and eyes; neither Thy end nor the middle nor the beginning do I see, O Lord of the Universe, O Universal Form.

Middle: what lies between two extremities.

Moreover,

किरीटिनं गदिनं चक्रिणं च
तेजोराशिं सर्वतो दीप्तिमन्तम् ।
पश्यामि त्वां दुर्निरीक्ष्यं समन्ताद्
दीप्तानलार्कद्युतिमप्रमेयम् ॥ १७ ॥

17. I see Thee with diadem, club, and discus; a mass of splendour shining everywhere, very hard to look at, all around blazing like burning fire and sun, and immeasurable.

Immeasurable: whose limits cannot be fixed.

Vishnu is one with the Unconditioned.

From this vision of Thy power of Yoga (wonder-working) I infer,

त्वमक्षरं परमं वेदितव्यम् त्वमस्य विश्वस्य परं निधानम् ।
त्वमव्ययः शाश्वतधर्मगोप्ता सनातनस्त्वं पुरुषो मतो मे ॥

18. Thou art the Imperishable, the Supreme Being worthy to be known. Thou art the great Abode of this Universe; Thou art the undying Guardian of the Eternal Dharma, Thou art the ancient Purusha, I deem.

To be known: by seekers of liberation.

The Univeral Form (continued.)

Moreover,

अनादिमध्यान्तमनन्तवीर्य-
मनन्तबाहुं शशिसूर्यनेत्रम् ।
पश्यामि त्वां दीप्तहुताशवक्त्रम्
स्वतेजसा विश्वमिदं तपन्तम् ॥ १९ ॥

19. I see Thee without beginning, middle or end, infinite in power, of manifold arms; the sun and the moon being Thy eyes, the burning fire Thy face; heating the whole Universe with Thy radiance.

द्यावापृथिव्योरिदमन्तरं हि
व्याप्तं त्वयैकेन दिशश्च सर्वाः ।
दृष्ट्वाऽद्भुतं रूपमुग्रं तवेदम्
लोकत्रयं प्रव्यथितं महात्मन् ॥ २० ॥

20. This space betwixt heaven and earth and all the quarters are filled by Thee alone. Having seen This, Thy marvellous and awful form, the three worlds are trembling, O High-souled Being.

Thee: in Thy Universal Form.

Now, in order to remove the doubt entertained by Arjuna (ii. 6) as to his success, the Lord proceeds to show that victory for Pa*nd*avas is certain. Seeing Him, Arjuna goes on:

अमी हि त्वां सुरसङ्घा विशन्ति
केचिद्भीताः प्राञ्जलयो गृणन्ति ।
स्वस्तीत्युक्त्वा महर्षिसिद्धसङ्घाः
स्तुवन्ति त्वां स्तुतिभिः पुष्कलाभिः ॥ २१ ॥

21. Into Thee, indeed, enter these hosts of Suras; some extol Thee in fear with joined palms; "May it be well!" thus saying, bands of great *R*ishis and Siddhas praise Thee with hymns complete.

These hosts of Suras: these warriors now fighting all, of them Devas,—the Vasus and others,—who have incarnated themselves as human beings for lightening the earth's burden. They are seen entering into Thee. Some of them only call out to Thee, unable even to flee. Having discovered portents and other forebodings of evil as the war approached, the great *R*ishis and Siddhas say 'May it be well for the world!' and offer their prayers to Thee in full hymns.

The wonderfulness of the Universal Form

Moreover,

रुद्रादित्या वसवो ये च साध्याः
विश्वेऽश्विनौ मरुतश्चोष्मपाश्च ।
गन्धर्वयक्षासुरसिद्धसङ्घाः
वीक्षन्ते त्वां विस्मिताश्चैव सर्वे ॥ २२ ॥

22. The Rudras, Adityas, Vasus, and Sadhyas, Visvas and Asvins, Maruts and Ushmapas, hosts of Gandharvas, Yakshas, Asuras, and Siddhas,—they are all looking at Thee, all quite astonished.

Ushmapas: a class of Pit*r*is. *Gandharvas:* such as Haha and Huhu. *Yakshas:* such as Kubera. *Asuras:* such as Virochana. *Siddhas*; such as Kapila.

The terribleness of the Universal Form.

For,

रूपं महत्ते बहुवक्त्रनेत्रम्
महाबाहो बहुबाहूरुपादम् ।
बहूदरं बहुदंष्ट्राकरालम्
दृष्ट्वा लोकाः प्रव्यथितास्तथाऽहम् ॥ २३ ॥

23. Having seen Thy immeasurable Form, possessed, O Mighty-armed, of many mouths and eyes, of many arms and thighs and feet, and of many stomachs, and fearful with many tusks, the worlds are terrified, and I also.

The worlds : all living creatures in the world.

Here follows the cause (of my terror):

नभःस्पृशं दीप्तमनेकवर्णम्
व्यात्ताननं दीप्तविशालनेत्रम् ।
दृष्ट्वा हि त्वां प्रव्यथितान्तरात्मा
धृतिं न विन्दामि शमं च विष्णो ॥ २४ ॥

24. On seeing Thee (Thy Form) touching the sky, blazing in many colours, with mouths wide open, with large fiery eyes, I am terrified at heart and find no courage nor peace, O Vishnu.

Many colours: fearful, putting on different shapes.

Wherefore?—

दंष्ट्राकरालानि च ते मुखानि दृष्ट्वैव कालानलसन्निभानि ।
दिशो न जाने न लभे च शर्म प्रसीद देवेश जगन्निवास ॥

25. Having seen Thy mouths which are fearful with tusks and resemble Time's Fires, I know not the four quarters, nor do I find peace; be Thou gracious, O Lord of Gods and Abode of the Universe!

Time's Fires : the fires which consume the worlds at the time of dissolution (pralaya). *I know not the four quarters* : I cannot distinguish the East and the West, I cannot discriminate the different quarters.

Arjuna's vision of the defeat of the enemy.

My fear, too, of defeat at the hands of others is gone: for

अमी च त्वां धृतराष्ट्रस्य पुत्राः
सर्वे सहैवावनिपालसङ्घैः ।
भीष्मो द्रोणः सूतपुत्रस्तथाऽसौ
सहास्मदीयैरपि योधमुख्यैः ॥ २६ ॥

वक्त्राणि ते त्वरमाणा विशन्ति
दंष्ट्राकरालानि भयानकानि ।
केचिद्विलग्ना दशनान्तरेषु
संदृश्यन्ते चूर्णितैरुत्तमाङ्गैः ॥ २७ ॥

26—27. And all the sons of Dh*r*itarash*t*ra, with hosts of princes, Bhishma, Dro*n*a and that son (Karna) of a charioteer, with the warrior chiefs of ours, enter hurrying into Thy mouth, terrible with tusks and fearful to behold. Some are found sticking in the gaps betwixt the teeth with their heads crushed to powder.

Sons : such as Duryodhana. *Ours* : such as Dhrish*t*a-dyumna. *Sticking* : like a piece of flesh.

How do they enter into Thy mouth?—Arjuna says :

यथा नदीनां बहवोऽम्बुवेगाः
समुद्रमेवाभिमुखा द्रवन्ति ।
तथा तवामी नरलोकवीराः
विशन्ति वक्त्राण्यभिविज्वलन्ति ॥ २८ ॥

28. As many torrents of rivers flow direct towards the sea, so do these heroes in the world of men enter Thy flaming mouths.

These: such as Bhishma .

Why and how do they enter ?—Arjuna says :

यथा प्रदीप्तं ज्वलनं पतङ्गाः विशन्ति नाशाय समृद्धवेगाः ।
तथैव नाशाय विशन्ति लोकास्तवापि वक्त्राणि समृद्धवेगाः ॥

29. As moths hurriedly rush into a blazing fire for destruction, just so do these creatures also hurriedly rush into Thy mouths for destruction.

The splendour of the Universal Form.

But,

लेलिह्यसे ग्रसमानः समन्ता-
ल्लोकान्समग्रान्वदनैर्ज्वलद्भिः ।
तेजोभिरापूर्य जगत्समग्रम्
भासस्तवोग्राः प्रतपन्ति विष्णो ॥ ३०॥

30. Thou lickest up devouring all worlds on every side with Thy flaming mouths, filling the whole world with flames. Thy fierce rays are blazing forth, O Vish*n*u.

Vishnu : all-pervading.

Because Thou art so fierce, wherefore,

आख्याहि मे को भवानुग्ररूपो
नमोऽस्तु ते देववर प्रसीद ।
विज्ञातुमिच्छामि भवन्तमाद्यम्
न हि प्रजानामि तव प्रवृत्तिम् ॥ ३१ ॥

31. Tell me who thou art, so fierce in form. I bow to Thee, O God Supreme; have mercy. I desire to know Thee, the Original Being. I know not indeed Thy doing.

The Lord's advent for destruction of worlds.

श्रीभगवानुवाच —

कालोऽस्मि लोकक्षयकृत्प्रवृद्धो
लोकान्समाहर्तुमिह प्रवृत्तः ।
ऋतेऽपि त्वां न भविष्यन्ति सर्वे
येऽवस्थिताः प्रत्यनीकेषु योधाः ॥ ३२ ॥

The Blessed Lord said :

32. I am the mighty world-destroying Time, now engaged in destroying the worlds. Even without thee, none of the warriors arrayed in hostile armies shalt live.

Warriors: Bhishma, Dro*n*a, Kar*n*a and others.

Such being the case.

तस्मात्त्वमुत्तिष्ठ यशो लभस्व
जित्वा शत्रून्भुङ्क्ष्व राज्यं समृद्धम् ।
मयैवैते निहताः पूर्वमेव
निमित्तमात्रं भव सव्यसाचिन् ॥ ३३ ॥

33. Therefore do thou arise and obtain fame. Conquer the enemies and enjoy the unrivalled dominion. By Myself have they been already slain; be thou a mere instrument, O Savyasachin.

Fame: that Bhishma and other atirathas (great warriors) arrayed in the hostile army, unconquerable even to Devas, have been defeated by Arjuna. Such a fame is the result only of good karma. *Enemies*: such as Duryodhana *Savyasachin*: Arjuna who could shoot arrows even with the left hand.

द्रोणं च भीष्मं च जयद्रथं च
कर्णं तथाऽन्यानपि योधवीरान् ।
मया हतांस्त्वं जहि मा व्यथिष्ठाः
युध्यस्व जेतासि रणे सपत्नान् ॥ ३४ ॥

34. Dro*n*a and Bhishma, Jayadratha, Kar*n*a and other brave warriors,—these, killed by Me, do thou kill; fear not, fight, thou shalt conquer the enemies.

The lord speaks of these warriors—whom Arjuna had any reason to fear—as killed by Himself. Now it is evident why there should be any hesitation (on the part of Arjuna) concerning Dro*n*a and Bhishma Dro*n*a was his teacher in the science of archery, was possessed of celestial weapons and was especially his (Arjuna's) own dear greatest Guru. Bhishma had his death at his own command and was possessed of celestial weapons. He once entered into a single combat with Parasu-Rama and was not defeated. As to Jayadratha, his father was engaged in austerity, firmly resolved that "whoever causes my son's head to drop down on earth, his head too shall fall." Kar*n*a, too, was furnished with an unerring Sakti (missile) given him by Indra. He was a son of the sun, born of a maiden. Wherefore he is also mentioned by name. *Enemies*: such as Duryodhana.

Arjuna's adoration of the Universal Form.

सञ्जय उवाच—

एतच्छ्रुत्वा वचनं केशवस्य
कृताञ्जलिर्वेपमानः किरीटी ।
नमस्कृत्वा भूय एवाह कृष्णम्
सगद्गदं भीतभीतः प्रणम्य ॥ ३५ ॥

Sanjaya said:

35. Having heard that speech of Kesava, the crowned one (Arjuna), with joined palms, trembling, prostrating himself, again addressed Krishna, stammering, bowing down, overwhelmed with fear.

When a man is overpowered with fear or with love, his eyes become full of tears, owing to the attack of pain or owing to the rise of joy: then his throat is choked up with phlegm, and this again causes indistinctness and dulness in speech. Thus did Arjuna speak in a stammering tone.

Sanjaya's speech on this occasion is very significant—How?—Sanjaya hoped that on seeing that his (Dhritarashtra's) son would certainly be killed for want of support if the unconquerable four, including Drona, should be killed by Arjuna, Dhritarashtra might despair of success and bring about peace. Thus he hoped there would be happiness to both. Even to this, Dhritarashtra did not listen, owing to mighty Destiny.

अर्जुन उवाच—

स्थाने हृषीकेश तव प्रकीर्त्या
जगत्प्रहृष्यत्यनुरज्यते च ।
रक्षांसि भीतानि दिशो द्रवन्ति
सर्वे नमस्यन्ति च सिद्धसङ्घाः ॥ ३६ ॥

Arjuna said:

36. It is meet, O Hrishikesa, that the world is delighted and rejoices by Thy praise; Rakshasas fly in fear to all quarters, and all hosts of Siddhas bow to Thee.

Praise: description of Thy glory. This verse may be also rendered so as to mean: The Lord is the proper object of delight and love, for the Lord is the Self of all and the Friend of all beings. *Siddhas*: such as Kapila. It is meet that such should be the case so far as Thou art concerned.

For the following reason also the Lord is the object of delight, etc.

कस्माच्च ते न नमेरन्महात्मन्
गरीयसे ब्रह्मणोऽप्यादिकर्त्रे ।
अनन्त देवेश जगन्निवास
त्वमक्षरं सदसत्तत्परं यत् ॥ ३७ ॥

37. And how should they not, O Mighty Being, bow to Thee, Greater (than all else), the Primal Cause even of Brahma, O Infinite Being, O Lord of Gods, O Abode of the Universe; Thou art the Imperishable, the Being and the non-Being, That which is the Supreme.

Brahma: the Hiranyagarbha. (Because Thou art the Mighty Being), therefore Thou art the proper object of delight and worship. Thou art the Supreme Being, as revealed in the Vedantas (Upanishads): Thou art the Sat and the A-sat. The existent, as well as the non-existent—*i.e.*, that with reference to which arises our consciousness of non-existence,—form the upadhis (conditions) of the Akshara, on account of which He is spoken of as the *Sat* or the *A-sat*, the existent or the non-existent. In reality, the Imperishable (Akshara) whom the Veda-knowers speak of transcends the *Sat* and the *A-sat*, and He is Thyself and none else.

He again extols the Lord thus:

त्वमादिदेवः पुरुषः पुराण-
स्त्वमस्य विश्वस्य परं निधानम् ।
वेत्ताऽसि वेद्यं च परं च धाम
त्वया ततं विश्वमनन्तरूप ॥ ३८ ॥

38. Thou art the Primal God, the Ancient Purusha; Thou art the Supreme Abode of all this, Thou art the Knower and the Knowable and the Supreme Abode. By Thee is all pervaded, O Being of infinite forms.

Primal God: because Thou art the creator of the Universe. *Purusha*: so called because He lies in the body. *Abode*: that in which the Universe rests during the Great Pralaya and such other periods. *Knower*: of all the knowable things. *Supreme Abode*: of Vishnu.

Moreover,

वायुर्यमोऽग्निर्वरुणः शशाङ्कः
प्रजापतिस्त्वं प्रपितामहश्च ।
नमो नमस्तेऽस्तु सहस्रकृत्वः
पुनश्च भूयोऽपि नमो नमस्ते ॥ ३९ ॥

39. Thou art Vayu, Yama, Agni, Varuna, the Moon, Prajapati, and the Great Grand-Father. Hail! Hail to Thee! a thousand times, and again and again hail! hail to Thee!

Prajapati: such as Kasyapa. *Great Grand-Father*: the father even of Brahma. *Again*: This shows Arjuna's dissatisfaction due to his extreme faith and devotion.

And,

नमः पुरस्तादथ पृष्ठतस्ते
नमोऽस्तु ते सर्वत एव सर्व ।
अनन्तवीर्यामितविक्रमस्त्वम्
सर्वं समाप्नोषि ततोऽसि सर्वः ॥ ४० ॥

40. Hail to Thee before and behind! Hail to Thee on every side! O All! Thou, infinite in power and infinite in daring, pervadest all, wherefore Thou art All.

Before: in the East. *On every side*: as Thou art present in all quarters. A man may be powerful, but he may not dare to slay the enemies, or he may be slow in daring; but Thou art infinite both in power and in daring. *Pervadest*: by Thy One Self. *O All*: without Thee nothing exists.

Arjuna's prayer for the Lord's forgiveness.

Because I have been a sinner for want of knowledge of Thy greatness, therefore,

सखेति मत्वा प्रसभं यदुक्तम्
हे कृष्ण हे यादव हे सखेति ।
अजानता महिमानं तवेदम्
मया प्रमादात्प्रणयेन वापि ॥ ४१ ॥

यच्चाऽवहासार्थमसत्कृतोऽसि
विहारशय्यासनभोजनेषु ।
एकोऽथवाऽप्यच्युत तत्समक्षम्
तत्क्षामये त्वामहमप्रमेयम् ॥ ४२ ॥

41-42. Whatever was rashly said by me from carelessness or love, addressing Thee as "O K*r*ish*n*a, O Yadava, O friend," looking on Thee merely as a friend, ignorant of this Thy greatness,—in whatever way I may have insulted Thee for fun while at play, on bed, in an assembly, or at meals, when alone, O Achyuta, or in company—that I implore Thee, Immeasureable, to forgive.

Looking on Thee merely as a friend: owing to misconception. *Greatness*: The Universal Form as Isvara. *Carelessness*: the mind being attracted elsewhere. *Love*: confidence born of affection. *That*: all those offences.

For,

पिताऽसि लोकस्य चराचरस्य
त्वमस्य पूज्यश्च गुरुर्गरीयान् ।
न त्वत्समोऽस्त्यभ्यधिकः कुतोऽन्यो
लोकत्रयेऽप्यप्रतिमप्रभावः ॥ ४३ ॥

43. Thou art the Father of this world, moving and unmoving. Thou art to be adored by this (world), Thou the Greatest Guru; (for) Thy equal exists not; whence another, superior to Thee, in the three worlds, O Being of unequalled greatness?

Thy equal exists not : for there cannot be two Isvaras or Lords; if there were more than one Isvara, the world could not get on as it now does.* When even Thy equal exists not, how can there exist a being superior to Thee?

Because it is so,

तस्मात्प्रणम्य प्रणिधाय कायम्
प्रसादये त्वामहमीशमीड्यम् ।
पितेव पुत्रस्य सखेव सख्युः
प्रियः प्रियायार्हसि देव सोढुम् ॥ ४४ ॥

44. Therefore, bowing down, prostrating my body, I implore Thee, adorable Lord, to forgive. It is meet Thou shouldst bear with me as the father with the son, as friend with friend, as the lover with the beloved.

As the father, etc, As a father forgives his son's offences.

Arjuna's prayer for the Lord's resumption of His usual form

अदृष्टपूर्वं हृषितोऽस्मि दृष्ट्वा
भयेन च प्रव्यथितं मनो मे ।
तदेव मे दर्शय देव रूपम्
प्रसीद देवेश जगन्निवास ॥ ४५ ॥

* When one Iswara desires to create, another may desire to destroy. There is no guarantee that all the different Isvaras would be of one mind; and as they would all be independent of each other, the effort of one *Isvara* in one direction would be neutralised by that of another in the opposite direction. The world could not exist as it exists now.—(A).

45. I am delighted, having seen what was unseen before; and (yet) my mind is confounded with fear. Show me that form only, O God; have mercy, O God of Gods, O Abode of the Universe.

What was unseen before: the Universal Form never before seen by me or anybody else. Therefore show me only that form (which Thou wearest) as my friend.

किरीटिनं गदिनं चक्रहस्त-
मिच्छामि त्वां द्रष्टुमहं तथैव ।
तेनैव रूपेण चतुर्भुजेन
सहस्रबाहो भव विश्वमूर्ते ॥ ४६ ॥

46. I wish to see Thee as before, crowned, possessd of the club, with the discus in the hand, in Thy former form only, having four arms, O Thousand-armed, O Universal Form.

Thy former form: as the son of Vasudeva. *Thousand-armed*: referring to the Universal Form manifested at present. Withdrawing Thy Universal Form, do Thou put on Thy former one.

The Lord resumes His usual form.

Seeing Arjuna afraid, the Lord withdrew the Universal Form; and consoling Arjuna with sweet words, He said:

श्रीभगवानुवाच—
मया प्रसन्नेन तवार्जुनेदम्
रूपं परं दर्शितमात्मयोगात् ।
तेजोमयं विश्वमनन्तमाद्यम्
यन्मे त्वदन्येन न दृष्टपूर्वम् ॥ ४७ ॥

The Blessed Lord said:

47. By Me, gracious to thee, O Arjuna, this Supreme Form has been shown,—by my sovereign power—full of splendour, the All, the Boundless, the Original Form of Mine, never before seen by any other than thyself.

The Lord praises that Form on the ground that 'Thou (Arjuna) shouldst be considered to have attained all thy ends by this vision of My Form.'

न वेदयज्ञाध्ययनैर्न दानै-
र्न च क्रियाभिर्न तपोभिरुग्रैः ।
एवंरूपः शक्य अहं नृलोके
द्रष्टुं त्वदन्येन कुरुप्रवीर ॥ ४८ ॥

48. Not by study of the Vedas and of the sacrifices, nor by gifts, nor by rituals, nor by severe austerities, can I be seen in this Form in the world of man by any other than thyself, O hero of the Kurus.

Though a regular study of the four Vedas includes that of the sacrifices also, the study of the sacrifices is separately mentioned in order to imply that a knowledge of the sacrifices is necessary.* *Rituals*: such as Agnihotra. *Austerity*: such as Chandrayana.†

---

* Some believe that the study of the Vedas consists in learning the texts by rote without understanding the meaning. It is therefore necessary to separately enjoin that the meaning of the Vedas. *i.e.*, of the nature of the sacrifices treated of in them, should also be learnt,—(B.)

† 'It consists in 'diminishing the daily consumption of food by one mouthful every day for the dark half of the month beginning with 15th at the full moon until the quantity is reduced to zero at the new moon and then increasing it in like manner during the fortnight of the moon's increase.'

मा ते व्यथा मा च विमूढभावो
दृष्ट्वा रूपं घोरमीदृङ्ममेदम् ।
व्यपेतभीः प्रीतमनाः पुनस्त्वम्
तदेव मे रूपमिदं प्रपश्य ॥ ४९ ॥

49. Be not afraid nor bewilderd on seeing such a terrible form of Mine as this; free from fear and cheerful at heart, do thou again see this My former form.

Former form: which is so dear to you,—four-armed, wearing a conch, discus and a club.

सञ्जय उवाच—

इत्यर्जुनं वासुदेवस्तथोक्त्वा
स्वकं रूपं दर्शयामास भूयः ।
आश्वासयामास च भीतमेनम्
भूत्वा पुनः सौम्यवपुर्महात्मा ॥ ५० ॥

Sanjaya said:

50. Having thus spoken to Arjuna, Vasudeva again showed His Own form; and the Mighty Being, becoming gentle in form, consoled him who was terrified.

His Own: as born in Vasudeva's family.

अर्जुन उवाच—

दृष्ट्वेदं मानुषं रूपं तव सौम्यं जनार्दन ।
इदानीमस्मि संवृत्तः सचेताः प्रकृतिं गतः ॥ ५१ ॥

Arjuna said.

51. Having seen Thy gentle human form, O Janardana, now I have grown serene, and returned to my nature.

Devotion as the sole means to the realization of the Universal form.

श्रीभगवानुवाच—

सुदुर्दर्शमिदं रूपं दृष्टवानसि यन्मम ।
देवा अप्यस्य रूपस्य नित्यं दर्शनकाङ्क्षिणः ॥ ५२ ॥

The Blessed Lord said:

52. Very hard to see is this Form of Mine which thou hast seen; even the Devas ever long to behold this Form.

Long to behold: though they long to see the form, yet they have not seen It as you have done, nor shall they ever see It.

नाहं वेदैर्न तपसा न दानेन न चेज्यया ।
शक्य एवंविधो द्रष्टुं दृष्टवानसि मां यथा ॥ ५३ ॥

53. Not by Vedas, nor by austerity, nor by gifts, nor by sacrifice, can I be seen in this Form as thou hast seen Me.

How canst Thou be seen?—Listen:

भक्त्या त्वनन्यया शक्य अहमेवंविधोऽर्जुन ।
ज्ञातुं द्रष्टुं च तत्त्वेन प्रवेष्टुं च परन्तप ॥ ५४ ॥

54. But by undistracted devotion can I, of this Form, be known and seen in reality, and entered into, O harasser of thy foes.

Undistracted devotion (Bhakti): that devotion which never seeks any other object except the Lord, and in virtue of which no object other than Vasudeva is cognised by any of the senses. *Of this Form*: of the Universal Form. By this sort of devotion it is possible not only to know Me as declared in the sastras, but also to intuitively realise Me as I am, and to enter into Me, *i.e.*, to obtain liberation.

The essence of the whole teaching of the Gita

Now the essential teaching of the whole Gita-sastra which conduces to Highest Bliss will be summed up here, the teaching being such as every one should follow:

मत्कर्मकृन्मत्परमो मद्भक्तः सङ्गवर्जितः ।
निर्वैरः सर्वभूतेषु यः स मामेति पाण्डव ॥ ५५ ॥

55. He who does works for Me, who looks on Me as the Supreme, who is devoted to Me, who is free from attachment, who is without hatred for any being, he comes to Me, O Pa*nd*ava.

A servant works for his master, but he does not look upon that master as the highest goal for him to reach after death; but My devotee works for Me aud also looks on Me as the Supreme Goal; I am this Supreme Goal. He is devoted to me; he serves Me alone in all manner of ways, with his heart and soul. He is not attached to wealth, to progeny, to friends, to wife, to kinsmen, or to pleasures; for them he has no attachment or love. He cherishes no feeling of enmity for any of the creatures, even though these latter may have done great injury to him. Such a man comes to Me. I am his highest Goal, and he seeks nothing else. This is the teaching I have to offer to thee, O Pa*nd*ava.

इति श्रीमद्भगवद्गीतासूपनिषत्सु ब्रह्मविद्यायां योगशास्त्रे
श्रीकृष्णार्जुनसंवादे विश्वरूपसन्दर्शनयोगो नाम
एकादशोऽध्यायः ॥

TWELETH DISCOURSE.

BHAKTI—YOGA.

Who are superior—the worshippers of Isvara, or the worshippers of Akshara ?

Now Arjuna is supposed to have addressed the Lord thus:—In the discourses beginning with the second and ending with the tenth which treats of Divine Glories, Thou hast taught the worship of the Supreme Self, the Imperishable (Akshara) Brahman, devoid of all upadhis (conditions); and Thou hast also taught here and there worship of Thyself as the Lord of the Universe, associated with the upadhi (condition) of that energy (sattva) which has the power of carrying on all evolutionary process and of knowing everything. And in the (eleventh) Discourse treating of the Universal Form, Thy Primal Form as Isvara manifesting itself as the whole Universe has also been shown by Thee for the same purpose of worship. And having shown that Form, Thou hast exhorted me to do works for Thy sake only (xi. 55), and so on. Wherefore, I ask of Thee with a desire to know which of these two ways is the better.

अर्जुन उवाच—

एवं सततयुक्ता ये भक्तास्त्वां पर्युपासते ।
ये चाप्यक्षरमव्यक्तं तेषां के योगवित्तमाः ? ॥ १ ॥

Arjuna said :

1. Those devotees who, always devout, thus contemplate Thee, and those also who (contemplate) the Imperishable, the Unmanifest,—which of them are better versed in Yoga ?

Thus: referring to what was said in the last preceding verse. 'He who does works for Me' (xi. 55) and so on. *Always devout*: engaged without intermission in doing works for the Lord's sake and in doing other things taught before, steadfast in mind. These devotees, seeking nobody else for their refuge, meditate on Thee in the Universal Form just manifested. There are others who, having abandoned all desires and renounced all actions, meditate on the Imperishable (akshara) Brahman—also described above,—who is unmanifest (avyakta, *i.e.*, incomprehensible to the senses), as devoid of all upadhis or conditions.—That indeed is said to be manifested (vyakta) which is visible to the senses, as the root of the word 'vyakta' implies; but this, the Imperishable (Akshara), is not so.—These others meditate on the Imperishable, the Unmanifested, as defined by other attributes to be enumerated below. Of the two classes, who are better versed in Yoga?

The worshippers of Isvara.

The Lord says: As to the worshippers of the Imperishable (Akshara) who see rightly and have abandoned desires, let them remain; we shall say later on what has to be said regarding them. But as regards the others:

श्रीभगवानुवाच—

मय्यावेश्य मनो ये मां नित्ययुक्ता उपासते ।

श्रद्धया परयोपेतास्ते मे युक्ततमा मताः ॥ २ ॥

The Blessed Lord said:

2. Those who, fixing their thought on Me, contemplate Me, always devout, endued with supreme faith, those in my opinion are the best Yogins.

Those devotees (bhaktas) who fix their mind on Me in the Universal Form, the Supreme Lord, and worship Me as the Governing Lord of all Masters of Yoga, who is omniscient, whose vision is free from the *timira* (purblindness) of attachment and other evil passions,—they who always contemplate Me steadfastly (in the manner described in the closing verse of the preceding discourse), endowed with supreme faith,—these, I think, are the best Yogins. Indeed, they pass their days and nights in incessant thought of Me. Wherefore it is but proper to speak of them as the best Yogins.

The worshippers of Akshara

Are not the others, then, the best Yogins?—Stop; hear thou what I have to say regarding them:

ये त्वक्षरमनिर्देश्यमव्यक्तं पर्युपासते ।
सर्वत्रगमचिन्त्यं च कूटस्थमचलं ध्रुवम् ॥ ३ ॥
संनियम्येन्द्रियग्रामं सर्वत्र समबुद्धयः ।
ते प्राप्नुवन्ति मामेव सर्वभूतहिते रताः ॥ ४ ॥

3—4. Those who ever contemplate the Imperishable, the Indefinable, the Unmanifest, the Omnipresent and the Unthinkable, the Unchangeable, the Immutable, the Eternal,—having restrained all the senses, always equanimous, intent on the welfare of all beings,—they reach Myself.

Because the Imperishable (Akshara) is unmanifest, He is not accessible to words and cannot therefore be defined. He is *unmanifest*, not manifest to any of the organs of knowledge. They contemplate the Imperishable everywhere all round.—Contemplation (Upasana) consists in approaching the object of worship by way of meditating it according to the Teaching (*s*astra) and dwelling for a long time steadily in the current of same thought (continuous) like a thread of descending oil.—The Imperishable who is the object of contemplation is thus qualified: He is omnipresent, pervading all like the aka*s*a. He is unthinkable, because He is unmanifest. Whatever is visible to the senses can be thought of by the mind also; but the Akshara is invisible to the senses and is therefore unthinkable. He is unchangeable (Ku*t*astha)—'Ku*t*a' means a thing which is good to all appearance but evil within. Accordingly it refers here to that seed of sa*m*sara—including avidya (nescience) and other things,—which is full of evil within, designated by various terms such as *Maya*, *Avyakrita* (undifferentiated), as in Sveta*s*vataropanishad (iv. 10) and in the Gita (vii. 14.) 'Ku*t*astha' means He who is seated in Maya as Its Witness, as Its Lord.—Or. 'Ku*t*astha' may mean 'remaining like a heap.' Hence He is immutable and eternal. They who contemplate the Imperishable, curbing all their senses, and always equanimous whether they come by the desirable or the undesirable,—they come to Myself.—It needs indeed no saying that they *come* to Me; for, it has been said that 'the wise man is deemed My very Self' (vii. 18). Neither is it necessary to say that they are the best Yogins,—seeing that they are one with the Lord Himself.

But,

क्लेशोऽधिकतरस्तेषामव्यक्तासक्तचेतसाम् ।
अव्यक्ता हि गतिर्दुःखं देहवद्भिरवाप्यते ॥ ५ ॥

5. Greater is their trouble whose thoughts are set on the Unmanifest; for, the Goal, the Unmanifest, is very hard for the embodied to reach.

Great indeed is the trouble of those who are engaged in

doing works for My sake, and so on; but greater still is the trouble of those who identify themselves with the Imperishable and contemplate the Supreme Reality,—the trouble arising from the necessity of having to abandon their attachment for the body. The Goal, the Imperishable, is very hard for the embodied to reach,—for those who are attached to their bodies. Therefore* their trouble is greater.

Salvation by worship of Isvara.

Later on, we shall describe the conduct in life of the worshippers of the Imperishable (Akshara-Upasakas.)

ये तु सर्वाणि कर्माणि मयि संन्यस्य मत्पराः ।
अनन्येनैव योगेन मां ध्यायन्त उपासते ॥ ६ ॥
तेषामहं समुद्धर्ता मृत्युसंसारसागरात् ।
भवामि न चिरात्पार्थ मय्यावेशितचेतसाम् ॥ ७ ॥

6—7. But those who worship Me, renouncing all actions in Me, regarding Me Supreme, meditating on Me with exclusive devotion (Yoga); for them whose thought is fixed on Me, I become ere long, O son of P*r*itha, the deliverer out of the ocean of the mortal sa*m*sara.

Me: the Isvara, the Lord. *Exclusive*: having no other object of worship except Myself, God in the Universal Form. *Devotion (Yoga)*: samadhi or steadfastness of mind. Those who are engaged in contemplating Me exclusively, I, the Lord, will lift up from the ocean of mortal sa*m*sara, since their thoughts are fixed on Me in the Universal Form.—Sa*m*sara is an ocean, because it is very hard to cross beyond it.

Because it is so, therefore,

---

* Because of the necessity there is for abandoning attachment to the body.

मय्येव मन आधत्स्व मयि बुद्धिं निवेशय ।
निवसिष्यसि मय्येव अत ऊर्ध्वं न संशयः ॥ ८ ॥

8. Fix thy mind in Me exclusively, apply thy reason to Me. Thou shalt no doubt live in Me alone hereafter.

Fix thy mind (manas)—thy purposes and thoughts—in Me, the Lord in the Universal Form. Fix in me thy reason (buddhi) also which resolves and determines.—What will be the result?—Listen: Thou shalt without fail abide in Me as Myself, on the death of this body. Thou shalt not doubt it.

Abhyasa-Yoga.

अथ चित्तं समाधातुं न शक्नोषि मयि स्थिरम् ।
अभ्यासयोगेन ततो मामिच्छाप्तुं धनञ्जय ॥ ९ ॥

9. If thou art unable to fix thy thought steadily on Me, then by yoga of constant practice do thou seek to reach Me, O Dhana*n*jaya.

If you cannot fix your thought on Me steadily in the manner I have mentioned, then seek thou to reach Me in the Universal Form, by yoga of constant practice (abhyasa-yoga). Practice (abhyasa) consists in withdrawing thought from all quarters and fixing it again and again on one particular object 'Abhyasa-yoga' means samadhana or steadfastness of mind acquired by such practice.

Service of the Lord.

अभ्यासेऽप्यसमर्थोऽसि मत्कर्मपरमो भव ।
मदर्थमपि कर्माणि कुर्वन्सिद्धिमवाप्स्यसि ॥ १० ॥

10. (If) thou art not equal to practise either, then be thou intent on (doing) actions for My sake.

Even doing actions for My sake, thou shalt attain perfection.

Even if thou doest mere actions for My sake without practising yoga, thou shalt attain perfection;—thou shalt first attain purity of mind, then yoga or steadfastness, then knowledge, and then perfection (moksha).

Abandonment of the fruits of actions.

अथैतदप्यशक्तोऽसि कर्तुं मद्योगमाश्रितः ।
सर्वकर्मफलत्यागं ततः कुरु यतात्मवान् ॥ ११ ॥

11. If thou art unable to do even this, then refuged in devotion to Me, do thou abandon the fruits of all actions, self controlled.

If thou canst not even be intent on doing actions for My sake as thou hast just been taught, then do thou perform actions renouncing them all in Me, and abandon the fruit of those actions.

Now He extols the abandoning of the fruits of all actions:

श्रेयो हि ज्ञानमभ्यासाज्ज्ञानाद्ध्यानं विशिष्यते ।
ध्यानात्कर्मफलत्यागस्त्यागाच्छान्तिरनन्तरम् ॥ १२ ॥

12. Better indeed is knowledge than practice; than knowledge is meditation more esteemed; than meditation the abandonment of the fruits of actions; on abandonment, peace follows immediately.

Knowledge is better than practice* accompanied with ignorance; † better than that knowledge is meditation (dhyana) with knowledge; better than meditation with knowledge is the abandonment of the fruits of actions, From such an abandonment of the fruits of actions, accompanied with the qualification ‡ mentioned above, cessation of samsara and of the cause thereof follows immediately; it admits of no delay.

Abandonment of the fruit of all actions is taught as a means to Bliss in the case of an ignorant person engaged in action, only when unable to tread the paths taught before, but not at first. Wherefore the act of abandoning the fruit of all actions is merely extolled by the declaration, in this verse, of the superiority of one over another; for it has been taught as the course to be adopted when a man is unable to follow the paths already taught.¶

In what way does it (the declaration) form a mere praise?

In the Kathopanishad (vi. 14) it is said that immortality results from the abandonment of all objects of desire; and this is a truth quite familiar ♆ to all. And all objects of desire are fruits of actions enjoined in the sruti and in the smriti. In the case of the enlightened person who is steadily

---

* *Abhyasa* (practice)—occuring in the text and the commentary—may mean either (1) the act of listening to the teaching of the srutis with a view to obtain knowledge, or, (2) the practice of dhyana with a firm resolve.—(A.)

† Two different readings are found here in the MSS. of the bhashya: (1) *viveka-purvakat*, and (2) *aviveka-purvakat*. The former would mean 'accompanied with discrimination.'

‡ The qualification being 'self-controlled.' (xii. 11).—(A.)

¶ The abandonment of the fruits of actions forms here the subject of praise. because it is the path intended to be taught in this connection —(A.)

♆ As taught in the sruti. (*Vide* Bri. Up 4—4—6)—(A.)

engaged in contemplation, peace immediately follows the abandonment of desires. Now mere abandonment of desires constitutes a factor of even an ignorant man's abandonment of the fruits of actions; and because of this point of similarity, mere abandonment of the fruits of all actions is praised—with a view to create a desire to follow the course—in the same way that, in saying that the ocean was drunk by the brahma*n*a sage Agastya, even the brahma*n*as of this age are praised for the mere reason that they too are brahma*n*as.

Thus, it has been taught that Karma-yoga accompanied with the abandonment of the fruits of actions is a means to Bliss.

The life of the Akshara-upasakas.

Here, it is by presupposing a distinction between Isvara and Atman, the Lord and the Self, that Yoga—which consiste in concentrating thought on the Lord, on the Universal Form,—and the performance of works for the sake of the Lord have been taught. As it is hinted—in the words 'If thou art unable to do this either' (xii. 11)—that Karma-Yoga is associated with ignorance (ajnana), we should understand that the Lord here means to say that Karmayoga is not meant for the worshipper of the Akshara, for him who sees no distinction (between the Lord and the Self). Similarly, the Lord shows the impossibility of the worship of the Akshara to a Karma-yogin. To explain: Having—in the words 'They reach Myself' (xii. 3)—declared that the worshippers of the Akshara are independent as regards the attainment of liberation (kaivalya), the Lord (xii. 7) has shewn—in the words 'for them I become the deliverer' (xii. 7)—that the others are dependent on the Lord, on a external Being. If these were deemed as the very Self of the Lord, they would be the very Akshara themselves owing to their realisation of the identity; so that it would have been inappropriate to speak of them as persons to be delivered by the Lord. Moreover,* the Lord who is preeminently a well-wisher of Arjuna recommends to him only Karma-yoga (iv. 15) based on an idea of distinction and quite dissociated from right knowledge. Nor would any man like to be subordinate to another after knowing himself to be the Lord through proper sources of right knowledge; for, the two are mutually opposed states. Therefore † it is with reference to the worshippers of the Akshara, to the s*am*nyasins who are devoted to right knowledge and have abandoned all desires, that He proceeds to teach those attributes—such as 'absence of hatred of any being'—which form the direct means to immortality.

अद्वेष्टा सर्वभूतानां मैत्रः करुण एव च ।
निर्ममो निरहङ्कारः समदुःखसुखः क्षमी ॥ १३ ॥

सन्तुष्टः सततं योगी यतात्मा दृढनिश्चयः ।
मय्यर्पितमनोबुद्धिर्यो मे भक्तः स मे प्रियः ॥ १४ ॥

13-14. He who hates no single being, who is friendly and compassionate to all, who is free from attachment and egoism, to whom pain and pleasure are equal, who is enduring, ever content and balanced in mind, self-controlled, and possessed of firm conviction, whose thought and reason are directed to Me, he who is (thus) devoted to Me is dear to Me.

---

* This is another reason why Karmayoga cannot be combined with Akshara-Upasana in one and the same person at one and the same time.—(A).

† Because the attributes mentioned below cannot, all of them, be cultivated by the followers of Karma, who are ignorant of the Self—(A).

He hates nothing, not even that which causes him pain. He regards all beings as himself. He is friendly and compassionate. He is full of compsssion for the distressed *i.e.*, he has offered security of life to all beings, he is a sa*m*nyasin. He does not regard anything as 'mine' and is free from egoism, from the notion of 'I'. Pain and pleasure do not cause in him hatred and attachment. He remains unaffected when abused or beaten. He is always content; he thinks he has enough whether he obtains or not the means of bodily sustenance. He is also satisfied whether he comes by a good thing or not. He is a yogin, always steadfast in thought. He has a firm conviction regarding the essential nature of the Self. This sa*m*nyasin has directed to Me exclusively his Manas—purposes and thoughts—as well as his Buddhi—the faculty of determining. Such a devotee is dear to Me. The same truth which was indicated in vii. 17—'I am very dear to the wise man and he is dear to Me'—is here described at length.

यस्मान्नोद्विजते लोको लोकान्नोद्विजते च यः ।
हर्षामर्षभयोद्वेगैर्मुक्तो यः स च मे प्रियः ॥ १५ ॥

15. He by whom the world is not afflicted and who is not afflicted by the world, who is free from joy, envy, fear and sorrow, he is dear to Me.

He: the sa*m*nyasin. *Joy* consists in the elation or exhilaration of the mind (anta*h*-kara*n*a) on attaining an object of desire, and is indicated by horripilation, tears, and so on.

अनपेक्षः शुचिर्दक्ष उदासीनो गतव्यथः ।
सर्वारम्भपरित्यागी यो मद्भक्तः स मे प्रियः ॥ १६ ॥

16. He who is free from wants, who is pure, clever, unconcerned, untroubled, renouncing all

undertakings, he who is (thus) devoted to Me is dear to Me.

He is indifferent to the body, the senses, the sense-objects and their mutual connections. He is possessed of purity both internal and external. He is able to decide rightly on the spot in matters demanding prompt attention. He does not take the side of a friend and the like. He habitually renounces all actions calculated to secure objects of desire, whether of this world or of the next.

Moreover,

यो न हृष्यति न द्वेष्टि न शोचति न काङ्क्षति ।
शुभाशुभपरित्यागी भक्तिमान्यः स मे प्रियः ॥ १७ ॥

17. He who neither rejoices, nor hates, nor grieves, nor desires, renouncing good and evil, he who is full of devotion is dear to Me.

He does not rejoice on attaining what is desirable. He does not fret on attaining what is undesirable. He does not grieve on having to part with a beloved object. He does not desire the unattained.

समः शत्रौ च मित्रे च तथा मानावमानयोः ।
शीतोष्णसुखदुःखेषु समः सङ्गविवर्जितः ॥ १८ ॥

तुल्यनिन्दास्तुतिर्मौनी सन्तुष्टो येनकेनचित् ।
अनिकेतः स्थिरमतिर्भक्तिमान्मे प्रियो नरः ॥ १९ ॥

18-19. He who is the same to foe and friend, and also in honor and dishonor; who is the same in cold and heat, in pleasure and pain; who is free from attachment; to whom censure and praise are equal; who is silent, content with anything, home-less, steady-minded, full of devotion; that man is dear to me.

He has no attachment for objects of any kind. He is content with the bare means of bodily sustenance. It is said (in the Mahabharata):

'Who is clad with anything, who is fed on any food, who lies down anywhere, him the Gods call a brahmana. (*Santi-parva, Moksha-Dhrma*, 245-12)

He has no fixed abode, he is 'houseless' as has been said in another smriti. His thought is fixed steadily on the Supreme Reality.

The enumeration, which was commenced in xii. 13, of the various attributes of the samnyasins—to the worshippers the Akshara who are constantly devoted to the knowledge of the Supreme Reality—is concluded as follows:

ये तु धर्म्यामृतमिदं यथोक्तं पर्युपासते ।
श्रद्दधाना मत्परमा भक्तास्तेऽतीव मे प्रियाः ॥ २० ॥

20. They, verily, who follow this immortal Law described above, endued with faith, looking up to me as the Supreme, and devoted, they are exceedingly dear to Me.

They: the samnyasins. *Immortal*: as leading to immortality. *Above*: in the portion beginning with xii. 13. *Looking up to Me as the Superme*: whose highest unsurpassed goal is Myself, the Imperishable Self. *Devoted*: resorting to the highest devotion, which consists in the knowledge of the Supreme Reality. What was implied in the words 'I am exceedingly dear to the wise man' (vii. 12) has been explained at length and concluded here thus: 'They are exceedingly dear to me.' The meaning of the verse is: Because he who follows the Immortal Law which has been now described becomes exceedingly dear to Vishnu, the Supreme Lord, therefore this Immortal Law should be zealouly followed by every seeker of Liberation, by every one who desires to attain to the Supreme Abode of Vishnu.

इति श्रीमद्भगवद्गीतासूपनिषत्सु ब्रह्मविद्यायां योगशास्त्रे
श्रीकृष्णार्जुनसंवादे भक्तियोगो नाम
द्वादशोऽध्यायः ।

THIRTEENTH DISCOURSE.

MATTER AND SPIRIT

The main subject of the discourse.

In the Seventh Discourse two Prak*r*itis (Natures) of the Supreme Lord were shown,—the one composed of the three gu*n*as and divided eightfold, forming the inferior (apara) Prak*r*iti, because of its being the cause of sa*m*sara or mundane life ; and the other, the superior (para) Prak*r*iti, forming the very life (jiva), the Kshetraj*n*a or 'the Knower of Matter' being essentially one with the Lord Himself. And through these two Prakritis, the Lord becomes the cause of the origin, sustenance and dissolution of the Universe. Now this discourse on Kshetra (Matter) is commenced with a view—by way of describing the two Prak*r*itis of Kshetra and Kshetraj*n*a —to determine the essential nature of their possessor, the Lord (Isvara).

Again, in the last preceding discourse, from verse 13 to the end, the path of the sa*m*nyasins who possess the knowledge of Truth,—*i.e.*, what sort of life they lead,—has been described Now arises the question : Possessed of what so of knowledge of truth do they become dear to the Lord by following the rule of life set forth above ?—The presen discourse is also intended as an answer to this question.

The body and the soul.

That Prak*r*iti which is composed of the three gu*n* transforms itself into all objective forms, such as the bodies (karya), the senses (kara*n*a), and sense-objects (vishaya), and is combined into various aggregates of the body and the senses, to subserve the two ends of Purusha or Spirit, *viz.*, enjoyment and liberation. Such an aggregate is this, our body. In reference to this body, the Lord says :

श्रीभगवानुवाच :—

इदं शरीरं कौन्तेय क्षेत्रमित्यभिधीयते ।
एतद्यो वेत्ति तं प्राहुः क्षेत्रज्ञ इति तद्विदः ॥ १ ॥

The Blessed Lord said :

1. This, the body, O son of Kunti, is called Kshetra ; him who knows it, they who know of them call Kshetraj*n*a.

In the words 'the body' the Lord specifies the thing referred to by the pronoun 'this.' *Kshetra*—the field, the body, matter—is so called because it is shielded from injury, or because it is destructible, or because it is liable to decay, or because the fruits of actions are reaped in it as in a field. This body is designated as 'Kshetra,' 'the field' 'matter.' He who knows this Kshetra, *i.e.*, he who comprehends it in understanding from head to foot, He who perceives it as distinct from himself by knowledge, natural or imparted by others,—him they designate as Kshetraj*n*a, 'the knower of the field,' 'the comprehender of matter,'—they who know of Kshetra and Kshetraj*n*a.

Identity of the soul with the Lord.

Thus Kshetra and Kshetraj*n*a have been described.—Is this all the knowledge that one has to acquire about them ?—No Listen :

क्षेत्रज्ञं चापि मां विद्धि सर्वक्षेत्रेषु भारत ।
क्षेत्रक्षेत्रज्ञयोर्ज्ञानं यत्तज्ज्ञानं मतं मम ॥ २ ॥

2. And do thou also know Me as Kshetrajna in all Kshetras, O Bharata. The knowledge of Kshetra and Khetrajna is deemed by Me as *the* knowledge.

Do thou also know the Kshetrajna, described above, to be Myself, to be the Supreme Lord, not a being of the world (samsara). The meaning is this :—The Kshetrajna who is in all Kshetras, and who is differentiated by the manifold upadhis or Kshetras, from Brahma down to a clump of grass, is, you should understand, really devoid of all the various upadhis (conditions) and is inaccessible to any such word or thought as 'sat' or 'asat,' existent or non-existent. As nothing else remains to be known apart from the true nature of Kshetra, Kshetrajna and the Isvara, that knowledge by which the two objects of knowledge, Kshetra and Kshetrajna, are known is considered by Me—the Lord, Vishnu—to be the right knowledge.

The soul is subject to evil only through ignorance.

(Objection) :—If only one Being, namely, Isvara, exists in all Kshetras, if there exists no being, no other enjoyer, distinct from Him, it would follow either that the Isvara is a samsarin ; or that there is no samsara because there is no samsarin—none else apart from the Isvara. Neither conclusion is acceptable ; for, then, it would follow that the scriptures which treat of bondage and liberation and their respective causes would have no purpose to serve. Moreover, the conclusion is opposed to all evidence, including sensuous perception (pratyaksha). In the first place, pleasure and pain and their causes, which together constitute the samsara, are known to us by immediate perception. And from our perception of variety in the world may also be inferred the

existence of s*am*sara arising from dharma and a-dharma. All this would be inexplicable if the Atman and the I*s*vara, the Self and the Lord, be identical.

(*Answer*):—No; for, that can be explained as due to a distinction between j*n*ana and aj*n*ana, between knowledge and ignorance. It has been said:

"These, what is known as wisdom and what is known as unwisdom, are quite distinct and lead to different goals."—(Ka*t*ha-Up. ii. 4.)

And so also a distinction through effect between vidya and avidya, wisdom and unwisdom, as producing quite opposite results,—the right and the sweet,—is pointed out (in the same Upanishad and in the same context), wisdom leading to the right, while the sweet is the effect of unwisdom. Accordingly, Vyasa says:

'Then there are these two paths, etc.,—(Mokshadharma. 24-6.)

'There are only these two paths,' &c.

Here (in the Gita) also two paths have been spoken of. Now we learn from the *s*ruti, sm*r*iti and reasoning, that unwisdom with its effect should be got rid of. As to the *s*ruti, the following passages may be quoted:

"If in this world a person knows (the Self), then the true end is gained; if a person in this world does not know (the Self), then there will be a great calamity."—(Kena-Upanishad, 2-5.)

'He who knows Him (the Supreme Self) thus becomes immortal here; there is no other way to reach the Goal.'—(Purusha-sukta.)

'The wise man is afraid of nothing'—(Taittiriya-Upanishad 2-4.)

As regards the ignorant person :—

'But to him there is the fear (of samsara).'—(Ibid. 2-7.)

'Those who live in the midst of avidya or ignorance ......go round and with an erring step, deluded as blind people led by the blind!'—(Katha-Upanishad, 2-5).

'He who knows Brahman is Brahman Itself.'—(Mundaka-Up. 3-2-9.)

"Whoever worships another Deity, thinking, 'He is another, another am I,' he does not know; for, he is like a beast for the Gods."—(Brihadaranyaka-Up. 1-4-10).

As to him who knows the Self,

'He becomes all this.'—(*Ibid.* 1-4-10).

"When men can roll up the sky like leather, (then only, not till then) can the end of sorrow be, without men knowing God." (Sveta. Up. 6-20).

And passages from the smriti—the Bhagavad-Gita v. 15, 19, and xiii. 28,—may also be quoted. By reasoning (nyaya) also we come to the same conclusion. It is said:

'Men avoid by knowledge serpents, thorns and wells; by ignorance some fall into them; see how estimable is the effect of knowledge.'—(Mokshadharma, 201-16).

So also* we see that an ignorant man regards the physical body, etc., as the Self, is impelled by attachment and hatred and the like, performs righteous and unrighteous deeds (Dharma and A-dharma), and is born and dead, while those are liberated who, knowing the Self to be distinct from the body and the like, give up attachment and hatred, and no longer engage in righteous or unrighteous deeds to which those passions may lead. This nobody can deny by argument.

* Here follows the nyaya or reasoning above referred to.—(A).

Such * being the case, the Kshetrajna, who is the Isvara Himself, appears to be a sa*m*sarin owing to a distinction in the upadhis set up by avidya, in the same way that the Atman or individual Self appears (by avidya) to be identical with the physical body, etc. It is a well-ascertained truth that that notion of identity of the individual Self with the not-Self,—with the physical body and the like,—which is common to all mortal creatures is caused by avidya, just as a pillar (in darkness) is mistaken (through avidya) for a human being. But thereby no essential quality of the man is actually tranferred to the pillar, nor is any essential quality of the pillar actually transferred to the man. Similarly; consciousness never actually pertains to the body; neither can it be that any attributes of the body—such as pleasure, pain and dulness—actually pertain to Consciousness, to the Self; for, like decay and death, such attributes are ascribed to the Self through avidya.

Kshetra is really unaffected by samsara.

(*Objection*) :—No, the two cases are dissimilar. The pillar and the man are *both objects* of cognition (*i.e.*, external to the Self) and are as such mistaken one for the other by the cogniser through avidya, whereas you say that the body and the Self, which are respectively the cognised and the cogniser, are mistaken one for the other. Thus the illustration differs from what has to be illustrated. Wherefore † the attribute of the body, though an object of cognition, actually pertains to the Self, the cogniser.

---

* Knowledge and ignorance being, as shewn above, distinct in kind and in effect, the Supreme Being and the individual Self must be essentially identical, though, through the upadhis such as Buddhi, the Self appears to be a sa*m*sarin—an illusion set up by avidya.—(A).

† The identifying of the Self with the body being no mere illusion (bhrama).

(*Answer*) :—No; for, then the Self would also become unconscious, etc. If the attributes—such as pleasure, pain, delusion, desire, hatred—of the body, etc., *i.e.*, of Kshetra (Matter) which is an object of cognition, could ever pertain to the Self, the cognizer, then it would be necessary to state a reason for the difference,—*i.e.*, to explain why a few attributes only of Kshetra (an object of cognition) which are ascribed to the Self by avidya actually pertain to the Self, while others such as decay and death do not. On the other hand, we are led to infer that those qualities of Kshetra do not actually pertain to the Self, because, like decay and death, they also are attributed to the Self, by avidya; also because they are objects shunned or sought for, and so on. Such being the case, inasmuch as sa*m*sara which consists in doing and enjoying, and which has its root in the cognized, is only attributed to the cognizer by avidya,—the cognizer is not thereby affected, just as the akasa or ether is not affected by the attributes of dirtiness and concavity which are ascribed to it by children through ignorance.

Thus, it cannot be imagined that the Kshetrajna, the Lord, though existing in all Kshetras, can ever so much as smell of the nature of a sa*m*sarin. Nowhere in our experience have we found anything improved or spoiled by a quality being falsely attributed to it through avidya.

As to the contention that the illustration is not quite analogous, we reply that it is wrong to say so.—Why?—For the intended point of agreement between the illustration and the thing illustrated consists in something being falsely attributed through ignorance. In this respect, both agree. But as to the contention that no false attribution of the qualities of the object to the subject is ever experienced, it has been shewn that even the contention fails in the case of decay and death.

Avidya inheres in the organ, not in the Self.

(*Objection*):—As possessed of avidya, Kshetrajna is a samsarin.

(*Answer*):—No; for avidya is born of Tamas. As partaking of the nature of a veil, avidya—whether causing perception of what is quite the contrary of truth, or causing doubt, or causing nescience or non-perception of a truth—is a Tamasic notion, *i.e.*, a notion born of Tamas; for, on the dawn of the light of discrimination, it disappears; and (for instance) we find the same three modes of avidya—such as non-perception, etc.,—arising also from *timira* (an eye-disease causing dimness of sight), which is Tamasic, as partaking of the nature of a veil.*

(*Objection*):—The avidya is an inherent property (dharma) of the cogniser.

(*Answer*):—No; for, we see that it is the organ of sight that is affected with the disease of *timira*.

(*To explain*):—You (the opponent) say: Avidya is an inherent property of the cogniser. As possessed of this avidya, Kshetrajna is a samsarin. It is therefore unjust to say that Kshetrajna is the Isvara Himself and not a samsarin.

We reply: It is not right to say so; for, we see that such diseases as lead to the perception of what is contrary to truth, and so on, pertain to the eye, to the organ. Neither the perception of what is contrary to truth, nor the cause thereof (*viz.*, the disease of *timira*), pertains to the percipient; for, when *timira* is removed by the treatment of the eye, the percipient is no longer subject to such perception, which is therefore not a property of the percipient. Similarly, non-perception, false perception, and doubt, as well as

* That is to say, the three forms or avidya are due to a certain disorder, and are not therefore attributes of the Self—(A).

their cause, properly pertain to the instrument, to one or another sense-organ, but not to the Kshetrajna, the cogniser. Moreover, they are all objects of cognition and cannot therefore form the properties of the cogniser, any more than the light of a lamp. And because they are cognisable, it follows also that they can be cognised only through some organ which is distinct from the cogniser; and no philosopher admits that, in the state of liberation wherein all the sense-organs are absent, there is any such evil as avidya. If they (false preception, etc.) were essential properties of the Self, the Kshetrajna, as the heat is an essential property of fire, there could be no getting rid of them at any time; and it is impossible for the immutable and formless Self, all-pervadtng like the akasa, to unite or part with any thing whatsoever. Wherefore we conclude that the Kshetrajna is ever identical with Isvara. The Lord also says, "Being beginningless and without qualities."* (xiii. 31).

Scriptural injunctions apply only to the state of bondage.

(*Objection*) :—Then, in the absence of samsara and samsarins, the conclusion is inevitable that the sastra or scripture serves no purpose, and so on.

(*Answer*)—No; for, it is admitted by all. The burden of explaining an objectionable point admitted into their systems by all those philosophers who argue the existence of Atman does not lie on only one of them.—In what way do all classes of philosophers admit into their systems this objectionable point?—All philosophers who admit the existence of a Self agree that liberated Selfs are not conscious of samsara or of the state of being bound to samsara; still, it is not believed that their systems are open to the objection that the sastra serves no purpose. So, according to our view, when

* The Lord teaches here that the Self is devoid of attributes.—(A).

the Kshetrajnas become one with the Lord, then let the sastra serve no purpose. It has, however, a purpose to serve where there is avidya. Just as, with the dualists (dvaitins) of all classes, the sastra has a purpose to serve only in the state of bondage but not in the state of liberation, so with us also.

Bondage and liberation are not real states of the Self.

Objection :—All dualistic philosophers (Dvaitins) hold that states of bondage and liberation are real conditions of the Self, real in the literal sense of the terms. Since thus there really exist something to be avoided and something attained, as also the means thereto, the sastra has some purpose to serve. But in the case of the non-dualists (Advaitins), the dual world is unreal ; and as the bondage of the self is caused by avidya, it is also unreal. Thus the sastra would have no subject to treat of and would therefore serve no purpose.

(Answer) :—No ; for, the Self cannot (really) exist in different states.—If bondage and liberation be states of the Self, they must be either simultaneous or successive. They cannot be simultaneous states of the Self as they are mutually opposed, just as motion and rest cannot be simultaneous states of one and the same thing. If successive, they are either caused or uncaused by another. If uncaused by another, there can be no liberation. If caused by another, they cannot be inherent in the Self and cannot therefore be real. And this is opposed to the hypothesis*. Moreover, if we would determine the order of their occurrence, the state of bondage should come first, without a beginning, but having an end ; and this is opposed to all evidence, Similarly, it has to be admitted that the state of liberation has a beginning and has

* That the states of bondage and liberation are real conditions of the Self.

no end ; which is alike opposed to all evidence. Nor is it possible to maintain the eternality of that which passes from one state to another.

Now, if, in order to avoid the objection of non-eternality, it be held that the states of bondage and liberation do not pertain to the Self, then even the dualists cannot avoid the objection that the *sastra* has no purpose to serve. The dualists and the non-dualists being thus similarly situated, the burden of answering the objection does not lie on the non-dualists alone.

Scriptural injunctions concern the unenlightened.

In point of fact, the objection that the *sastra* would have no purpose to serve cannot be brought against non-dualism ; for, the *sastra* is concerned with the ignorant who view things as they present themselves to their consciousness.—It is, indeed, the ignorant who identify themselves with the cause and the effect, * with the not-Self. But not the wise ; for, these latter do not identify themselves with the cause and the effect, since they know that the Self is distinct from the cause and the effect. Not even the dullest or the most insane person regards water and fire, or light and darkness, as indentical ; how much less a wise man. Wherefore, the injunctions and prohibitions of the *sastra* do not apply to him who knows the Self to be distinct from the cause and the effect. Of course, when a certain person has been commanded to do an action in the words "Do this, O Devadatta," no other person, such as Vishnu-mitra, though standing near and hearing the word of command, thinks that he (Vishnu-mitra) has been so ordered ; he might, however, think so if he did

* The cause is agency and the effect is enjoyment ; or the cause is karma, adrishta, and the effect is the body to which karma has given rise.—(A.)

not understand to whom the injunction has been addressed. So, too, in the case of the cause and the effect here.

(*Objection*) :— Notwithstanding his knowledge that the Self is unconnected with the cause and the effect, it is quite possible for a wise man to regard himself—in reference to the connection (between the Self and the body, etc.,) once set up by avidya (prak*ri*ti)—as still bound by the injunctions of the *s*astra, thinking that he has been enjoined to adopt a certain course of action by which to attain a desirable end, and to avoid a certain other course of action which leads to an evil ; just as a father and his sons * regard every one among themselves as bound by the injunctions and prohibitions addressed to every other, notwithstanding their knowledge that they are all persons distinct from each other.

(*Answer*) :—No ; it is only prior to the knowledge of the Self unconnected with causes and effects that it is possible for one to identify the Self with them ; for, it is only after having duly observed the injunctions and prohibitions of the *s*astra—but not before †—that a person attains to the knowledge that the Self is quite unconnected with causes and effects. Hence the conclusion that the injunctions and prohibitions of the *s*astra concern only the ignorant.

(*Objection*) :—Neither those who know that the Self is independent of the body, etc., nor those who regard the mere body as the Self are, (according to non-dualists), concerned with the injunctions such as "He who desires svarga must sacrifice," "Let none eat *kalanja*" ; thus, there being no person who would observe scriptural injunctions, the *s*astra would have no purpose to serve.

(*Answer*) :—Performance of enjoined acts and abstention from prohibited acts are possible in the case of those who

* *Vide* Briha. Up. 1-5-17.

† *Vide* Vedanta-Sutras III. iv 26-27.

know of the Self only through the Scriptures.—He who knows Brahman and has realised the identity of the Kshetrajna with the Lord does not certainly engage in the Vidic rites. Neither does the person who denies the existence of the Self and of the other world engage in such rites. But, he who derives his idea of the Self only from the scriptural injunctions,—*i.e.*, who believes in the existence of the Self* because the teaching of the *s*astra enjoining certain actions and prohibiting (certain others) would otherwise be inexplicable, but who does not directly know the Self in His essential nature,—cherishes a longing for the results of the Vedic rites and devoutly performs them : a fact which is evident to us all. Wherefore, it cannot be said that the *s*astra would have no purpose to serve.

(*Objection*) :—On seeing the wise not performing Vedic rites, their followers also may not perform them ; and thus the *s*astra would serve no purpose at all.

(*Answer*) :—No ; for very rare is the person who attains wisdom. It is, indeed, only one among many that attains wisdom. As we now see. Nor do the ignorant follow the wise men ; for, attachment and other evil passions necessarily lead to action. We do see people engaging in the practice of Black Magic. † Lastly, action is natural to man, as has been said already, "It is nature that acts." (v. 14).

Therefore, sa*m*sara is only based on avidya and exists only for the ignorant man who sees the world as it appears to him. Neither avidya nor its effect pertains to Kshetraj*na* pure and simple. Nor is illusory knowledge able to affect the

* Knowing nothing more than that the Self exists and survives the body ; this conviction being formed on the basis of the teaching of the Kar*m*a-ka*n*da.

† This fact shews that the ignorant do not always follow the wise men. In spite of protests of wise men, we find some ignorant men resorting to Sorcery or Black Magic.

Real Thing. The water of the mirage, for instance, can by no means render the saline soil miry with moisture. So, too, avidya can do nothing to Kshetrajna. Wherefore it has been said, 'Do thou also know Me as Kshetrajna' (xiii. 2); and 'By unwisdom wisdom is covered' (v. 15).

Learned but deluded.

(Objection):—How is it that the learned (pandits) also feel—"I am so and so*," "this† is mine,"—like the samsarins?

(Answer):—Listen: Their learning consists in regarding the body itself as their Self! ‡

If, on the other hand, they really see the immutable Kshetrajna, they would desire neither pleasure nor action with the attachment 'let it be mine'; for, pleasure and action are but changes of state.

Thus, then, it is the ignorant man who, longing for results, engages in action. The wise man, on the contrary, who sees the immutable Self, cherishes no longing for results and does not therefore engage in action; and when, as a consequence, the activity of the aggregate—of the body and the senses—ceases, we say, only figuratively, that *he* abstains from action.

There is, again, another sort of learning professed by some other (class of panndits), which may be stated as follows—The Lord Himself is Kshetrajna, and Kshetra is quite distinct from Kshetrajna who perceives it; but I am a

---

* Referring to superior birth, etc.

† Referring to wife, children, etc.

‡ That is to say, those who hold this belief are not pandits in the proper sense of the term. We do admit the existence of such a belief; only we regard it as pratibhasika, as due to illusion, while, in point of *absolute* truth, the Self is unaffected by samsara.

samsarin subject to pleasure and pain. To bring about the cessation of samsara I should first acquire a discriminative knowledge of Kshetra and Kshetrajna then attain a direct perception of the Kshetrajna, the Lord, by means of dhyana or meditation of the Lord, and then dwell in the true nature of the Lord.* He who is given to know thus and he who teaches thus †, neither of them is the Kshetrajna.

He who holds this view and hopes to make out that the sastra concerning bondage and liberation has a meaning is the meanest of the learned. He is the slayer of the Self. Ignorant in himself, he confounds others, devoid as he is of the traditional key (sampradaya) to the teaching of the sastras. Ignoring what is directly taught ‡, he suggests what is not taught. Therefore, not being acquainted with the traditional interpretation, he is to be neglected as an ignorant man, though learned in all sastras.

The relation of the Self to samsara is a mere illusion

Now as to the objections that Isvara would be a samsarin if He be one with Kshetrajna, and that if Kshetrajnas be one with the Isvara there can be no samsara because there is no samsarin: these objections have been met by saying that knowledge and ignorance are distinct in kind and in effects, as admitted by all.§—To explain: The Real Entity (*viz.*, Isvara) is not affected by the defect (samsara) attributed to Him through ignorance of that Real Entity. This has

---

* The individual Ego is distinct from the Lord, and should strive to attain to the state of Isvara by means of the knowledge which can be brought about through dhyana.—(D).

† *i.e.*, The pupil and the Teacher—(A.)

‡ In such passages as "That Thou art" "This Self is Brahman,"—(Mandukya—*Up*.)

§ That is to say, by saying that the Lord and the soul are one in reality, while illusion makes Kshetrajna a samsarin—(A).

also been illustrated by the fact that the water of the mirage does not wet the saline soil. And the objection raised on the ground that in the absence of a samsarin there can be no samsara has been answered by explaining thal the samsara and the samsarin are creatures of avidya.

(*Objection*) :—The very fact that Kshetrajna is possessed of avidya makes Him a samsarin; and the effect thereof—happiness and misery and so on—is directly perceived.

(*Answer*) :—No ; for, what is perceived is an attribute of Kshetra (matter); and Kshetrajna, the cogniser, cannot be vitiated by the blemish due to it. To explain: whatever, blemish—not inhering in Kshetrajna—you ascribe to Him, it comes under the cognised, and therefore forms a property of Kshetra, and not a property of Kshetrajna. Nor is Kshetrajna affected by it, since such intimate association of the cogniser and the cognised is impossible. If there should be such an association, then that blemish could not be cognised. That is to say, if misery and nescience were properties of the Self, how could they be objects of immediate perception *? Or, how could they ever be regarded as the properties of the Self? † Since it has been determined that all that is knowable is Kshetra (xiii. 5-6), and that Kshetrajna is the knower and none else (xiii. 1). it is nothing but sheer ignorance which may lead one to contradict it by saying that nescience and misery and the like are the attributes and specific properties of Kshetrajna and that they are immediately perceived as such.

---

* If the Self could perceive His own properties, He could also perceive Himself; which is absurd, since one and the same thing cannot be both the agent and the object of an action.

† Whatever is perceived, as for instance form and colour, cannot be a property of the perceiver.

The perception of the relation of avidya, etc., to the Self is due to illusion.

* Now asks (*the opponent*) :—Whose is this avidya ?

[*To explain* :—This avidya which accounts for the mistaken notion is not an independent entity and should inhere in something else which has an independent existence. But it cannot inhere in Chit or Consciousness which is vidya by nature, and there is no independent entity outside Chit. Hence the question.—(A).]

(*Reply*) :—By whomsoever it is seen.

[*To explain*: Do you ask to know whether avidya inheres as an attribute in something else which is an independent entity, or to know in particular what that entity is wherein it inheres? In the first case, there is no occasion for the question at all, for, if avidya be cognised, then, since it cannot exist by itself, it must be cognised as inhering in something else. If, on the other hand, avidya be not cognised, then how do you know that avidya exists at all ?

The opponent perhaps means to ask what that entity is wherein avidya inheres. Hence the question that follows. (A).]

(*Opponent*) :—By whom is it seen ?

(*Reply*)—As regards this we say: There is no use asking the question. "By whom is avidya seen?" For, if avidya is perceived, you perceive also the one who has that avidya. When its possessor is perceived, it is not proper to ask, "Whose is it?" When the possessor of cows is seen, there is no occasion for the question "whose are the cows?"

* In the following discussion, the opponent tries to drive the Advaitin to the conclusion that the Kshetrajna is tainted with Avidya and cannot therefore be identical with the Isvara, while the Advaitin avoids it by shewing that the Kshetrajna can really have no connection whatever with Avidya which, cognised as it is by Him, is always distinct from him.

[*To explain*: Since avidya is an object of cognition, and since the Self wherein it inheres reveals Himself in one's own consciousness—there is no occasion for the question.—(A)].

(*Opponent*) :—The illustration is not analogous to the case in point. Since the cows and their possessor are objects of immediate perception, their relation is also on object of immediate perception ; and so the question has no meaning. But not so are avidya and its possessor *both* object of immediate perception. If they were, the question ld have been meaningless.

(*Reply*) :—If you know to what particular entity, not immediately perceived, avidya is related, of what avail is it to you ?

[The meaning is :—Though the possessor of avidya is not immediately perceived, still, you know in what entity avidya inheres. Where is then any occasion for your question ?

The opponent does not understand the real drift of the reply and proceeds as follows :—(A)]

(*Opponent*) :—Since avidya is the cause of evil, it is a thing that should be got rid of. [So, I ask to know whose is avidya.—(B)].

(*Reply*) :—He who has avidya will get rid of it, [and it can be no other—(A).]

(*Opponent*) :—Why, it is I who have avidya, and I should try and get rid of it—(A.)].

(*Reply*) :—Then you know avidya and the Self, its possessor, [so that your question has no meaning—(A)].

(*Opponent*) :—I know, but not by immediate perception. [Hence my question—(A)].

(*Reply*) :—Then you know the Self by inference.* How can you perceive the relation between the Self and avidya? It is not indeed possible for you to perceive your Self as related to avidya, at the same moment (that your Self cognises avidya); for, the cogniser (Self) acts at the moment as the percipient of avidya.‡ Neither can there be a (separate) cogniser of the relation between the cogniser (the Self) and avidya, nor a separate cognition of that (relation); for then you would commit the fallacy of *infinite regress* (anavastha). — If the relation between the cogniser (the Self) and the cognised could be congnised, another cogniser should be supposed to exist; then another cogniser of that cogniser; then another of that again; and so on; and thus the series would necessarily be endless. If, on the other hand, avidya —or, for that matter, anything else—is the cognised, then it is ever the cognised only. So also the cogniser is ever the cogniser; he can never become the cognised. Such being the case, † Kshetrajna, the cogniser, is not at all tainted by nescience, misery and the like.

(*Objection*) :—There is in the Self this blemish, *viz.*, that He is the cogniser of Kshetra or matter which is full of blemishes.

(*Answer*) :—No; for, it is only by a figure of speech that the Self, the immutable Consciousness, is spoken of as the

---

* The inference meant here may be stated as follows:—I must be the possessor of avidya, because I feel the effects of avidya such as misery. If I have no avidya, I should not feel its effects; for those who have no avidya, as for instance the liberated souls, do not feel the effects of avidya—(A).

‡ The Self cannot be both the perceiver and the perceived at the same time.—(A).

‡ Because the Self cannot be cognised by anything beyond, there is on proof whatever that avidya inheres in the Self. And the Self reveals himslef in every phase of consciousness.—(A).

cogniser, just as, in virtue of its heat, fire is said, by a figure, to do the act of heating. We have shewn how here, in ii. 19, iii. 27 and v. 15 and other places, the Lord has taught that the Self has in Himself no concern with action or with its accessories or with its results, that they are imputed to the Self by avidya, and that they are therfore said to belong to the Self only by a figure of speech. And we shall also explain how the same truth is taught in the sequel.

(*Objection*): —Well if the Self has in Himself no concern with action or with its accessories or with its results, and if they are ascribed (to the Self) by avidya, then it would follow that the rituals (karmas) are intended only for the ignorant, not for the wise.*

(*Answer*) :—Yes,† it does follow, as we shall explain when commenting on xviii. 11. And in the section (xviii. 50, *et seq.*) where the teaching of the whole *sastra* is summed up, we shall dwell more particularly on this point. No need here to expatiate further on the subject ; so we conclude for the present.

Summary of the Doctrine.

Here follows a verse which forms a summary of the teaching of the Discourse on Kshetra (*i.e.*, thirteenth Discourse), which is already contained in brief in the verses xiii. 1, 2 ; for it is but proper to give beforehand a summary of the whole doctrine to be explained at length in the sequel.

तत्क्षेत्रं यच्च यादृक् च यद्विकारि यतश्च यत् ।
स च यो यत्प्रभावश्च तत्समासेन मे शृणु ॥ ३ ॥

---

* And this is opposed to the *sastra* which often says that one should perform the sacrificial rituals with knowledge,—(A).

‡ The Sastra demands from the ritualist the knowledge of the existence of a Self beyond the body, not also the knowledge that that Self is free from all attributes, such as hunger.

3. And what that Kshetra is, and of what nature, and what its changes; and whence is what; and who He is and what His powers; this hear thou briefly from Me.

"*That Kshetra*" refers to what was spoken of as 'this body' (xiii 1). *What that Kshetra is:* what it is in itself. *Of what nature*: what it is in its properties. *And whence is what*: what effects arise from what causes. *Who He is* etc.: Who He is that was spoken of as Kshetrajna and what His powers (prabhavas, saktis, such as the power of seeing) are which arise from the upadhis or environments (such as the eye). Do thou hear My speech describing briefly the true nature of Kshetra and Kshetrajna in all these specific aspects: and on hearing that speech, thou wilt understand the truth— The (five) and's imply that one should understand Kshetra and Kshetrajna in all these aspects.

The Doctrine extolled.

The Lord now extols what He has proposed to teach,—namely, the doctrine of the true nature ef Kshetra and Kshetrajna,—with a view to interest the mind of the hearer .

ऋषिभिर्बहुधा गीतं छन्दोभिर्विविधैः पृथक् ।
ब्रह्मसूत्रपदैश्चैव हेतुमद्भिर्विनिश्चितैः ॥ ४ ॥

4. Sung by sages, in many ways and distinctly, in various hymns, as also in the suggestive words about Brahman, full of reasoning and decisive.

Sages (Rishis): such as Vasishtha. *Hymns*: such as the Rik. The true nature of Kshetra and Kshetrajna has also been taught in the Brahma-sutras, *i.e.*, in the passages treating of Brahman,—such as "Only as the Self, let a man contemplate Him" (Bri. Up. 1-4-7),—in the words through which alone Brahman is known. They are full of reasoning. They admit of no doubt, *i.e.*, they are productive of certain knowledge.

Matter in all its forms.

To Arjuna who has, by this praise (of the doctrine), been prepared to hear it, the Lord says:

महाभूतान्यहङ्कारो बुद्धिरव्यक्तमेव च ।
इन्द्रियाणि दशैकं च पञ्च चेन्द्रियगोचराः ॥ ५ ॥

5. The Great Elements, Egoism, Reason, as also the Unmanifested, the ten senses and one, and the five objects of the senses ;

The *Great Elements* (Mahabhutas) are so called because they pervade all vikaras, all modifications of matter. The elements here referred to are the subtle ones (sukshma), not the gross (sthula) elements, which latter will be spoken of as "the objects of the senses."

Egoism (Ahamkara): self-consciousness, consciousness of ego, the cause of 'the Great Elements'. *Reason* (Buddhi) is defined by determination and is the cause of Ahamkara. The cause of Reason (Buddhi) is the *Avyakta*, the Unmanifested, the Avyakrita or Undifferentiated, the Energy of the Lord (Isvara-Sakti) spoken of in vii. 14. So much alone is Prakriti, divided eightfold.* *The ten senses* are made up of the five "buddhi-indriyas", senses of knowledge—such as hearing,—so called because they produce knowledge, and of the five "karma-indriyas," senses of action such as speech and hand, so called because they bring about action. *And the one*: the manas, which is composed of thoughts and

---

* The Isvara-Sakti here referred to is the root of the insentient matter, spoken of as Maya in vii. 14, not the root of consciousness (chaitanya) ; *i.e*, the Mulaprakriti in its eight modifications.—(A).

purposes (samkalpa) and so on, is the eleventh sense. *The five objects of the senses* are sound, etc. The Sankhyas speak of these as the twenty-four principles (tattvas).

इच्छा द्वेषः सुखं दुःखं सङ्घातश्चेतना धृतिः ।
एतत्क्षेत्रं समासेन सविकारमुदाहृतम् ॥ ६ ॥

6. Desire, hatred, pleasure, pain, the aggregate, intelligence, courage ;—the Kshetra has been thus briefly described with its modifications.

Now, the Lord proceeds to teach that even those which the Vaiśeshikas speak of as the inherent attributes of Atman (the Self) are merely the attributes of Kshetra (matter), but not the attributes of Kshetrajna (the knower of matter).—*Desire* (ichchha) is that which impels a person who has once experienced a certain object of pleasure to seek—on again perceiving an object of the same class,—to get hold of this latter as conducive to pleasure. This, namely *desire*, is a property of the inner sense (antah-karana); and it is Kshetra (matter) because it is knowable. So also, *hatred* is that which leads a person, who once experienced a certain object of pain, to dislike an object of the same class on perceiving this latter. This, namely *hatred*, is only Kshetra (matter), because it is knowable. *Pleasure* is the agreeable, the tranquil, made up of the Sattva principle. Even this is Kshetra, because it is knowable. *Pain* is the disagreeable; and it is Kshetra because it is knowable. *The aggregate* is the combination of the body and the senses. *Intelligence* is a mental state which manifests itself in the aggregate—just as fire manifests itself in a burning metallic mass,—pervaded by the semblance of the consciousness of the Self. It is Kshetra, because it is knowable. *Courage* is that by which the body and the senses are upheld when they get depressed; and it is Kshetra because it is knowable.—*Desire* and other qualities mentioned here stand for all the qualities of the inner sense (anta*h*-kara*n*a). The Lord concludes the present subject as follows: the Kshetra has been thus briefly described, with its modifications such as Mahat (Buddhi).

Virtues conducive to Self-knowledge.

The Kshetra, of which the various modifications in their totality have been spoken of as "this body" (xiii. 1), has been described in all its different forms, from 'the Great Elements to 'courage' (xiii. 5-6).* The characteristic marks of Kshetrajna will be shortly described. In xiii. 12, the Lord Himself will describe Kshetrajna in detail,—that Kshetrajna through a knowledge of whose powers immortality can be attained. But, now, the Lord prescribes, as means to that knowledge, virtues such as humility, which qualify a person for a knowledge of the Knowable, intent on which a sa*m*nyasin is said to be a jnana-nish*t*ha, a firm devotee in the path of knowledge, and which are designated as knowledge (jnana) because they are the means of attaining knowledge.

अमानित्वमदम्भित्वमहिंसा क्षान्तिरार्जवम् ।
आचार्योपासनं शौचं स्थैर्यमात्मविनिग्रहः ॥ ७ ॥

7. Humility, modesty, innocence, patience, uprightness, service of the teacher, purity, steadfastness, self-control;

Humility: absence of self-esteem. *Modesty*: not proclaiming one's own virtues. *Innocence*: doing no injury to any living being. *Patience*: not being affected: when others have done any injury. *Service of the teacher*: doing acts of service to the preceptor (acharya) who teaches the means

* The cosmic body and the individual bodies (samashtideha and vyash*t*idehas) have been described here with a view to shew that he alone who has grown indifferent (virakta) to them is qualified for knowledge.—

of attaining moksha. *Purity* : washing away the dirt from the body by means of water and earths, the *inner* purity of *mind* consisting in the removal from it of the dirt of attachment and other passions by cultivating the idea * that is inimical to them. *Steadfastness* : concentration of all efforts exclusively in the path of salvation. *Self-control* : control of the self, of the aggregate of the body and the senses. This aggregate is spoken of as the self, because it is of some service to the true Self. † Self-control consists in directing exclusively to the right path the body and the mind which are by nature attracted in all directions.

Moreover,

इन्द्रियार्थेषु वैराग्यमनहङ्कार एव च ।
जन्ममृत्युजराव्याधिदुःखदोषानुदर्शनम् ॥ ८ ॥

8. Absence of attachment for objects of the senses, and also absence of egoism ; perception of evil in birth, death and old age, in sickness and pain ;

Absence of attachment : for sense-objects such as sound, for pleasures seen or unseen. *Perception*, etc. : thinking of what evil there is severally in birth, etc. Thus the evil in *birth* lies in having to dwell in the womb and to issue out through the uterus. Similarly in *death*. The evil of *old age* consists in the decay of intelligence, power and strength, and in being treated with contempt. So also may be seen the evil caused by *sickness* such as head-disease or the evil caused by *pain*, whether adhyatmika, *i.e.*, arising in one's own person, or adhibhautika, *i.e.*, produced by external agents, or adhidaivika, *i.e.*, produced by supernatural beings.

---

* The recognition of evil in all objects of senses.—(A).

† There is another reading of the commentary which means that 'the aggregate' is inimical to the Self and should therefore be restrained.

Or, the passage may be thus interpreted :—Pain itself is evil. Birth, etc., should be regarded as painful, as shewn above. Birth is a misery ; death is a misery ; old age is a misery ; and sickness is a misery. Birth, etc., are all miseries, because they produce misery ; they are not miseries in themselves.

From this perception of the evil of pain in birth, etc., there arises indifference to the pleasures of the body and of the senses ; and then the senses turn towards the Innermost Self to obtain a glimpse of the Self. Because the perception of the evil of pain in birth, etc., conduces to knowledge, it is itself spoken of as knowledge.

असक्तिरनभिष्वङ्गः पुत्रदारगृहादिषु ।
नित्यं च समचित्तत्वमिष्टानिष्टोपपत्तिषु ॥ ९ ॥

9. Unattachment, absence of affection for son, wife, home and the like, and constant equanimity on the attainment of the desirable and the undesirable ;

Unattachment : absence of liking for things which may form objects of attachment. *Affection* is an intense form of attachment and consists in complete identification with another, as in the case of a man who feels happy or miserable when another is happy or miserable and who feels himself alive or dead when another is alive or dead. *The like :* others who are very dear, other dependants. Unattachment and absence of affection are termed knowledge because they lead to knowledge. *Constant equanimity* consists in not being delighted on attaining the desirable, and in not chafing on attaining the undesirable. This equanimity also is (conducive to) knowledge.

मयि चानन्ययोगेन भक्तिरव्यभिचारिणी ।
विविक्तदेशसेवित्वमरतिर्जनसंसदि ॥ १० ॥

10. Unflinching devotion to Me in Yoga of non-separation, resort to solitary places, distaste for the society of men ;

Yoga of non-separation : aprithak-samadhi, a steady unflinching meditation on the One with the idea that there is no Being higher than the Lord, Vasudeva, and that therefore He is our sole Refuge. And this devotion is (conducive to) knowledge. *Solitary places :* which are naturally free, or made free, from impurities, as also from fear of serpents, thieves and tigers : such as a jungle, the sandbank of a river, the temple of a God, and so on. It is in solitude that the mind becomes calm ; so that meditation of the Self and the like is possible only in a solitary place. Wherefore resort to solitude is said to be (conducive to) knowledge. *Society of men* : of the ordinary unenlightened and undisciplined people, not of the enlightened and disciplined men, because the society of these latter is an aid to knowledge. Distaste for the society of ordinary men is knowledge, because it leads to knowledge.

Moreover,

अध्यात्मज्ञाननित्यत्वं तत्त्वज्ञानार्थदर्शनम् ।
एतज्ज्ञानमिति प्रोक्तमज्ञानं यदतोऽन्यथा ॥ ११ ॥

11. Constancy in Self-knowledge, perception of the end of the knowledge of truth. This is declared to be knowledge, and what is opposed to it is ignorance.

Self-knowledge : knowledge of the Self and the like. *Perception*, etc : Knowledge of truth results from the mature development of such attributes as (humility xiii. 7), which are the means of attaining knowledge. The end of this knowledge is moksha, the cessation of mortal existence, of samsara. The end should be kept in view; for, it is only when one perceives the end of the knowledge of truth that one will endeavour to cultivate the attributes which are the means of attaining that knowledge. These attributes—from 'humility' to 'perception of the end of the knowledge of truth'—are declared to be knowledge, because they are conducive to knowledge. What is opposed to this—*viz.*, pride, hypocrisy, cruelty, impatience, insincerity and the like—is ignorance, which should be known and avoided as tending to the perpetuation of samsara.

Brahman the Knowable.

What is it that has to be known by this knowledge?—In answer to this question the Lord proceeds with xiii. 12, etc.

(Objection):—Humility and the like are only forms of self-control (*yama* and *niyama*); by them cannot be perceived the Knowable. Never indeed have we found humility and other attributes (mentioned above) serving to determine the nature of anything. And in all cases, it is only the knowledge or consciousness of an object that has been found to determine the nature of that object of knowledge. And, certainly, no object can be determined through the knowledge of another object, any more than fire can be perceived through the knowledge of a pot.

(Answer):—This objection does not apply here; for, we have said that humility and the like are spoken of as knowledge because they conduce to knowledge, or because they are secondary or auxiliary causes of knowledge.

ज्ञेयं यत्तत्प्रवक्ष्यामि यज्ज्ञात्वाऽमृतमश्नुते ।
अनादिमत्परं ब्रह्म न सत्तन्नासदुच्यते ॥ १२ ॥

12. That which has to be known I shall describe; knowing which one attains the Immortal. Beginningless is the Supreme Brahman. It is not said to be 'sat' or 'asat.'

That which has to be known, I shall fully describe as It is.—The Lord then goes on to describe what the result of that knowledge will be, in order to call the hearer's attention by way of creating in him a desire to know of It. It, the unsurpassed One, the Brahman, just spoken of as 'That which has to be known,' has no beginning.

With a view to avoid tautology * some split the expression '*anadimatparam*' into '*anadi matparam*', and explain it differently; thus: Brahman is beginningless, and I am Its Para-Sakti, the Supreme Energy called Vasudeva.

(But we say)—True, tautology might thus be avoided, provided the given interpretation were possible. But the interpretation does not hold good, for it is intended here to expound the nature of Brahman by denying all specific possessed of a particular kind of energy and at the same time as devoid of all specific attributes. Therefore tautology should be explained as due to the exigencies of the metre.

Brahman is beyond speech and thought.

After saying that He is going to speak of what, as leading to immortality, is worth knowing, and after having thus called the hearer's attention by creating a desire for the knowledge, the Lord says: It is not said to be 'sat (existent)' or 'asat (non-existent).'

---

* Tautology involved in taking "anadimat" as one compound, as the Bhashyakara has done.

(*Objection*) :—After proclaiming very loudly that He is going to speak of the Knowable, it does not become the Lord to describe It as neither 'sat' nor 'asat.'

(*Answer*) :—No ; it is quite the right thing that has been said.—How ?—Thus : being inaccessible to speech, Brahman, the Knowable, is defined in all Upanishads only by a denial of all specialities,—'Not thus' (B*ri* Up. 2-3·6) and 'not gross, not subtle' *Ibid*, 3-8·8)—in the terms "It is not this."

(*Objection*) :—That thing (alone) exists which can be spoken of as existing. If the Knowable cannot be spoken of as existing, then It cannot exist. And it is a contradiction in terms to say that. It is knowable and that It cannot be spoken of as existing.

(*Answer*) :—Neither is It non-existent, since It is not an object of the consciousness of non-existence.

(*Objection*) :—Every state of consciousness involves either the consciousness of existence or that of non-existence. Such being the case, the Knowable should be comprehended either by a state of consciousness accompanied with the consciousness of existence, or by a state of consciousness accompanied with the consciousness of non-existence.

(*Answer*) :—No ; for, being beyond the reach of the senses, It is not an object of consciousness accompained with the idea of either (existence or non-existence). That thing, indeed, which can be perceived by the senses, such as a pot, can be an object of consciousness accompanied with the idea of existence, or an object of consciousness accompanied with the idea of non-existence. Since, on the other hand, the Knowable is beyond the reach of the senses and as such can be known solely through that instrument of knowledge which

* If not, you cannot escape the conclusion that Brahman is undefinable—(A).

is called 'Sabda' (the Word, *i.e.*, Revelation), It cannot be, like a pot, etc., an object of consciousness accompanied with the idea of either (existence or non-existence) and is therefore not said to be ' sat ' or ' asat '.

Now, as regards the allegation that it is a self-contradiction in terms to say that the Knowable is not said to be ' sat ' or ' asat ', (we say that) there is no contradiction ; for, the sruti says.

' It is other than the known and above the unknown '—(Kena Up. 2-3.)

(*Objection*) :—Even the passage of the sruti just quoted is self-contradictory, * just as the sruti is self-contradictory when, after putting up the hall for the sacrifice, it says " (who knows) there exists (any good) in the next world ?" (Taittiriya-Samhita, 6-1-1).

(*Answer*) :—No ; the passage which says that " It is other than the known and above the unknown, " teaches, by itself, something which should be accepted as true, † whereas the passage quoted by the opponent—" who knows if there exist any good in the next world ?"—is a mere artha-vada, a statement which, to be understood in its full import, should be read along with the injunction to which it is subsidiary. ‡

Moreover, it stands to reason to say that Brahman cannot be expressed in words such as ' sat ; ' for. every word employed to denote a thing denotes that thing—when heard

* If so we do not accept the passage as authoritative, since that passage alone is accepted as authoritative which contradicts no accepted authority.—(A).

† That is to say. we should not reject the passage as teaching no new truth. ; for it teaches this new truth, namely, that Brahman is no other than one's own Inner Self, and it should therefore be accepted as authoritative in itself.—(A).

‡ Hence it is no authority in itself—(A).

by another—as associated with a certain *genus*, or a certain *act*, or a certain *quality*, or a certain mode of *relation*. Thus: *cow* and *horse* imply genera, *cook* and *teacher* imply acts, *white* and *black* imply qualities, *wealthy* and *cattle-owner* imply possession. But Brahman belongs to no genus* wherefore It cannot be denoted by such words as 'sat (existent)'. Being devoid of attributes, It possesses no qualities. If It were possessed of qualities, then It could be denoted by a word implying a quality. Being actionless, It cannot be indicated by a word implying an act. The Sruti says:

"It is without parts, actionless and tranquil." (*Svet.* Up. 6-19).

It is not related to anything else; for It is one, It is without a second, It is no object (of any sense), It is the very Self. Wherefore, it is but right to say that It can be denoted by no word at all; and the passages of the sruti like the following point to the same thing:

Whence (*i.e.*, away from Brahman, unable to approach Brahman) all words return,"—(Tait. Up. 2-4-1.)

Brahman is the source of all activity.

When it is said that Brahman the Knowable is not accessible to the word or thought of 'sat' (existent), one may perhaps suppose It to be 'asat' or none-existent. To prevent this supposition the Lord proceeds to declare Its existence as, manifested through the upadhis, through the senses of all living beings.

[*To explain*: Since nothing is found which is devoid of all conditions and quite beyond all speech and thought,—nay, since everything we experience is of a contrary nature,—one may suppose that Brahman as described above must be a

---

* Brahman is described in the sruti as belonging to no class, as possessing no colour, and so on.—(A).

void or non-entity (*sunya*). To prevent this supposition, the Lord proceeds to teach that Brahman exists (1) as the Inner Self (Pratyak), (2) as the source of all activity of the senses and the like, (3) as the source whence arises our consciousness of existence with reference to all duality which is imaginary, (4) as Isvara or the Lord of the universe. First of all, here, the Lord proves, by way of inference, the existence of Brahman as the Inner Self-consciousness: there must be some self-conscious principle (pratyak-chetana) behind insentient principles in activity, such as the physical body; for, we invariably find self-consciousness lying behind all insentient objects in activity, such as a carriage in motion.—(A)]

सर्वतःपाणिपादं तत्सर्वतोऽक्षिशिरोमुखम् ।
सर्वतः श्रुतिमल्लोके सर्वमावृत्य तिष्ठति ॥ १३ ॥

13. With hands and feet everywhere, with eyes and heads and mouths everywhere, with hearing everywhere, That exists enveloping all.

The Knowable has hands and feet everywhere. The existence of Kshetrajna is indicated by the upadhis of the sense-organs* of all living beings. Kshetrajna (the self-conscious principle living behind the sense-organs) is so called because of the upadhi of Kshetra; and this Kshetra is of various forms, such as hands, feet, etc. All the variety caused in Kshetrajna by the variety in the upadhis of Kshetra is but illusory, and it has therefore been said—in the words "It not said to be 'sat' or 'asat'"—that It should be known as devoid of all variety. Though what is caused (in Kshetrajna) by upadhis is illusory, still it is spoken of—in the words that 'It has hands and feet everywhere'—as though it were an attribute of the Knowable, only with a view to indicate Its

* Because there must be self-consciousness at the back of thei ivity.— A).

existence. Accordingly there is the saying of the *sampradaya-vids*—of those who know the right traditional method of teaching—which runs as follows: "That which is devoid of all duality is described by *adhyaropa* and *apavada*," *i.e.*, by superimposition and negation, by attribution and denial. Hands, feet and the like, constituting the limbs of all bodies in all places, derive their activity from the Energy inherent in the Knowable *, and as such they are mere marks of Its existence and are spoken of as belonging to It only by a figure of speech.—All the rest should be similarly interpreted. It (Brahman) exists in the world, in the whole animal creation, pervading all.

Brahman is unconditioned.

The purpose of this verse is to prevent the supposition that the Knowable is (*really*) possessed of the upadhis—the sense-organs such as hands, feet, and the like,—which are merely superimposed (upon It).

सर्वेन्द्रियगुणाभासं सर्वेन्द्रियविवर्जितम् ।
असक्तं सर्वभृच्चैव निर्गुणं गुणभोक्तृ च ॥ १४ ॥

14. Shining by the functions of all the senses, (yet) without the senses; unattached, yet supporting all; devoid of qualities.

All the senses: the buddhi-indriyas and karma-indriyas, the organs of knowledge and the organs of action. The inner senses,—manas and buddhi,—which alike form the upadhis of the Knowable, are included in the term 'all the senses' Moreover, even hearing and other senses form upadhis only through the upadhi of the anta*h*-kara*n*a, the inner sense. Thus, we should understand that Brahman manifests Itself

* *i.e.*, they act in virtue of the mere presence of that Energy.—(A).

through the upadhis of external and internal senses, through the functions of all the senses, *viz.*, determination, purposes and thoughts, hearing, speech and the like. That is to say, the Knowable functions, as it were, through the functions of all the senses. The sruti says :

" It meditates as it were, It moves as it were." (Bri. Up. 4-3-7)

Why should it not mean that It actually functions ?—Says the Lord : It is not possessed of any of the senses. Wherefore, the Knowable does not actually function when the senses are functioning. And as regards the verse,

" Without hands and feet He is swift, He grasps ;
He sees without the eye, He hears without the ear."
(Svet. Up. 3-19).—

there, the sruti implies that the Knowable has the power to accommodate itself to the varying fuctions of all the senses which are Its upadhis, but not that It actually possesses swift motion and such other activities. The verse should be interpreted * like the passsage "The blind one saw the gem. (Taitt. Aranyaka, i. 11). Because It is devoid of the senses therefore It is unattached, devoid of all attachments.

Brahman, the basic Reality in all illusory phenomena.

Though It is so, yet It supports all. Indeed, everything is based on the ' sat,' the Existent ; for everywhere the idea of ' sat ' is present. Not even the mirage and the like exist without a basis. Hence it is said that It supports all.

Brahman, the perceiver of the Gunas

There is this yet another gate to a knowledge of the existence of the Knowable : Though devoid of the gunas,—Sattva, Rajas, and Tamas—yet, the Knowable is the enjoyer

* That is to say, the *arthavada* passage should not be understood in its literal sense ; it must be so interpreted as not to contradict the main subject of the section.—(A).

the perceiver, of the *gunas* which, assuming the forms of sound and other (objects of the senses), transform themselves into pleasure, pain and delusion.

Brahman is all.

Moreover,

बहिरन्तश्च भूतानामचरं चरमेव च ।
सूक्ष्मत्वात्तदविज्ञेयं दूरस्थं चान्तिके च तत् ॥ १५ ॥

15. Without and within (all) beings; the unmoving as also the moving. Because subtle, That is incomprehensible; and near and far away is That,

Without: What lies outside the body which is inclusive of the skin and which is regarded through ignorance as one's own self. And '*within*' refers to the Inner Self, Pratyagatman, lying inside the body.—The statement that It is 'without and within' may imply Its absence in the middle.* To prevent this implication, the Lord says that It is 'the unmoving as also the moving.' It is Brahman, the Knowable, that appears as the bodies, moving and unmoving, just as a rope appears as a snake.

Brahman is comprehended only by the wise.

(*Objection*):—If all things we perceive, the moving and the unmoving, were the Knowable, then how is it that Brahman is not directly comprehended by everybody, as 'This It is'?

(*Answer*):—True, It manifests Itself as everything; but It is subtle † like the *akasa*. Wherefore, on account of Its subtlety, It is incomprehensible to the unenlightened, though

---

* *i.e.*, in the body which intervenes between the Pratyagatman and external objects.

† Beyond the reach of the senses.

knowable in Itself. It is, however, always known to the enlightened, as revealed in the following texts :

'All this is the Self and the Self alone' (Bri. Up. 2-4-6.).
'All this is Brahman and Brahman alone.' (*Ibid.* 2-5-1.)

It is far away when unknown; for It is unattainable by the unenlightened even in millions of years. And to the enlightened It is very near, because It is their own Self.

Brahman is the one Self in all.

Moreover,

अविभक्तं च भूतेषु विभक्तमिव च स्थितम् ।
भूतभर्तृ च तज्ज्ञेयं ग्रसिष्णु प्रभविष्णु च ॥ १६ ॥

16. And undivided, yet remaining divided as it were in beings; supporter of beings, too is That, the Knowable; devouring, yet generating.

It is undivided in the different bodies, It is one like the akasa. Still, it appears to be different in all the different bodies, inasmuch as It manifests Itself only in the bodies.

Brahman is the Cause of the Universe.

The Knowable supports beings during *sthiti*, the period of sustenance of the Universe; and It devours them at *pralaya*, *i.e.*, at the time of dissolution. It generates them at the time of *utpatti*, the origin of the Universe, just as a rope gives rise to an illusory snake.

Brahman is the Illuminator of all.

(*Objection*) :—If the Knowable, though existing everywhere, is not perceived, then It is but darkness (Tamas).

(*Answer*) :—No,—What then ?—

Moreover :

ज्योतिषामपि तज्ज्योतिस्तमसः परमुच्यते ।
ज्ञानं ज्ञेयं ज्ञानगम्यं हृदि सर्वस्य धिष्ठितम् ॥ १७ ॥

17. The Light even of lights, That is said to be beyond darkness. Knowledge, the Knowable, the Goal of knowledge, (It) is implanted in the heart of every one.

That, the Knowable, is the Light even of lights * such as the sun. Indeed these latter shine only when illumined by the light of the consciousness of the Self. The Chants say :

'That Light by which illumined the sun shines'—

(Taitt. Br. 3-12-9.)

'By Its light all this shines'—(*Svet.* Up. 6-14).

So says the smriti also here (in the Bhagavad-Gita xv. 12) It is said to be uncontaminated by Tamas, by ajnana, by nescience.

The Light is in the heart of every one.

Now, with a view to cheer up Arjuna who seemed dejected at the thought of the knowledge (of Brahman) being very difficult of attainment, the Lord says: Knowledge, such as humility (xiii, 7-11); the Knowable, as described in xiii. 12-17; and the same thing, *viz.*, the Knowable, which, when known, forms the fruit of knowledge and is therefore said to be the *Goal of knowledge*, and which as a thing to be known forms the Knowable: these three (Knowledge, the Knowable, and the Goal of knowledge) are implanted pre-eminently in the heart (buddhi) of every living being; it is indeed there that the three are distinctly manifested.

---

* The existence of Brahman, the Knowable, can be recognised as the Light illumining the sun, etc.' and reason (buddhi), etc.—(A).

Seek the Light through devotion.

Here follows the verse which concludes the the subject treated of:

इति क्षेत्रं तथा ज्ञानं ज्ञेयं चोक्तं समासतः ।
मद्भक्त एतद्विज्ञाय मद्भावायोपपद्यते ॥ १८ ॥

18. Thus the Kshetra, as well as knowledge and the Knowable, have been briefly set forth. My devotee, on knowing this, is fitted for My state.

Thus the *Kshetra*, described above (xiii. 5-6), beginning with the 'Great elements' and ending with 'firmness;' *knowledge*, comprising the attributes which have been enumerated, beginning with 'humility' and ending with 'perception of the end of the knowledge of truth' (xiii. 7-11); and the Knowable, described in xiii. 12-17;—these have been set forth in brief.

Such, indeed, is the whole doctrine, the doctrine of the Vedas and the doctrine of the Gita, taught in brief.

(*Question*):—Who is fit to attain this right knowledge?

(*Answer*):—He who is devoted to Me, who regards Me—Vasudeva, the Supreme Lord, the Omniscient, the Supreme Guru—as the Self (Soul, Essence) of everything, *i.e.*, he who is possessed (as it were) with the idea that all that he sees or hears or touches is nothing but the Lord, Vasudeva. Thus devoted to Me, and having attained the right knowledge described above, he is fit to attain to My state, *i.e.*, he attains moksha.

Prakriti and Purusha are eternal.

In the seventh discourse were described two Prakritis, the superior and the inferior, corresponding to Kshetra and

Kshetrajna; and it was said that they are the womb of all creatures (vii. 6).—It may now be asked, how can it be said that the two Prakritis, Kshetra and Kshetrajna, are the womb of all beings?—This question will now be answered:

प्रकृतिं पुरुषं चैव विध्यनादी उभावपि ।
विकारांश्च गुणांश्चैव विद्धि प्रकृतिसम्भवान् ॥ १९ ॥

19. Know thou that Prakriti as well as Purusha are both beginningless; and know thou also that all forms and qualities are born of Prakriti.

Prakriti and Purusha, Matter and Spirit, are the two Prakritis of the Isvara, the Lord. These two, Prakriti and Purusha—you should know—have no beginning. As the Isvara is the eternal Lord, it is but right that His Prakritis also should be eternal. The Lordship of the Isvara consists indeed in His possession of the two Prakritis by which He causes the origin, preservation and dissolution of the universe. The two Prakritis are beginningless, and they are therefore the cause of samsara.

Some construe the passage so as to mean that the two Prakritis are not primeval. It is by such an interpretation, they hold, that the causality of the Isvara can be established. If, on the other hand, Prakriti and Purusha were eternal, it would follow that they are the cause of the universe, and that the Isvara is not the creator of the universe.

It is wrong to say so; for the Isvara would then be no Isvara, inasmuch as there would be nothing for Him to rule over prior to the birth of Prakriti and Purusha. Moreover, if samsara had no cause (other than Isvara), there could be no cessation * thereof; and thus the sastra (the scripture) would have not purpose to serve. Likewise, there could be neither bondage nor salvation.†

Prakriti and Purusha as the Cause of samsara.

If, on the other hand, the Prakritis of the Isvara be eternal, all this can be explained.—How?—Know thou that all forms, all emanations (vikaras) from buddhi down to the physical body, and all qualities (gunas) such as those which manifest themselves as pleasure, pain, delusion and other mental states to be described hereafter, spring from Prakriti, Maya, composed of the three gunas, that Energy of the Isvara which constitutes the cause of (all) emanations. Know thou that they are all modifications of Prakriti.‡

What then are these forms and qualities which are said to be born of Prakriti?—Says the Lord:

कार्यकारणकर्तृत्वे हेतुः प्रकृतिरुच्यते ।
पुरुषः सुखदुःखानां भोक्तृत्वे हेतुरुच्यते ॥ २० ॥

20. As the producer of the effect and the instruments §, Prakriti is said to be the cause; as

* If the Isvara were the sole cause of the universe, quite independently of the two Prakritis, the samsara would be endless, inasmuch as there is nothing to prevent even the emancipated souls from being hurled into samsara, so long as there is *Isvara*, as the sole cause of samsara.—(A).

† Before the birth of the two Prakritis, there could be no bondage and consequently no moksha. If at any time there were neither bondage nor moksha, there could bo no cause which would ever bring them into existence.—(A).

‡ Prakriti is that out of which all forms and qualities come into existence. Since Prakriti is thus eternal and is the source of all forms (vikaras) and qualities (gunas). Atman remains ever changeless and without qualities.—(A).

§ Or, (according to another interpretation), the effect and the cause.

experiencing pleasure and pain, Purusha is said to be the cause.

The effect (karya) is the physical body, and the instruments (kara*n*as) are the thirteen * located in the body. The five elements (bhutas) which buildup the body, and the five sense-objects which are the emanations of Prak*r*iti as mentioned above, are included under the term 'effect;' and all qualities, such as pleasure, pain and delusion, which are born of Prak*r*iti, are included under the term 'instruments,' since those qualities are seated in the instruments, the senses. In the production of the physical body, of the senses and their sensations, Prak*r*iti is said to be the cause, for, it generates them all. Thus, as producing the physical body and the senses, Prak*r*iti is the cause of sa*m*sara.

In the place of 'kara*n*a' which means instrument, some read 'kâra*n*a' which means cause.—Whatever is a modification of another is the effect or emanation (vikara) of that other; and that from which it emanates is the cause (kâra*n*a) Prak*r*iti is the source of the cause and the effect, which comprise the same things (that were denoted by the terms 'the effect and the instruments'). Or, it may be that the sixteen *vikaras*† or emanations are here spoken of as the effect; and the seven ‡ which are at once Prak*r*iti and vik*r*iti, cause and effect, and which are therefore called Prak*r*iti-Vik*r*ritis, are spoken of as the cause. In the production of these, the cause is Prak*r*iti, as generating them all.

---

* Five organs of sensation, five of activity, Manas, Buddhi, and Aha*m*kara.

† The ten sense-organs, Manas and the five sense-objects.—(A).

‡ *viz*, Mahat, Aha*m*kara, and the five Tanmatras or rudimental elements. Each of these is an emanation from its predecessor and is in turn the cause, of its successor. As producing all these, the Mulaprakriti is their cause, their basis.—(A).

And now will be shown how Purusha is the cause of samsara. '*Purusha.*' '*Jiva,*' '*Kshetrajna,*' '*Bhoaktri* (Enjoyer)' * are all synonymous terms. Purusha is said to be the cause, as perceiving pleasure, pain, and other objects of experience.

(*Objection*) :—Why should Prakriti and Purusha be regarded as the cause of samsara by way of generating causes and effects and experiencing pleasure and pain?

(*Answer*) :—How could there be samsara at all without Prakriti transforming itself as causes and effects, as the body and the senses, as pleasure and pain, and without the conscious Purusha experiencing them? † When, on the other hand there is a conjunction—in the form of avidya or nescience—of Purusha, the experiencer, with Prakriti, the opposite, the object of experience, in all its transformations as the body and the senses, as pleasure and pain, as causes and effects, then only is samsara possible. Wherefore it is but right to say that Prakrriti and Purusha are the case of samsara; the one generating the body and the senses, the other experiencing pleasures and pains.

(*Objection*) :—What, then, is this samsara? ‡

(*Answer*) :—Samsara is the experience of pleasure and pain; and Purusha is the samsarin, as the experiencer of pleasure and pain.§

---

* The three last terms are respectively intended to show that Purusha here referred to is not the Paramatman or the Highest Self, is an intelligent (chetana) principle, is a conditioned being.—(A)

† For, the Atman who is ever free (nitya-mukta) from samsara, cannot of Himself be subject to samsara.—(A).

‡ The objector means: If Atman be immutable (avikriya), not subject to changes of state, then it is not proper to say that He is ever subject to samsara.—(A).

§ That is to say: while experiencing pleasure or pain, the Self, the experiencer remains quite unchanged. It is this experience (bhoga) which constitutes His samsara, and which makes Him a samsarin,—(A).

Avidya and Kama are the cause of rebirths.

It has been said that Purusha is the sa*m*sarin as experiencing pleasure and pain. What is the (experiencing of pleasure and pain) due to ?—The Lord says :

पुरुषः प्रकृतिस्थो हि भुङ्क्ते प्रकृतिजान्गुणान् ।
कारणं गुणसङ्गोऽस्य सदसद्योनिजन्मसु ॥ २१ ॥

21. Purusha, when seated in Prak*r*iti, experiences the qualities born of Prak*r*iti. Attachment to the qualities is the cause of his birth in good and evil wombs.

Because Purusha, the experiencer, is seated in Prak*r*irti, in avidya or nescience,—that is to say, because he identifies himself with the body and the senses which are emanations of Prak*r*iti,—he experiences the qualities born of Prak*r*iti, manifesting themselves as pleasure, pain and delusion ; he thinks, " I am happy, I am miserable, I am deluded, I am wise." Over and above avidya (the cause of birth), His attachment to (*i.e.*, identification of Himself with) what He experiences,—namely, the qualities of pleasure, pain and delusion,—forms the main cause of Purusha's birth. The sruti says :

" As is his desire, so is his will." (*Bri.Up.* 4-4-5.)

Accordingly the Lord says here :—The experiencer's attachment for qualities leads him to births in good and evil wombs.

Or the second half of the verse may be construed, by supplying the word 'sa*m*sara,' so as to mean : Attachment for qualities is the cause of His sa*m*sara through births in good and evil wombs.

Good wombs are those of Devas and the like ; evil wombs are those of lower animals. We may also add, as implied here—being opposed to no teaching,—the wombs of men which are (partly) good and (partly) evil.

The sense of the passage may be explained as follows: Avidya,—spoken of as (Purusha's) being 'seated in Prakriti,'—and Kama or attachment for qualities, together constitute the cause of Samsara.*

Self-Knowledge removes the cause of Samsara.

The twofold cause has been taught here for avoidance, (*i.e.*, in order that we may try to remove it). The means of bringing about the removal of the (twofold) cause are Jnana and Vairagya, *i.e.*, knowledge and indifference conjoined with samnyasa or renunciation † as has been clearly taught in the Gita-sastra. This knowledge, the knowledge of Kshetra and Kshetrajna, has been imparted in the beginning of this discourse. And it has also been imparted in xiii. 12, *et. seq.*, both by eliminating foreign elements (xiii. 12) and by attributing alien properties (xiii. 13, *et. seq.*)

Now again the Lord proceeds to teach directly what that knowledge is:

उपद्रष्टाऽनुमन्ता च भर्ता भोक्ता महेश्वरः ।
परमात्मेति चाप्युक्तो देहेऽस्मिन्पुरुषः परः ॥ २२ ॥

22. Spectator and Permitter, Supporter, Enjoyer, the Great Lord, and also spoken of as the Supreme Self, (is) the Purusha Supreme in this body.

Spectator (Upadrashtri): a bystander and a witness, Himself not acting. When priests and the sacrificer are engaged in a sacrificial act, there is another, an expert in sacrificial matters, sitting by their side, not taking part in the

*Avidya being the *upadana* or material cause and kama the *nimitta* or efficient cause.—A.

† Vairagya leads to samnyasa; and knowledge coupled with samnyasa brings about the cessation of avidya and kama.—A.

act, and discerning what is good and what is bad in the acts of the sacrificer and of the priests; just so, not taking part in the activities of the body and the senses, the Self is distinct from them, a near witness of the body and the senses and all their acts.—Or, it may be also explained thus: The body, the sense of sight, Manas, Buddhi, and the Self are the seers. Of these, the body is the most external seer; and viewed from the body inwards, the Self is the innermost and nearest seer, and beyond Him there is no seer in the interior. Thus, being the nearest seer, He is spoken of as 'Upadrash*tri*.' Or, the Self is Upadrash*tri* because, like the Upadrash*tri* in the sacrificial rite, He watches all. He is also the Permitter (Anuman*tri*,) expressing approbation or satisfaction concerning the acts of those who are engaged in action.—Or, though Himself not engaged in action while the body and senses are active, He seems to be active in co-operation with them.—Or, being their mere witness, He never stands in the way of those that are engaged in their respective activities. *Supporter* (Bhart*ri*): The Self is called the Supporter, because the body, the senses, Manas and Buddhi—which aggregate together to serve the purposes of some one else, *viz.*, the Intelligent Self, and which are, or which convey, mere reflections of the Intelligence—are what they are, only as made by that Intelligent Self. *Enjoyer* (Bhokt*ri*): The Self is the enjoyer because by the Self who is 'nitya-chaitanya-svarupa', *i.e.*, whose inherent nature is eternal intelligence, just as heat is the inherent nature of fire, are clearly perceived, in their mutual relations, all states of mind (buddhe*h*-pratyaya*h*), constituted of pleasure, pain and delusion, which, as they come into being, are permeated as it were by the intelligent Self. *The Great Lord*: As one with the whole universe and independent of all, He is the Great One as well as the Lord.

The Supreme Self (Paramatman): the Self who has been defined as the Spectator, etc., is Supreme, because He is superior to all those things—from the physical body up to the Avyakta—which are through ignorance mistaken for the Inner Self. Whence He is spoken of as 'Paramatman' in the *sruti* also,—Where is He?—Purusha, who transcends the Avyakta, as will be described hereafter in xv. 17, is here in this body.

The Self treated of in xiii. 2 has been described at length, and the subject has been concluded. As to him who knows the Self thus described:

य एवं वेत्ति पुरुषं प्रकृतिं च गुणैः सह ।
सर्वथा वर्तमानोऽपि न स भूयोऽभिजायते ॥ २३ ॥

23. He who thus knows Purusha and Prak*r*iti together with qualities, whatever his conduct, he is not born again.

He who knows Purusha in the manner mentioned above,* *i.e.*, he who directly perceives Him as his very Self, 'This I am,' he who knows Prak*r*iti or Avidya described above † with all its modifications, *i.e.*, he who knows the Prak*r*iti as resolved into nothing (abhava) by vidya or knowledge,—whatever life he may lead, (*i.e.*, whether he is engaged in the prescribed duties or forbidden acts), he is not born again; that is, he will not have to put on another body on the death of this, *i.e*, at the end of the birth in which he has attained wisdom. How much more so the wise man who stands firm in the path of duty!

(*Objection*):—What acts are neutralised by knowledge?—Absence of rebirth subsequent to the attainment of knowledge

---

* As the basic Reality underlying all manifestations such as Jiva, *Isvara*, and so on.—A.

† As beginningless, as indefinable (anirvachya), as the source of all evil.—A.

has indeed been taught here. But, inasmuch as it is not right (to suppose) the annihilation, before producing their respective effects, of those acts which were done (in the present birth) before the attainment of knowledge or of those acts which may be done thereafter, or of those which had been done in the many past birhs, there should be at least three (more) births; for it is not right to suppose the annihilation of these acts any more than to suppose the annihilation of the deeds whose fruits are being reaped in the present birth. And we see no distinction between (those two groups of) acts*. Accordingly, the three classes of acts will give rise to a single birth. Otherwise, the possibility of annihilation of what has been done would lead to uncertainty everywhere, and the sastra (all scriptural injunctions) would become useless. Wherefore it is not right to say that 'he is not born again.'

(*Answer*) :—No, (it is right), as the following passages of the sruti show:

'His deeds perish.'—(Mund. Up. 2-2-8.)

'He who knows Brahman, becomes Brahman Itself.'—(*Ibid.*, 3-2-9).

'For him there is only delay so long as he is not delivered from the present body).—(Chhand. Up. 6-14-2).

'As the soft fibres of the ishika reed are burnt in the fire, so all his actions are burnt.'—(*Ibid.*, 5-24-3).

Consumption of all acts has been taught here also in iv. 37

---

* As all acts alike result from ajnana, they must all alike be neutralised by knowledge, so that there is no force in the possible argument that the acts which can be neutralised by knowledge are those which have not yet begun their effects, not those which have already begun their effects by way of generating the present body.—A.

and will be taught also hereafter.* And this also stands to reason; for, only those acts which spring from avidya (nescience), from desire (kama) and such other affections, which are the seeds † of all evil, can cause future births; and it has also been stated by the Lord here and there in the Gita that those actions which are accompanied with egotism and desire—but not other action—are productive of results. It is also said elsewhere,

"As the fire-burnt seeds do not sprout again, so the body cannot be formed again, by wisdom-burnt affections."

(*Objection*):—Granted that knowledge consumes acts done subsequently to the attainment of knowledge, inasmuch as they are accompanied with knowledge; but it is not possible to explain how it can consume acts done in this life before the attainment of knowledge, and those done in the several past births.

(*Answer*):—Do not say so, because of the qualification 'all acts' (iv. 37)

(*Objection*):—It may mean all those acts only which are done subsequently to the attainment of knowledge.

(*Answer*):—No, for, there is no reason for the limitation.

Now as regards the contention that just as the actions which have begun their effects by way of bringing about the

---

* In xviii. 66. the Lord teaches Arjuna to abandon all-Dharmas, thus showing that knowledge consumes all actions—A.

† These seeds of evil, termed klesas are avidya, asmita, raga, dvesha, and abhinivesa. Only those acts of dharma and adharma which are occasioned by these klesas can bring about incarnate existence. But as to the acts of a wise man, their seeds have been fried in knowledge: those acts are said to exist only in so far as they present themselves to his consciousness, pratitimatradehah. Being karmabhasas, mere semblances of karma, they are not effective causes and cannot bring about births; a burnt cloth, for instance, cannot serve the purposes of a cloth, —A.

present birth do not perish in spite of knowledge, so also even those acts which have not yet begun to produce their effects cannot perish, (we say) it is wrong.—How?—For, the former have, like an arrow discharged, begun their effects. Just as an arrow once discharged from a bow at an aim does not, even after piercing through the aim, cease to act till it drops down on the exhaustion of the whole force with which it was propelled,* so also, though the purpose of the bodily existence has been gained, the effects of actions which have produced the body continue as before till the exhaustion of their inherent energy. (On the other hand), just as the same arrow when not yet propelled with the energy which is the cause of its activity, *i.e.*, when not discharged, can be withdrawn, though already fixed in the bow, so also, the acts which have not yet begun their effects, which only abide in their own seat,† can be neutralised by the knowledge of truth. Thus it is but right to say that when the body of a wise man perishes 'he is not born again'

The four paths to Self-knowledge.

Now, there are several paths to Self-knowledge, and they are mentioned here as follows:

ध्यानेनात्मनि पश्यन्ति केचिदात्मानमात्मना ।
अन्ये साङ्ख्येन योगेन कर्मयोगेन चापरे ॥ २४ ॥

---

* *i.e.*, provided its action is not checked by some overpowering obstacle in the way. And Self-knowledge is no such obstacle in the way of the karma which has brought about the present birth; for, even while that knowledge arises, it arises with its power checked by that karma, as the latter has already begun to operate. Accordingly, the effects of the prarabdha-karma should be worked out in full.—A.

† Svasraya, sabhasa-antah-karana, *i.e.*, the inner sense or Manas containing the reflection of Spiritual Intelligence.—A.

24. By meditation some behold the Self in the self by the self others by Sankhya Yoga, and others by Karma-Yoga.

Meditation (Dhyana) consists in withdrawing by concentration hearing and other senses into the Manas away from sound and other sense-objects, then withdrawing Manas into the Inner Intelligence, and then contemplating (that inner Intelligence). Hence the comparison, "the crane meditates as it were; the earth meditates as it were......the mountains meditate as it were" (Chha, Up. 7-6-1). Dhyana is a continuous and unbroken thought like a line of flowing oil. By meditation the Yogins behold* the Self, the Inner Intelligence, in the self (Buddhi) by the self, by their own intelligence, *i.e.*, by the anta*h*-kara*n*a refined by Dhyana.—*Sankhya* consists in thinking thus: 'these, Sattva, Rajas and Tamas, are Gu*n*as,' Atman is the witness of their acts, eternal, and distinct from the Gu*n*as.' By Sankhya Yoga † some‡ behold the Self in the self by the self.—Karma is Yoga §, *i.e.*, that Karma or action which is performed in the service of the Lord (I*s*vara). Such a course of *action* is *Yoga*—only by a figure of speech—inasmuch as it *leads* to Yoga. Some ¶ behold the Self by this Yoga of action, which, causing purity of the mind (sattva), gives rise to knowledge.

---

* These Yogins, who are of the highest class of aspirants (uttam*a*dhik*a*rins) behold the Self, by meditation, to be identical with the Param*a*tman.—A.

† S*a*nkhya is knowledge got through intellectual investigation (vichara). As leading to Yoga, it is spoken of as Yoga itself.—A,

‡ These are the aspirants of the middling class (madhyam*a*dhik*a*rins) —A.

§ As causing purity of mind, Karma leads to Yoga, to the concentration of mind.—A.

¶ These are the lowest class of aspirants.—A.

अन्ये त्वेवमजानन्तः श्रुत्वाऽन्येभ्य उपासते ।
तेऽपि चातितरन्त्येव मृत्युं श्रुतिपरायणाः ॥ २५ ॥

25. Yet others, not knowing thus, worship, having heard from others; they, too, cross beyond death, adhering to what they heard.

But there are yet others, who, not able to know the Self described above by any one of the several methods already pointed out, learn from others, from acharyas or teachers who tell them "Do thou thus meditate upon this"; they then engage in worship, *i.e.*, they contemplate the idea in full faith. Even they cross beyond death, *i.e.*, beyond sa*m*sara which is associated with death—even they whose best equipment when commencing to tread the path of moksha consists in what they have heard, *i.e.*, who solely depend upon the authority of other's instructions and are themselves ignorant. How much more so, then, those who can independently appreciate evidence and discriminate.

Nothing exists outside the Self.

The knowledge of the identity of Kshetrajna with the Isvara—of the individual soul with the Lord—as taught in xiii. 2 has been spoken of in xiii. 12 as the means to moksha.—For what reason is it so?—The Lord proceeds to explain the reason.

For,

यावत्सञ्जायते किञ्चित्सत्त्वं स्थावरजङ्गमम् ।
क्षेत्रक्षेत्रज्ञसंयोगात्तद्विद्धि भरतर्षभ ॥ २६ ॥

26. Whatever being is born, the unmoving or the moving, know thou, O best of the Bharatas,

that to be owing to the union of Kshetra and Kshetrajna.*

(*Objection*) :—Of what sort is this union of Kshetra and Kshetrajna meant to be? The union of Kshetrajna with Kshetra cannot certainly be a relation through contact (sa*m*yoga) of each other's parts, as between a rope and a vessel, inasmuch as Kshetrajna is, like the akasa, without parts. Nor can it be of the nature of samavaya or inseparable inherence, inasmuch as it cannot be admitted that Kshetra and Kshetrajna are related to each other as cause and effect.

(*Answer*) :—The union between Kshetra and Kshetrajna, between the object and the subject, which are opposed to each other in nature, is of the nature of mutual adhyasa; *i. e.*, it consists in confounding them as well as their attributes with each other owing to the absence of a discrimination between the nature of Khetra and that of Kshetrajna, like the union of a rope and a mother-of-pearl respectively with a snake and silver when they are mistaken the one for the other owing to the absence of discrimination. The union of Kshetra and Kshetrajna which is of the nature of adhyasa—which consists in confounding the one with the other—is a sort of illusion (mithyajnana); and this illusion vanishes—because of its opposition to the right knowledge —when a man attains to a knowledge of the distinction between Kshetra and Kshetrajna as defined in the sastra, when he is able to separate Kshetrajna from Kshetra like the ishika reed from the munja-grass and to realise that Brahman, the Knowable, which is devoid of all upadhis as

* Everything is born of the union of Kshetra and Kshetraj*n*a; there exists no being whatever apart from Kshetrej*n*a who is one with the Paramatman; therefore knowledge of that unity alone can lead to moksha.—A.

described in the words "It is not said to be existent or non-existent" (xiii. 12) is his own Self, when he is convinced that, like the elephants and palaces projected by a juggler's art, or like a thing seen in a dream, or like a gandharva-nagara (an imaginary city in the sky). Kshetra is non-existent and only *appears* to be existent. As the cause of birth has vanished in the case of such a man, it stands to reason that the wise man is not born again (xiii. 23).

The one Self in all.

It has been said (xiii. 23) that the effect of right knowledge is the cessation of births through the removal of avidya (nescience) and the like* which form the seed of sa*m*sara. It has also been said that the cause of birth is the union of Kshetra and Kshetrajna caused by avidya. Therefore, the right knowledge which alone can remove avidya, though already described, will again be described in other words as follows:

समं सर्वेषु भूतेषु तिष्ठन्तं परमेश्वरम् ।
विनश्यत्स्वविनश्यन्तं यः पश्यति स पश्यति ॥ २७ ॥

27. He sees who sees the Supreme Lord, remaining the same in all beings, the undying in the dying.

The Supreme Lord exists, without any difference, in all living beings, from Brahma down to the unmoving object (sthavara). He is the Lord Supreme as compared with the body, senses, Manas, Buddhi, the Avyakta (the unmanifested, *i.e.*, the causal body, the kâra*n*a-*s*arira, avidya) and the individual soul (Atman, Jiva). All living beings are perishable while the Supereme Lord is imperishable. Thus there is a great disparity between the Supreme Lord and the created

* *i. e.*, effects (sa*m*skara) of avidya—A.

beings. For, of all changing states of a being (bhava-vikaras), the change of state called birth is the root; all the other changes ending with destruction occur subsequently to birth. There can be no change of state subsequent to destruction, since the object itself does not exist. Attributes can exist only when the substance exists. Wherefore, the denial of the final change of state comprehends the denial of all the preceding changes as well as their effects. Thus it may be seen that the Supreme Lord is quite unlike all beings and that He is one and immutable in all. He sees (rightly) who sees the Supreme Lord as now described.

(*Objection*) :—The whole world sees; why this one in particular?

(*Answer*) :—True, the world sees; but it sees erroneously. Hence the particularisation 'he alone sees.' A man whose eye is affected with *timira* sees more moons than one; and with reference to him, he who sees one moon may be specified thus, 'he alone sees.' Similarly here, he who sees the one undivided Self as described above is distinguished—from those who erroneously see many distinct selfs—in the words 'he alone sees.' Others, though seeing, yet do not see, inasmuch as they see erroneously like those who see more moons than one.

Knowledge of the one Self leads to moksha.

To praise the Right Knowledge described above by way of stating its results the Lord proceeds as follows:

समं पश्यन्हि सर्वत्र समवस्थितमीश्वरम् ।
न हिनस्त्यात्मनाऽऽत्मानं ततो याति परां गतिम् ॥ २८ ॥

28. Because he who sees the Lord, seated the same everywhere, destroys not the self by the self, therefore he reaches the Supreme Goal.

He who realises that the Isvara described in the last preceding verse is the same—*i. e.*, he who sees that he dwells in all creatures alike—destroys not his own self by himself. Because he does not destroy the self, he reaches the Supreme Goal, he attains moksha.*

(*Objection*) :—No living being whatever destroys itself by itself. Where then is the necessity for the denial "He destroys not the self by the self," any more than for the prohibition † "fire should be consecrated not on earth, not in the sky, not in heaven" (Tait. Sa*m*. 5-2-7) ?

(*Answer*) :—This objection does not apply here ; for, the necessity may be explained on the ground that ignorant men are guilty of ignoring the Self. An ignorant man ignores the Self who is quite manifest to all, self-manifested, and directly visible, and he regards the not-Self (physical body, etc.) as himself. Having performed good and evil works (dharma and a-dharma), he kills even this self (the physical body, etc.) which he had accepted and accepts another new self ; he kills this again and accepts another and so on ; thus he goes on killing every new self that he has accepted. An ignorant man is, accordingly, a slayer of the self. Even the real Self is always killed by avidya, inasmuch as there is no perceptible effect of His existence. Thus, all ignorant men are but

---

* Knowledge destroys ignorance, and with it all evil is destroyed. On the destruction of nescience (aj*n*ana) and false knowledge (mithya-j*n*ana), the two veil that have hidden the true nature of the Self, the sage attains the highest goal, the highest end of man, the Supreme Bliss (Param*a*nanda)—A.

† The prohibition of the construction of the altar on Earth has a meaning, because it is possible to erect one on earth. But the prohibition of the construction of altars in this sky and in the heaven has no meaning, as there is no occasion for the procedure. It has been therefore determined that the prohibition in this latter case should not be understood literally. Similarly we cannot understand the denial here literally. —A.

the slayers of the self. He who, on the other hand, sees the Self as described above, kills not self by self in either of the ways shown above. Wherefore, he reaches the supreme good; he reaps the fruit spoken of above.

Prakriti acts, not the Self.

It has been said that he who sees the Lord (the Self) remaining the same in every being destroys not the self by the self. This may be objected to on the ground that there are many selfs, differentiated by differences in their respective deeds (karma) and qualities. To remove this objection the Lord says:

प्रकृत्यैव च कर्माणि क्रियमाणानि सर्वशः ।
यः पश्यति तथाऽऽत्मानमकर्तारं स पश्यति ॥ २९ ॥

29. He sees, who sees all actions performed by Prakriti alone and the Self not acting.

Prak*r*iti is the Lord's Maya composed of three gu*n*as. So the Mantra reads.

"Let him know that Maya is the Prak*r*iti and that the Great Lord is the possessor of Maya."—(Svetasvatara-Up. 4-10.)

By Prak*r*iti,—*i.e.*, Maya, the Sakti or inherent energy of the Lord, not the other, *i.e.*, not the (Pradhana, the self-existent) Prak*r*iti (of the Sankhyas) described as transforming Itself into causes and effects such as the Mahat,—are done all sorts of actions, whether done in speech, thought, or deed. He sees, who realises this truth and also the truth that the Self (Kshetrajna) is devoid of all upadhis or conditions:—*i.e.*, he sees the supreme truth. There is no evidence to show that there is any variety in Him who is non-agent, unconditioned, and free from all specialities, just as there is no variety in the akasa.

The Self is the source and the abode of all.

The same Right Knowledge is again expounded in other words:*

यदा भूतपृथग्भावमेकस्थमनुपश्यति ।
तत एव च विस्तारं ब्रह्म सम्पद्यते तदा ॥ ३० ॥

30. When a man realises the whole variety of beings as resting in the One, and is an evolution from that (One) alone, then he becomes Brahman.

When, in accordance with the teachings of the *sastra* and the teacher, he sees that all the various classes of beings abide in the One, in the Self, *i.e.*, when he intuitively realises that all that we perceive is only the Self†, and when he further sees that the origin, the evolution, (of all) is from that One, the Self,—as stated in the passage "From the Self is life, from the Self is desire, from the Self is love, from the Self is akasa, from the Self is light, from the Self are waters, from the Self is manifestation and disappearance, from the Self is food." (Chha. Up. 7-26-1)—then he becomes Brahman indeed.‡

* With a view to prevent the supposition that Prakriti and its modifications are quite distinct from Purusha, quite external to him, as the Sankhyas say.—A.

† To explain: on seeing that the whole universe of being in all its variety, from Prakriti down to the ultimate particulars (visesha), is evolved from the Self, has derived its being from the Self, he realises the essential unity of the universe with the Self. To realise this unity, one must merge the Prakriti also in unity with the Self: for it is not possible to merge the universe of forms in unity with the pure Self except by merging also the Prakriti, the root of the whole universe, in the Self. —A.

‡ That is to say, he realises the all-pervading nature of the Self, inasmuch as the cause of all limitation has been absorbed into unity with Self.—A.

The Self is unaffected by the fruits of acts.

If the one Self be the Self in all the bodies, then He must be necessarily affected by their defects. To avoid this conclusion it is said:

अनादित्वान्निर्गुणत्वात्परमात्माऽयमव्ययः ।
शरीरस्थोऽपि कौन्तेय न करोति न लिप्यते ॥ ३१ ॥

31. Having no beginning, having no qualities, this Supreme Self, imperishable, though dwelling in the Body, O son of Kunti, neither acts nor is tainted.

The Self has no beginning, no cause. That which has a cause perishes by itself, whereas This (Self) does not perish, because, as having no cause, He is without parts. Further, He does not perish because He is without qualities; for that which has qualities perishes by loss of qualities; whereas the Self does not perish, because He is devoid of qualities. Thus the Supreme Self imperishable. He suffers no destruction. Therefore, though dwelling in the body,—the Self is said to dwell in the body because the Self is manifested in the body,—yet He does not act. Because He does not act, He is not affected by the results of acts. The meaning is this:—He that is an agent is affected by the fruit of the act; but this (the Self) is a non-agent and is therefore not tainted by the fruit of action.

(*Objection*):—Who, then, in the bodies acts and is tainted? If, on the one hand, an embodied self, distinct from the Supreme Self, acts and is tainted, then the identity of Kshetrajna with the Isvara spoken of in such places as xiii. 2 would be inexplicable. If, on the other hand, there be no embodied self distinct from the Isvara, then tell me who acts and is tainted: or say that the Isvara is not Supreme.* On the ground that the doctrine or the Upanishads taught by the Lord is thus in every way difficult to understand and difficult to explain, it has been abandoned by the Vaiseshikas, as well as by the Sankhyas, the Arhatas, and the Buddhists.

(*Answer*):—As regards this objection, the following answer† has been afforded by the Lord Himself.—"It is Nature that acts" (v. 14). The idea that there is one who acts and is tainted is a mere illusion (avidya) and nothing else. Action does not really exist in the One Supreme Self. It has, for this very reason, been pointed out by the Lord here and there that there is no necessity of performing works (karma) for those devotees of Wisdom, for the order of Paramahamsa-Parivrajakas, who adhere to this doctrine of Supreme Truth (Paramartha-Sankhya-darsana) and have risen above *avidya* and *vyavahara*, nescience and all experience (due to avidya).

Like what does He not act, like what is he not tainted?— Here follows the illustration:

यथा सर्वगतं सौक्ष्म्यादाकाशं नोपलिप्यते ।
सर्वत्रावस्थितो देहे तथाऽऽत्मा नोपलिप्यते ॥ ३२ ॥

32. As the all-pervading akasa is, from its subtlety‡, never soiled, so the Self seated in the body everywhere is not soiled.

---

* If the *Isvara* be the doer and enjoyer, He is no longer the *Isvara*, any more than ourselves.—A.

† The answer is this: The Supreme is in reality neither the doer nor the enjoyer. Agency and enjoyment are attributed to Him by avidya. Therefore the Lord's teaching should be accepted as true.—A.

‡ Because *akasa* is so subtle that it pervades all without obstruction, it is not at all affected by mire, etc., which it pervades.—A.

The Self illumines all.

Moreover,

यथा प्रकाशयत्येकः कृत्स्नं लोकमिमं रविः ।
क्षेत्रं क्षेत्री तथा कृत्स्नं प्रकाशयति भारत ॥ ३३ ॥

33. As the one sun illumines all this world, so does the embodied One, O Bharata, illumines all bodies.

The embodied one (Kshetrin), the Supreme Self (Paramatman), is one and illumines all bodies, the whole material being (Kshetra), from the Avyakta (the unmanifested material cause of the universe) down to the unmoving objects, from the 'Great Elements' down to 'firmness' (xiii. 5-6 .—The illustration by means of the sun serves here a double purpose with reference to the Self,—showing that, like the sun, the Self is *One* only in all bodies, and that like the sun He is unsoiled.

The doctrine summed up.

The teaching of the whole discourse is concluded as follows:

क्षेत्रक्षेत्रज्ञयोरेवमन्तरं ज्ञानचक्षुषा ।
भूतप्रकृतिमोक्षं च ये विदुर्यान्ति ते परम् ॥ ३४ ॥

34. They who by the eye of wisdom perceive the distinction between Kshetra and Kshetrajna, and the dissolution of the Cause of beings,—they go to the Supreme.

---

* The Lord proceeds to show that the Self, being the cogniser, cannot be affected by the attributes of the cognised.—A.

They who in this manner perceive the exact distinction, now pointed out, between Kshetra and Kshetrajna, by the eye of wisdom, by means of that knowledge of the Self which has been generated by the teachings of the *sastra* and the master (*acharya*), and who also perceive the non-existence of Prakriti, Avidya, Avyakta, the material cause of beings,—they reach Brahman, the Real, the Supreme Self, and assume no more bodies.

इति श्रीमद्भगवद्गीतासूपनिषत्सु ब्रह्मविद्यायां योगशास्त्रे
श्रीकृष्णार्जुनसंवादे क्षेत्रक्षेत्रज्ञविभागयोगो नाम
त्रयोदशोऽध्यायः ।

FOURTEENTH DISCOURSE.

THE THREE GUNAS.

The subject of the discourse.

It has been said that all that is born is produced by the conjunction of Kshetra ana Kshetrajna.—How can it be so?—The present discourse is intended as an answer to this question.

Or the connection may be explained thus: With a view to show that it is Kshetra and Kshetrajna, both dependent on the Isvara,—but not independent in themselves as the Sankhyas hold,—that constitute the cause of the universe, it has been stated that the dwelling (of the Kshetrajna) in the Kshetra (*i.e.*, his self-identification with Kshetra) and his attachment for the Gunas from the cause of samsara (xiii. 21.)—In what Gunas and in what way is He attached? What are the Gunas? How do they bind him? How is liberation from the Gunas attained? What are the characteristics of a liberated soul?—With a view to answer these questions, the Lord proceeds as follows:

Knowledge of the origin of the universe is necessary for Salvation.

श्रीभगवानुवाच—

परं भूयः प्रवक्ष्यामि ज्ञानानां ज्ञानमुत्तमम् ।
यज्ज्ञात्वा मुनयः सर्वे परां सिद्धिमितो गताः ॥ १ ॥

The Blessed Lord said:

1. I shall again declare that sublime knowledge, the best of all knowledges; which having learnt, all the sages have passed to high perfection from here.

Though declared more than once in the preceding discourses, I shall again declare that knowledge which is sublime as concerning itself with the Supreme Being, and which is the best of all knowledges as productive of the best result. '*All knowledges*' does not refer to those which have been spoken of as knowledge in the verses xiii. 7-10 but to those kinds of knowledge which relate to sacrifices and other such things to be known. These (latter kinds of knowledge) do not lead to salvation, whereas the knowledge which is going to be imparted in this discourse does lead to salvation. So, the Lord praises this latter knowledge by the epithets 'sublime' and 'best,' in order to rouse interest in the minds of the hearers. And having learnt this knowledge, all the sages (munis)—the sa*m*nyasins, those who are devoted to contemplation (manana) —have passed from here—from this bondage of the body—to high perfection, known as moksha or liberation.

The Lord now proceeds to declare that this knowledge unfailing leads to perfection:

इदं ज्ञानमुपाश्रित्य मम साधर्म्यमागताः ।
सर्गेऽपि नोपजायन्ते प्रलये न व्यथन्ति च ॥ २ ॥

2. They who, having resorted to this knowledge, have attained to unity with Me, are neither born in the creation, nor disturbed in the dissolution.

'Unity' (sadharmya) here means 'identity.' It does not mean 'equality in attributes,' since in the Gita-sastra no distinction is made between the Isvara and tbe Kshetrajna. And a declaration of the (true main end (of knowledge) is here necessary to praise the knowledge.* They who, having resorted to this knowledge,—*i.e.*, having practised the neces-

* If equality were meant here, then it would only be a statement of the fruit of dhyana, not that of knowledge, of which the Lord is here speaking.—A.

sary means whereby to attain that knowledge,—have attained to idenity with Me, the Supreme Lord, are neither born at the time of creation nor disturbed at the time of dissolution; *i.e.*, they are not affected even at the time of Brahma's dissolution.

Evolution of the universe from the union of Spirit and Matter.

The Lord now proceeds to explain what sort of conjunction of Kshetrajna is the cause of all beings:

मम योनिर्महद्ब्रह्म तस्मिन् गर्भं दधाम्यहम् ।
सम्भवः सर्वभूतानां ततो भवति भारत ॥ ३ ॥

3. My womb is the great Brahman; in that I place the germ; thence, O Bharata, is the birth of all beings.

My womb: My own Prakriti,—*i.e.*, the Prakriti which belongs to Me, the Maya made up of the three Gunas, the material cause of all beings This Prakriti is spoken of as great because it is greater than all effects; and as the source and nourishing energy of all Its modifications, It is termed Brahman. In that Great Brahman I place the germ, the seed of the birth of the Hiranyagarbha, the seed which gives birth to all beings. I who am possessed of the two potencies (Saktis), the two Prakritis of Kshetra and the Kshetrajna, unite the Kshetrajna with Kshetra, the Kshetrajna conforming Himself to the upadhis of avidya (nescience), kama (desire), and karma (action). This act of impregnation gives rise to the birth of all beings through the birth of the Hiranyagarbha.

सर्वयोनिषु कौन्तेय मूर्तयः सम्भवन्ति याः ।
तासां ब्रह्म महद्योनिरहं बीजप्रदः पिता ॥ ४ ॥

4. Whatever forms are produced, O son of Kunti, in any wombs whatsoever, the Great Brahman is their womb, I the seed-giving Father.

Wombs : such as the Devas, the Pitris, men, cattle, beasts. *Forms* : such as the bodies which are the condensed aggregations of several parts and limbs. Of these forms, the Great Brahman (Prakriti) which passes through all states of matter is the cause; and I, the Isvara, am the Father, the author of impregnation of the seed in the womb.

The gunas bind the soul.

What are the gunas? How do they bind?—The answer follows:

सत्त्वं रजस्तम इति गुणाः प्रकृतिसम्भवाः ।
निबध्नन्ति महाबाहो देहे देहिनमव्ययम् ॥ ५ ॥

5. Sattva, Rajas, Tamas,—these gunas, O mighty-armed, born of Prakriti, bind fast in the body the embodied, the indestructible.

Sattva (goodness), *Rajas* (vigour, activity, passion) and *Tamas* (darkness)—thus are the gunas named.—'Guna' is a technical term. It does not mean a property, attribute or quality, such as colour, as opposed to the substance in which it is said to inhere.* No separate existence of a guna and a gunin—of an attribute and a substance—is meant here. Accordingly, the gunas here meant are so called because, like the attributes of substances, they are ever dependent on another, namely, the Kshetrajna, as they are only forms of avidya or nescience; and they bind fast *as it were* the Kshetrajna. They are said to bind Kshetrajna because

* The Gunas are the primary constituents of the Prakriti and are the bases of all substances; they cannot therefore b said to be qualities inhering in these substances,—A.

they come into being with Kshetrajna as the basis of their existence. Born of the Lord's Maya, they bind fast as it were in the body the embodied* one, the indestructible Self.† That the Self is indestructible has been shown in xiii. 31. *Mighty-armed*: with powerful arms reaching down to the knees.

(*Objection*) :—It has been said that the embodied one is not tainted (xiii. 31). How then, on the contrary, is it said here that the gunas bind him ?

(*Answer*) :—We have met this objection by adding 'as it were,' 'they bind him *as it were*.'

The nature and functions of the gunas.

Of these three gunas, Sattva is thus defined :

तत्र सत्त्वं निर्मलत्वात्प्रकाशकमनामयम् ।
सुखसङ्गेन बध्नाति ज्ञानसङ्गेन चानघ ॥ ६ ॥

6. Of these, Sattva, which, from its stainlessness, is lucid and healthy, binds by attachment to happiness and by attachment to knowledge, O sinless one.

It is stainless like a pebble-stone, and therefore lucid and healthy.‡ *Sattva* binds the Self by making Him think 'I am happy ;'—it binds Him by causing in Him attachment to happiness §, by bringing about a union of the subject (the

* Him who identifies himself with the body.—A.

† They make it appear that the Self undergoes all the changes that take place in them.—A.

‡ It is *stainless*, because it is able to ward off all veiling ; *lucid*, as able to reflect Consciousness ; *health*, because it is so pure as to perfectly mirror the Spiritual Bliss...A.

§ The happiness and knowledge here spoken of are those modifications of the Sattva in which *Atman's* inherent happiness and consciousness are manifested.—A.

Self) with the object (happiness). It makes Him think "Happiness has accrued to me." This attachment to happiness is an illusion; it is avidya. An attribute of the object cannot indeed belong to the subject; and it has been said by the Lord that all the qualities from 'desire' to 'courage,' (xiii. 6) are all attributes of Kshetra (matter), the object. Thus it is through avidya alone—which forms an attribute (dharma) of the Self as the non-discrimination between the object and the subject,—that Sattva causes the Self to be attached *as it were* to happiness which is not His own, causes Him, who is free from all attachment, to be engrossed as it were in happiness; causes to feel happy as it were Him who does not possess the happiness. Similarly, Sattva binds the Self by attachment to knowledge. From its mention here along with 'happiness,' 'knowledge' meant here must be an attribute of the antahkarana—of the Kshetra (matter), of the *Object*,—not of the Self; for if it were an attribute of the Self, it cannot be an attachment and cannot be a bondage. Attachment to knowledge arises in the same way that attachment to happiness arises.

रजो रागात्मकं विद्धि तृष्णासङ्गसमुद्भवम् ।
तन्निबध्नाति कौन्तेय कर्मसङ्गेन देहिनम् ॥ ७ ॥

7. Know thou Rajas (to be) of the nature of passion, the source of thirst and attachment; it binds fast, O son of Kunti, the embodied one by attachment to action.

Rajas is of the nature of passion, coloring (the soul) like a piece of red chalk, etc. Know it to be that from which arise thirst and attachment,—*thirst* after what has not been attained, *attachment* or mental adherence to what has been attained. It binds fast the embodied Self by attachment to action, by making Him attached to actions productive of visible and invisible results.*

तमस्त्वज्ञानजं विद्धि मोहनं सर्वदेहिनाम् ।
प्रमादालस्यनिद्राभिस्तन्निबध्नाति भारत ॥ ८ ॥

8. But, know thou Tamas to be born of unwisdom, deluding all embodied beings ; by heedlessness, indolence and sloth, it binds fast, O Bharata.

The third *guna*, *Tamas*, causes delusion or non-descrimination.

Again the action of the *gunas* is briefly described as follows:

सत्त्वं सुखे सञ्जयति रजः कर्मणि भारत ।
ज्ञानमावृत्य तु तमः प्रमादे सञ्जयत्युत ॥ ९ ॥

9. Sattva attaches to happiness, Rajas to action, O Bharata, while Tamas, enshrouding wisdom, attaches, on the contrary, to heedlessness.

Tamas, by its very nature as a veil, covers the judgment caused by Sattva and attaches one to heedlessness, *i.e.*, to the non-performance of necessary duties.

The mutual action of the gunas.

When do the *gunas* produce the effects described above?†—The answer follows:

---

* Though the self is not the agent, Rajas makes Him act with the idea 'I am the doer.'—A.

† The question is: Do they produce their effects simultaneously, or at different times, each in its turn? In the former case, do they act in mutual concord or discord?—The answer is that they act at different times, each in its turn.—A.

रजस्तमश्चाभिभूय सत्त्वं भवति भारत ।
रजः सत्त्वं तमश्चैव तमः सत्त्वं रजस्तथा ॥ १० ॥

10. Sattva arises, O Bharata, predominating over Rajas and Tamas; and Rajas, over Sattva and Tamas ; so Tamas, over Sattva and Rajas.

When Sattva increases, predominating over both Rajas and Tamas, then, asserting itself, Sattva produces its own effect, knowledge and happiness. Similarly, when the gu*n*a of Rajas increases, predominating over both Sattva and Tamas, then it gives rise to its own effect, *viz*., action such as husbandry. Similarly, when the gu*n*a called Tamas increases, predominating over both Sattva and Rajas, then it produces its own effects, the covering of wisdom, etc.

How to know when a particular guna is predominant.

What is the characteristic mark by which to know when a particular gu*n*a is predominant ?—The answer follows :

सर्वद्वारेषु देहेऽस्मिन्प्रकाश उपजायते ।
ज्ञानं यदा तदा विद्याद्विवृद्धं सत्त्वमित्युत ॥ ११ ॥

11. When at every gate in this body there shoots up wisdom-light, then it may be known that Sattva is predominant.

All the senses such as hearing are for the Self the gateways of perception. When at all these gates in this body there arises what is called light, illumination (prakasa)—*i.e.*, the presence of anta*h*-kara*n*a, of buddhi,—then we have what is called knowledge (j*n*ana). When the light of knowledge thus springs up, then, by that mark of knowledge, it may be known that Sattva is predominant.

The characteristic marks of predominant Rajas are these :

लोभः प्रवृत्तिरारम्भः कर्मणामशमः स्पृहा ।
रजस्येतानि जायन्ते विवृद्धे भरतर्षभ ॥ १२ ॥

12. Greed, activity, the undertaking of works, unrest, desire—these arise when Rajas is predominant, O lord of the Bharatas.

Greed: desire to appropriate the property of another. *Activity*: action in general. *Unrest*: giving vent to joy, attachment etc. *Desire*: thirst after all things in general. These are the characteristic marks seen when Rajas is predominant.

अप्रकाशोऽप्रवृत्तिश्च प्रमादो मोह एव च ।
तमस्येतानि जायन्ते विवृद्धे कुरुनन्दन ॥ १३ ॥

13. Darkness, heedlessness, inertness, and error,—these arise when Tamas is predominant, O descendant of Kuru.

Darkness: absence of discrimination. *Inertness*: Extreme inactivity, the result of darkness. Heedlessness and error are also the effects of darkness.

Life after death as governed by the gunas.

Whatever result is obtained after death,—even that is caused by attachment and desire and is all due to the gunas. This is taught as follows:

यदा सत्त्वे प्रवृद्धे तु प्रलयं याति देहभृत् ।
तदोत्तमविदां लोकानमलान्प्रतिपद्यते ॥ १४ ॥

14. If the embodied one meets death when

Sattva is predominant, then he attains to the spotless regions * of the knowers of the Highest.

The embodied : the Self. *The Highest* : the Mahat and the like principles (Tattvas).

रजसि प्रलयं गत्वा कर्मसङ्गिषु जायते ।
तथा प्रलीनस्तमसि मूढयोनिषु जायते ॥ १५ ॥

15. Meeting death in Rajas, he is born among those attached to action; and, dying in Tamas, he is born in the wombs ot the irrational.

If he meets death when Rajas is predominant, he is born among men, who are attached to action. *The irrational*: cattle and the like.

Here follows a summary of what has been taught in the preceding verses:

कर्मणः सुकृतस्याहुः सात्त्विकं निर्मलं फलम् ।
रजसस्तु फलं दुःखमज्ञानं तमसः फलम् ॥ १६ ॥

16. The fruit of good action, they say, is Sattvic † and pure; while the fruit of Rajas is pain, and ignorance is the fruit of Tamas.

Good action : Sattvic action. *They* : the wise. *Rajas* means Rajasic action, as this section treats of actions. The fruit of Rajasic actions is only pain, which is Rajasic : for, the effect should be consonant with the cause. *Tamas* means Tamasic action, a-dharma or sin.

---

* The Brahma-loka and the like, where Rajas and Tamas never predominate, as we are told in the scriptures (agamas).—A.

† *i.e.*, brought about by Sattva; devoid of impurities such as may arise from Rajas and Tamas.—A.

The functions of the gunas summed up.

And what arises from the gu*n*as ?

सत्त्वात्सञ्जायते ज्ञानं रजसो लोभ एव च ।
प्रमादमोहौ तमसो भवतोऽज्ञानमेव च ॥ १७ ॥

17. From Sattva arises wisdom, and greed from Rajas; heedlessness and error arise from Tamas, and also ignorance.

From Sattva : When Sattva asserts itself.

Moreover,

ऊर्ध्वं गच्छन्ति सत्त्वस्था मध्ये तिष्ठन्ति राजसाः ।
जघन्यगुणवृत्तिस्था अधो गच्छन्ति तामसाः ॥ १८ ॥

18. Those who follow Sattva go upwards: the Rajasic remain in the middle; and the Tamasic, who follow in the course of the lowest gu*n*a, go downwards.

Those who follow the course of Sattva-gu*n*a will be born in the region of the Devas or the like. The Rajasic will dwell among men; The Tamasic—those who follow the course of Tamas, the lowest gu*n*a—will go down, *i.e.*, they will be born in the wombs of cattle and the like creatures.

Realisation of the Self beyond the gunas leads to immortality.

It has been briefly taught in the preceding discourse that the cause of sa*m*sara—of the Purusha's birth in the wombs of high and low creatures—is the attachment which the Purusha, whom under the influence of the illusory knowledge that leads him to identify himself with Prakriti, has for objects of experience, *i.e.*, for the gu*n*as which assume the forms of pleasure, pain and delusion;—the attachment which makes him feel "I am happy, miserable, deluded." The same thing has been described at length here (xiv. 5 *et. seq.*): the nature of the gu*n*as, their functions, how they bind by their functions, the destination of the persons enslaved by the functions of the gu*n*as; all about the cause of bondage rooted in illusion. Now, with a view to teach that moksha accrues from right knowledge, the Lord says:

नान्यं गुणेभ्यः कर्तारं यदा द्रष्टाऽनुपश्यति ।
गुणेभ्यश्च परं वेत्ति मद्भावं सोऽधिगच्छति ॥ १९ ॥

19. When the seer beholds not an agent other than the gu*n*as and knows Him who is higher than the gu*n*as, he attains to My being.

When a man is enlightened and realises that there is no agent other than the gu*n*as which transform themselves into the bodies, senses and sense-objects, when he sees that it is the gu*n*as that in all their modifications constitute the agent in all actions; when he sees Him who is distinct from the gu*n*as, who is the Witness of the gu*n*as and of their functions, then he attains to My being: *i.e.*, seeing that All is Vasudeva, he becomes Vasudeva.*

Now the Lord proceeds to teach how he attains to it.

गुणानेतानतीत्य त्रीन्देही देहसमुद्भवान् ।
जन्ममृत्युजरादुःखैर्विमुक्तोऽमृतमश्नुते ॥ २० ॥

20. Having crossed beyond these three gu*n*as, which are the source of the body, the embodied one is freed from birth, death, decay and pain, and attains the immortal.

* Then his identity with Brahman becomes manifest.—A.

The wise man crosses, while still alive, beyond the three gunas which constitute the upadhi of Maya † and the seed out of which the body is evolved. He is emancipated, while still alive, from birth, death, decay and pain, and attains to immortality: in this way he attains to My being.

The marks of a liberated soul.

When it was said that (the wise man) crosses beyond the gunas and attains to immortality while still alive, Arjuna found an occasion for a question and asked:

अर्जुन उवाच—

कैर्लिङ्गैस्त्रीन्गुणानेतानतीतो भवति प्रभो ।
किमाचारः कथं चैतांस्त्रीन्गुणानतिवर्तते ॥ २१ ॥

Arjuna said:

21. By what marks, O Lord, is he known who has crossed beyond those three gunas? What is his conduct, and how does he pass beyond those three gunas.

Having been thus asked by Arjuna as to what are the characteristic marks of one who has crossed beyond the gunas and as to the means of crossing the gunas, the Lord proceeds to answer the two questions. First as to the question 'by what marks is he known who has crossed beyond the gunas?' listen to what follows:

श्रीभगवानुवाच:—

प्रकाशं च प्रवृत्तिं च मोहमेव च पाण्डव ।
न द्वेष्टि संप्रवृत्तानि न निवृत्तानि काङ्क्षति ॥ २२ ॥

† The three gunas are the constituents of Maya, the upadhi, and are the source of all evil.—A.

The Blessed Lord said:

22. Light and activity and delusion present, O Pa*n*dava, he hates not, nor longs for them absent.

Light is the effect of Sattva, *activity* of Rajas, and *delusion* of Tamas. He does not hate these when present, when they clearly present themselves, as objects of consciousness. It is only in the absence of right knowledge that a man hates them thus: 'I have now a Tamasic idea by which I am deluded; there has arisen in me the Rajasic activity which is painful, and urged on by this Rajas I have fallen from my true nature, and painful is this fall from my true nature; and the Sattvic gu*n*a, which is luminous, binds me by way of ascribing discrimination to me and causing attachment to happiness.' But the man who has risen above the gu*n*as does not thus hate them when they present themselves to his consciousness. Unlike a man of Sattva (or Rajas or Tamas) who longs for the Sattvic (or Rajasic or Tamasic) states which first presented themselvss to his consciousness and then disappeared, he who has risen above the gu*n*as does not long after things which have disappeared.—This is a mark which others cannot perceive; it serves as a mark for the individual himself, as it can be perceived by himself alone; no man indeed can perceive the hatred or the desire which presents itself to another man's consciousness.

The conduct in life of the Liberated one.

Now follows the answer to the question, what is his conduct who has risen above the gu*n*as?

उदासीनवदासीनो गुणैर्यो न विचाल्यते ।
गुणा वर्तन्त इत्येव योऽवतिष्ठति नेङ्गते ॥ २३ ॥

23. He who, seated as a neutral, is not moved by gu*n*as ; who, thinking that gu*n*as act, is firm and moves not ;

समदुःखसुखः स्वस्थः समलोष्टाश्मकाञ्चनः ।
तुल्यप्रियाप्रियो धीरस्तुल्यनिन्दात्मसंस्तुतिः ॥ २४ ॥

24. He to whom pain and pleasure are alike, who dwells in the Self, to whom a clod of earth and stone and gold are alike, to whom the dear and the undear are alike, who is a man of wisdom, to whom censure and praise are same ;

The Self-knowing sa*m*nyasin, like a neutral man who inclines to neither party,* treads firmly the path † by which he seeks to rise above the gu*n*as ; he does not swerve from the state of discrimination. This is made clearer by what follows next : the gu*n*as transforming themselves into the body, senses and sense-objects, act and react upon each other. Thus thinking, he remains unshaken. *i.e.*, he remains in his own true nature.—There is another reading which makes this part mean "thus thinking, he acts.‡" *Who dwells in the Self* : who is calm.

Moreover :

मानापमानयोस्तुल्यस्तुल्यो मित्रारिपक्षयोः ।
सर्वारम्भपरित्यागी गुणातीतः स उच्यते ॥ २५ ॥

* This is to illustrate how the Self-knower, in virtue of his knowledge of the immutability of the Self, ceases to regard himself as the doer of actions and does not engage in any action.—A.

† This path is Self-knowledge.—A.

‡ This action is the continuation of a mere semblance of action which, he knows, does not pertain to him—A.

25. The same in honour and disgrace, the same towards friends and enemies, abandoning all undertakings,—he is said to have crossed beyond the gu*n*as.

The same: unaffected. Though neutral from their own standpoint, some appear to others as if they were on the side of friends or on the side of foes; but this man appears to be same to friends and foes. He renounces all actions, productive of visible and invisible results, except those which are necessary for the bare maintenance of the body.

Devotion to the Lord leads to liberation.

The attributes described in xiv. 23, 24, 25, form a rule of conduct laid down for the sa*m*nyasin who seeks moksha, so long as they are to be achieved by effort; but when they are firmly ingrained in his nature, as may be perceived by himself, they form marks indicating that the devotee has risen above the gu*n*as.*

The Lord proceeds next to answer the question 'How does one pass beyond these three gu*n*as?'

मां च योऽव्यभिचारेण भक्तियोगेन सेवते ।
स गुणान्समतीत्यैतान् ब्रह्मभूयाय कल्पते ॥ २६ ॥

---

* These attributes, such as indifference to the various modifications and functions of the gu*n*as, have to be acquired with special effort prior to the attainment of Self-knowledge (vidya): and the aspirant for Self-knowledge should therefore cultivate these virtues, as they are the means of attaining it. But, on the rise of Self-knowledge, when the aspirant becomes a Jivanmukta (one who is liberated while still living in the body,) all the attributes mentioned here form part and parcel of his nature and serve as marks of liberation which he can perceive for himself.—A.

26. And he who serves Me with unfailing Devotion of Love, he, crossing beyond those three gu*n*as, is fitted for becoming Brahman.

A sa*m*nyasin (yati), or even a man of works (karmin), who serves Me—the I*s*vara, Narayana—dwelling in the heart of all beings, with a never-failing Bhakti-Yoga,* in devotion to discriminative knowledge,—this Bhakti-Yoga being indeed the result of the Grace and Mercy of the Lord,—he crosses beyond the three gu*n*as mentioned above and is fit for becoming Brahman, *i.e.*, for moksha.

Unity of Atman.

How can it be so †?—Listen:

ब्रह्मणो हि प्रतिष्ठाऽहममृतस्याव्ययस्य च ।
शाश्वतस्य च धर्मस्य सुखस्यैकान्तिकस्य च ॥ २७ ॥

27. For I am the abode of Brahman, the Immortal and the Immutable, the Eternal Dharma, and the unfailing Bliss.

For, in Me, in the Pratyagatman, in the true Inner Self, abides Brahman, the Supreme Self (Paramatman) who is immortal and immutable; who is the Eternal Dharma, *i.e.*, who is attainable by the Dharma of Jnana-Yoga or wisdom-devotion; who is the unfailing Bliss, the Supreme Bliss, the Bliss Immortal. Because I,—the Pratyagatman, the Immor-

* Bhakti-Yoga is that Supreme Love (Parama-preman) which leads to communion with the Supreme. To serve God in Bhakti-Yoga means to constantly contemplate Him by completely withdrawing the mind from all external objects, from the non-Self. In virtue of the Divine Grace, he is endued with right knowledge. Thus enlightened, he becomes Brahman while still alive.—*A*.

† *i.e.*, how can the sage be himself Brahman?

tal Self,—am the abode of the Supreme Self, therefore by Right Knowledge one sees that the Pratyagatman is the very Supreme Self. It is this truth which has been declared in the preceding verse in the words "he is fitted for becoming Brahman."

The meaning of the passage may be explained as follows: It is through His Isvara-Sakti,—through the power He has to manifest Himself as Isvara or the Lord of the universe,—that Brahman shews His grace to His devotees, and so on. I am only that power or Sakti in manifestation, and am therefore Brahman Himself; for Sakti—power, potentiality, energy—cannot be distinct from the one in whom it inheres.

The verse may also be explained as follows:

By 'Brahman,' is here meant the Conditioned Brahman, who alone can be spoken of by any such word as 'Brahman.'—I, the Unconditioned and the Unutterable, am the abode of the Conditioned Brahman, who is Immortal and Indestructible. I am also the abode of the Eternal Dharma of Wisdom-Devotion, and the abode of the unfailing Bliss born of that Devotion.

इति श्रीमद्भगवद्गीतासूपनिषत्सु ब्रह्मविद्यायां योगशास्त्रे
कृष्णार्जुनसंवादे गुणत्रयविभागयोगो नाम
चतुर्दशोऽध्यायः ॥

FIFTEENTH DISCOURSE.

THE SUPREME SPIRIT.

The Tree of Samsara.

Because all living beings are dependent on Me for the fruits of (their) actions, and the wise for the fruit of their knowledge, therefore those who serve Me with Bhakti-Yoga (Devotion of Love) cross beyond the gu*n*as by My Grace, through the attainment of knowledge, and attain liberation (moksha); much more so those who rightly understand the real nature of the Self. Wherefore the lord proceeds in the present discourse to teach the real nature of the Self, though unasked by Arjuna.

First he describes the nature of sa*m*sara or mundane existence by a figurative representation as a tree * in order to produce vairagya or absence of all attachment. For, he alone who is free from all attachment, and no other person, is fit for attaining the knowledge of the real nature of the Lord.

श्रीभगवानुवाच—

ऊर्ध्वमूलमधःशाखमश्वत्थं प्राहुरव्ययम् ।
छन्दांसि यस्य पर्णानि यस्तं वेद स वेदवित् ॥ १ ॥

1. They speak of the indestructible Asvattha having its root above and branches below, whose leaves are the metres. He who knows it knows the Vedas.

---

*Sa*m*sara is represented as a tree because it can be cut off like a tree.—A.

As Brahman with Maya * or the unmanifested potentiality is subtle in point of time, as He is the Cause †, as He is eternal, as He is great, He is spoken of as the one above. The One above is the root of this Tree of Samsara, which is therefore said to have its root above. The Sruti says:

" With roots above and branches below, this Asvattha is eternal." (Katha-Up. 3-2-1).

In the Purana also it is said:

" The root from which the Eternal Tree of Brahman ‡ has sprung is the Avyakta, the Unmanifested. It has developed by the strength of the same (Avyakta). Its trunk is Buddhi, the sense-apertures Its hollows, the great elements Its boughs, the sense-objects Its leaves and branches, dharma and a-dharma Its fair blossoms, pleasure and pain Its fruits affording livelihood to all creatures. And this is the resort § of Brahman (the Highest Self), and that Highest Self is (the essence) of that Tree of Brahman. Having cut asunder and split the Tree with the mighty sword of knowledge || and then attained to the Bliss of the Self, none comes back from there again."

---

* Brahman who is Kutastha (immutable) cannot by Himself be the cause.—A.

† This is to shew how Brahman is "subtle in point of time." Brahman is the Cause because He is the invariable antecedent of all effects.—A.

‡ *i.e.*, the Tree occupied, presided over, led, governed, guided, by Brahman. It is said to be eternal because it cannot be cut except by knowledge.—A.

§ It is in this Tree of samsara that Brahman abides.—This portion is interpreted to mean "Brahman is the resort of this Tree of samsara: for this infinite universe has its basis in Brahman and in nothing else. It is indeed Brahman Himself that, owing to avidya, manifests Himsel in the form of this universe.—A.

|| The knowledge "I am Brahman."—A.

They speak of the illusory sa*m*sara as a tree rooted above. The Mahat, the Aha*m*kara (Egoism), the Tanmatras (the Elemental Essences), etc., are its branches as it were, and these extend downwards; whence the tree is said to have its branches below. They call this tree 'Asvattha' because it will not abide the same even till tomorrow, because it undergoes destruction every moment. The illusion (Maya) of sa*m*sara having existed in time without beginning, they say that this Tree of sa*m*sara is eternal; for, it rests, as is well known, on a continuous series of births which is without beginning or end and is thus eternal. The Tree of Sa*m*sara is further qualified thus: The metres (chhandases) are its leaves as it were; they are so called because, like leaves, the metres (Vedas) such as Rik, Yajus and Saman *protect* ('*chad*' to cover) the Tree of Sa*m*sara. Just as the leaves of a tree serve to protect the tree, so do the Vedas* serve to protect the Tree of Sa*m*sara, as treating of dharma (merit) and a-dharma (demerit), with their causes and fruits. He who knows the Tree of Sa*m*sara and its Root as described above is a knower of the Teaching of the Vedas. Indeed nothing else, not even an iota, remains to be known beyond this Tree of Sa*m*sara and its Root. He who knows It is therefore omniscient.—This is to extol the knowledge of the Tree of Sa*m*sara and its Root.

Now follows another figurative representation of the members of this Tree of Sa*m*sara:

अधश्चोर्ध्वं प्रसृतास्तस्य शाखाः
गुणप्रवृद्धा विषयप्रवालाः ।
अधश्च मूलान्यनुसन्ततानि
कर्मानुबन्धीनि मनुष्यलोके ॥ २ ॥

* The ritualistic sections of the Veda treat of the path of ascent and descent of the soul; they protect sa*m*sara by concealing its defects.—A.

2. Below and above are its branches spread, nourished by the *gunas*, sense-objects its buds; and below in the world of man stretch forth the roots ending in action.

From man down to unmoving objects below, and from him up to the abode of Brahma, the Creator of the Universe, whatever regions are attained as the suitable reward of knowledge and action,—each varying according to the character of knowledge or of action,—they are the spreading branches as it were of that Tree; they are nourished and fattened by the *gunas* of Sattva, Rajas and Tamas, which form their material basis (upadana). The sense-objects such as sound are the buds, as it were, sprouting from the branches of the physical and other bodies which are the result of actions.—The Highest Root of the Tree of Samsara has been mentioned already, and now will be mentioned the secondary roots as it were (of the universe), as leading to acts of dharma or a-dharma: *viz.*, the latent impressions (vasanas) of the feelings of attachment and aversion, etc., which were caused by the fruits of actions. These roots are spread in this world of man below*—below the regions of Devas and the like—and give rise to acts of dharma and a-dharma, these acts springing up on the up-springing of those vasanas. Those roots are spread especially in the world of man. It is while here, as is well-known to all, that men concern themselves with action †.

Cut the Tree and seek the Goal.

And as to the Tree of Samsara just described,

---

* *i.e.*, in the linga-sariras of men these feelings of attachment and aversion are constantly present.—A.

† That is to say, it is while in the human body especially, that one is fit to engage in action.—A.

न रूपमस्येह तथोपलभ्यते नान्तो न चादिर्न च सम्प्रतिष्ठा ।
अश्वत्थमेनं सुविरूढमूलमसङ्गशस्त्रेण दृढेन छित्त्वा ॥ ३ ॥
ततः पदं तत्परिमार्गितव्यं यस्मिन्गता न निवर्तन्ति भूयः ।
तमेव चाद्यं पुरुषं प्रपद्ये यतः प्रवृत्तिः प्रसृता पुराणी ॥ ४ ॥

3. Its form is not perceived as such here, neither its end nor its origin nor its existence. Having cut asunder this firm-rooted Asvattha with the strong sword of dispassion.

4. Then That Goal should be sought for, whither having gone none return again. "I seek refuge in that Primeval Purusha whence streamed forth the Ancient Current."

As such: as described above. Its form as such is perceived by nobody here: for it is very much like a dream, a mirage a *gandharva-nagara* (an imaginary city in the sky) produced by a juggler's art; indeed, it appears and disappears.* It has therefore no finality, no end †. Neither has it a beginning: nobody knows 'It has proceeded from this point.' Its existence—*i.e.*, its nature between the origin and

* One may suppose that the Tree of Samsara, constantly kept up as it is by attachment etc., has no beginning and is not liable to destruction in itself, and that it is not even possible for one to cut it asunder. To remove this idea, the Lord says that the Tree of Samsara described above, though not perceived through our sense-organs, should be inferred to be as described above from the teachings of the sastra (scripture). So it is possible for one to cut it asunder by means of knowledge.—A.

† In the absence of knowledge, samsara has no end, inasmuch as illusion, vasanas (latent tendencies acquired in the past) and works give rise to one another, by action and reaction. Samsara is firmrooted: and one should therefore put forth a very-strong effort to uproot it, by resorting to renunciation through practice of indifference.—A.

the end—is perceived by nobody. *Dispassion:* freedom from attachment to children, to wealth, and to the world. *Strong:* strengthened by a resolute bent of mind towards the Supreme Self and sharpened again and again on the whetstone of the practice of true discrimination. *Cut asunder:* uprooted the Tree of sa*m*sara with its seed.

Then the aspirant should seek for and know the abode of Vish*n*u beyond that Tree. Those who have reached this Goal never return to sa*m*sara.—How is that Goal to be sought after?—It is sought after thus: "I seek refuge in Him, the Primeval Purusha," who is spoken of as the Goal; *i.e.*, He is to be sought for by way of seeking refuge in Him. -Who is this Purusha?—It is that Purusha from whom the emanation of the Tree of the illusory Sa*m*sara streamed forth, just as illusory sights (maya) issue from out of a juggler.

The Path to the Goal.

What sort of persons reach that Goal?—Listen:

निर्मानमोहा जितसङ्गदोषा
अध्यात्मनित्या विनिवृत्तकामाः ।
द्वन्द्वैर्विमुक्ताः सुखदुःखसंज्ञै-
र्गच्छन्त्यमूढाः पदमव्ययं तत् ॥ ५ ॥

5. Free from pride and delusion, with the evil of attachment conquered, ever dwelling in the Self, their desires having completely turned away, liberated from the pairs of opposites known as pleasure and pain, the undeluded reach that Goal Eternal.

Dwelling, etc: constantly engaged in the contemplation of the nature of the Supreme Self. *Their desires, etc:* they become sa*m*nyasins, all desires having fled without leaving any taint behind. *That*: described above.

The Goal is the Lord's Glorious Being.

The Goal is again specified thus:

न तद्भासयते सूर्यो न शशाङ्को न पावकः ।
यद्गत्वा न निवर्तन्ते तद्धाम परमं मम ॥ ६ ॥

6. That the sun illumines not, nor the moon, nor fire; That is My Supreme Abode, to which having gone none return.

The sun, though possessed of the power of illumining all, does not illumine that Abode, the Abode of Light. That Abode to which having gone none return, and which the sun and other (luminous bodies) do not illumine, is the Highest Abode of Vish*n*u.

Jiva is a ray of the Lord.

It has been said 'to which having gone none return.' But, as everybody knows, going ultimately leads to returning, union to disunion. How can it be said that there is no returning of those who have reached that Abode?—Listen; how that may be is thus explained:

ममैवांशो जीवलोके जीवभूतः सनातनः ।
मनःषष्ठानीन्द्रियाणि प्रकृतिस्थानि कर्षति ॥ ७ ॥

7. A ray of Myself, the eternal Jiva in the world of Jivas, attracts the senses, with manas the sixth, abiding in Prak*r*iti.

An integral portion of Myself—of the Supreme Self, of Narayana,—is the eternal Jiva (individual soul) in sa*m*sara, manifesting himself in every one as the doer and enjoyer. He is like the sun reflected in water; the reflected sun is but a portion of the real sun; and on the removal of water the reflected sun returns to the original sun and remains as that very. sun.—Or, it is like the akasa (space) in the jar, which is limited by the upadhi of the jar. This akasa of the jar is but a portion of the infinite akasa and becomes one with the latter on the destruction of the jar which is the cause of limitation; then it returns no more. Thus the statement "to which having gone none return" is quite explicable.

(*Objection*):—How can there be a portion of the Supreme Self who has no parts? If He has parts, He would be liable to destruction on the separation of parts.

(*Answer*):—Our theory is not open to this objection; for, it is only a portion limited by the upadhi set up by avidya; it is a portion as it were, an imaginary portion. This truth was established at length in the thirteenth discourse.*

How Jiva dwells in the body and departs from it.

How does the Jiva of individual Soul, who is only an imaginary portion of Myself, live in the world? or how does he leave it?†—Listen: He draws round himself the (five) senses, such as hearing, with the manas, the sixth sense—those six senses which abide in the Prakriti, *i.e.*, in their respective seats such as the orifice of the ear.

When (does he draw them round himself)?

शरीरं यदवाप्नोति यच्चाप्युत्क्रामतीश्वरः ।

गृहीत्वैतानि संयाति वायुर्गन्धानिवाशयात् ॥ ८ ॥

8. When the Lord acquires a body, and when He leaves it, He takes these and goes, as the wind takes scents from their seats.

---

* It has been shewn there that, as a matter of fact, Jiva is not a portion of Paramatman, that he is identical with the Supreme Self.—A.

† *i.e.*, if Jiva is the Supreme Self, how is it that he is spoken of as a sa*m*sarin, or as departing from this world?—A.

When the Jiva, the Lord of the aggregate of the body and the rest, is to leave the body, then (he draws round himself the senses and the manas). When he leaves a former body and enters another, he does so, taking these—the (five) senses with the manas the sixth—with him as the wind takes with it the scents of flowers.

What then are those (senses)?

श्रोत्रं चक्षुः स्पर्शनं च रसनं घ्राणमेव च ।
अधिष्ठाय मनश्चायं विषयानुपसेवते ॥ ९ ॥

9. The ear, the eye and the touch, the taste and the smell, using these and the manas, he enjoys the sense-objects.

Using the manas along with each sense separately, the Dweller in the body enjoys the sense-objects such as sound.

The Self is visible only to the eye of knowledge.

उत्क्रामन्तं स्थितं वापि भुञ्जानं वा गुणान्वितम् ।
विमूढा नानुपश्यन्ति पश्यन्ति ज्ञानचक्षुषः ॥ १० ॥

10. Him who departs, stays and enjoys, who is conjoined with gu*n*as, the deluded perceive not; they see, who possess the eye of knowledge.

Him who thus dwells in the body, who leaves the body once acquired, who stays in the body, who perceives sound and other objects, who is always in association with gu*n*as, *i.e.*, whom all dispositions of mind—such as pleasure, pain delusion—invariably accompany, the deluded do not recognise. They do not see Him, though in this way He comes quite within the range of their vision, because they are deluded in various ways, their minds being forcibly attracted by the enjoyment of objects seen and unseen.* Ah! such is human perversity.—Thus does the Lord regret.—But those whose wisdom-eye † has been opened by an authoritative source of knowledge, *i.e.*, who possess the power of discrimination, do recognise Him.

No self-knowledge without Yoga.

A few, however,

यतन्तो योगिनश्चैनं पश्यन्त्यात्मन्यवस्थितम् ।
यतन्तोऽप्यकृतात्मानो नैनं पश्यन्त्यचेतसः ॥ ११ ॥

11. Those who strive, endued with Yoga, perceive Him dwelling in the self; though striving, those of unrefined self, devoid of wisdom, perceive Him not.

Those who strive, well balanced in their mind, behold Him, the Self, dwelling in their own mind (buddhi): they recognise Him, "This I am." But though striving to know Him by means of proper authorities such as the scriptures (sastra), men of unrefined self—whose self (mind) has not been regenerated by austerity (tapas) and subjugation of the senses, who have not abandoned their evil ways, whose pride has not been subdued,—behold Him not.‡

---

* Though *A*tman is nearest and therefore most easily perceivable, still, all do not see Him, because of their complete subservience to sense-objects.—A.

† The wisdom-eye here spoken of refers to the scriptures (*sastra*) aided by reflection and reason (nyayanug*r*ihita), which form a means to knowledge.—A.

‡ A mere study of scriptures, aided by reason and reflection, will not be of much avail to those whose minds are still impure and who therefore have not yet realised the distinction between the permanent and the impermanent, the real and the unreal.—A.

Immanence of the Lord, (1) as the all-illumining Light of Consciousness.

That Goal (the Supreme Self) which even such luminaries as fire and sun, the illuminators of all, do not illumine : which having reached, the seekers of moksha never return towards sa*m*sara ; of which the Jivas (individual souls) are only parts manifesting themselves in conformity to the upadhis, as the akasa (space) in a jar is but a portion of the all-pervading akasa,—with a view to show that that Goal is the essence of all and the real basis (*i.e.*, object) of all experience, the Lord proceeds in the next four verses to give a brief summary of His manifestations.

यदादित्यगतं तेजो जगद्भासयतेऽखिलम् ।
यच्चन्द्रमसि यच्चाग्नौ तत्तेजो विद्धि मामकम् ॥ १२ ॥

12. That light which residing in the sun illumines the whole world, that which is in the moon and in the fire, that light do thou know to be Mine.

Light : splendour. *Mine* : Vish*n*u's.

Or, '*light*' may be understood to mean the light of consciousness (chaitanya).

(*Objection*) :—The light of consciousness exists in all alike, in the moving and unmoving objects : then why this qualification of light as 'residing in the sun,' etc ?

(*Answer*) :—This objection does not apply here ; for, the qualification may be explained on the ground that the better manifestation (of consciousness in the sun, etc.) is due to a higher proportion of Sattva. In the sun and other bodies (mentioned here) the Sattva is very brilliant and luminous ; wherefore it is in them that the light of consciousness is better manifested. Hence the qualification ; not that the light is a specific attribute of those bodies only. To illustrate it by an example from ordinary experience : A man's face is not reflected in a wall, in a piece of wood or the like ; but the same face is reflected in a miror in a greater or less degree of clearness, according as the mirror is more or less transparent.

(2) As the all-sustaining Life.

Moreover,

गामाविश्य च भूतानि धारयाम्यहमोजसा ।
पुष्णामि चौषधीः सर्वाः सोमो भूत्वा रसात्मकः ॥ १३ ॥

13. Penetrating the earth I support all beings by (My) Energy ; and having become the watery moon I nourish all herbs.

Energy (ojas): the energy of the Isvara. It is devoid of desires and passions. It permeates the earth for supporting the world. Held by that energy, the massive earth does no fall down and is not shattered to pieces. So it is chanted as follows :—

"Whereby the vast heaven and the earth are firmly held." "He held the earth firm."—(Taittiriya-Samhita, 4-1-8). Thus do I, penetrating the Earth, support the moving and unmoving objects. Moreover, becoming the savoury moon I nourish all the herbs germinating on the Earth, such as rice and wheat, and make them savoury. Soma (the moon) is the repository of all savours. It is indeed the savoury moon tha nourishes all herbs by infusing savours into them.

(3) As the Digestive-Fire in all living organisms.

Moreover,

अहं वैश्वानरो भूत्वा प्राणिनां देहमाश्रितः ।
प्राणापानसमायुक्तः पचाम्यन्नं चतुर्विधम् ॥ १४ ॥

14. Abiding in the body of living beings as Vaisvanara, associated* with Pra*n*a and Apana, I digest the fourfold food.

Vaisvanara : the fire abiding in the stomach, as said in the sruti :

"This fire is Vaisvanara, which is within man and by which this food is digested."—(B*r*i. Up. 5-9-1.)

Fourfold food : the food which has to be eaten by mastication, that which has to be sucked out, the food which has to be eaten by devouring, and that which is eaten by licking.

He who regards that the eater is the Vaisvanara Fire, that the food eaten by Fire is the Soma (moon), and that thus the two together form Fire-Soma (Agni-shoman), is free from all taint of impurity in food.†

(4) As the Self in the hearts of all.

Moreover,

सर्वस्य चाहं हृदि सन्निविष्टो मत्तः स्मृतिर्ज्ञानमपोहनं च ।
वेदैश्च सर्वैरहमेव वेद्यो वेदान्तकृद्वेदविदेव चाहम् ॥ १५ ॥

15. And I am seated in the hearts of all : from Me are memory, knowledge, as well as their loss ; it is I who am to be known by all the Vedas, I am indeed the author of the Vedanta as well as the knower of the Vedas.

---

* Kindled by Pra*n*a.—A.

† Incidentally the Lord teaches here that he who at the time of eating contemplates that the whole universe which is in the form of eater and eaten is made up of Agni and Soma is untouched by the evil arising from bad food.—A.

I dwell in the hearts (buddhi) of all sentient beings as their Self.* Wherefore from Me †, the Self of all sentient beings, are memory, knowledge, ‡ as well as their loss. Just as knowledge and memory occur in righteous persons as a result of their good deeds (punyakarmani), so as a result of their sins, loss of memory and knowledge occur in the sinful. I, the Supreme Self, am to be known in all the Vedas. It is I who cause the Teaching of the Vedanta (Upanishads) to be handed down in regular succession, and it is I who know the Vedic Teaching.

The Lord beyond the perishable and the imperishable universe.

From xv. 12, *et. seq.*, a summary has been given of the glories of Narayana, the Blessed Lord, as manifested through superior upadhis.§ Now, in the following verses, the Lord proceeds to determine the true nature of the same (Blessed Lord), who is pure and unlimited, being quite distinct from all perishable (kshara) and imperishable (akshara) upadhis. First, then, the Lord arranges all that is taught in the preceding as well as in the succeeding discourses in three groups and says :

द्वाविमौ पुरुषौ लोके क्षरश्चाक्षर एव च ।
क्षरः सर्वाणि भूतानि कूटस्थोऽक्षर उच्यते ॥ १६ ॥

16. There are these two beings in the world

---

* I am the witness of all that is good and evil in their hearts.—A.

† Who am the wire-puller (Sutra-dhara) standing behind the machine of the universe, who presides over all actions.—A.

‡ *Memory* of what was experienced in the past births. and *knowledge* of things transcending the ordinary limits of space, time, and visible nature.—A.

§ Such as the sun.—A.

the perishable and the imperishable: the perishable comprises all creatures, the immutable is called the imperishable.

In sa*m*sara, there are two categories, we see, arranged in two separate groups of beings, spoken of as 'purushas.'* One group consists of the perishable (kshara): and the other is the imperishable (akshara)—the contrary of the first—*viz.*, the Mâya-Sakti, the Illusion-Power of the Lord, the germ from which the perishable being takes its birth, the seat of all the latent impressions (sa*m*skaras) of desires, actions, etc., pertaining to the numerous mortal creatures. As to what the two beings (Purushas) comprise, the Lord Himself says: The perishable comprises the whole universe of changing forms; the imperishable is what is known as immutable (ku*t*astha)—that which remains immovable like a heap. Or, 'ku*t*a' means illusion, and 'ku*t*astha' means that which manifests itself in various forms of illusion and deception. As the seed of sa*m*sara is endless †, it is said to be imperishable.

Distinct from these two,—the perishable and the imperishable,—and untainted by the evils of the two upadhis of the perishable and the imperishable, eternal, pure, intelligent and free by nature is the Highest Spirit.

उत्तमः पुरुषस्त्वन्यः परमात्मेत्युदाहृतः ।
यो लोकत्रयमाविश्य बिभर्त्यव्यय ईश्वरः ॥ १७ ॥

17. But distinct is the Highest Spirit spoken of as the Supreme Self, the indestructible Lord who penetrates and sustains the three worlds.

* They are spoken of as 'purushas' because they are the upadhis of the purusha, the one Spirit.—A.

† In the absence of Brahma-j*n*ana the seed does not perish.—(A).

But the Highest Spirit is quite distinct from the two. He is the Supreme Self. He is Supreme as compared with the other selves set up by avidya, such as the physical body; and He is the Self as constituting the unfailing Inner Consciousness of all beings. He is therefore known as the Supreme Self in the Vedantas (Upanishads). The Highest Spirit is further specified thus: He is the Eternal Omniscient Lord, Narayana, who penetrates by His Vital Energy (Bala-Sakti)* the three worlds—the Earth (Bhuh), the Mid-region (Bhuvah) and Heaven (Suvah)—and supports them by His mere existence in them.

'Purushottama,' the Highest Spirit, is a well-known name of the Lord described above. Now the Lord, while showing, by a declaration of the etymology of the word, that the name is significant, shows what He really is, "I am the unsurpassed Lord."

यस्मात्क्षरमतीतोऽहमक्षरादपि चोत्तमः ।
अतोऽस्मि लोके वेदे च प्रथितः पुरुषोत्तमः ॥ १८ ॥

18. Because I transcend the perishable and am even higher than the imperishable, therefore am I known in the world and in the Veda as 'Purushottama,' the Highest Spirit.

Because I transcend the perishable, the Tree of illusory samsara called Asvattha, because I am higher than even the imperishable which constitutes the seed of that Tree of the illusory samsara, because I am thus superior to the perishable and the imperishable, I am known in the world and in the Veda as the Highest Spirit: devotees know Me as such, and the poets, too, incorporate this name in their poems and other works.

---

* 'Bala' means energy, the energy of Consciousness or sentienc (chaitanya), and 'sakti' means Maya which lies therein.—A.

The Glory of Self-knowledge.

Now the Lord speaks of the fruit accruing to him who realises the Self as described above :

यो मामेवमसम्मूढो जानाति पुरुषोत्तमम् ।
स सर्वविद्भजति मां सर्वभावेन भारत ॥ १९ ॥

19. He who, undeluded,* thus knows Me, the Highest Spirit, he, knowing all, worships Me with his whole being, O Bharata.

Me: the Lord as above specified. *Knows*: 'that I am He.' *With his whole being*: with his whole thought devoted exclusively to the Self of all.

A knowledge of the true nature of the Lord having been imparted in this discourse,—a knowledge which leads to moksha,—it is now extolled as follows:

इति गुह्यतमं शास्त्रमिदमुक्तं मयाऽनघ ।
एतद्बुद्ध्वा बुद्धिमान् स्यात्कृतकृत्यश्च भारत ॥ २० ॥

20. Thus, this most Secret Science has been taught by Me, O sinless one; on knowing this, (a man) becomes wise, O Bharata, and all his duties are accomplished.

Though the whole of the Gita is called Science (Sastra) yet from the context it appears that the fifteenth discourse alone is here spoken of as the Science, for the purpose of extolling it. In fact the whole teaching of the Gita-Sastra has been summed up in this discourse. Not the teaching of the Gita-Sastra only, but the whole teaching of the Veda is here embodied: and it has been said that 'he who knows it

---

* Never looking upon the physical body, *etc*., as himself or as belonging to himself.—A.

(the A*s*vattha) knows the Veda ' (xii. 1). and that 'It is who am to be known by all the Vedas ' (xv.15). On knowing this science as taught above—but not otherwise--a man becomes wise. He has accomplished all duties. Whatever duty a brahma*n*a of superior birth has to do, all that duty has been done when the real truth about the Lord is known ; that is to say, by no other means can a man's duty have been accompalished. And it has been said " All actions, without exception, O son of P*r*itha, are comprehended in wisdom " (iv. 33). And here is the saying of Manu :

"This is the fulfilment of the birth, especially for a brahma*n*a ; for, by attaining to this does the twice-born become the accomplisher of all duties, and not otherwise " (xii. 93).

Since you have heard from Me this truth about the Supreme Being, you are a happy man, O Bharata.

इति श्रीमद्भगवद्गीतासूपनिषत्सु ब्रह्मविद्यायां योगशास्त्रे
श्रीकृष्णार्जुनसंवादे पुरुषोत्तमप्राप्तियोगो नाम
।पञ्चदशोऽध्यायः ।

SIXTEENTH DISCOURSE.

SPIRITUALITY AND MATERIALISM

Spiritual disposition.

In the ninth discourse were indicated three kinds of nature (prakriti) belonging to sentient beings, namely, the nature of the Gods, that of the Asuras, and that of the Rakshasas. The sixteenth discourse proceeds to describe them at length. Of these the nature of the Gods (Daivi Prakriti) leads to liberation from samsara, and those of the Asuras and the Rakshasas lead to bondage. Accordingly the nature of the Gods will be described with a view to its acceptance, and the other two with a view to their rejection.*

श्रीभगवानुवाच—

अभयं सत्त्वसंशुद्धिर्ज्ञानयोगव्यवस्थितिः ।

दानं दमश्च यज्ञश्च स्वाध्यायस्तप आर्जवम् ॥ १ ॥

The Blessed Lord said :

1. Fearlessness †, purity of heart, steadfastness in knowledge and Yoga ; alms-giving, self-restraint and worship, study of one's own (scriptures), austerity, uprightness ;

Purity of heart : purity of the antah-karana (sattva), *i. e.*, abandonment of deception, dissimulation, falsehood and the

---

* These are respectively the Sattivic, Rajasic, and Tamasic natures, manifested in men according to the karma of their previous births. They are the tendencies (vasanas) showing themselves out in actions and spoken of in XV. 2 as the secondary roots of samsara.—A.

† Devout observance of scriptural precepts without doubting.—A.

like, in all transactions; that is to say, transacting business in perfect honesty. *Knowledge* consists in understanding the nature of things, such as the Self, as taught in the Scripture (sastra) and by the Teacher (Acharya). *Yoga* consists in making what has been thus learnt an object of one's own direct perception, by concentration (one-pointedness) through the subjugation of the senses. This—*viz.*, fearlessness, purity of heart, and steadfastness in knowledge and Yoga—forms the Daivi or Sattvic nature by pre-eminence. Whatever attributes among those (mentioned in xvi. 1—3) can possibly pertain to the disciples treading a particular path,* they constitute the *Sattvic nature* of the disciples in that particular path. *Alms-giving:* distributing food and the like as far as lies in one's power. *Self-control:* the subjugation of external senses; that of the antah-karana (internal sense, manas) being mentioned in the next verse. *Worship:* including the fire worship (agnihotra) and the like enjoined in the sruti, as also the worship of the Gods (Deva-yajna) and the like enjoined in the smriti. *Study*, etc: study of the Rig-Veda and the like having in view some unseen results (adrishta). *Austerity:* bodily mortification and other penances, which will be mentioned in the sequel. *Uprightness:* this should be a constant attitude.

Moreover,

अहिंसा सत्यमक्रोधस्त्यागः शान्तिरपैशुनम् ।
दया भूतेष्वलोलुप्त्वं मार्दवं ह्रीरचापलम् ॥ २ ॥

2. Harmlessness, truth, absence of anger,

---

* Karma-Yoga or Jnana-Yoga. The first three of the attributes mentioned here can be found in Jnana-Yogins only, the rest being common to Jnana-Yogins and Karma-Yogins. The latter, though wanting in the first three attributes, are neverthless classed among Sattvic men.

renunciation, serenity, absence of calumny, compassion to creatures, uncovetousness, gentleness, modesty, absence of fickleness;

Harmlessness: abstaining from injury to sentient beings. *Truth*: speaking of things as they are, without giving utterance to what is unpleasant or what is false, *Absence of anger*: suppression of anger arising when beaten or reviled. *Renunciation*: 'tyaga' (*lit.*, giving up) is thus explained, since 'almsgiving' has already beenmentioned. *Serenity*; tranquillity of mind (anta*h*-kara*n*a). *Compassion to creatures*: to those in suffering. *Uncovetousness*: unaffectedness of the senses when in contact with their object. *Absence of fickleness*: not to speak or m ove hands and legs in vain.

Moreover,

तेजः क्षमा धृतिः शौचमद्रोहो नातिमानिता ।
भवन्ति सम्पदं दैवीमभिजातस्य भारत ॥ ३ ॥

3. Energy, forgiveness; fortitude, purity, absence of hatred, absence of pride; these belong to one born for a divine lot, O Bharata.

'*Tejas*' means energy, not brightness of the skin. *Forgiveness*: unaffectedness when beaten or reviled. We have explained 'absence of anger' to mean suppression of anger when it arises. Thus 'forgiveness' and 'absence of anger' should be distinguished from each other. *Fortitude*: that state of mind (anta*h*-kara*n*a) which removes the exhaustion of the body and senses when they droop down, and upheld by which the body and senses no longer get dejected. *Purity*: of the two sorts, the external and the internal; the one being accomplished by means of earths and water, the other consisting in the taintlessness of mind and heart, in freedom from impurities such as desception and passion. *Absence of* *hatred*: absence of a desire to injure others. *Pride:* consists in supposing oneself worthy of a high honor. These—from 'fearlessness' to 'absence of pride'—are found in one who is born for a divine lot, *i.e.*, who is worthy of the powers of the Devas, *i.e.*, for whom there is happiness in store.

Materialistic disposition.

Here follows a description of the demoniac (asuric) nature.

दम्भो दर्पोऽभिमानश्च क्रोधः पारुष्यमेव च ।
अज्ञानं चाभिजातस्य पार्थ सम्पदमासुरीम् ॥ ४ ॥

4. Ostentation, arrogance and self-conceit anger as also insolence, and ignorance, belong to one who is born, O Partha, for a demoniac lot.

Ostentation: pretending to be righteous. *Arrogance*: pride of learning, wealth, high connection, etc. *Insolence*: in speech; *e.g.* to speak of the blind as having eyes, of the ugly as handsome, of a man of low birth as one of high birth, and so on. *Ignorance*: misconception of duties and the like.

Results of the two dispositions.

The effects of the two natures are spoken of as follows:

दैवी सम्पद्विमोक्षाय निबन्धायासुरी मता ।
मा शुचः सम्पदं दैवीमभिजातोऽसि पाण्डव ॥ ५ ॥

5. The divine nature is deemed for liberation, the demoniac for bondage. Grieve not, O Pa*n*-*d*ava; thou art born for a divine lot.

Liberation: from the bondage of sa*m*sara. The demoniac (asuric) nature leads to an unfailing bondage and so does the fiendish (Rakshasic) nature.—Now, seeing some such question as "Am I possessed of demoniac nature, or of divine nature?" occur in the mind of Arjuna on hearing what has been said, the Lord again says: grieve not; thou art born for a divine lot; *i.e.*, thou hast happiness in prospect.

The materialists.

द्वौ भूतसर्गौ लोकेऽस्मिन्दैव आसुर एव च ।
दैवो विस्तरशः प्रोक्त आसुरं पार्थ मे शृणु ॥ ६ ॥

6. There are two creations of beings in this world, the divine and the demoniac. The divine has been described at length; hear from Me, O Partha, of the demoniac.

Creation means what is created. The men who are created with the two kinds of nature, the divine and the demoniac, are here spoken of as the 'two creations.' It is said in the sruti,

'Verily there are two classes of Prajapati's creatures, Devas and Asuras.' (B*r*i. Up. 1-3-1).

Every being in this world is included in the one or the other of the two creations, the divine and the demoniac. The purpose of repeating again what has been already said is stated thus:—The divine has been declared at length, beginning with xvi. 1, but not the demoniac; therefore, do thou hear and understand the demoniac nature to be described at length by Me in the sequel here in order that you may avoid it.

The demoniac nature will be described,—to the very end of the discourse—as an attribute of some living men; for, only when it is recognised in the visible, its avoidance is possible.

प्रवृत्तिं च निवृत्तिं च जना न विदुरासुराः ।
न शौचं नापि चाचारो न सत्यं तेषु विद्यते ॥ ७ ॥

7. Neither action nor inaction do the demoniac men know; neither purity nor good conduct nor truth is found in them.

They do not know what acts they should perform to achieve the end of man, nor from what acts they should abstain to avert evil. Not only do they not know 'action and inaction,' there is neither purity nor good conduct nor truth in them. Indeed, the demons are persons who are wanting in purity and good conduct, who are hypocrites and liars.

The materialist's view of the world.

Moreover :

असत्यमप्रतिष्ठं ते जगदाहुरनीश्वरम् ।
अपरस्परसम्भूतं किमन्यत्कामहैतुकम् ॥ ८ ॥

8. They say, "the universe is unreal, without a basis, without a Lord, born of mutual union, brought about by lust; what else?"

These demons of men say. "As we are unreal, so this whole universe is unreal. Neither are dharma and a-dharma its basis. There exists no Isvara ruling the universe according to dharma and a-dharma. Universe is, therefore, they say, without a Lord. The whole universe is, moreover, caused by the mutual union of man and woman under the impulse of lust. It is brought about only by lust. What else can be the cause, of the universe? There is no other cause whatever, no invisible cause, of the universe, no such thing as karma." This is the view of the materialists (Lokayatikas), that sexual passion is the sole cause of all living creatures.

Men's life as guided by materialism.

एतां दृष्टिमवष्टभ्य नष्टात्मानोऽल्पबुद्धयः ।
प्रभवन्त्युग्रकर्माणः क्षयाय जगतोऽहिताः ॥ ९ ॥

9. Holding this view, these ruined souls of small intellect, of fierce deeds, rise as the enemies of the world * for its destruction.

Ruined souls: having lost all chances of going to the higher worlds. Their intellect is small, as it concerns itself only with sense-objects. *Of fierce deeds:* intent on injuring others.

काममाश्रित्य दुष्पूरं दम्भमानमदान्विताः ।
मोहाद्गृहीत्वाऽसद्ग्राहान्प्रवर्तन्तेऽशुचिव्रताः ॥ १० ॥

10. Filled with insatiable desires, full of hypocrisy, pride and arrogance, holding unwholesome views through delusion, they work with unholy resolve;

चिन्तामपरिमेयां च प्रलयान्तामुपाश्रिताः ।
कामोपभोगपरमा एतावदिति निश्चिताः ॥ ११ ॥

11. Beset with immense cares ending only with death, sensual enjoyment their highest aim, assured that that is all †;

They give themselves up to care.‡ *Sensual enjoyment:* Enjoyment of sense-objects such as sound. They are convinced that this sensual enjoyment is the highest end of man.

---

* *World.* Sentient beings.—*A.*

† Sensual enjoyment is the supreme source of happiness: there is no such thing as the happiness of another world.—A.

‡ The immeasurable care as to the means of acquiring and preserving the innumerable objects of desire.—A.

आशापाशशतैर्बद्धाः कामक्रोधपरायणाः ।
ईहन्ते कामभोगार्थमन्यायेनार्थसञ्चयान् ॥ १२ ॥

12. Bound by hundreds of bands of hope, given over to lust and wrath, they strive to secure by unjust means hoards of wealth for sensual enjoyment.

They are attracted here and there, bound by a hundred bands of false hopes. They secure wealth for sensual enjoyment, not for (performing acts of) dharma. *By unjust means:* by robbing other men's wealth.

The materialist's aspirations.

Their aspiration is expressed as follows:

इदमद्य मया लब्धमिमं प्राप्स्ये मनोरथम् ।
इदमस्तीदमपि मे भविष्यति पुनर्धनम् ॥ १३ ॥

13. This to-day has been gained by me; this desire I shall attain; this is mine, and this wealth also shall be mine in future.

In future: in the coming year this wealth also shall be mine, and thereby I shall be known to be a man of wealth.

असौ मया हतः शत्रुर्हनिष्ये चापरानपि ।
ईश्वरोऽहमहं भोगी सिद्धोऽहं बलवान्सुखी ॥ १४ ॥

14. "That enemy has been slain by me, and others also shall I slay. I am a lord, I enjoy, I am successful, strong and healthy."

That unconquerable enemy, say Devadatta by name, has been slain by me and others also shall I slay. What can these poor men do? There is none equal to me in any respect

—How?—I am a lord, I enjoy, I am successful in every way, blessed with children and grandchildren; I am no ordinary man, I am alone strong and healthy.

आढ्योऽभिजनवानस्मि कोऽन्योऽस्ति सदृशो मया ।
यक्ष्ये दास्यामि मोदिष्य इत्यज्ञानविमोहिताः ॥ १५ ॥
अनेकचित्तविभ्रान्ता मोहजालसमावृताः ।
प्रसक्ताः कामभोगेषु पतन्ति नरकेऽशुचौ ॥ १६ ॥

15. "I am rich and well-born. Who else is equal to me? I will sacrifice, I will give, I will rejoice." Thus deluded by unwisdom.

16. Bewildered by many a fancy, entangled in the snare of delusion, addicted to the gratification of lust, they fall into a foul hell.

Well-born: born in a family learned in the scriptures for seven generations. Even in this respect none is equal to me. I will surpass others even in respect of sacrificial rites. I will give (money) to actors and obtain a high delight. *Many a fancy:* such as those described above. Delusion is a snare, as it is of the nature of an enclosure or envelope. They are addicated to sensual gratification; and with sins thus accumulated they fall into a foul hell, such as Vaitara*n*i.

The materialist's sacrificial rites.

आत्मसम्भाविताः स्तब्धा धनमानमदान्विताः ।
यजन्ते नामयज्ञैस्ते दम्भेनाविधिपूर्वकम् ॥ १७ ॥

17. Self-honored, stubborn, filled with the pride and intoxication of wealth, they perform sacrifices in name with hypocrisy, without regard to ordinance.

Self-honored: Esteeming themselves as possessed of all good qualities; they are not esteemed as such by the righteous. They perform sacrifices without regard to the several parts and obligations enjoined in the scriptural ordinances.

The materialist's neglect of Divine Commandments.

अहङ्कारं बलं दर्पं कामं क्रोधं च संश्रिताः ।
मामात्मपरदेहेषु प्रद्विषन्तोऽभ्यसूयकाः ॥ १८ ॥

18. Given over to egotism, power, haughtiness, lust, and anger, these malicious people hate Me in their own and others' bodies.

Egotism: they esteem themselves very high for qualities which they really possess and for those which they falsely attribute to themselves. This egotism is what is called avidya; and it is the hardest thing (to overcome), the source of all perversitiss (doshas), of all evil acts. *Power*: accompanied with lust and passion, and seeking to humiliate others. *Haughtiness*: when this arises one transgresses the path of virtue; it is a peculiar vice seated in the anta*h*kara*n*a.. *Lust*: sexual passion, and the like. *Anger*: at something unpleasant. They are given over to these and other great vices. Moreover, they hate Me, the Isvara, abiding in their own and other bodies as the Witness of their thoughts and actions. To hate Me is to transgress My commands.* They are malicious, jealous of the virtue of those who tread the right path.

The materialist's fall.

तानहं द्विषतः क्रूरान्संसारेषु नराधमान् ।
क्षिपाम्यजस्रमशुभानासुरीष्वेव योनिषु ॥ १९ ॥

*Not caring to know and follow the *Isvara's* commands as embodied in the Sruti and the Smriti.—A.

19. These cruel haters, worst of men, I hurl these evil-doers for ever in the worlds into the wombs of the demons only.

These: enemies of the right path and haters of the righteous. *Worst*: because they are guilty of unrighteous deeds (a-dharma). *Worlds*: paths of samsara passing through many a hell. *Wombs of the demons*: wombs of the most cruel beings such as tigers, lions and the like.

आसुरीं योनिमापन्ना मूढा जन्मनि जन्मनि ।
मामप्राप्यैव कौन्तेय ततो यान्त्यधमां गतिम् ॥ २० ॥

20. Entering into demoniac wombs, the deluded ones, in birth after birth, without ever reaching Me, O son of Kunti, pass into a condition still lower than that.

These deluded creatures are born, birth after birth, only in Tamasic wombs and pass into lower and lower states. Without ever reaching Me, the Isvara, they fall into a condition which is still lower (than they are in at present). *Without reaching Me*: Certainly there is no room whatever even for the supposition that they will ever reach Me. The meaning, therefore, is, 'without ever attaining to the right path taught by Me.'*

The three Gates of Hell to be avoided.

Here follows a summary of the whole demoniac (asuric) nature in which, in its three forms, the whole variety of asuric nature, though endless, is comprehended; which being avoided, the whole asuric nature becomes avoided, and which is the source of all evil.

* The meaning on the whole is this, The asuric nature, as leading to a series of evils, is inimical to all human progress. A man should, therefore, try and shake it off while he is yet a free agent, while he has not yet passed into a birth which would make him entirely dependent on others.—A.

त्रिविधं नरकस्येदं द्वारं नाशनमात्मनः ।
कामः क्रोधस्तथा लोभस्तस्मादेतत्त्रयं त्यजेत् ॥ २१ ॥

21. Triple is this, the gate to hell, destructive of the self : LUST, WRATH, and GREED. Therefore, these three, one should abandon.

The gate to hell : the gate leading to hell (naraka). By merely entering at the gate, the self is ruined, *i. e.*, is fit for no human end whatever. Since this gate is ruinous to the self, let every one abandon these three : *lust*, *wrath* and *greed*.

Here follows the praise of this abandonment.

एतैर्विमुक्तः कौन्तेय तमोद्वारैस्त्रिभिर्नरः ।
आचरत्यात्मनः श्रेयस्ततो याति परां गतिम् ॥ २२ ॥

22. A man who is released from these, the three gates to darkness, O son of Kunti, does good to the self, and thereby reaches the Supreme Goal.

Gates to darkness : leading to hell (naraka) which is full of pain and delusion. He who is released from lust, wrath and greed will act for the good of the self, because of the absence of that by which obstructed he has not hitherto so acted. By so doing he even attains moksha.

Let the Law guide thy Life.

The scripture (sastra) is the authority on which all this renunciation of asuric nature and the observance of what is good are based. One would engage in these only on the authority of the scriptures (sastra), not otherwise. Therefore,

यः शास्त्रविधिमुत्सृज्य वर्तते कामकारतः ।
न स सिद्धिमवाप्नोति न सुखं न परां गतिम् ॥ २३ ॥

23. He who, neglecting the scriptural ordinance, acts under the impulse of desire, attains not perfection, nor happiness, nor the Supreme Goal.

Scripturarl ordinance : the command of the Veda in the form of injunctions and prohibitions, giving us to know what ought to be done and what ought not to be done. *Perfection* : fitness for attaining the end of man. *Happiness* : in this world. *Supreme Goal* : Svarga or Moksha (as the case may be).

तस्माच्छास्त्रं प्रमाणं ते कार्याकार्यव्यवस्थितौ ।
ज्ञात्वा शास्त्रविधानोक्तं कर्म कर्तुमिहार्हसि ॥ २४ ॥

24. Therefore, the scripture is thy authority in deciding as to what ought to be done and what ought not to be done. Now, thou oughtest to know and perform thy duty laid down in the scripture-law.

Authority: source of knowledge. *Scripture-Law* : The scripture itself is the Law, which says "thou shalt act so and so, thou shall not act so and so." *Now* : referring to the stage where the disciple is fit for Karma-Yoga.

इति श्रीमद्भगवद्गीतासूपनिषत्सु ब्रह्मविद्यायां योगशास्त्रे
कृष्णार्जुनसंवादे दैवासुरसम्पद्विभागयोगो नाम
षोडशोऽध्यायः ॥

SEVENTEENTH DISCOURSE.

THE THREEFOLD FAITH.

The ignorant, but faithful.

The Lord's words (xvi. 24) having given Arjuna an occasion for a question, he said :

अर्जुन उवाच—

ये शास्त्रविधिमुत्सृज्य यजन्ते श्रद्धयाऽन्विता. ।
तेषां निष्ठा तु का कृष्ण सत्त्वमाहो रजस्तमः ॥ १ ॥

Arjuna said :

1. Whoso worship, setting aside the ordinance of the scripture, endued with faith,—what faith is theirs ? Is it Sattva, or Rajas, or Tamas ?

Whoso : not exactly specified. It must refer to those who, endued with faith, *i.e.*, thinking that there is something beyond,—on observing the conduct of the learned,—worship the Gods and the like, unaware of the procedure laid down in the scriptures, the sruti and the smriti. Those, on the other hand, who while knowing the injunctions of the scripture, set them aside and worship the Gods, etc., contrary to those injunctions,—they cannot indeed be meant here, because of the qualification that they are 'endued with faith.' We cannot suppose that those men are endued with faith who, while knowing the scriptural injunctions about the worship of the Gods, etc., set them aside, without caring for

* The Lord has described the future lots of astikas and nastikas, o believers and unbelievers, of persons who, seeing with the eye of the scriptures, do or do not believe in their teachings. Now Arjuna proceeds to ask as to the fate of the believers who do not know the scriptures.—A.

them,* and engage in the worship of the Gods which is not in accordance with the injunctions. Therefore it is only the persons of the other class described above that are here referred to. Arjuna's question may be thus stated : Is the worship offered by them to the Gods, etc., based in Sattva, or Rajas, or Tamas ?

The three kinds of Faith.

Seeing that such a general question cannot be answered without reference to the several particular aspects of it, the Blessed Lord said :

श्रीभगवानुवाच—

त्रिविधा भवति श्रद्धा देहिनां सा स्वभावजा ।

सात्त्विकी राजसी चैव तामसी चेति तां शृणु ॥ २ ॥

The Blessed Lord said :

2. Threefold is that faith born of the individual nature of the embodied,—Sattvic, Rajasic, and Tamasic. Do thou hear of it.

Faith, of which thou hast asked, is of three sorts. It is born of the *individual nature* (svabhava): *i.e.*, the samskara or tendency made up of the self-reproductive latent impressions of the acts—good and bad, Dharma and Adharma—which were done in the past births and which manifested themselves at the time of death. *Sattvic*: faith in the worship of the Gods (Devas) which is an effect of Sattva. *Rajasic*: faith in the worship of the Yakshas and the Rakshasas, which is an effect of Rajas. *Tamasic*: faith in the worship of the Pretas and the Pisachas, which is an effect of Tamas. Do thou understand the threefold faith which is going to be described.

* And who are therefore to be classed among demons (asuras), as shewn in the preceding discourse.—A.

As to this threefold Faith,

सत्त्वानुरूपा सर्वस्य श्रद्धा भवति भारत ।
श्रद्धामयोऽयं पुरुषो यो यच्छ्रद्धः स एव सः ॥ ३ ॥

3 The faith of each is in accordance with his nature, O Bharata. The man is made up of his faith; as a man's faith is, so is he.

Each: every living being. *Nature* (Sattva): the antahkarana with its specific tendencies or samskara. *Man*: Jiva, samsarin. *So*: in accordance with that faith.

So the Sattvic faith or the like has to be inferred from its characteristic effects, namely, the worship of the Gods or the like. The Lord says:

यजन्ते सात्त्विका देवान्यक्षरक्षांसि राजसाः ।
प्रेतान्भूतगणांश्चान्ये यजन्ते तामसा जनाः ॥ ४ ॥

4. Sattvic men worship the Gods; Rajasic the Yakshas * and the Rakshasas; the others—Tamasic men,—the Pretas and the hosts of Bhutas.

Hosts of Bhutas: as also the seven Matrikas.

Men of Rajasic and Tamasic Faiths.

Thus, by a general principle laid down in the scripture, Sattvic and other devotions have been determined through their respective effects. Now only one in a thousand is Sattvic and devoted to the worship of the Gods, while the Rajasic and Tamasic creatures form the majority. How?

---

* *Gods*: such as the Vasus. *Yakshas*: such as Kubera. *Rakshasas*: such as Nairrita. *Pretas*: those who, while they had been on earth as brahmanas, etc., neglected their proper duties, and who, after death, attained Vayu-dehas (ærial bodies). We may understand that all these beings, when worshipped, answer the prayers of the devotees by granting their respective desires.—A.

अशास्त्रविहितं घोरं तप्यन्ते ये तपो जनाः ।
दम्भाहङ्कारसंयुक्ताः कामरागबलान्विताः ॥ ५ ॥
कर्शयन्तः शरीरस्थं भूतग्राममचेतसः ।
मां चैवान्तःशरीरस्थं तान्विद्ध्यासुरनिश्चयान् ॥ ६ ॥

5. Those men who practise terrific austerities not enjoined by the scripture, given to hypocrisy and egotism, endued with the strength of lust and passion ;

6. Weakening all the elements in the body—fools they are—and Me who dwell in the body within ; know thou these to be of demoniac resolves.

Terrific: causing pain to himself and to other living beings. *Endued*, etc: This portion of the text may also be interpreted to mean 'possessed of lust, passion and strength.' *Elements*: organs. *Me*: Narayana, the Witness of their thoughts and deeds. To weaken Me is to neglect My teaching. Know thou that they are demoniac (asuric) in their resolves, so that you may avoid them. This is a word of advice to Arjuna.

Threefold Food, Worship, Austerity and Gift.

Now will be shown what sort of food—which is divided into three classes, *viz.*, that which is savoury and oleaginous, and so on—is dear to the Sattvic, Rajasic and Tamasic men repectively, so that a man may know that he is one of Sattva or of Rajas or of Tamas as indicated by his own partiality for one or another particular class of food—such as the savoury and the oleaginous—and then give up the Rajasic and Tamasic food and resort to Sattvic one. Similarly, the object of the threefold division here made of sacrifice and the like according to the Sattva and other gu*n*as is to show how a man may find out and give up the Rajasic and Tamasic ones and resort exclusively to the Sattvic ones. The Lord says:

आहारस्त्वपि सर्वस्य त्रिविधो भवति प्रियः ।
यज्ञस्तपस्तथा दानं तेषां भेदमिमं शृणु ॥ ७ ॥

7. The food also which is dear to each is threefold, as also worship, austerity and gift. Do thou hear of this, their distinction.

Each: Every living being that eats. *This*: that which is going to be described. *Their*: of food (ahara), etc.

The three kinds of Food.

आयुःसत्त्वबलारोग्यसुखप्रीतिविवर्धनाः ।
रस्याः स्निग्धाः स्थिरा हृद्या आहाराः सात्त्विकप्रियाः ॥ ८ ॥

8. The foods which increase life, energy, strength, health, joy and cheerfulness, which are savoury and oleaginous, substantial and agreeable, are dear to the Sattvic.

Oleaginous: oily, fatty. *Substantial*: which can last long in the body.

कट्वम्ललवणात्युष्णतीक्ष्णरूक्षविदाहिनः ।
आहारा राजसस्येष्टा दुःखशोकामयप्रदाः ॥ ९ ॥

9. The foods that are bitter, sour, saline, excessively hot, pungent, dry and burning, are liked by the Rajasic, causing pain, grief and disease.

Excessively: should be construed with all thus, *excessively* bitter, *excessively* hot, etc.

यातयामं गतरसं पूतिपर्युषितं च यत् ।
उच्छिष्टमपि चामेध्यं भोजनं तामसप्रियम् ॥ १० ॥

10. The food which is stale, tasteless, putrid and rotten, refuse and impure, is dear to the Tamasic.

Stale: Half-cooked. 'Yatayama' (*lit.* cooked three hours ago) meaning 'powerless' is thus explained, to avoid tautology; for the next word 'gatarasa' (tasteless) means the same, *i.e.*, 'powerless.' *Rotten*: the cooked food over which one-night has passed. *Refuse*: left after a meal. *Impure*: unfit for offering.

The three kinds of Worship.

Now the three sorts of worship will be described:

अफलाकाङ्क्षिभिर्यज्ञो विधिदृष्टो य इज्यते ।
यष्टव्यमेवेति मनः समाधाय स सात्त्विकः ॥ ११ ॥

11. That worship is Sattvic which is offered by men desiring no fruit, as enjoined in the Law, with a fixed resolve in the mind that they should merely worship.

That they should merely worship: that their duty lies in the mere performance of the worship itself, that no personal end has to be achieved by that means.

अभिसन्धाय तु फलं दम्भार्थमपि चैव यत् ।
इज्यते भरतश्रेष्ठ तं यज्ञं विद्धि राजसम् ॥ १२ ॥

12. That which is offered, O best of the Bharatas, with a view to reward and for ostentation, know it to be a Rajasic worship.

विधिहीनमसृष्टान्नं मन्त्रहीनमदक्षिणम् ।
श्रद्धाविरहितं यज्ञं तामसं परिचक्षते ॥ १३ ॥

13. They declare that worship to be Tamasic which is contrary to the ordinances, in which no food is distributed, which is devoid of mantras and gifts, and which is devoid of faith.

Distributed : to brahmanas. *Devoid of mantras* : with hymns defective in utterance and accent. *Gifts* : prescribed fees (to priests).

Physical Austerity.

Now the three kinds of austerity will be described :

देवद्विजगुरुप्राज्ञपूजनं शौचमार्जवम् ।
ब्रह्मचर्यमहिंसा च शारीरं तप उच्यते ॥ १४ ॥

14. Worshipping the Gods, the twice-born, teachers and wise men,—purity, straightforwardness, continence, and abstinence from injury are termed the bodily austerity.

The bodily austerity : that which is accomplished by th body, *i.e.*, in which the body is the chief of all factors of action,—the doer, etc.,—of which the Lord will speak in xviii. 15.

Austerity in Speech.

अनुद्वेगकरं वाक्यं सत्यं प्रियहितं च यत् ।
स्वाध्यायाभ्यसनं चैव वाङ्मयं तप उच्यते ॥ १५ ॥

15. The speech which causes no excitement and is true, as also pleasant and beneficial, and also the practice of sacred recitation, are said to form the austerity of speech.

Excitement : pain to living beings. *Pleasant and beneficial* : having respectively to do with the seen and the unseen. 'Speech' is specified by the attributes of 'causing no excitement' and so on. An invariable combination of all these attributes is here meant. That speech addressed to others which, though causing no pain, is devoid of one, two or three of the other attributes—*i.e.*, is not true, not pleasant and not beneficial—cannot form the austerity of speech; so, that speech which, though true, is wanting in one, two, or three of the other attributes cannot form the austerity of speech: so, an agreeable speech which is wanting in one, two, or three of the other attributes cannot form the austerity of speech. So, the speech which, though beneficial, is wanting in one, two, or three of the other attributes cannot form the austerity of speech.—What forms the austerity then?—The speech that is true, that causes no excitement, that is agreeable and good, forms the austerity of speech;* as for example, "Be tranquil, my son, study (the Vedas) and practise yoga, and this will do thee good." *Practice of sacred recitation* : according to ordinances.

Mental Austerity.

मनःप्रसादः सौम्यत्वं मौनमात्मविनिग्रहः ।

भावसंशुद्धिरित्येतत्तपो मानसमुच्यते ॥ १६ ॥

16. Serenity of mind, good-heartedness, silence, self-control, purity of nature,—this is called the mental austerity.

---

* *i. e.*, the austerity practised specially in regard to speech, *i.e.*, in which speech plays the leading part.—A.

Good-heartedness : the state of mind which may be inferred from its effects, such as the brightness of the face, etc. *Silence* : even silence in speech is necessarily preceded by a control of thought, and thus the effect is here put for the cause, *viz*, the control of thought. *Self-control* : a general control of the mind. This is to be distinguished from *silence* (mauna) which means the control of thought so far as it concerns speech. *Purity of nature* : Honesty of purpose in dealings with other people.

The three kinds of Austerity according to Gunas.

The Lord proceeds to show that the foregoing austerity,—bodily, vocal and mental,—as practised by men, is divided into the classes according to Sattva and other gu*n*as.

श्रद्धया परया तप्तं तपस्तत्त्रिविधं नरैः ।
अफलाकाङ्क्षिभिर्युक्तैः सात्त्विकं परिचक्षते ॥ १७ ॥

17. This threefold austerity, practised by devout* men with utmost faith, desiring no fruit, they call Sattvic.

Threefold : having respectively to do with the three seats —body, speech, and mind. *With faith* : believing in the existence of things (taught in the scriptures.)

सत्कारमानपूजार्थं तपो दम्भेन चैव यत् ।
क्रियते तदिह प्रोक्तं राजसं चलमध्रुवम् ॥ १८ ॥

18. That austerity which is practised with the object of gaining good reception, honour and worship, and with hypocrisy †, is said to be of this ‡ world, to be Rajasic, unstable and uncertain.

* Balanced in mind : unaffected in success and failure.—A.

† With no sincere belief, for mere show,—A.

‡ Yielding fruit only in this world.—A.

Good reception : in such words as 'Here is a good brahmana of great austerities.' *Honour* : the act of rising to greet, of making a reverential salutation, etc. *Worship* : the washing of feet, adoring and feeding. *Unstable* : as productive of a transient effect.

मूढग्राहेणात्मनो यत्पीडया क्रियते तपः ।
परस्योत्सादनार्थं वा तत्तामसमुदाहृतम् ॥ १९ ॥

19. The austerity which is practised out of a foolish notion, with self-torture, or for the purpose of ruining another, is declared to be Tamasic.

The three kinds of Gift.

Now the threefold nature of gift will be described.

दातव्यमिति यद्दानं दीयतेऽनुपकारिणे ।
देशे काले च पात्रे च तद्दानं सात्त्विकं स्मृतम् ॥ २० ॥

20. That gift which is given—knowing it to be a duty to give—to one who does no service, in place and in time and to a worthy person, that gift is held Sattvic.

Given to one, etc. : to one who cannot return the good, or to one from whom, though able to return the good, no such return is expected. *Place* : Kurukshetra &c. *Time* : Sa*m*kranti (passage of the sun from one Zodiacal sign to another), etc. *Worthy* : as learned in the six sciences (angas) etc.

यत्तु प्रत्युपकारार्थं फलमुद्दिश्य वा पुनः ।
दीयते च परिक्लिष्टं तद्दानं राजसं स्मृतम् ॥ २१ ॥

21. And that gift which is given with a view to a return of the good, or looking for the fruit, or reluctantly, that gift is held to be Rajasic.

With a view etc.: hoping that he (the donee) will in time return the service, or that the gift will secure for himself some (now) unseen reward.

अदेशकाले यद्दानमपात्रेभ्यश्च दीयते ।
असत्कृतमवज्ञातं तत्तामसमुदाहृतम् ॥ २२ ॥

22. The gift that is given at a wrong place or time, to unworthy persons, without respect or with insult, that is declared to be Tamasic.

At a wrong place and time: at a place which is not sacred and which is associated with mlechhas (Non-aryans) with unholy things and the like, and at a time which is not auspicious—*i.e.*, which is not marked with any such speciality as the sun's passage from one zodiacal sign to another. *Unworthy persons:* such as fools or rogues. *Without respect:* without agreeable speech, without the washing of feet, or without worship, though the gift be made in proper time and place.

How to perfect the defective acts.

The following instructions are given with a view to perfecting sacrifices, gifts, austerities, etc.

ओं तत्सदिति निर्देशो ब्रह्मणस्त्रिविधः स्मृतः ।
ब्राह्मणास्तेन वेदाश्च यज्ञाश्च विहिताः पुरा ॥ २३ ॥

23. "OM, TAT, SAT": this has been taught to be the triple designation of Brahman*. By that

* When a sacrificial rite or the like is found defective it will be perfected on the utterance of one of the three designations.—A.

were created of old* the brahma*n*as and the Vedas and the sacrifices.

Taught: in the Vedanta by the knowers of Brahman. *By that* etc: by the triple designation, etc. This is said in praise of (the triple) designation.

तस्मादोमित्युदाहृत्य यज्ञदानतपःक्रियाः ।
प्रवर्तन्ते विधानोक्ताः सततं ब्रह्मवादिनाम् ॥ २४ ॥

24. Therefore, with the utterance of '*Om*,' are the acts of sacrifice, gift and austerity, as enjoined in the scriptures, always begun by the students of Brahman†.

Acts of sacrifice: acts in the form of sacrifice, etc.

तदित्यनभिसन्धाय फलं यज्ञतपःक्रियाः ।
दानक्रियाश्च विविधाः क्रियन्ते मोक्षकाङ्क्षिभिः ॥ २५ ॥

25. With 'Tat,' without aiming at the fruits, are the acts of sacrifice and austerity and the various acts of gift performed by the seekers of moksha.

With 'Tat': with the utterance of 'Tat', which is a designation of Brahman. *The fruits*: of sacrifice, etc. *Acts of gift*: gifts of land, gold, etc.

The use of 'Om' and of 'Tat' has been explained. Now the use of 'Sat' is given as follows:

सद्भावे साधुभावे च सदित्येतत्प्रयुज्यते ।
प्रशस्ते कर्मणि तथा सच्छब्दः पार्थ युज्यते ॥ २६ ॥

* At the beginning of creation by the Prajapati.—A.

† 'Brahman' here means 'Veda.'—A.

26. The word 'Sat' is used in the sense of *reality* and of *goodness*; and so also, O Partha, the word 'Sat' is used in the sense of an *auspicious act*.

In expressing the reality of an object which is unreal—as for example, the birth of a son who is unreal—and in expressing that a man is one of good conduct who is not so, this designation of Brahman, *viz.*, the word 'Sat,' is employed. It is also used with reference to the act of marriage and the like*.

यज्ञे तपसि दाने च स्थितिः सदिति चोच्यते ।
कर्म चैव तदर्थीयं सदित्येवाभिधीयते ॥ २७ ॥

27. Devotion to sacrifice, austerity and gift is also spoken of as 'Sat'; and even action in connection with these is called 'Sat.'

Sacrifice: the act of sacrifice. *Spoken of*: by the learned. *These*: sacrifice, gift and austerity. Or, 'tadarthiyam karma' may be interpreted to mean action for the sake of the Lord whose triple designation is the subject of treatment here. These acts of sacrifice, gift and austerity,—even such of them as are not of the Sattvic class and are imperfect,—turn out to be Sattvic and perfect ones, on applying to them with faith the triple designation of Brahman.

* It may be further explained thus: A son when born is said to come into existence. From the stand-point, however, of the Absolute, he never exists. Thus the word 'Sat' meaning 'real' properly applicable to Brahman who alone is real, is applied also to a son who is unreal or is only relatively real. Similarly, the word 'Sat,' properly applicable to Brahman who is absolutely Good and absolutely Auspicious, is applied to a man whose conduct is not good or is only relatively good, or to an act which is not auspicious or which is only relatively auspicious. This is only to illustrate how the imperfectly performed acts of sacrifice, gift and austerity the designation of Brahman may be applied—as enjoined here—with a view to make them perfect.

Works without faith are fruitless.

Because all these acts become perfect when done in full faith, therefore,

अश्रद्धया हुतं दत्तं तपस्तप्तं कृतं च यत् ।
असदित्युच्यते पार्थ न च तत्प्रेत्य नो इह ॥ २८ ॥

28. Whatever is sacrificed, given, or done, and whatever austerity is practised, without faith, it is called 'asat,' O Partha ; it is naught here or hereafter.

Given: to the brahma*n*as. *Deed:* such as adoration and obeisance. *Asat:* as they are quite outside the path by which I (the Isvara) may be reached. *It is naught:* though costing much trouble, it is of no use here as it is despised by the wise; nor can it produce any effect hereafter.

The teaching of the discourse summed up.

[The teaching of this discourse may be thus summed up:—There are devotees, who, though ignorant of the scriptures, are yet endued with faith, and who, accordnig to the nature of their faith, may be classed as Sattvic, Rajasic, or Tamasic. These should cultivate pure Sattva by avoiding Rajasic and Tamasic kinds of food, worship, gift and austerity, and resorting exclusively to Sattvic ones. When their acts of worship, gift, and austerity are found defective, they may be perfected by uttering the three designations of Brahman, 'Om,' 'Tat,' and 'Sat.' With their reason (buddhi) thus purified, they should engage in the study of scriptures and in the subsequent stages of investigation into the nature of Brahman. Thereby they attain a direct perception of Truth and are finally liberared.—A.]

इति श्रीमद्भगवद्गीतासूपनिषत्सु ब्रह्मविद्यायां योगशास्त्रे
श्रीकृष्णार्जुनसंवादे श्रद्धात्रयविभागयोगो नाम
सप्तदशोऽध्यायः ॥

EIGHTEENTH DISCOURSE.

CONCLUSION.

'Samnyasa' and 'Tyaga' distinguished.

In the present discourse the Lord proceeds to teach, by way of summing up, the doctrine of the whole of the Gita-Sastra, as also the whole of the Vedic Doctrine. Verily, the whole of the doctrine taught in the preceding discourses is to be found in this discourse. Arjuna, however, asks to know only the distinction in meaning between '*samnyasa*, and '*tyaga*'.

अर्जुन उवाच—

संन्यासस्य महाबाहो तत्त्वमिच्छामि वेदितुम् ।
त्यागस्य च हृषीकेश पृथक्केशिनिषूदन ॥ १ ॥

Arjuna said:

1. 'Of sa*m*nyasa' O Mighty-armed, I desire to know the truth, O H*r*ishike*s*a, as also of 'tyaga', severally, O Slayer of Ke*s*in.

Samnyasa: the connotation of the term '*samnyasa*.' *Tyaga*: the connotation of the term '*tyaga*'. *Severally*: as distinguished from each other. Ke*s*in was an Asura whom the Lord, the son of Vasudeva, slew, and the Lord is therefore addressed as 'Ke*s*i-nishudana,' the Slayer of Ke*s*in'

The words 'sa*m*nyasa' and 'tyaga' have been used here and there in the preceding discourses, their connotations, however, not being clearly distinguished. Wherefore, with a view to determining them, the Lord addresses Arjuna, who desired to know of them, as follows:

श्रीभगवानुवाच :—

काम्यानां कर्मणां न्यासं संन्यासं कवयो विदुः ।
सर्वकर्मफलत्यागं प्राहुस्त्यागं विचक्षणाः ॥ २ ॥

The Blessed Lord said:

2. Sages understand 'samnyasa' to be the renouncement of interested works; the abandonment of the fruits of all works, the learned declare, is 'tyaga'

A few sages understand by 'samnyasa' the abandonment of *kamya-karmani*, of works (such as the Asvamedha, Horse-sacrifice) accompanied with a desire for fruits. The learned declare that 'tyaga' means abandonment of the fruits of all the works that are performed,—*nitya* and *naimittika*, ordinary and extra-ordinary duties,—*i.e.*, of the fruits that may accrue to the performer.

The abandonment of interested works and the abandonment of fruits (of works) being intended to be expressed (by the two words) the meaning of the words 'samnyasa' and 'tyaga' is in any way one and the same so far as the general idea is concerned, namely, *abandonment*. They are not quite so distinct in meaning as the words 'jar' and 'cloth'*.

(Objection):—The *nitya* and *naimittika* works ordinary and exta-ordinary duties, are said to produce no fruits. How is it that the abandoning of their fruits is here spoken of? It is like speaking of the abandoning of a barren woman's son.

* To explain the two words as meaning two altogether distinct things would be in contravention to the accepted usage. As explained here, the two words convey the same general idea with some distinction. —A.

(*Answer*) :—No such objection may be raised here, since, in the opinion of the Lord, ordinary and occasional duties produce their own fruits, as He will show in xviii. 12, where, indeed, while teaching that sa*m*nyasins alone (those alone who have renounced all desire for the fruits of works) have no connection whatever with those fruits, the Lord teaches also that those who are not sa*m*nyasins will have to reap the fruits of the ordinary works which they are bound to perform.

Should the ignorant perform works or not?

त्याज्यं दोषवदित्येके कर्म प्राहुर्मनीषिणः ।
यज्ञदानतपःकर्म न त्याज्यमिति चापरे ॥ ३ ॥

3. That action should be abandoned as an evil, some philosophers declare; while others (declare) that acts of sacrifice, gift and austerity should not be given up.

Some philosophers, following the doctrine of the Sankhyas, etc., declare that all action should be given up as an evil, even by those who are fit for Karma-Yoga. *As an evil*: this may be interpreted to mean either that all Karma should be given up as involving evil since it is the cause of bondage; or that it should be given up like passion and other such evil tendencies. With regard to the same class of persons (*viz.*, those who are fit for Karma-Yoga), others say that the acts of sacrifice, gift and austerity ought not to be abandoned.

It is the Karma-Yogins that form the subject of discussion here; and it is with reference to them that these divergent views are held, but not with reference to the jnana-nish*t*has (wisdom-devotees), the sa*m*nyasins who have risen (above all worldly concerns). Those persons who have been raised above the path of Karma in iii. 3 are not spoken of in this connection.

(*Objection*):—Just as the persons who are qualified for works form the subject of discussion here—in the section where the whole doctrine of the *sastra* is summed up,—though their path has already been specified in iii. 3. so also the Sankhyas, the devotees of wisdom, may also form the subject of discussion here.

(*Answer*):—No, because of the inconceivability of their abandoning of duty from delusion or on account of pain. (To explain): The Sankhyas (men of knowledge) perceive in the Self no pain whatever arising from bodily trouble, since desire, pain, etc., are said to be the attributes of Kshetra or matter. Wherefore they do not abandon action for fear of bodily trouble and pain. Neither do they perceive action in the Self. If they could ever perceive action in the Self, then it would be possible to imagine their abandoning of obligatory works from delusion. In fact, they abandon works because they see that action pertains to gu*n*as and think 'I do nothing at all' (v. 8). How those men who know the truth renounce works has been described in v. 13. etc. Therefore it is only the other class of persons who are ignorant of the true nature of the Self and are qualified for works, and in whose case the supposition of the abandoning of duty from delusion or for fear of bodily trouble is possible,—it is only these that are censured as Tamasic and Rajasic relinquishers (tyagins) in order to praise the abandoning of the fruits of action resorted to by the followers of works who do not know the Self. And the sa*m*nyasin proper has been distinguished by the Lord, when defining the man who has transcended gu*n*as —as one "renouncing all undertakings...who is silent, content with anything, homeless, steady-minded......" (xii. 16—18). And the Lord will hereafter describe (his devotion) as "that supreme consummation of knowledge" (xviii 50) Thus, it is not the sa*m*nyasins, who are the devotees of wisdom, that are referred to here. It is only the abandoning of the fruits of works that, by reason of its being Sattvic, is spoken of as samnyasa in contradistinction to the Tamasic and Rajasic (abandoning of works); but not samnyasa proper, that pre-eminent renunciation of *all* works.

(*Objection*) :—Since xviii. 11 states the reason why renunciation of all action is an impossibility, it is only the samnyasa proper that is spoken of in this connection.

(*Answer*) :—No, because the passage referred to as a statement of the reason is only intended to praise (something else enjoined). Just as the passage "on abandonment of peace closely follows" (xii, 12) is only a praise of the abandonment of the fruits of works, since it is addressed to Arjuna who is ignorant of the Self and who could not therefore follow the several paths previously spoken of, so also, the passage here referred to goes to praise the abandonment of the fruits of action. It is not possible for any one to point out an exception to the proposition. "Renouncing all actions by thought, and self-controlled, the embodied one rests happily in the nine-gated city, neither at all acting nor causing to act." (v. 13). Wherefore these alternative views regarding samnyasa and tyaga concern those persons only for whom works are intended. On the other hand, the Sankhyas, those who see the Supreme Reality, have only to follow the path of knowledge, accompanied with the renunciation of all works; and they have nothing else to do, and do not therefore form the subject of the alternative views set forth here. And so we established this proposition while commenting on ii. 21 and at the commencement of the third discourse.

The Lord's decree is that the ignorant should perform works.

Now, as to these divergent views,

निश्चयं शृणु मे तत्र त्यागे भरतसत्तम ।
त्यागो हि पुरुषव्याघ्र त्रिविधः सम्प्रकीर्तितः ॥ ४ ॥

4. Learn from Me the truth about this abandonment, O best of the Bharatas; abandonment, verily, O best of men, has been declared to be of three kinds.

Do thou learn from My words the truth as to the alternatives of abandonment and renunciation referred to. *Abandonment* (tyaga): the Lord has used this single word here, implying that the meaning of 'tyaga' and 'samnyasa' is one and the same. *Of three kinds*: Tamasic, etc. *Declared*: in the sastras. Because it is hard to know the fact that the threefold (Tamasic, etc.) abandonment denoted by the words 'tyaga' and 'samnyasa' is possible in the case of him alone who does not know the Self and for whom works are intended,—not in the case of him who sees the Supreme Reality,—therefore no one, other than Myself, is able to teach the real truth about the subject. Wherefore, learn from Me what My—the Lord's—decree is as to the real teaching of the sastra.

What is the decree then?—The Lord says:

यज्ञदानतपःकर्म न त्याज्यं कार्यमेव तत् ।
यज्ञो दानं तपश्चैव पावनानि मनीषिणाम् ॥ ५ ॥

5. Practice of worship, gift, and austerity should not be given up; it is quite necessary; worship, gift and austerity are the purifiers of the wise.

The three sorts of action should be performed, for, they cause purity in the wise, *i.e.*, in those who have no desire for fruits.

The obligatory works should be performed without attachment.

एतान्यपि तु कर्माणि सङ्गं त्यक्त्वा फलानि च ।
कर्तव्यानीति मे पार्थ निश्चितं मतमुत्तमम् ॥ ६ ॥

6. But even those actions should be performed, setting aside attachment and the fruits; this, O son of Pritha, is My firm and highest belief.

Those actions, &c: the acts of worship, gift and austerity which have been said to be purifiers, should be performed, setting aside attachment for them and abandoning their fruits.

A proposition was started in the words, 'Learn from Me the truth about this' (xviii. 4); and as a reason for it, it has been stated that worship, etc., are the purifiers: so that the words "even those actions should be performed.........this is My firm and highest belief" form a mere conclusion of the proposition started in xviii. 4. "Even those actions should be performed" cannot be a fresh proposition: for, it is better to construe the passage as related to the immediate subject of the present section. The word "even" implies that these actions should be performed by a seeker of liberation, though they form the cause of bondage in the case of one who has an attachment for the actions and a desire for their fruits. The words 'even those' cannot certainly refer to actions other (than the acts of worship, etc.)

But others explain: Since obligatory (nitya) actions bear no fruits, it is not right to speak of "setting aside attachment and the fruits." Therefore in the words "even those actions" etc., the Lord teaches that even those works which are intended to secure objects of desire—*i.e.*, even *kamaya* or interested works, as opposed to *nitya* or obligatory works—should be performed; how much more then the obligatory acts of worship, gift and austerity.

It is wrong to say so; for it has been declared here that even obligatory actions are productive of fruits, in the words "worship, gift and austerity are the purifiers of the wise" (xviii. 5). To a seeker of liberation who would give up even the obligatory works, looking upon them as the cause of bondage, where is an occasion to engage in interested works? "Even these actions" cannot refer to interested (kamya) works, inasmuch as these have been despised as constituting an inferior path (ii. 49) and decisively declared to be the cause of bondage (iii. 9, ii. 45, ix. 20, 21), and are too far removed from the present section.

Tamasic and Rajasic renunciations of works.

Therefore for a seeker of liberation who is ignorant and is (therefore) bound to perform works,

नियतस्य तु संन्यासः कर्मणो नोपपद्यते ।
मोहात्तस्य परित्यागस्तामसः परिकीर्तितः ॥ ७ ॥

7. Verily, the abandonment of an obligatory duty is not proper; the abandonment thereof from ignorance is declared to be Tamasic.

Not proper: since it is admitted to be a purifier in the case of an ignorant man. To hold that a duty is obligatory and then to abandon it involves a self-contradiction. Therefore, this sort of abandonment is due to ignorance and is said to be Tamasic, inasmuch a signorance is Tamas.

Moreover,

दुःखमित्येव यत्कर्म कायक्लेशभयात्त्यजेत् ।
स कृत्वा राजसं त्यागं नैव त्यागफलं लभेत् ॥ ८ ॥

8. Whatever act one may abandon because it is painful, from fear of bodily trouble, he practises Rajasic abandonment, and he shall obtain no fruit whatever of abandonment.

He does not obtain moksha, which is the fruit of the renunciation of all actions accompanied with wisdom.

Renunciation in works is Sattvic.

What then is the Sattvic abandonment?—The Lord says:

कार्यमित्येव यत्कर्म नियतं क्रियतेऽर्जुन ।
सङ्गं त्यक्त्वा फलं चैव स त्यागः सात्त्विको मतः ॥ ९ ॥

9 Whatever obligatory work is done, by Arjuna, merely because it ought to be done, by abandoning attachment and also the fruit, that abandonment is deemed to be Sattvic.

Abandoning etc. :—These words of the Lord form, as we have said, the authority which declares that obligatory (nitya) works produce fruits.

Or thus :—An ignorant man may even suppose that though the fruits of obligatory works are not declared in the Scripture, the obligatory works, when performed, do produce their fruits for the doer in the form of self-regeneration, or by way of warding off *pratyavaya* or the sin of non-performance. But even this supposition is prevented by the words "abandoning the fruits." Hence the appropriateness. *That abandonment* : the abandoning of all attachment for, and of the fruits of, obligatory works.

(Objection) :—It is the threefold abandonment of *works* —referred to as 'samnyasa' (xviii. 7)—that forms the subject of the present section (xviii. 4, etc.). Out of the three, the Rajasic and Tamasic (sorts of abandonment of works) have been treated of. How is it that the abandonment of attachment and of the *fruits* of works is spoken of as the third? It is something like saying, "Three Brahmanas have come;

two of them are proficient in sha*d*angas or the six auxiliary sciences, and the third is a Kshatriya."

(*Answer*) :—No such objection can be raised here ; for, the object of this section is to praise (the abandonment of the fruits of works, as compared with the abandonment of works, *i e.*, by comparing the two abandonments), both being alike abandonments. In fact the abandonment of works and the abandonment of desire for the fruits do agree in so far as they alike imply abandonment. Accordingly, by despising the two sorts of the abandonment of *works*, as Rajasic and Tamasic abandonments, the abandonment of *desire for the fruits* of the works is praised as being the Sattvic abandonment, in the words 'that abandonment is deemed to be Sattvic.'

From Renunciation in works to Renunciation of all works.

When the man who is qualified for (Karma-Yoga) performs obligatory works without attachment and without a longing for results, his inner sense (anta*h*-kara*n*a) unsoiled by desire for results and regenerated by (the performance of) obligatory works, becomes pure. When pure and tranquil, the inner sense is fit for contemplation of the Self. Now, with a view to teach how the man whose inner sense has been purified by the performance of obligatory works and who is prepared to acquire the Self-knowledge may gradually attain to jnana-nish*th*a or devotion in knowledge, the Lord proceeds as follows :

न द्वेष्ट्यकुशलं कर्म कुशलं नानुषज्जते ।
त्यागी सत्त्वसमाविष्टो मेधावी छिन्नसंशयः ॥ १० ॥

10. He hates not evil action, nor is he attached, to a good one,—he who has abandoned, pervaded by Sattva and possessed of wisdom, his doubts cut asunder.

Evil action: the Kamya-karma, the interested action, which becomes the cause of *samsara* by producing a body. He does not hate evil action, thinking "of what avail is it?" *Good one:* nitya-karma, obligatory action. He cherishes no attachment for it by way of thinking that it leads to moksha by purifying the heart and thereby conducing to knowledge and to devotion in knowledge.—Of whom is this said?—Of him who has abandoned attachment and desire, and who, having abandoned attachment to action and desire for its fruit, performs obligatory works (nitya-karma)—When does he hate no evil action? When is he not attached to a good one?—When he is permeated with Sattva, which causes a discriminative knowledge of the Self and the not-Self. As he is permeated with Sattva, he becomes gifted with wisdom, with knowledge of Self. As he becomes possessed of wisdom, his doubt caused by avidya is cut asunder by the conviction that to abide in the true nature of the Self is alone the means of attaining the Highest Bliss, and that there is no other means.

That is to say, when a man who is qualified (for Karma-Yoga) practises Karma-Yoga in the manner described above and thereby becomes gradually refined in the self (antah-karana), then he knows himself to be that Self; who, as devoid of birth or any other change of condition, is immutable; he renounces all action in thought; he remains without acting or causing others to act; he attains devotion in wisdom, *i.e.*, he attains freedom from action. Thus, the purpose of the Karma-Yoga described above has been taught in this verse.

Renunciation of Fruits is alone possible for the Ignorant.

For the unenlightened man, on the other hand, who wears a body by way of identifying himself with it, who not yet disabused of the notion that the Self is the agent of action, firmly believes that he is himself the agent,—for him who is thus qualified for Karma-Yoga, abandonment of all works is impossible, so that his duty lies only in performing prescribed works by abandoning their fruits,—not in abandoning those works. To impress this point, the Lord proceeds thus:

न हि देहभृता शक्यं त्यक्तुं कर्माण्यशेषतः ।
यस्तु कर्मफलत्यागी स त्यागीत्यभिधीयते ॥ ११ ॥

11. Verily, it is not possible for an embodied being to abandon actions completely; he who abandons the fruits of actions is verily said to be an abandoner.

An embodied being: a body-wearer, *i.e*, he who identifies himself with the body. No man or discrimination can be called a body-wearer, for it has been pointed out (ii. 21, *etc.*) that such a man does not concern himself (in actions) as their agent. So the meaning is: it is not possible for an ignorant man to abandon actions completely. When an ignorant man who is qualified for action performs obligatory works, abandoning merely the desire for the fruits of his actions, he is said to be an abandoner (tyagin) though he is a performer of works. This—the title "abandoner,"—is applied to him for courtesy's sake. Accordingly, the abandonment of all actions is possible for him alone who, realising the Supreme Reality, is not a 'body-wearer' *i.e.*, does not regard the body as the Self.

Effects of the true Renunciation after Death.

Now, what is the benefit which accrues from the abandonment of all actions?—The Lord says:

अनिष्टमिष्टं मिश्रं च त्रिविधं कर्मणः फलम् ।
भवत्यत्यागिनां प्रेत्य न तु संन्यासिनां क्वचित् ॥ १२ ॥

12. The threefold fruit of action,—evil, good, and mixed,—accrues after death to non-abandoners, but never to abandoners.

Fruit: brought forth by the operation of various external factors. It is a doing of avidya; it is like the glamour cast by a juggler's art, very delusive, inhering, to all appearance, in the Innermost Self; by its very etymology, the word 'phala', fruit, implies something that vanishes, something unsubstantial. *Action* (karma): Dharma and Adharma. *Evil*: such as hell (naraka), the animal kingdom, etc. *Good*: such as the Devas. *Mixed*: Good and evil mixed together in one; the humanity. These three sorts of fruits accrue after death to non-abandoners, to the unenlightened, to the followers of Karma-yoga, to the, abandoners (sa*m*nyasins) not strictly so called,* but never to the real sa*m*nyasins, engaged exclusively in the path of knowledge (jnana-nish*t*ha) and belonging to the highest order of sa*m*nyasins, the Parama-ha*m*sa-Parivrajakas. Indeed, exclusive devotion to Right Knowledge cannot but destroy avidya and other seeds of sa*m*sara.

Accordingly, a complete abandonment of all works is possible for him alone who has attained to Right Knowledge, inasmuch as he sees that action and its accessories and its results are all ascribed to the Self by Avidya: but, for the unenlightened man indentifying himself with the body, etc., which constitute action, its agent and accessories, complete

* That is to say, those who perform works without desire for their fruits will necessarily reap, after death, the ftuits of their respective actions.—A.

abandonment of action is not possible. This truth, the Lord proceeds to teach in the following verses:

Factors in the Production of an Act.

पञ्चैतानि महाबाहो कारणानि निबोध मे ।

साङ्ख्ये कृतान्ते प्रोक्तानि सिद्धये सर्वकर्मणाम् ॥ १३ ॥

13 These five factors in the accomplishment of all action, know thou from Me, O mighty-armed, as taught in the Sankhya which is the end of action.

These: which are going to be mentioned. *Learn:* this exhortation is intended to secure steady attention on the part of the hearer to what follows, as well as to indicate the difference (in the view which is going to be presented) as to the nature of those things. In the words "taught in the Sankhya," the Lord praises them, as they are things that ought to be known. *Sankhya:* Vedanta (the Upanishads) in which all the things that have to be known are expounded. It is qualified by the epithet "krita-anta," the end of action, that which puts an end to all action (karma). The verses ii. 46, and iv. 33 teach that all action ceases when the knowledge of the Self arises; so that the Vedanta, which imparts Self-knowledge, is 'the end of action.'

अधिष्ठानं तथा कर्ता करणं च पृथग्विधम् ।

विविधाश्च पृथक्चेष्टा दैवं चैवात्र पञ्चमम् ॥ १४ ॥

14. The seat and actor and the various organs, and the several functions of various sorts, and the Divinity also, the fifth among these;

The seat: the body which is the seat of desire, hatred, happiness, misery, knowledge and the like; *i.e.*, the seat of their manifestation *Actor*: the enjoyer, partaking of the character of the upadhi with which it may be associated. *The various organs*: such as the sense of hearing, by which to perceive sound, etc. *Functions*: of the air (vayu), such as outbreathing and inbreathing. *Of various sorts*: twelve in number. *Divinity*: such as the Aditya aad other Gods by whose aid the eye and other organs discharge their functions.

शरीरवाङ्मनोभिर्यत्कर्म प्रारभते नरः ।
न्याय्यं वा विपरीतं वा पञ्चैते तस्य हेतवः ॥ १५ ॥

15. Whatever action a man does by the body, speech and mind, right or the opposite, these five are its causes.

Right: not opposed to dharma, taught in the sastra. *The opposite*: what is opposed to dharma and opposed to sastra. Even those actions,—the act of twinkling and the like,—which are the necessary conditions of life are denoted by the expression "the right or the opposite", since they are but the effects of the past dharma and a-dharma. *Its causes*: the causes of every action.

(*Objection*):—The body, etc. (xviii. 14), are necessary factors in every action. Why do you speak of (a distinction in actions) in the words "whatever action a man does by the *body*, *speech* or *mind*?"

(*Answer*):—This objection cannot be urged against us. In the performance of every action, whether enjoyed or forbidden, one of the three—body, speech or mind—has a more prominent share than the rest; while seeing, hearing, and other activities, which form mere concomitants of life, are subordinate to the activity of that one. All actions are thus classed into three groups and are spoken of as performed by body, or speech, or mind. Even at the time of fruition, the fruit of an action is enjoyed through the instrumentality of body, speech and mind, one of them being more prominent than the rest. Hence no gainsaying of the assertion that all the five are the causes of action (xviii. 14.)

The agency of the self is an illusion.

तत्रैवं सति कर्तारमात्मानं केवलं तु यः ।
पश्यत्यकृतबुद्धित्वान्न स पश्यति दुर्मतिः ॥ १६ ॥

16 Now, such being the case, verily, he who as untrained in understanding, looks on the pure Self as the agent, that man of perverted intelligence sees not.

Now: with reference to what we are speaking of. *Such being the case*: every action being accomplished by the five causes described above. *Now......case:* this shows the reason why the person here referred to is said to be a man of perverted intelligence. The unenlightened one, in virtue of his ignorance, identifies the Self with the five causes and looks upon the pure Self as the agent of the action, which is really accomplished by those five causes.—Why does he regard them so?—For, his understanding (buddhi) has not been trained in the Vedanta, has not been trained by a master's teaching, has not been trained in the principles of reasoning. Even he who, while maintaining the existence of the disembodied Self, looks upon the pure Self as the agent, is a man of untrained understanding; he does not therefore see the truth about the Self and action. He is therefore a man of perverted intelligence,—his intelligence takes a wrong direction, is vicious, continually leading to birth and death. Though seeing, yet he does not see (the truth), like a man whose *timira*-affected eye sees many moons, or like one who regards that the moon moves when the clouds are in motion, or like a man who, seated in a vehicle, regards himself as running—when it is the others (the bearers) that run.

Realisation of the Non Agency of the Self Leads to Absolution from the Effects of All Works.

Who then is the wise man that sees rightly ?—The answer follows :

यस्य नाहङ्कृतो भावो बुद्धिर्यस्य न लिप्यते ।
हत्वाऽपि स इमांल्लोकान्न हन्ति न निबध्यते ॥ १७ ॥

17. He who is free from egotistic notion, whose mind is not tainted,—though he kills these creatures, he kills not, he is not bound.

He whose mind has been well trained in the scriptures, well-trained by a master's instructions, and well-trained in the sound principles of reasoning, is free from the egotistic notion that 'I am the agent.' He thinks thus: It is these five—the body, etc., ascribed to the Self through avidya—that are the causes of all action, not I. I am the witness of their actions. I am "without breath, without mind, pure, higher than the Indestructible which is Supreme" (Mu*n*d. Up. 2·1·2). I am pure and immutable. He whose anta*h*-kara*n*a (buddhi), which is an upadhi of the Self, is not tainted, does not repent thus : "I have done this : thereby I shall go to naraka (hell)." He is wise: he sees rightly: though he kills all these living creatures, he commits no act of killing, nor is he bound by the fruit of a-dharma as an effect of that act.

(*Objection*) :—Even supposing that this is intended as a mere praise, the statement that "though he kills all these creatures, he does not kill" involves a self-contradiction.

(*Answer*) :—This objection cannot stand ; for, the statement can be explained by distinguishing the two standpoints of worldly conception and absolute truth. From the stand-point of worldly conception, which consists in thinking 'I am the killer' by identifying the Self with the physical body etc., the Lord says, "though he kills;" and from the stand-point of absolute truth explained above, He says. 'he kills not, he is not bound.' Thus both are quite explicable.

(*Objection*) :—The Self *does* act in conjunction with the body, etc., as implied by the use of the word 'pure' in xviii. 16, 'he who looks on the pure Self as the agent.'

(*Answer*) :—This contention is untenable; for the Self being, by nature, immutable, we cannot conceive Him to act in conjunction with the body, etc. What is subject to change can alone conjoin with others, and thus conjoined can become the agent. But there can be no conjunction of the immutable Self with anything whatsoever, and He cannot therefore act in conjunction with another. Thus, the isolated condition being natural condition. And His immutability is quite evident to all, as taught by the *sruti*, *smriti* and reason. In the Gita itself, for instance, it has been over and over again taught in the words, "He is unchangeable" (ii. 25): "actions are wrought by gunas" (III. 27); "though dwelling in the body, he acts not" (xiii 31). And the same thing is also taught in the passages of the *sruti* such as "It meditates as it were, It moves as it were" (Bri Up. 4-3-7). By reasoning also we may establish the same, thus:—That the Self is an entity without parts, is not dependent on another, and is immutable, is the royal road (*i.e.*, is undisputed). Even if it be admitted that the Self is subject to change, He should only be subject to a change of His own; the actions of the body, etc, can never be attributed to the agency of the Self. Indeed, the action of one cannot go to another that has not done it. And what is attributed to the Self by avidya cannot really pertain to Him, in the same why that the mother-of-pearl cannot become silver, or (to take another illustration) in the same way that surface and dirt ascribed by children through ignorance to akasa cannot really pertain to akasa. Accordingly, any changes that may take place in the body, etc., belong to them only, not to the Self. Wherefore, it is but right to say that in the absence of egotism and of all taint in the mind, the wise man neither kills nor is bound.

Having started this proposition in the words "he slays not, nor is he slain;" (ii. 19) having stated in ii. 20 as the reason therefore the immutability of the Self, having in the beginning of the sastra (ii. 21) briefly taught that to a wise man there is no need for works, and having introduced the subject here and there in the middle and expatiated upon it, the Lord now concludes it in the words that the wise man "kills not, nor is bound" with a view to sum up the teaching of the sastra. Thus in the absence of the egotistic feeling of embodied existence, the samnyasins renounce all avidya-generated action. and it is therefore right to say that the threefold fruit of action "evil, good and mixed" (xviii. 12), does not accrue to the samnyasins; and the further conclusion also is inevitable that quite the reverse is the lot of others. This teaching of the Gitasastra has been concluded here. To show that this essence of the whole Vedic Teaching should be investigated and understood by wise men of trained intelligence, it has been expounded by us here and there in several sections in accordance with the scripture (sastra) and reason.

The impulses to action.

Now will be mentioned the impulses to action :

ज्ञानं ज्ञेयं परिज्ञाता त्रिविधा कर्मचोदना ।
करणं कर्म कर्तेति त्रिविधः कर्मसङ्ग्रहः ॥ १८ ॥

18. Knowledge, the object known, the knower, (form) the threefold impulse to action; the organ, the end, the agent, from the threefold basis of action.

Knowledge: any knowledge, knowledge in general. Similarly *the object known* refers to objects in general, to all objects of knowledge. *The knower*: the experiencer, partaking of the nature of the upadhi, a creature of avidya. This triad forms the threefold impulse to all action, to action in general. Indeed, performance of action with a view to avoid a thing or to obtain another and so on, is possible only when there is a conjunction of the three,—knowledge, etc. The actions accomplished by the five (causes of action),—by the body, etc.,—and grouped into three classes according to their respective seats—speech, mind, body,—are all traceable to the interplay of the organ, etc.: and this is taught in the second part of the verse. *The organ*: that by which something is done; *external* organs being the organ of hearing, etc., and the internal organs being buddhi (intelligence), etc. *The end*: that which is sought for, that which is reached through action by the agent. *The agent*: he who sets the organs going, partaking of the nature of the upadhi (in which he works). In these three all action inheres, and they are therefore said to form the threefold basis of action.

The impulses are threefold according to the gunas.

Inasmuch as action, the several factors of action, and the fruit, are all made up of the gu*n*as, the Lord now proceeds to teach the threefold distinction of each, according to the three distinct gu*n*as, Sattva, Rajas and Tamas:

ज्ञानं कर्म च कर्ता च त्रिधैव गुणभेदतः ।
प्रोच्यते गुणसङ्ख्याने यथावच्छृणु तान्यपि ॥ १९ ॥

19. Knowledge and action, and the agent, are said in the science of gu*n*as to be of three kinds only, according to the distinction in gu*n*as. Hear thou duly of them.

Action (karma): 'karma' here means action (kriya). It is not used in the technical sense of the word denoting the object of an action, what is sought to be attained by means of action. *Agent*: the performer of acts. They are of three kinds only—This restriction is intended to imply the absence of dintinctions other than that caused by the gu*n*as.—*Gunas*: such as Sattva. The science of gu*n*as here referred to is Kapila's system of philosophy.—Even Kapila's science of gu*n*as is certainly an authority so far as it concerns gu*n*as and their experiencer (bhokt*r*i). Though they are opposed to us as regards the supreme truth, *viz*., the oneness or non-duality of Brahman, still the followers of Kapila are of acknowledged authority in the exposition of the functions of gu*n*as and of their products, and their science is therefore accepted here as an authority as serving to extol the teaching which follows. Hence no inconsistency. *Hear, etc*: Pay attention to the teaching which follows here, concerning knowledge and the rest, as well as their various distinctions caused by different gu*n*as, as I describe them duly, according to science, according to reason.

Sattvic Knowledge.

Here follows the threefold character of knowledge:

सर्वभूतेषु येनैकं भावमव्ययमीक्षते ।
अविभक्तं विभक्तेषु तज्ज्ञानं विद्धि सात्त्विकम् ॥ २० ॥

20. That by which a man sees the one Indestructible Reality in all beings, inseparate in the separated,—that knowledge know thou as Sattvic.

Reality (Bhava): the one Self. *Indestructible*: which cannot be exhausted either in itself or in its properties; Kutastha or immutable. *All beings*: from *Avyakta*, or the unmanifested matter, down to the *sthavara* or unmoving objects. That Reality, the Self, is not different in different bodies; like the akasa, the Self admits of no division. Know thou this direct and right perception of the non-dual Self as Sattvic.

Rajasic Knowledge.

The dualistic fallacious systems of philosophy are Rajasic and Tamasic, and therefore they cannot directly bring about the cessation of *samsara*

पृथक्त्वेन तु यज्ज्ञानं नानाभावान्पृथग्विधान् ।
वेत्ति सर्वेषु भूतेषु तज्ज्ञानं विद्धि राजसम् ॥ २१ ॥

21. But that knowledge which by differentiation, sees in all the creatures various entities of distinct kinds, that knowledge know thou as Rajasic.

By differentiation: regarding them as different in different bodies. *Entities*: Selfs. *Which sees*, etc.: This should be interpreted to mean 'by which one sees,' since knowledge cannot be an agent.

Tamasic Knowledge.

यत्तु कृत्स्नवदेकस्मिन् कार्ये सक्तमहैतुकम् ।
अतत्त्वार्थवदल्पं च तत्तामसमुदाहृतम् ॥ २२ ॥

22. But that which clings to one single effect as if it were all, without reason, having no real object, and narrow, that is declared to be Tamasic.

Tamasic knowledge is engrossed in one single effect,—such as the body or an external idol—as though it is all-comprehensive, thinking 'this body is the Self' or 'that is God,' and that there is nothing higher than that. Jiva (soul), for example, dwelling in the body is regarded by the naked *S*rama*n*akas,* etc., as being of the size of that body, and the I*s*vara is regarded (by some) to be the mere stone or piece of wood † This knowledge is not founded on reason and does not perceive things as they are. Because it is not founded on reason, it is *narrow*, as extending over a limited area, or as producing very small results. This knowledge is said to be Tamasic, because it is found only in Tamasic beings possessing no faculty of discrimination.

Sattvic Action.

The threefold nature of action is next described :

नियतं सङ्गरहितमरागद्वेषतः कृतम् ।
अफलप्रेप्सुना कर्म यत्तत्सात्त्विकमुच्यते ॥ २३ ॥

23. An action which is ordained, which is free from attachment, which is done without love or hatred by one not desirous of the fruit, that action is declared to be Sattvic.

Ordained : Obligatory (nitya). It is not an action done by one impelled by love or hatred.

Rajasic Action.

यत्तु कामेप्सुना कर्म साहङ्कारेण वा पुनः ।
क्रियते बहुलायासं तद्राजसमुदाहृतम् ॥ २४ ॥

* The Jains. Some MSS. read *Kshapanakas*.

† The material of which the image is made.

24. But the action which is done by one longing for pleasures, or done by the egotistic, costing much trouble, that is declared to be Rajasic.

Pleasures: as fruits of action. *The Egotistic*: not as distinguished from one who has realised the true nature of the Self (who is absolutely free from egotism), but as distinguished from one who is free from pride in the sense in which an ordinary srotriya (a devotee of the Vedic Religion) of the world is expected to be free from egotism. For, he who is absolutely without egotism, *i.e.*, one who has realised the Self, cannot even be imagined to long for the fruit of an action; or to do an action costing much trouble. Even the doer of a Sattvic action is ignorant of the Self and is egotistic; much more so are the Rajasic and Tamasic doers. In common parlance, a srotriya who is ignorant of the Self is said to be free from egotism; we say "He is a modest (unegotistic) Brahmana." It is only from this class of persons that the doer of a Rajasic action is distinguished as being egotistic.

Tamasic Action.

अनुबन्धं क्षयं हिंसामनपेक्ष्य च पौरुषम् ।
मोहादारभ्यते कर्म यत्तत्तामसमुच्यते ॥ २५ ॥

25. The action which is undertaken from delusion, without regarding the consequence, loss, injury, and ability, that is declared to be Tamasic.

Loss: Loss of power and of wealth accruing from the action done. *Injury* to living beings. *Ability*: one's own ability to complete the work.

Sattvic Agent.

Now the Lord proceeds to treat of the distinction among agents.

मुक्तसङ्गोऽनहंवादी धृत्युत्साहसमन्वितः ।
सिद्ध्यसिद्ध्योर्निर्विकारः कर्ता सात्त्विक उच्यते ॥ २६ ॥

26. Free from attachment, not given to egotism, endued with firmness and vigour, unaffected in success and failure, an agent is said to be Sattvic.

Success: Attainment of the fruit of the action done. *Unaffected:* as having been impelled to act merely by the authority of the sastra, not by a desire for the fruits.

Rajasic Agent.

रागी कर्मफलप्रेप्सुर्लुब्धो हिंसात्मकोऽशुचिः ।
हर्षशोकान्वितः कर्ता राजसः परिकीर्तितः ॥ २७ ॥

27. Passionate, desiring to attain the fruit of action, greedy, cruel, impure, subject to joy and sorrow, such an agent is said to be Rajasic.

Greedy: thirsting for another's property, not giving away one's own property to worthy persons, etc. *Cruel:* doing harm to others. *Impure:* devoid of external and internal purity. *Subject to joy and sorrow:* rejoicing on the attainment of what is desirable, and feeling sorry on the attainment of what is not desirable or on having to part with what is desirable. Joy or sorrow may arise at the success or failure of the action in which he is engaged

Tamasic Agent.

अयुक्तः प्राकृतः स्तब्धः शठो नैष्कृतिकोऽलसः ।
विषादी दीर्घसूत्री च कर्ता तामस उच्यते ॥ २८ ॥

28. Unsteady, vulgar, unbending, deceptive, wicked, indolent, desponding, and procrastinating, (such) an agent is said to be Tamasic.

Vulgar: quite uncultured in intellect (buddhi), who is like a child. *Unbending*: not bowing like a stick to anybody. *Deceptive*: concealing his real power. *Wicked*: setting others at variance with each other. *Indolent*: not doing even what ought to be done. *Desponding*: always depressed in spirit. *Procrastinating*: postponing duties too long, always sluggish, not doing even in a month what ought to be done to-day or to-morrow.

Intellect and Firmness are threefold according to gunas.

बुद्धेर्भेदं धृतेश्चैव गुणतस्त्रिविधं शृणु ।
प्रोच्यमानमशेषेण पृथक्त्वेन धनञ्जय ॥ २९ ॥

29. The threefold division of intellect and firmness according to qualities, about to be taught fully and distinctively (by Me), hear thou, O Dhananjaya.

Qualities: Gunas, such as Sattva. The first half of the verse contains in an aphoristic form what is going to be taught. *Dhananjaya*: the conqueror of wealth. Arjuna is so called because he acquired much wealth,—human and divine, material and spiritual,—during his tour of conquest through the four quarters of the earth.

Sattvic Intellect.

प्रवृत्तिं च निवृत्तिं च कार्याकार्ये भयाभये ।
बन्धं मोक्षं च या वेत्ति बुद्धिः सा पार्थ सात्त्विकी ॥ ३० ॥

30. That which knows action and inaction, what ought to be done and what ought not to be done, fear and absence of fear, bondage and liberation, that intellect is Sattvic, O Partha.

Action (pravritti): the cause of bondage, the karma-marga, the path of action as taught in the sastra. *Inaction* (nivritti): the cause of liberation, the path of samnyasa.—As 'action' (pravritti) and 'inaction' (nivritti) occur in connection with 'bondage' (bandha) and 'liberation' (moksha), they have been interpreted to mean the paths of action and renunciation (karma and samnyasa). *What...done*: the necessity for doing or not doing—by one who relies on the sastra—at particular places and times, actions producing visible or invisible results, according as they are enjoined or prohibited by the scriptural or social ethics. *Fear* etc.: the cause of fear and the cause of fearlessness, either visible or invisible. *Bondage and liberation*: together with their causes. *Knowledge* is a vritti or function or state of intellect (buddhi), whereas intellect is what functions or undergoes change of state.* Even *firmness* (dhriti) is only a paricular function or state of intellect.

Rajasic Intellect.

यया धर्ममधर्मं च कार्यं चाकार्यमेव च ।
अयथावत्प्रजानाति बुद्धिः सा पार्थ राजसी ॥ ३१ ॥

31. That by which one wrongly understands dharma and a-dharma, and also what ought to be done and what ought not to be done, that intellect, O Partha, is Rajasic.

Dharma is what is ordained in the scriptures and *a-dharma* is what is prohibited in them. *What...done*: the same that was mentioned already. (xviii. 30). † *Wrongly*: in opposition to what is determined by all (authorities).

---

* This is to show how the knowledge (jnana) whose threefold nature has been described already (xviii, 20-22) is different from the intellect (buddhi) whose threefold nature is here described.—A.

† Dharma and a-dharma here spoken of refer to the 'apurva' *i.e.*, the forms which actions assume after their performance till their effects become perceptible; whereas karya and a-karya refer to the performance or the non-performance of the acts. Hence no tautology.—A.

Tamasic Intellect.

अधर्मं धर्ममिति या मन्यते तमसा वृता ।
सर्वार्थान् विपरीतांश्च बुद्धिः सा पार्थ तामसी ॥ ३२ ॥

32. That which, enveloped in darkness, sees adharma as dharma and all things perverted, that intellect, O Partha, is Tamasic.

It takes quite a perverted view of all things to be known.

Sattvic Firmness.

धृत्या यया धारयते मनःप्राणेन्द्रियक्रियाः ।
योगेनाव्यभिचारिण्या धृतिः सा पार्थ सात्त्विकी ॥ ३३ ॥

33. The firmness which is ever accompanied by Yoga, and by which the activities of thought, of life-breaths and sense-organs, O Partha, are held fast, such a firmness is Sattvic.

Yoga: samadhi or concentration of mind. *Held fast*: restrained from rushing into ways which are opposed to the sastra. It is only when they are restrained by firmness (of the intellect) that they do not rush into ways which are opposed to the sastra. The meaning of the passage is this: He who, by unflinching firmness, restrains the activities of thought (manas), of life-breaths and sense-organs, restrains them by Yoga.*

Rajasic Firmness.

यया तु धर्मकामार्थान् धृत्या धारयतेऽर्जुन ।
प्रसङ्गेन फलाकाङ्क्षी धृतिः सा पार्थ राजसी ॥ ३४ ॥

* That is to say, one can restrain these activities by the firmness only which is every accompanied by samadhi, by concentration of mind in the Brahman. By mere firmness, which is not so accompanied by samadhi, one cannot invariably restrain them.—A.

34. But the firmness with which one holds fast to dharma and pleasures and wealth, desirous of the fruit of each on its occasion, that firmness, O Partha, is Rajasic.

Dharma etc.: when a person is firmly convinced at heart that dharma, pleasure and wealth ought always to be secured and is desirous of the fruit of each whenever that one (dharma or pleasure or wealth) occupies his attention, the firmness of such a person is Rajasic.

Tamasic Firmness.

यया स्वप्नं भयं शोकं विषादं मदमेव च ।
न विमुञ्चति दुर्मेधा धृतिः सा पार्थ तामसी ॥ ३५ ॥

35. That with which a stupid man does not give up sleep, fear, grift, depression and lust, that firmness, O Partha, is Tamasic.

The stupid man holds sensual gratification in high esteem and never gives up lasciviousness. He regards sleep, etc., as things that ought always to be resorted to.

Pleasure is threefold according to gunas.

The threefold division of actions and of the several factors (karakas) concerned in action, has been described. Here follows the threefold division of pleasure which is the effect of actions.

सुखं त्विदानीं त्रिविधं शृणु मे भरतर्षभ ।
अभ्यासाद्रमते यत्र दुःखान्तं च निगच्छति ॥ ३६ ॥

36. And now hear from Me,—O lord of the Bharatas,—of the threefold pleasure, in which one

delights by practice and surely comes to the end of pain*.

Hear: Pay steady attention to. *Practice*: familiarity, frequency. *The end*: cessation or alleviation.

Sattvic Pleasure.

यत्तदग्रे विषमिव परिणामेऽमृतोपमम् ।
तत्सुखं सात्त्विकं प्रोक्तमात्मबुद्धिप्रसादजम् ॥ ३७ ॥

37. That which is like poison at first, at the end, like nectar that pleasure is declared to be Sattvic, born of the purity of one's own mind.

Like poison at first: on its first occurrence it is attended with pain as it is preceded by much trouble in the acquisition of *jnana* or spiritual knowledge, of *vairagya* or indifference to worldly objects, of *dhyana* and *samadhi*. At the end, the pleasure is like nectar, arising from mature knowledge and indifference to external objects. *Declared*: by the wise. *Born, etc*: born of the purity of one's own buddhi or antah-karana: or born of the perfectly clear knowledge of the Self. Being so born, the pleasure is Sattvic.

Rajasic Pleasure.

विषयेन्द्रियसंयोगाद्यत्तदग्रेऽमृतोपमम् ।
परिणामे विषमिव तत्सुखं राजसं स्मृतम् ॥ ३८ ॥

38. That pleasure which arises from the contract of the sense-organ with the object, at first like nectar, in the end like poison, that is declared to be Rajasic.

---

* The second half of this verse is construed by other commentators, such as Sridhara and Madhusudana, with the next verse. Though the *bhashya* does not make it clear how it should be construed, I have, following Anandagiri, made the whole verse appear to be a description of the threefold pleasure— Tr

In the end like poison: after indulgence. the (sensual) pleasure proves to be like poison, because it leads to deterioration in strength, vigour, colour, wisdom, intellect, wealth and energy; and because it leads to a-dharma, and, as an effect thereof, to hell (naraka).

Tamasic Pleasure:

यदग्रे चानुबन्धे च सुखं मोहनमात्मनः ।
निद्रालस्यप्रमादोत्थं तत्तामसमुदाहृतम् ॥ ३९ ॥

39. The pleasure which at first and in the sequel is delusive of the self, arising from sleep, indolence, and heedlessness, that pleasure is declared to be Tamasic.

In the sequel: after the termination.

No man or god is free from gunas.

Here follows the verse which concludes the present subject:

न तदस्ति पृथिव्यां वा दिवि देवेषु वा पुनः ।
सत्त्वं प्रकृतिजैर्मुक्तं यदेभिः स्यात्त्रिभिर्गुणैः ॥ ४० ॥

40. There is no being on earth, or again in heaven among the Devas, that can be free from these three gu*n*as born of Prak*r*iti.

Being: animate or inanimate. *Gunas*: such as Sattva. *On Earth*: among men.

The sequel sums up the whole Doctrine.

The whole sa*m*sara, manifested as action, instruments of action, and results, made up of the gu*n*as (Sattva, Rajas, and Tamas), and set up by avidya,—the evil of sa*m*sara has been thus described as well as its root. It has also been figuratively represented as a tree, in xv. 1, *et seq.* It has also been said that after having cut the tree of *samsara* asunder with the strong sword of non-attachment, "Then That Goal should be sought after" (xv. 3, 4). From this it may follow that, as everything is made up of the three *gunas*, a cessation of the cause of *samsara* cannot be brought about. Now, it is with a view to show how its cessation can be brought about, with a view, further, to sum up the whole teaching of the Gita-sastra, and with a view to show what the exact teaching of the Vedas and the *smritis* is which should be followed by those who seek to attain the highest end of man,—it is with this view that the next section, from xviii. 41 onward, is commenced.

Duties of the four castes ordained according to nature.

ब्राह्मणक्षत्रियविशां शूद्राणां च परन्तप ।
कर्माणि प्रविभक्तानि स्वभावप्रभवैर्गुणैः ॥ ४१ ॥

41. Of Brahma*n*as and Kshatriyas and Vai*s*yas, as also of Sudras, O Parantapa, the duties are divided according to the qualities born of nature.

Sudras are separated from others—who are all mentioned together in one compound word—because Sudras are of one birth and are debarred from the study of the Vedas. *Divided:* the duties are allotted to each class, as distinguished from those pertaining to the other classes.—By what standard?—According to the qualities (*gunas*) born of nature. Nature (svabhava) is the Isvara's Prak*r*iti, the Maya made up of the three *gunas*. It is in accordance with the *gunas* of the Prak*r*iti that duties—such as serenity and the like—are assigned to the Brahma*n*as, etc. respectively.

Or to explain in another way: The source of the Brahma*n*a's nature (svabhava) is the *guna* of Sattva; the source of the Kshatriya's nature is Rajas and Sattva, the latter being subordinate to the former; the source of the Vaisya's nature is Rajas and Tamas, the latter being subordinate to the former; the source of the Sudra's nature is Tamas and Rajas, the latter being subordinate to the former. For, as we see, the characteristic features of their nature are serenity, lordliness, activity, and dullness respectively.

Or to interpret yet in another way :—Nature (svabhava) is the tendency (Samskara, Vasana) in living beings acquired by them in the past births, and manifesting itself in the present birth by way of being ready to yield its effects : and this nature is the source of the gunas, it being impossible for the gunas to manifest themselves without a cause. The assertion that nature (Samskara, Vasana) is the cause (of the gunas) means that it is a kind of specific cause.* The duties, such as serenity, are assigned to the four classes in accordance with the gunas of Sattva, Rajas and Tamas, which are brought into manifestation by their respective natural tendencies, and which lead to those duties as their natural effects.

(Objection) :—The duties of Brahmanas, etc., are enjoined by the sastra and are assigned to them by the sastra. How then can it be said that they are divided according to Sattva and other gunas ?

(Answer) :—There is no room here for any such objection. By the sastra, too, are the duties—such as serenity—assigned to the Brahmanas, etc., only in accordance with their respective gunas, such as Sattva, but not independently of them. Wherefore it is said that duties are assigned according to gunas, though it has also been said that they are assigned by the sastra

What then are those duties ?—The answer follows :

* Nimitta-karana or secondary cause, as opposed to the Upadana-karana or matearial cause of the gunas, namely, Prakriti.—A.

शमो दमस्तपः शौचं क्षान्तिरार्जवमेव च ।
ज्ञानं विज्ञानमास्तिक्यं ब्रह्मकर्म स्वभावजम् ॥ ४२ ॥

42. Serenity, self-restraint, austerity, purity, forgiveness, and also uprightness, knowledge, wisdom, faith,—these are the duties of the Brahmanas, born of nature.

'Serenity' and 'self-restraint' have already been explained (xvi. 1, 2). *Austerity*: physical austerity, and so on, mentioned above (xvii, 14, 15. 16). *Purity*: already explained. *Faith*: in the teaching of the scriptures. *Born of nature*: this means the same here as in the latter portion of xviii. 41.

शौर्यं तेजो धृतिर्दाक्ष्यं युद्धे चाप्यपलायनम् ।
दानमीश्वरभावश्च क्षात्रं कर्म स्वभावजम् ॥ ४३ ॥

43. Bravery, boldness, fortitude, promptness, not flying from battle, generosity and lordliness are the duties of the Kshatriyas, born of nature.

Fortitude: that by which upheld one is not subject to depression, under any circumstances whatever. *Promptness*: the performing, without confusion, of duties which present themselves quite unexpectedly and demand ready action. *Not flying from battle*: not turning away from foes. *Lordliness*: exercise of ruling power over those who are to be ruled.

कृषिगोरक्ष्यवाणिज्यं वैश्यकर्म स्वभावजम् ।
परिचर्यात्मकं कर्म शूद्रस्यापि स्वभावजम् ॥ ४४ ॥

44. Ploughing, cattle-rearing, and trade are the duties of the Vaisyas, born of nature. And of the nature of service is the duty of the Sudra, born of nature.

Devotion to one's own duty leads to perfection.

These duties, respectively enjoined on the several castes, lead, when rightly performed, to Svarga as their natural result, as stated in the smritis, such as the following : "Men of several castes and orders, each devoted to his respective duties, reap the fruits of their actions after death, and then by the residual (karma) attain to births in superior countries, castes and families, possessed of comparatively superior dharma, span of life, learning, conduct, wealth, happiness and intelligence." (Apastamba-Dharmasutra, 2-2-2, 3). And in the Purana also are specified the different results and worlds which the several castes and orders attain. But, from the operation of a new cause * the following result accrues.

स्वे स्वे कर्मण्यभिरतः संसिद्धिं लभते नरः ।
स्वकर्मनिरतः सिद्धिं यथा विन्दति तच्छृणु ॥ ४५ ॥

45. Devoted each to his own duty, man attains perfection ; how one, devoted to one's own duty, attains success, that do thou hear.

Each to his own duty : as ordained according to his nature. *Man :* he who is qualified (for Karma-Yoga). *Perfection* (samsiddhi) : which consists in the body and senses being qualified for the devotion of knowledge (jnana-nishtha) after all their impurities have been washed away by the performance of one's own duty.—Can this perfection be attained directly by the mere performance of one's own duty † ?—No.—How then ?—Learn how it can be attained :

---

* That is, when the same duties are performed, not for the sake of their immediate results, but for the sake of Moksha.—A.

† The questioner understands 'perfection' in the sense of absolute perfection *i. e.*, Moksha. It is, of course, impossible to attain Moksha by works alone.—A.

यतः प्रवृत्तिर्भूतानां येन सर्वमिदं ततम् ।
स्वकर्मणा तमभ्यर्च्य सिद्धिं विन्दति मानवः ॥ ४६ ॥

46. Him from whom is the evolution of (all) beings, by whom all this is pervaded,—by worshipping Him with his proper duty, man attains perfection.

'Pravritti' (in the text) may mean either *evolution* or *activity*; and it proceeds from the Isvara, the Antaryamin, the Ruler within. *Beings*: living creatures. *His proper duty*: each according to his caste, as described above. Worshipping the Lord by performing his duty, man attains perfection, in so far only as he becomes qualified for the devotion of knowledge (jnana-nishtha).

Such being the cause, therefore,

श्रेयान् स्वधर्मो विगुणः परधर्मात्स्वनुष्ठितात् ।
स्वभावनियतं कर्म कुर्वन्नाप्नोति किल्बिषम् ॥ ४७ ॥

47. Better is one's own duty (though) destitute of merits, than the duty of another well performed. Doing the duty ordained according to nature one incurs no sin.

Just as a poisonous substance does not injure the worm born in that substance, so, he who does the duty ordained according to his own nature incurs no sin.

One ought not to abandon one's own duty.

It has been said that he who does the duty ordained according to his nature incurs no sin like a worm born in poison, that the duty of another brings on fear, and that he who does not know the Self cannot indeed remain even for a moment without doing action. Wherefore,

सहजं कर्म कौन्तेय सदोषमपि न त्यजेत् ।
सर्वारम्भा हि दोषेण धूमेनाग्निरिवावृताः ॥ ४८ ॥

48. The duty born with oneself, O son of Kunti, though faulty, one ought not to abandon; for, all undertakings are surrounded with evil, as fire with smoke.

Born with oneself: born with the very birth of man. *Faulty*: as everything is composed of the three *gunas*. *All undertakings*: whatever the duties are; by context, one's own as well as other's duties; for. the reason here assigned is that they are all made up of the three *gunas*.

Though a man may perform another's duty, abandoning what is called his own duty, the duty born with himself, he is not free from fault; and another's duty brings on fear.* And since it is not possible for any man who does not know the Self to give up action entirely, therefore he ought not to abandon action (karma).

Is entire renunciation of action possible?

(Now, let us enquire): Is it because of the impossibility of entire abandonment of action that no one ought to renounce one's own (nature-born) duty, or is it because some sin † accrues from the abandoning of the duty born with oneself?

(*Question*):—Now, of what good is this enquiry?

(*Answer*):—In the first place, if the duty born with oneself ought not to be abandoned (merely) because of the impossibility of renouncing action entirely, then it would follow that there can be nothing but merit in renouncing it entirely.

---

* Therefore, it is not right to do another's duty.—A.

† The sin (pratyavaya) arising from the neglect of the duty enjoined in the *sruti* as obligatory.—A.

The Sankhya, Buddhistic and Vaiseshika theories.

(*Objection*) :—Yes; but an entire renunciation is not possible.—Is the soul (Purusha) always mobile like the gu*n*as of the Sankhyas? Or, is action itself the actor (soul), like the five Skandhas of the Buddhists, undergoing destruction every moment? In either case, an entire renunciation of action is impossible.*

Now there is also a third theory—When the thing (soul) acts, then it is active; when it does not act, then it is actionless. Such being the case, it is possible to renounce action entirely. And there is this peculiarity in this theory: neither is the thing (soul) ever mobile, nor is action itself the actor (the soul); but it is a permanent fixed substance, wherein action which was non-existent before arises, and wherein action which has been existent ceases, while the substance remains pure (actionless), with the potentiality (of the activity) in it, and as such forms the actor.—Thus say the followers of Ka*n*ada. What objection is there to this theory?

Refutation of the Vaiseshika theory.

(*Answer*) :—There is certainly this objection, that it is contrary to the Lord's teaching.—How do you know?—For, the Lord has said 'there can be no existence of the non-existent' (ii. 16) and so on. But according to the followers of Ka*n*ada, the non-existent comes into existence, and the existent becomes non-existent. Wherefore their theory is contrary to the Lord's teaching.

(*Objection*) :—How can it be objected to if it agrees with reason, though it may be opposed to the Lord's teaching?

(*Answer*) :—We reply:

---

* Inasmuch as it would imply that the soul undergoes change in its very nature:—A.

This view is certainly objectionable, because it is opposed to all evidence.—How?—If a dvyanuka (an aggregate of two atoms) or other substance is absolutely non-existent before its production, and if, remaining for a time after production, it again becomes non-existent, then it follows that what was non-existent becomes existent, and what is existent will become non-existent; that non-entity becomes an entity and an entity becomes non-entity. In that case it must be that a non-entity (abhava) which is to become an entity (bhava) is like a rabbit's horn before becoming an entity, and that it becomes an entity by the action of the threefold cause,—of the material, the non-material or accidental, and the efficient causes, (samavayi-asamavayi-nimitta-karanas). Now it is not possible to hold (in the present case) that a non-entity is born and needs a cause; for, it does not apply to other non-entities, such as a rabbit's horn If a pot or the like, which is to be produced (as an effect), be of the nature of an entity, then we can understand that when it is to be produced as an effect, it needs a cause so far merely as regards its manifestation.

Moreover, if the non-existent should become existent and the existent should become non-existent, then nobody can be certain as to anything whatsoever in matters of evidence and things ascertainable by evidence, inasmuch as there can be no certainty that the existent will continue to be existent and the non-existent will continue to be non-existent.

Moreover, when they (the followers of Kanada) say that a dvyanuka or such other substance is produced as an effect, they speak of it as connected with its cause and as existent. Having been non-existent before production, it becomes, in virtue of the operation of its cause connected with that cause—the ultimate *atoms*—and with *existence*, by the relation known as samavaya, *i.e.*, intimate or inseparable relation

When (thus) related, *i.e.*, when it is inseparably connected with the cause, it becomes existent. Here they may be asked to explain how the non-existent can have a cause of its own. We cannot indeed think of a thing which can cause the birth of a barren woman's son or his relation to anything else.

(*Objection*) :—The Vaiseshikas do not hold that the non-existent is related to anything. It is substances, such as dvyanukas, that are said to be intimately related to their causes.

(*Answer*) :—No; because they are not supposed to exist prior to this relation.—The Vaiseshikas do not argue that a pot or the like exists prior to the action of the potter, the potter's stick and wheel. Neither do they hold that clay assumes by itself the form of a pot. Wherefore, as the only other alternative, they have to admit that the non-existent (pot) becomes related (to the cause).

(*Objection*) :—It is not opposed to reason to hold that, though non-existent, it may be related by *samavaya* or intimate relation (to the cause).

(*Answer*) :—No so; for, no such thing can be admitted in the case of a barren woman's son.—If we are to hold that the antecedent non-existence (pragabhava) of a pot or the like becomes related to the cause, but not the barren woman's son, notwithstanding that both are alike non-entities (abhava), it is necessary to show how one non-entity can be distinguished from the other. Non-existence of one, non-existence of two, non-existence of all, antecedent non-existence (pragabhava), non-existence after destruction (pradhvamsabhava), mutual non-existence (anyonyabhava), absolute non-existence (atyanta-bhava),—nobody can point out any definite distinction among these in themselves. In the absence of a distinction, it is unreasonable to hold that only the antecedent non-existence of a pot becomes a pot through the action of a potter, etc., that it becomes related to a cause of its own, *viz.*, the pot-shreds which are existent, that when thus related it can very well be spoken of as being produced and so on, but that such is not the case with regard to the non-existence after destruction (pradhva*m*sabhava) of the same pot, though both alike are non-existent. It is unreasonable to hold that other non-existences (abhavas), such as non-existence after destruction, can never become (an existent effect) and so on, whereas antecedent non-existence alone, such as that of dvya*n*uka and the like substances, can become (an existent effect) and so on, though it is an abhava or non-existent quite as much as non-existence after destruction or absolute non-existence.

(*Objection*) :—We do not hold that the non-existent becomes the existent.

(*Answer*) :—Then the existent becomes existent,—for instance, a pot becomes a pot, a cloth becomes a cloth. This, too, is opposed to all evidence, like the theory that non-existent becomes existent.

Refutation of the Parinama-Vada.

As to the Pari*n*ama (transformation) theory of the Sankhyas, even that theory does not differ from the theory of the Vaiseshikas, inasmuch as it postulates the production of properties non-existent before, as well as their destruction. Even admitting their explanation that by manifestation or disappearance (an effect is said to come into existence or undergo destruction), the theory is all the same opposed to evidence, as may be found if we enquire whether the manifestation and disappearance are previously existent or non-existent.

For the same reason, we have to condemn that theory also which says that production etc., of an effect, are only different states of the cause itself.

The Lord's theory of illusion.

As the only other alternative, there remains this theory, that the One Existence, the sole Reality, is by avidya, imagined variously, as so many things undergoing production, destruction and the like changes, like an actor on the stage. This doctrine of the Lord has been stated in ii. 16; the consciousness of the existent (sat) being constant and the consciousness of all the rest being inconstant.

The enlightened alone can renounce action entirely.

(*Objection*) :—Then, the Self being immutable, where is the impossibility of renouncing all action entirely?

(*Answer*) :—Action is the property or attribute of the gu*n*as, be they regarded as real things, or as things set up by avidya. It is ascribed to the Self through avidya, and it has therefore been said that no ignorant man (avidvan) can renounce action entirely even for a moment (iii. 5). On the other hand, he who knows the Self is able to renounce action entirely, inasmuch as avidya has been expelled by vidya or wisdom; for, there can be no residue left of what is ascribed by avidya. Indeed, no residue is left of the second moon created by the false vision of the *timira*-affected eye, even after the removal of *timira*. Such being the case, the statements contained in v. 13, xviii. 45, 46 are quite reasonable.

Perfection in Karma-Yoga leads to absolute Perfection.

It has been said that the perfection reached by means of Karma-Yoga consists in becoming qualified for j*n*ana-nish*t*ha, the Path of Wisdom; and it is with a view to describe, as the fruit thereof, the *naishkarmyasiddhi*,—perfection in the form of absolute freedom from action, known as j*n*ana-nishtha,—that the Lord now proceeds to teach as follows:

असक्तबुद्धिः सर्वत्र जितात्मा विगतस्पृहः ।
नैष्कर्म्यसिद्धिं परमां संन्यासेनाधिगच्छति ॥ ४९ ॥

49. He whose reason is not attached anywhere, whose self is subdued, from whom desire has fled, he by renunciation attains the supreme state of freedom from action.

He whose reason (budhi, anta*h*-kara*n*a) is free from attachment to sons, wife, and other objects of attachment, whose self (anta*h*-kara*n*a) is brought under his own control, from whom desire for the body, for life, and for pleasures has fled,—a person of this sort who knows the Self attains to the supreme perfection, to absolute freedom from action (naishkarmyasiddhi), by sa*m*nyasa. In virtue of his knowledge of the unity of the actionless (nishkriya) Brahman and the Self, all actions have fled from him. This is known as the state of absolute freedom from action; and it is a siddhi or perfection. — *Naishkarmyasiddhi* may also mean the attainment (siddhi) of *naishkarmya*, the state in which one remains as the actionless Self. It is supreme as distinguished from the perfection attainable by Karma-Yoga; it is the state of immediate liberation (sadyo-mukti). This state is attained by sa*m*nyasa or right knowledge,—or better still, by the renunciation of all actions for which one is prepared by his right knowledge, and so says the Lord in v. 13.

Now, the Lord proceeds to teach how a man who, having attained perfection (as described above in xviii. 46) by performing his duty (as taught above) in the service of the Lord, has come by the discriminative knowledge of the Self, can attain the perfection known as *naishkarmya* or absolute freedom from action, *i.e.*, a firm unswerving stand in the knowledge of the pure Self.

सिद्धिं प्राप्तो यथा ब्रह्म तथाऽऽप्नोति निबोध मे ।
समासेनैव कौन्तेय निष्ठा ज्ञानस्य या परा ॥ ५० ॥

50. How he who has attained perfection reaches Brahman, that in brief do thou learn from Me, O son of Kunti,—that supreme consummation of knowledge.

The perfection he has already attained consists in the body and the senses being prepared for devotion to knowledge as a result of the Grace of the Lord worshipped through his duty. Reference to this (perfection) serves as a prelude to what follows.—What is that perfection to which that reference forms a prelude ?—It is the process of jnana-nishtha, or devotion to knowledge, by which he attains Brahman, the Supreme Self. That process, the way to the attainment of jnana-nishtha, do thou understand with certainty from my speech.—Is it to be described at length ?—No, says the Lord ; it will be described only in brief.

Absolute perfection is the consummation of Self-knowledge.

What the attainment of Brahman—referred to in the words " how he reaches Brahman,"—is, the Lord proceeds to specify in the words " that supreme consummation of knowledge." Consummation (nishtha) means perfection, the final or highest stage.

* (*Question*) :—Consummation of what ?

* The following discussion in the form of questions and answers is ntended to show that the consummation of knowledge is a well-defined end as spoken of here. It is the consummation of Brahma-jnana (knowledge of Brahman). Brahma-jnana is not different from Self-knowledge, and the nature of the Self is defined here in ii. 20 and in the Upanishads : and it can also be ascertained by reasoning upon scriptural texts, which describe hi as " devoid of attachment and immutable ".—A.

(*Answer*) :—Of Brahma-jnana or knowledge of Brahman.

(*Question*) :—Of what nature is the consummation of Brahma-jnana ?

(*Answer*) :—Of the same nature as Atmajnana or Self-knowledge.

(*Question*) :—Of what nature is the Self-knowledge ?

(*Answer*) :—Of the same nature as the Self.

(*Question*) :—Of what nature is the Self ?

(*Answer*) :—Of the nature described by the Lord and in the passages of the Upanishads, and (ascertainable) by nyaya or reasoning (upon the scriptural texts).

Is Self-knowledge possible at all ?

(*Objection*) :—Knowledge or cognition (jnana) is of the form of its object. But it is nowhere admitted that the Self is an object of cognition or has a form.

(*Answer*) :—The Self has a form, as taught in the scriptural passages, 'In colour like the sun' (*S*ve. Up. 3-8) ; 'Luminous in form' (Chha. Up. 3-14-2); 'Self-luminous' (Bri. Up. 4-3-9).

(*Objection*) :—No ; those passages are intended to remove the idea that the Self is of the nature of darkness (Tamas).—When the Self is said to be neither of the form of a substance nor of an attribute, it would follow that the Self is of the nature of darkness : and the preventing of this idea is the aim of the descriptions such as 'In colour like the sun.' Form is specifically denied, the Self being described as 'formless' (Ka*t*ha-Up. 3-15). Neither is the Self an object of cognition, as taught in passages like the following : "His form stands not in (our) ken, nor can any one see Him with the eye" (*S*ve. Up. 4-20) ; "Without sound and touch" (Ka*t*ha-Up. 3-15). Wherefore it is wrong to speak of a cognition of the form of the Self.

Such being the case, how can there be a cognition of the Self? Indeed, all cognition, whatever be its object, is of the form of that object. And it has been said that the Self is formless. If both the Self and the cognition thereof be formless, how is the constant meditation of Self-knowledge or the consummation thereof to be attained?

The Self reveals Himself in Pure Reason.

(*Answer*) :—Do not think so: for it can be shown that the Self is extremely pure, extremely clear, and extremely subtle. And Buddhi (reason) being as pure, etc., as the Self, it can put on the semblance of that aspect of the Self which is manifested as consciousness. Manas puts on a semblance of Buddhi, the sense-organs put on a semblance of Manas, and the physical body again puts on a semblance of the sense-organs. Wherefore common people look upon the mere physical body as the Self. And the Lokayatikas (materialists) who argue that consciousness is a property of the physical body declare that the Purusha or Soul is identical with the physical body endued with consciousness. Similarly, others again argue that consciousness is a property of the senses; others again argue that consciousness is a property of Buddhi. There are a few who hold that there is something within even beyond the Buddhi, *viz.*, the Avyakta (the Unmanifested) also called the Avyak*r*ita (the Undifferentiated), in the form of Avidya; and they say that the Avyak*r*ita is the Self.* Everywhere, from Buddhi down to the physical body, the cause of illusory indentification of each with the Self is its wearnig a semblance of the consciousness of the Self; and it is therefore unnecessary to impart directly a knowledge of the Self.—What then is necessary?—What is necessary is the mere elimination of the not-Self associated with the Self,—

* Those who study and contemplate upon the Cause of the universe regard the Antaryamin, the Avyak*r*ita endued with consciousness, as the Self.—A.

names, forms and the like; but it is unnecessary to try and teach what the consciousness of the Self is like, inasmuch as it is invariably comprehended in association with all objects of perception which are set up by avidya. Accordingly, the Vijnanavadins, the Buddhistic Idealists, hold that there is nothing real except ideas, and that these ideas require no external evidence (to prove their existence), inasmuch as it is admitted that they are self-cognized. Therefore we have only to eliminate what is falsely ascribed to Brahman by avidya; we have to make no more effort to acquire a knowledge of Brahman as He is quite self-evident. Though thus quite self-evident. easily knowable, quite near, and forming the very Self, Brahman appears—to the unenlightened, to those whose reason (Buddhi) is carried away by the differentiated phenomena of names and forms created by avidya—as unknown, difficult to know, very remote, as though He were a separate thing. But to those whose reason (Buddhi) has turned away from external phenomena, who have secured the grace of the Guru and attained the serenity of the self (manas), there is nothing else so blissful, so well-known, so easily knowable, and quite so near as Brahman. Accordingly, the knowledge of Brahman is said to be immediately comprehended and unopposed to dharma (ix. 2.)

Some conceited philosophers hold that reason (Buddhi) cannot grasp the Self, as He is formeless, and that therefore the Devotion of Right Knowledge is impossible of attainment.

True, it is unattainable to those who have not been properly initiated into the traditional knowledge by the Gurus (the Great Ones), who have not learned and studied the (teachings of the) Vedanta, whose intellect is quite engrossed in the external objects of senses, and who have not been trained in the right sources of knowledge. But, for those who are differently situated, (*i.e.*, who have been duly initiated etc.,) it is quite impossible to believe in the reality of the dual—the perceiver and the perceived—of our external perception, because they perceive no reality other than the consciousness of the Self. And we have shewn in the preceding sections that this—not the reverse—is the truth, and the Lord also has declared the same in ii. 69. Wherefore it is only a cessation of the perception of the differentiated forms of the external world that can lead to a firm grasp of the real nature of the Self. For, the Self is not a thing unknown to anybody at any time, is not a thing to be reached or got rid of or acquired. If the Self be quite unknown, all undertakings intended for the benefit of oneself would have no meaning. It is not, indeed, possible to imagine that they are for the benefit of the physical body or the like which has no consciousness; nor is it possible to imagine that pleasure is for pleasure's sake and pain is for pains's sake. It is, moreover, the Self-knowledge which is the aim of all endeavour.* Wherefore, just as there is no need for an external evidence by which to know one's own body, so there is no need for an external evidence by which to know the Self who is even nearer than the body. Thus it is clear that, to those who can discriminate, the Atma-jnana-nish*t*ha (devotion to Self-knowledge) is easy of attainment.

Cognition and the Cogniser are self-revealed.

Those also who had that cognition (j*n*ana) is formless and is not known by immediate perception must admit that, since an object of knowledge is apprehended through cognition, cognition is quite as immediately known as pleasure or the like.

Moreover, it cannot be maintained that cognition is a thing which one seeks to know.—If cognition were unknown, it would be a thing which has to be sought after just as an

* All action enjoined in the *sruti* is intended only as a means to Sel knowledge. *Vide*, Vedanta-Sutras III. iv. 26-27—A.

object of cognition is sought after. Just as, for example, a man seeks to reach by cognition the cognisable object such as a pot, so also would he have to seek to reach cognition by means of another cognition. But the fact is otherwise. Wherefore *cognition* is self-revealed, and therefore, also, is the *cogniser* self-revealed.

Therefore it is not for the *knowledge* (of Brahman or the Self) that any effort* is needed; it is needed only to prevent us from regarding the not-Self as the Self. Therefore, Devotion to Knowledge (j*n*ana-nish*t*ha) is easily attainable.

The Path to Absolute Perfection.

How is this consummation of knowledge † to be attained? Listen:

बुद्ध्या विशुद्धया युक्तो धृत्याऽऽत्मानं नियम्य च ।
शब्दादीन्विषयांस्त्यक्त्वा रागद्वेषौ व्युदस्य च ॥ ५१ ॥

51. Endued with a pure reason, controlling the self with firmness, abandoning sound and other objects, and laying aside love and hatred ;

Pure: free from illusion (maya), from doubt and misconception. *Reason* (buddhi): the determining faculty. *The Self*: the aggregate of the body and the senses. *Abandoning etc*: (as we should understand from the context) all superfluous luxuries, all objects except those only which are necessary for the bare maintenance of the body, and *laying aside love and hatred* even for those objects which appear necessary for the maintenance of the body.

---

* With a view to bring into existence something that does not already exist by means of an act enjoined in the Sruti.—A.

† A continuous current of the knowledge of Brahman; the reason merging in Brahman through the elimination of all alien attributes ascribed to Him.—A.

Then,

विविक्तसेवी लघ्वाशी यतवाक्कायमानसः ।
ध्यानयोगपरो नित्यं वैराग्यं समुपाश्रितः ॥ ५२ ॥

52. Resorting to a sequestered spot, eating but little, speech and body and mind subdued, always engaged in meditation and concentration, endued with dispassion ;

Resorting, etc.: ever accustomed to resort to such sequestered spots as a jungle, the sandbank of, a river, the mountain-cave. *Eating but little*: as conducive to the serenity of thought by keeping off sleep and such other evils. This devotee of wisdom should also restrain his speech, body and mind. With all the senses thus quieted, he should always and devoutly practise *Dhyana* or mediation upon the nature of the Self, and *Yoga* or concentration of the mind on the Self. *Always:*: this implies that he has to do nothing else, no *mantrajapa* (repetition of chants or mystic formulae), etc. *Dispassion* : absence of desire for visible and invisible objects. This should be a constant attitude of the mind.

Moreover,

अहङ्कारं बलं दर्पं कामं क्रोधं परिग्रहम् ।
विमुच्य निर्ममः शान्तो ब्रह्मभूयाय कल्पते ॥ ५३ ॥

53. Having abandoned egotism, strength, arrogance, desire, enmity, property, free from the notion of "mine," and peaceful, he is fit for becoming Brahman.

Egotism: identifying the Self with the body, etc. *Strength*: that strength which is combined with passion and desire, but not the physical or any other strength : the latter being natural, its abandonment is not possible. *Arrogance* : which follows the state of exultation and leads to the transgression of dharma, as said in the sm*r*iti :

"When a man exults, he becomes arrogant, and when he becomes arrogant, he transgresses dharma"—

(Apastamba-Dharmasutra, 1-13-4).

Property : though a man is free from all passions of the mind and the senses, he may own so much of external belongings as is necessary for bodily sustenance and for the observance of his duties (dharma); but even this the aspirant abandons; *i.e.*, he becomes a Paramaha*m*sa-Parivrajaka, a sa*m*nyasin of the fourth or highest order. He does not regard even the bodily life as his. *Peaceful* : free from exultation and care. Such a devotee of wisdom is fit to become Brahman.

The consummation of Knowledge attained by Devotion.

In this way,

ब्रह्मभूतः प्रसन्नात्मा न शोचति न काङ्क्षति ।
समः सर्वेषु भूतेषु मद्भक्तिं लभते पराम् ॥ ५४ ॥

54. Becoming Brahman, of serene self, he neither grieves nor desires, treating all beings alike ; he attains supreme devotion to Me.

How who has reached Brahman and attained self-serenity does not grieve regarding his failure to accomplish an object or regarding his wants. It is not indeed possible to suppose that he who knows Brahman can have a longing for any object unattained ; therefore the words "he neither grieves nor desires" is tantamount to saying that such is the nature of the man who has become Brahman.—Another reading makes the passage mean "he neither grieves nor exults."—*Treating all beings alike* : he regards the pleasure and pain of all creatures equally with his own, *i.e.*, that they would affect them just as they affect himself).—It is not meant here that he sees the identity of the Self in all, as this will be mentioned in the next verse.—Such a devotee to wisdom attains highest devotion to me, the Supreme Lord,—the fourth or the highest of the four kinds of devotion,—*viz.*, the Devotion of Knowledge, —spoken of in vii. 16.

Then,

भक्त्या मामभिजानाति यावान्यश्चास्मि तत्त्वतः ।
ततो मां तत्त्वतो ज्ञात्वा विशते तदनन्तरम् ॥ ५५ ॥

55. By Devotion he knows Me in truth, what and who I am; then, knowing Me in truth, he forthwith enters into Me.

By Bhakti, by the Devotion of Knowledge, he knows Me as I am in the diverse manifestations caused by upadhis. He knows who I am, he knows that I am devoid of all the differences caused by the upadhis, that I am the Supreme Purusha, that I am like unto akasa; he knows Me to be non-dual, the one Consciousness (Chaitanya), pure and simple, unborn, undecaying, undying, fearless, deathless. The knowing Me in truth, he enters into Myself immediately after attaining knowledge.

It is not meant here that the act of knowledge and the act of entering are two distinct acts.—What then is the act of entering?—It is the knowledge itself; for, there is nothing to be effected (by knowledge) other than itself, as the Lord has taught. "Do thou also know Me as Kshetrajna." (xiii. 2).

(*Objection*) :—The statemet that "by the supreme devotion of knowledge he knows Me," involves a contradiction.—How?—Thus: when the knowledge of a certain object arises in the knower, then and then alone the knower knows that object; no devotion to that knowledge, no repetition of the knowledge, is necessary. Therefore, the statement that "he knows Me, not by knowledge, but by *devotion* to knowledge, by a repetition of knowledge," involves a contradiction.

(*Answer*):—This objection does not apply here; for, the word "devotion (nishtha)" means that the knowledge aided by all the favourable conditions of its rise and development and freed from obstacles culminates in a firm conviction by one's own experience. When the knowledge of the unity of the individual Self (Kshetrajna) and the supreme Self (Paramatman), generated by the teachings of the Scriptures and the master under conditons favourable to the rise and ripening of that knowledge—*viz.*, purity of mind, humility and other attributes (xiii, 7. *et seq.*)—and accompanied with the renunciation of all works which are associated with the idea of distinctions such as the agent and other factors of action, culminates in a firm conviction by one's own experience, then the knowledge is said to have attained supreme consummation. This jnana-nishtha (Devotion of Knowledge) is referred to as the Supreme or fourth kind of Devotion, Bhakti (vii. 17), —supreme as compared with the remaining three kinds of Devotion, with that of the distressed, etc., (vii. 16). By this supreme devotion the aspirant knows the Lord as He is, and immediately afterwards all consciousness of difference between the Isvara and the Kshetrajna disappears altogether. Thus there is no contradiction involved in the statement that "by the Devotion of Knowledge (the aspirant knows) Me."

Renunciation of all works is necessary for absolute perfection.

Then alone can the well-ascertained teaching of all scriptures—*viz.*, the Upanishads, Itihasas, Puranas and Smritis—enjoining retirement have a meaning. The scriptural texts are such as the following:

"Knowing It, they renounce and lead a mendicant life." —(Bri. Up. 3-5-9).

"Wherefore they say that renunciation is excellent among these austerities."—(Yajniki-Up. 79.)

"Renunciation excels."—(*Ibid.* 78),

"Samnyasa is the renunciation of actions."

"Having abandoned Vedas, this world and the next," etc.—(Apastamba-Dharmasutra, 2-23-13).

"Renounce dharma and a-dharma."

And so on. Here, in the Gita also, passages of similar import (such as v. 12) occur. It cannot be held that these passages are meaningless. Nor can it be held that they are *arthavadas*, mere explanatory or incidental remarks (not meant as obligatory injunctions); for they occur in the sections which specially treat of renunciation.

Moreover, (renunciation of works is necessary) because Moksha consists in the realisation of the immutability of one's own Inner Self. He who wishes to reach the eastern sea should not indeed travel in the opposite direction, *i.e.*, by the same road that the man who wishes to go to the western sea chooses. And the Devotion of Knowledge (jnana-nishtha) consists in an intent effort to establish a continuous current of the idea of the Inner Self (Pratyagatman); and there would be a conflict if that devotion were to be conjoined with ritual (karma), which is like going towards the western sea. It is a firm conviction of philosophers that the difference between the two is as wide as that between a mountain and a mustard seed. Hence the conclusion that the Devotion of Knowledge (jnana-nishtha) should be practised by renouncing all action.

Devotion to the Lord by works enjoined.

The perfection accruing as the fruit of that Bhakti-Yoga, which consists in worshipping the Lord through one's own duties qualifies the aspirant for the Devotion of Knowledge which culminates in moksha. This Bhakti-Yoga, the Yoga of Devotion to the Lord, is extolled here, in this section which sums up the teaching of the sastra, with a view to firmly impress that teaching.

सर्वकर्माण्यपि सदा कुर्वाणो मद्व्यपाश्रयः ।
मत्प्रसादादवाप्नोति शाश्वतं पदमव्ययम् ॥ ५६ ॥

56. Doing continually all actions whatsoever, taking refuge in Me,—by My Grace he reacheth the eternal undecaying Abode.

Doing all actions including even the prohibited actions, whoso seeks refuge in Me, Vasudeva, the Lord, with his whole self centred in Me, reaches the eternal Abode of Vishnu by the Grace of the Lord.

Wherefore,

चेतसा सर्वकर्माणि मयि संन्यस्य मत्परः ।
बुद्धियोगमुपाश्रित्य मच्चित्तः सततं भव ॥ ५७ ॥

57. Mentally resigning all deeds to Me, regarding Me as the Supreme, resorting to mental concentration, do thou ever fix thy heart in Me.

Mentally: with discriminative faith.* *All actions*: producing visible and invisible results. *Me*: the Lord. As taught in ix. 27, do thou dedicate all thy actions to Me. *Regarding*: regarding Me, Vasudeva, as the highest goal; his whole self centered in Me. *Regarding, &c*: resorting to the *Buddhi-Yoga* (samahita-buddhitva, steady-mindedness, firm faith as thy sole refuge.

* *i.e.*, the faith that knowledge alone obtainable by the Lord's Grace,—but not works, finally leads to salvation.—A.

मच्चित्तः सर्वदुर्गाणि मत्प्रसादात्तरिष्यसि ।
अथ चेत्त्वमहङ्कारान्न श्रोष्यसि विनङ्क्ष्यसि ॥ ५८ ॥

58. Fixing thy heart in Me, thou shalt, by My Grace, cross over all difficulties; but if from egotism thou will not hear (Me), thou shalt perish.

Difficulties: the impassable obstacles arising from (avidya), the cause of saṁsara. *Egotism*: the idea that thou art a learned man. If thou wilt not abide by my advice, then thou shalt be ruined.

Neither shouldst thou think, "I am independent; why should I obey the dictates of another"?

यदहङ्कारमाश्रित्य न योत्स्य इति मन्यसे ।
मिथ्यैष व्यवसायस्ते प्रकृतिस्त्वां नियोक्ष्यति ॥ ५९ ॥

59. If, indulging egotism, thou thinkest 'I will not fight,' vain is this, thy resolve; nature will constrain thee.

Thinkest, resolvest. *Vain*: for, thy nature as a Kshatriya will constrain thee to do so.

Also because,

स्वभावजेन कौन्तेय निबद्धः स्वेन कर्मणा ।
कर्तुं नेच्छसि यन्मोहात्करिष्यस्यवशोऽपि तत् ॥ ६० ॥

60. Bound (as thou art), O son of Kunti, by thy own nature-born act, that which from delusion thou likest not to do, thou shalt do, though against thy will.

Nature-born: such as prowess, &c., mentioned above (xviii. 43). *Against thy will*: in subjection to some external force.

For,

ईश्वरः सर्वभूतानां हृद्देशेऽर्जुन तिष्ठति ।

भ्रामयन्सर्वभूतानि यन्त्रारूढानि मायया ॥ ६१ ॥

61. The Lord dwells in the hearts of all beings, O Arjuna, whirling by Maya all beings (as if) mounted on a machine.

The Lord (Isvara): the Ruler, Narayana. *Arjuna* pure in the internal self, of a pure antah-karana. The word "Arjuna" is used in the sense of 'pure' in the Rig-Veda. "The dark day and the *light* day." (6-9-1). He causes all beings to revolve as if—'as if' being understood—mounted on machines, like wooded dolls mounted on a machine. *By Maya*: by causing illusion. 'Whirling' should be construed with 'dwells.'

तमेव शरणं गच्छ सर्वभावेन भारत ।

तत्प्रसादात्परां शान्तिं स्थानं प्राप्स्यसि शाश्वतम् ॥ ६२ ॥

62. Fly unto Him for refuge with all thy being, O Bharata; by His Grace shalt thou obtain supreme peace (and) the eternal resting place.

Seek thou that Lord as thy sole Refuge with thy whole being for relief from the distress of samsara. Then by His Grace, thou shalt obtain supreme peace and attain to My—*i.e.*, Vishnu's—Supreme Eternal Abode.

इति ते ज्ञानमाख्यातं गुह्याद्गुह्यतरं मया ।

विमृश्यैतदशेषेण यथेच्छसि तथा कुरु ॥ ६३ ॥

63. Thus has wisdom, more secret than all that is secret, been declared to thee by Me; reflect thou over it all and act as thou pleasest.

Me: the Omniscient Lord. *It*: the Sastra, the teaching declared above. *All*: everything that has been taught.

Devotion to the Lord is the Secret of success in Karma-Yoga.

Listen to what I am again going to say:

सर्वगुह्यतमं भूयः शृणु मे परमं वचः ।
इष्टोऽसि मे दृढमिति ततो वक्ष्यामि ते हितम् ॥ ६४ ॥

64. Hear thou again My word supreme, the most secret of all; because thou art My firm friend, therefore will I tell thee what is good.

Again: though it has been more than once declared. I do not tell thee either from fear or from hope of reward: thou art My firm friend, thou art ever beloved of Me; and for this reason I shall tell thee of the supreme good, the means of attaining knowledge. This last is, indeed, the highest of all kinds of good.

What is it?—The Lord says:

मन्मना भव मद्भक्तो मद्याजी मां नमस्कुरु ।
मामेवैष्यसि सत्यं ते प्रतिजाने प्रियोऽसि मे ॥ ६५ ॥

65. Fix thy thought on Me, be devoted to Me, worship Me, do homage to Me. Thou shalt reach Myself. The truth do I declare to thee; (for) thou art dear to Me.

Thou shalt reach Myself: thus acting—*i.e.*, looking up to Vasudeva alone as thy aim, means, and end—thou shalt come to Me. In this matter I make a solemn promise.—The meaning of the verse is this. Thus, knowing that the Lord's declarations are true, and being convinced that moksha is a necessary result of devotion to the Lord, one should look to the Lord as the highest and sole Refuge.

Right Knowledge and Renunciation.

Having thought in conclusion that the supreme secret of the Devotion of Karma-Yoga is the regarding of the Lord as the sole Refuge, the Lord now proceeds to speak of the Right Knowledge, the fruit of the Devotion of Karma-Yoga, as taught in the essential portions of all the Vedantas (Upanishads):

सर्वधर्मान्परित्यज्य मामेकं शरणं व्रज ।
अहं त्वा सर्वपापेभ्यो मोक्षयिष्यामि मा शुचः ॥ ६६ ॥

66. Abandoning all righteous deeds, seek me as thy sole Refuge; I will liberate thee from all sins; do thou not grieve.

Righteous deeds (dharma); including unrighteous deeds (a-dharma) also, since *naishkarmya* or freedom from all action is intended to be taught here. Here may be cited such passages of the sruti and the smriti as the following

"Not he who has not abstained from evil deed...can attain It."—(Katha-Up. 1-2-24).

"Abandon dharma and a-dharma.,'

So, the passage means "renouncing *all* works." *Me alone*: the Isvara, the Self of all, dwelling the same in all. *Seek Me as thy sole Refuge*: in the belief "I myself am that Isvara;" *i e*, do thou understand that there is naught else except Me. When thou art firm in this faith, I shall liberate thee from all sins, from all bonds of dharma and a-dharma, by manifesting Myself as thy own Self. So it has been already said here,

"I destroy the darkness born of ignorance by the luminous lamp of wisdom, abiding in their self."—(x. II.)

Wherefore do thou not grieve.

What is the means to the Highest Bliss,—Knowledge or Works?

What has been determined in the Gita-sastra as the means of attaining the Highest Bliss (nis-sreyasa)? Is it Knowledge (jnana), or Works (karma), or both together?

Whence this doubt?

It has been said "Knowing which one attains the Immortal" (xiii. 12), and "Then knowing Me in truth, he forthwith enters into Me" (xiii. 55): these and other passages teach that the Highest Bliss is attained by mere knowledge. Such passages again as "Thy concern is with action alone" (ii. 47), and "Do thou also perform action," (iv. 15), teach that performance of works is quite obligatory Since it has been taught that both knowledge and works are obligatory, there may arise a doubt as to whether also the two conjoined may not constitute the means to the Highest Bliss.

What is the good of this enquiry at all?

It is this, *viz.*, to determine which one of them forms the means to the Highest Bliss. Wherefore, the subject is very wide and is worth investigating.

Self-Knowledge alone is the means to the Highest Bliss.

Pure Self-knowledge alone is the means to the Highest Bliss; for, as removing the notion of variety, it culminates in liberation (kaivalya.) Avidya is the perception of variety involving actions, factors of action, and the ends of actions. It is always present in the Self. "Mine is action: I am the agent; I do this act for such and such a result:" in this form, avidya has been active in time without a beginning. The remover of this avidya is the knowledge of the Self arising in the following form. "Here I am, free, a non-agent, actionless, devoid of results"; for such a knowledge removes the notion of variety which causes one to engage in action.—The word "alone" (in the opening line of this paragraph) is intended to exclude the two other alternatives: neither by works alone, nor by works and knowledge conjoined together, is the Highest Bliss attained. Since, moreover, the Highest Bliss is not an effect to be accomplished by action, works cannot be the means to it. Indeed, the Eternal Reality is not produced either by knowledge or by works.

(Objection):—Then, even the pure knowledge serves no purpose!

(Answer):—Not so; for, by removing avidya, it culminates in emancipation, which is a visible result.—We know from experience that knowledge which removes the darkness of avidya culminates in emancipation as its result; for instance, in the case of a rope (mistaken for a serpent), as soon as the light of the lamp removes the darkness which caused the error, the rope is no longer mistaken for a serpent. The result of illumination culminates indeed in the emancipation of the rope, in freeing the rope from the various mistaken notions of serpent, etc., which then cease altogether. So, too, as regards the Self-knowledge.

Knowledge cannot be conjoined with Works.

Now when the agent and other factors of action are operating in the act of cutting or in the act of churning fire,—each act producing a visible result,—they cannot (at the same time) operate in another act productive of another result different from severance or the kindling of a fire; so also when the agent and other factors of action are concerned in the act of knowledge-devotion (jnana-nishtha),—whereof alike the result is visible,—they cannot at the same time operate to bring about another act productive of a result other than the emancipation of the Self. Wherefore, the Devotion of Knowledge cannot be conjoined with works.

(*Objection*):—They may be conjoined, just as the act of eating and the acts of fire worship (agnihotra), etc, are conjoined.

(*Answer*):—No; for, emancipation being the result of knowledge, (the devotee of knowledge) cannot desire the result of works.—When there is an all-spreading flood of water close by, nobody would ever think of constructing wells and tanks to any purpose. So also when knowledge leading to emancipation as its result has been attained, nobody would ever desire any other result or seek to do an act by which to obtain that other result. He who is engaged in an act by which he hopes to acquire a whole kingdom will not certainly engage in an act which can at best secure for him a piece of land, nor will he cherish a desire for it. Therefore works are not the means to the Highest Bliss. Neither is a conjunction of knowledge and works possible. Nor can it be held that knowledge which leads to emancipation requires the aid of works; for as removing avidya, knowledge is opposed to works. Indeed, darkness cannot remove darkness. Therefore, knowledge alone is the means to the Highest Bliss.

Refutation of the theory that salvation is attained by works alone.

(*Objection*):—No. For, by neglect of *nitya* or obligatory works one incurs sin (pratyavaya); and *kaivalya* or emancipation is eternal.

(*To explain*):—It is wrong to say that emancipation is attained by knowledge alone; for by neglect of the *nitya-karma* or obligatory works enjoined in the sruti, a man incurs sin which leads him to hell, etc.

(*Counter-objection*):—Thus, then, since moksha is not to be attained by works, there can be no hope of attaining moksha at all.

(*Rejoinder*) :—There is no room for any such objection, inasmuch as *moksha is eternal.* The sin of omission (pratyavaya) is avoided by the observance of the *nitya-karma* or obligatory works; by avoiding the prohibited acts, no obnoxious bodies are generated; by avoiding the *kamya-karma* or interested acts no desirable body either generated; and when the present body perishes on the exhaustion of the fruits of the works which have given rise to the body, no more causes then exist which can generate another body; and when attachment and other passions are expunged from the heart, the emancipation of the Self—*i.e.*, the realisation by the Self of His own true nature—is attained without any effort.

(*Conter-objection*) :—Those of the acts done in the past innumerable births, which have not yet begun their effects, and of which some lead to heaven and others to hell, and so on, have not been extinguished, because their effects have not been enjoyed.

(*Rejoinder*) :– No; for we argue that the fruits of those works are reaped in the form of the trouble and pain involved in the performance of the *nitya-karma.* Or the *nitya-karma* may, like the prayaschitta or expiatory act, serve to destroy past sins. The works which have begun their effects being exhausted by the enjoyment of their fruits, and no new works being undertaken, it follows that emancipation is attained without any effort.

(*Answer*):—No ; for the sruti says that there exists no other road to moksha than knowledge:

> "Knowing Him alone, one crosses beyond death;
> there exists no other road to the Abode." (*S*vet. Up. 3.8).

*S*ruti says, further, that moksha is as impossible for the unwise man as it is impossible for men to compress the akasa like leather (*Ibid.* 6—20). And the Puranic tradition also ays that 'one attains emancipation by knowledge.'

Moreover, the good deeds (punya-karma) which have not yet begun their effects cannot be said to have been exhausted. Just as the existence of sins which have not begun their effects is possible, so also the existence of good (punya) deeds which have not yet begun their effects is possible; and as these cannot be exhausted without generating another body, moksha is not possible.

Neither is it possible to generate no new merit and demerit (dharma and adharma in this body), inasmuch as destruction of love and hatred and delusion which lead to acts of merit and demerit cannot be effected except by means of Self-knowledge. Because the sruti says that the *nitya-karma* produces merit (punya) as its result, and because the smriti says that, by performing their proper duties, the several castes and orders attain to a high immeasurable happiness, the exhaustion of works is not possible.

Refutation of the theory that the Nitya-Karma leads to no future births.

Now, as to the contention: As painful in itself, the nitya-karma is itself the fruit of sinful deeds committed in the past; apart from itself, the nitya-karma bears no distinct fruit, because the sruti speaks nowhere of its fruits, the mere circumstance of a man being alive forming a sufficient ground for its necessary performance.

We say, no; for, it is impossible for those deeds to yield their fruits which have not yet begun to work out their effects. Neither can there be any variety in the pain (involved in the performance of the nitya-karma).

(*To explain*) :—It is wrong to say that the fruits of sinful deeds committed in the past births are reaped in the form of the trouble and pain involved in the performance of the nitya-karma. We cannot indeed understand how the fruit of the deeds which did not sprout up for fruition at the time of death can be reaped in the birth caused by another set of deeds. Otherwise, there would be nothing unreasonable in the supposition that infernal suffering is possible in the very birth that has been generated by *Agnihotra* (fire-sacrifice) for the enjoyment of the fruit thereof *i. e.*, for the enjoyment of heaven (svarga).

Moreover, the pain involved in the performance of the nitya-karma cannot answer to that variety of suffering (which should result from the variety) of acts of sin. While many acts of sin productive of as many distinct kinds of suffering may possibly exist, to suppose that their effects consist in the mere trouble and pain involved in the observance of the nitya-karma would lead to the further supposition—which it is impossible to hold—that the suffering inflicted by the pairs of opposites, diseases and the like, has no cause of its own, and that the trouble and pain involved in the observance of the nitya-karma is alone the effect of past sins, but not the pain of carrying stones on the head or the like.

Besides, it is irrelevant to say that the trouble and pain involved in the observance of the nitya-karma constitutes the result of the sinful deeds done in the past.—How?—It has been urged that no extinction of the past sin which has not begun to bear fruit is possible; whereas you say that the fruit of the deed which *has begun* to bear fruit—not the fruit of the deed which *has not begun* to bear fruit—is reaped in the form of the trouble and pain involved in the observance of the nitya-karma. If, on the other hand, you mean that the whole sin committed in the past has begun to bear fruit, then there is no ground for the specification that the mere trouble and pain involved in the observance of the nitya-karma are the fruits (of those sinful deeds which have not begun to produce their effects). It would then also follow that the enjoining of the nitya-karma has no purpose to serve; for, the sinful deeds which have begun their effects can be extinguished by merely undergoing the effects so produced.

Moreover, if pain be the result of the nitya-karmas enjoined in the sruti that pain may arise from the trouble involved in the observance of the nitya-karma itself as from any other active exercise: it is therefore unreasonable to suppose that it is the result of another action.

Again as enjoined on a man on the mere ground of his being alive, the nitya-karma cannot be, any more than a prayaschitta or expiatory act, the effect of sins committed in the past. An expiatory act, enjoined by a reason of a certain act of sin having been committed, is not the fruit of that sinful act. If, on the other hand, the pain of the expiatory act be the effect of the very sinful act which forms its occasion, then, it would follow that the trouble and pain involved in the performance of the nitya-karma occasioned by the man's being alive, etc., is the effect of that very state of being alive which has occasioned the necessity; the nitya-karma and prayaschitta being alike necessitated by the particular occasions respectively.

Moreover. the trouble and pain involved in the performance of a *nitya-agnihotra* (fire-worship done as a duty) and a *kamya-agnihotra* (fire worship done with a motive) being equal, and no special reason being found as to why the trouble and pain involved in the performance of the nitya-karma alone should constitute the result of sins committed in the past, but not the tronble and pain involved in the performance of the kâmya-karma, it would follow that the latter also is the result of sins committed in the past. Such being the case, it is wrong to infer, on the ground of consistency (arthâpatti), that because no mention is made in the sruti of the nitya-karma's results and because the injunction thereof is otherwise inexplicable, the trouble and pain involved in the performance of the nitya-karma is the result of sins committed in the past. The injunction being otherwise inexplicable, we should even infer that the nitya-karma is productive of results distinct from the pain and trouble involved in its performance.

The opponent is also guilty of inconsistency. When it is once admitted that through the performance of the nitya-karma the fruit of another deed is reaped, this reaping forms itself the fruit of the nitya-karma, and it is therefore inconsistent to hold at the same time that the nitya-karma produces no fruits of its own.

Moreover, when the kâmya-agnihotra is performed, the nitya-agnihotra is also said to have been performed simultaneously, as included in that self-same act; and therefore the fruit of the kâmya-agnihotra should become exhausted with the trouble and pain involved in the nitya-agnihotra, inasmuch as the kâmya-agnihotra is not a distinct act from the nitya-agnihotra. If, on the other hand, the effect of the kâmya-agnihotra be something distinct, such as svarga, then it would follow that the trouble and pain of its performance must also be distinct; but it is not so, for it is opposed to facts. In point of fact, the trouble and pain involved in the performance of the nitya-karma is not distinct from that of the kâmya-karma.

Furthermore, an action which is neither enjoined nor prohibited (in the sruti) is productive of immediate results; but an act which is enjoined or prohibited by the sastra cannot be productive of immediate result. If this latter were productive of immediate results, then no effort would be made with a view to attain an unseen result, even though it be svarga or the like, so long as it is held that in the case of Agnihotra or the like—despite the absence of all distinction in the nature of the Act—the fruits of the act when performed as a nitya-karma are reaped in the form of the mere trouble and pain involved in its performance, whereas when performed as a kâmya-karma the self-same act produces a superior result—such as svarga—merely because there is a longing for its results, although the latter act is not superior to the former in any of the subsidiary parts in the mode of performance. Wherefore it is in no way reasonable to contend that the nitya-karma does not lead to results in the unseen future.

The Paths of Knowledge and Works are meant for distinct classes of aspirants.

So*, knowledge alone can cause total destruction of good or evil deeds caused by avidya—not the performance of the nitya-karma. For, avidya and kama (nescience and desire) constitute the seed of all action. Accordingly it has been declared that Karma-Yoga pertains to the ignorant and that Jnana-nistha or knowledge-devotion accompanied with renunciation of all works pertains to the wise. *Vide* ii. 19, 21: iii. 3, 26, 28; v. 8, 13; vii. 18; ix. 21, 22; x, 10. From the last verse here quoted it should be inferred that ignorant men who are devoted to action cannot approach the Lord. And therefore, notwithstanding that ignorant men, who are followerss of works, are most devout, rendering service to the Lord, they resort only to one of the several paths mentioned xii. 6-11) in their descending order, the lowest of them being that which consists in abandoning the fruits of action. But as regards those who are devoted to the Undefinable and the Indestructible, the attributes they cultivate are mentioned in xii. 13-20; and their path of knowledge is also described in the three discourses commencing with the (thirteenth dis-

* Because the nitya-karma, like the kamya-karma, yields its fruits in the invisible future by way of taking the devotee to the regions of Pitris and the like, it is not intended for the removal of sins; and therefore self-knowledge alone, it must be admitted, conduces to tha end.—A.

course on the Kshetra.* The triple result of action,—such as the evil, good and mixed fruit,—(xviii. 12) does not accrue to those who have renounced all works generated by the five causes such as the body (xviii. 14), who know that the Self is one and non-agent, who are engaged in the higher devotion of knowledge, who have known the true nature of the Lord,—to the Paramahamsa-Parivrajakas (*i.e.*, the samnyasins of the fourth or highest order) who have obtained refuge in the unity of the Self and the Divine Being. But it does accrue to others who are ignorant, who follow the path of works, who are not samnyasins. Thus should we assign the paths of duty taught in the Gita-sastra.

Action is a creature of Avidya

(*Objection*) :—It cannot be proved that all action is caused by avidya.

(*Answer*) :—No ; it can be proved, as in the case of brahmanicide (brahmahatya).—The nitya-karma is no doubt taught in the sastra; but it concerns the ignorant alone. Just as the act of brahmanicide, which, is prohibited in the sastra, is known to be a source of evil, is committed only by him who is ignorant and influenced by passion and other evil tendencies,—his concern in it being otherwise inexplicable—so also, all *nitya*, *naimittika*, and *kamya* karmas, *i. e.*, all works comprising the constant and occasional duties as well as all interested sacrificial rites, concern only him who is ignorant (of the Self.)

(*Objection*)) :—So long as it is not known that the Self is distinct from the body, it is not likely that any man would undertake to perform the nitya-karma, etc.

(*Answer*) :—Not so ; for, we see that a man engages in an act thinking " I do " the act, which, being of the nature of motion, is really done by the agency of the not-Self, (of the body, etc.)

* Vide xiii. 7-11, xiv. 22-26, xv. 3-5.—A.

(*Question*) :—The regarding of the aggregate of the body, etc., as the Self is only a gau*n*a-pratyaya or a figuratively expressed notion ; it is not an illusion (mithya).

(*Answer*) :—Not so; for, then its effects, too, must be gau*n*a, must have been figuratively spoken of.

(*To explain the objection*) :—When we speak of the aggregate of the body, etc.,—which are things *belonging* to the Self,—as the Self, our words should be understood in a figurative sense, as when for instance, addressing the father the sruti says "thyself art be who is spoken of as thy son." In common parlance, too, we say "this cow is my very life." In the present case there is certainly no *mithyapratyaya* or illusory notion. It is only when the distinction between the two is not perceived,—as when a pillar is mistaken for a man, —that we have an instance of illusion.

(*To explain the answer*) :—Not so. A gau*n*a-pratyaya cannot lead to a real effect ; for, a figurative expression,—the sign of similarity being understood,—is merely intended to extol the subject. For example. such expressions as "Devadatta is a lion" and "the student is fire" are intended merely to extol the subjects, Devadatta and the student, because of their respective resemblance to the lion and fire in point of *fierceness* and *yellowishness* ; but no effect of the existence of a real lion or of a real fire is accomplished in virtue of that figurative expression or idea. On the other hand, one actually experiences the evil effects of an illusory notion.

Furthermore, one knows what the subject in reality is when it is figuratively spoken of as some other thing : one knows that Devadatta is no lion and that the student is no fire. So also, if the bodily aggregate be figuratively spoken of as the Self, the act done by the bodily aggregate would not be regarded as an act done in reality by the Self, by the real subject of the notion "I." Indeed, no act done by a gau*n*a (figurative) lion or fire can become an act done by a real lion or fire. Neither is any purpose whatever of an actual lion or fire served by fierceness or yellowishness, it being merely intended to extol (the subject).

Moreover, he who is thus praised knows that he is not a lion, that he is not fire.; he never regards an act of a lion or of fire as his. So, (if in the present case the bodily aggregate were figuratively spoken of as the Self), one would think rather that the act of the (bodily) aggregate "is not mine," *i.e.*, not the real Self's, than that "I am the agent, mine is the action."

And as regards the theory that the Self actually does an act,—his memory, desire and effort forming causes of action, —we say that such is not the case, because they proceed from illusion. In fact, memory desire and effort proceed from impressions produced by the experience of desirable and undesirable effects of actions set up by illusion. Just as in this birth dharma and a-dharma and the experience of their fruits are due to the identifying of the Self with the aggregate of the body, etc., to affection and aversion and so on, so also in the last previous birth and in the birth previous to that, and so on. Thus we are to infer that sa*m*sara, past and future, is caused by avidya and is without a beginning. Wherefore it follows that the final cessation of sa*m*sara is attained through devotion to knowledge accompanied with renunciation of all works.

Because attachment to the body is an aspect of avidya, therefore, when avidya ceases, the body also must cease to be, and then sa*m*sara necessarily ceases.—The identifying of the Self with the aggregate of the body, etc., is an aspect of avidya; for, nobody in the world who knows that he is distinct from a cow, &c., and that the cow, &c., are distinct from him, regards them as himself. Only an ignorant man identifies the Self with the aggregate of the body, etc., for want of discrimination, in the same way that one mistakes the branchless trunk of a tree for a man :—but not he who knows the truth by discrimination.

As to the son being spoken of as the father himself in the sruti, "thyself art he who is spoken of as thy son," it is a gau*n*a-pratyaya, a figuratively expressed notion, because of their relation as the generator and the offspring. By what is only figuratively spoken of as the Self, no real purposes of the true Self can be accomplished, any more than the son can eat for the father. No real purposes, for instance, of a real lion and a real fire can be achieved by what are only figuratively spoken of as a lion and fire.

(*Objection*) :—Since the scriptural ordinances are of undisputed authority in transcendental matters, the purposes of the Self can certainly be achieved by what are figuratively spoken of as the Self—*viz.*, the body, the senses, and so on.

(*Answer*) :—No : for, they are selfs set up by avidya. The body and the senses and the like are not figuratively spoken of as the Self. On the other hand, being really not Self, they are regarded as selfs by illusion ; for, they are regarded as the Self so long as there is illusion, and they cease to be regarded as the Self when illusion disappears. It is only children, the ignorant people, who, for want of knowledge think, "I am tall, I am yellowish," and thus regard the aggregate of the body, etc., as the Self. On the other hand those who can discriminate and understand that "I am distinct from the aggregate of the body," etc., do not identify themselves with the aggregate of the body, etc. This notion of identity is therefore—because it does not exist in the absence of illusion—caused by illusion ; and it is not a gau*n*a-pratyaya. It is only when similarity and difference are distinctly seen between two things—as between a lion and Devadatta, or between a student and fire,—that those two things may be figuratively spoken of in word as identical or so regarded in thought, but not when similarity and difference are not perceived. And as regards the appeal made to the authority of sruti, we say that no such appeal should be made, inasmuch as sruti is an authority in transcendental matters, in matters lying beyond the bounds of human knowledge. Sruti is an authority only in matters not perceived by means of ordinary instruments of knowledge, such as pratyaksha or immediate perception ;—*i.e.*, it is an authority as to the mutual relation of things as means to ends, but not in matters lying within the range of pratyaksha ; indeed, sruti is intended as authority only for knowing what lies beyond the range of human knowledge. Wherefore it is not possible to suppose that the notion of " I " which arises in connection with the aggregate of the body, etc., and which is evidently due to illusion, is only a figurative idea. A hundred srutis may declare that fire is cold or that it is dark ; still they possess no authority in the matter. If sruti should at all declare that fire is cold or that it is dark, we would still suppose that it intends quite a different meaning from the apparent one ; for its authotity cannot otherwise be maintained : we shonld in no way attach to sruti a meaning which is opposed to other authorities or to its own declaration.

The theory of Avidya does not militate against the authority of Karma-Kanda.

(*Objection*) :—As a man does an action only when he is subject to illusion, it would follow that when he ceases to be an agent * the sruti (which treats of works) would prove false.

(*Answer*) :—No ; for, sruti is still true in the matter of Brahma-vidya.

(*Objection*) :—If the sruti which treats of works should

* *i.e.*, on the cessation of avidya.—A.

be no authority, the *sruti* which teaches Brahmavidya, too, can be no authority.

(*Answer*) :—Not so; for, there can arise no notion that can remove (Brahmavidya).—The notion that the Self is identical with the aggregate of the body, etc., is removed when the true nature of the Self is known from the *sruti* which teaches Brahmavidya; but not so can this knowledge of the true Self be ever removed in any way by anything whatsoever; for, knowledge of the Self is necessarily associated with its result (*i.e.*, the absence of avidya) like the knowledge that fire is hot and luminous.

Our theory, mareover, does not drive us to the conclusion that the *sruti* teaching works proves useless; for by restraining the first natural activities one by one and thereby gradually inducing fresh and higher activities, it serves to create an aspiration to reach the Innermost Self. Though the means is *mithya* or illusory, still it is true, because the end is true, as in the case of the *arthavadas* or explanatory statements subsidiary to a main injunction. And even in ordinary affairs, when we have to induce a child or a lunatic to drink milk or the like, we have to tell him that thereby his hair will grow, and so on,—Or, we may even argue that the *sruti* treating of works is an authority in itself * under other circumstances (*i.e.*, before the attainment of Self-knowledge), just as *pratyaksha* or sense-perception caused by attachment to the body is held to be authoritative prior to (the attainment of) Self-knowledge.

Refutation of the theory of the Self's agency by mere presence.

Another theory runs as follows :—Though not directly engaged in action, the Self does act by mere presence. This by itself constitutes the real agency of the Self. A king, for

* *Sakhat*, directly, *i.e.*, indipendently of Brahmavidya.—A,

instance, though himself not acting, is said to fight when his soldiers fight, in virtue of his mere presence, and he is said to be victorious or defeated. Similarly the commander of an army acts by mere word. And we find that the king and the commander are connected with the results of the act. To take another example: the acts of the *ritviks* or officiating priests are supposed to belong to the *yajamana* or sacrificer. So the acts of the body, etc., we may hold, are done by the Self, inasmuch as their results accrue *to* the Self. To take yet another example: since the loadstone or magnet makes a piece of iron revolve, real agency may rest with what is not actually engaged in an act. And so also in the case of the Self.

(*We reply*):—It is not right to say so; for it would be tantamount to saying that that which does not act is a *karaka* or an agent.

(*The opponent says*):—Yes, *karaka* or agency may be of various kinds.

(*We reply*):—No; for we find that the king, etc., (as instanced above) are direct agents also. In the first place, the king may be personally engaged in fighting. He is a direct agent as causing others to fight, as paying them wages, and also as reaping the fruits accruing from success and defeat. The sacrificer, too, is a real agent as offering the main oblation and as giving presents Wherefore, we should understand that to speak, by courtesy, of a man as an agent when he is not actually engaged, amounts to a figure of speech. If real agency, which consists in one being actually engaged in the act, were not found in the case of such agents as the king and the sacrificer, then we might suppose that even agency by mere presence constitutes real agency, as in the case of a magnet causing a piece of iron to revolve. On the contrary, we do find the king and the sacrificer actually engaged in some acts. Wherefore agency by mere presence is merely a gau*n*a or figurative agency. Such being the case, even the connection with results can only be gauna or unreal. By a gau*n*a or figurative agent no real action is performed. Therefore it is quite unreasonable to say that the activity of the body, etc., makes the actionless Self a real doer and enjoyer.

The theory of Avidya concluded.

But all this becomes explicable when traced to illusion as its case, as in the case of dreams and the juggler's art (maya). And no agency or enjoyership or any other evil of the sort is experienced in sleep, samadhi and similar states in which there is a break in the continuity of the illusory notions identifying the Self with the body, etc. Wherefore the illusion of sa*m*sara is due solely to an illusory notion and is not absolutely real.

Therefore we conclude that Right Knowledge conduces to absolute cessation of sa*m*sara.

Qualification for instruction in the Gita Doctrine.

Having concluded the whole doctrine of the Gita-*s*astra in this discourse, and having also briefly and conclusively started the doctrine especially here at the end to impress it the more firmly, the Lord proceeds now to state the rule as to the handing down of the instruction.

इदं ते नातपस्काय नाभक्ताय कदाचन ।
न चाशुश्रूषवे वाच्यं न च मां योऽभ्यसूयति ॥ ६७ ॥

67. This (which has been taught) to thee is never to be taught to one who is devoid of austerities, nor to one who is not devoted, nor to one who does not do service, nor to one who speaks ill of Me.

* "Susrushu" *literally* means one who desires to hear.

This *sastra* has been taught to you by Me for your good, for the destruction of *samsara*. *Not devoted:* without devotion to the Guru and to the Deva. *Never:* under no circumstances whatever. It should not be declared to him who, devoted and full of austerities as he may be, renders no service. *One speaks ill of Me:* he who looks upon Me, Vasudeva, as an ordinary man, and who in his ignorance declares Me guilty of self-adulation and does not like to be told that I am the Isvara. He, too, is not fit; and the *sastra* should not be taught to him. By implication we should understand that the *sastra* is to be taught to him who does not speak ill of the Lord, who is a man of austerities, who is devoted, and who renders service. Now as it has been elsewhere said that it should be taught "either to a man of austerities, or to an intelligent man," it should be declared to a man of austerities who is devoted and renders service, or to an intelligent man possessed of the two attributes; it should not be taught to a man of austerities or to an intelligent man if he is not devoted and does not render service. It should not be taught to him who is jealous of the Lord, though he may be possessed of all attributes. It should be thought to one who is devoted and renders service to the Guru. This is the rule as to how the *sastra* should be handed down.

The merit of teaching the Doctrine.

Now the Lord proceeds to state what fruits will accrue to him who hands down the instruction:

य इदं परमं गुह्यं मद्भक्तेष्वभिधास्यति ।
भक्तिं मयि परां कृत्वा मामेवैष्यत्यसंशयम् ॥ ६८ ॥

68 He who with supreme devotion to Me will teach this Supreme Secret to My devotees, shall doubtless come to Me.

This Supreme Secret: the Secret Doctrine taught above in the form of a dialogue between Kesava and Arjuna. It is Supreme because it conduces to the Highest Bliss. *Teach:* establish by teaching both the text itself and the doctrine, as I have established it by teaching it too thee. By repetition of 'devotion' here it is meant that by devotion alone one becomes worthy of being taught the sastra.—How should he teach it?—I in the faith that he is thus doing service to the Eternal Lord, to the Parama-Guru, the Supreme Teacher. As the fruit of this act, such a teacher will go to the Lord, he will be liberated.

न च तस्मान्मनुष्येषु कश्चिन्मे प्रियकृत्तमः ।
भविता न च मे तस्मादन्यः प्रियतरो भुवि ॥ ६९ ॥

69. Nor is there any among men who does dearer service to Me than he; nor shall there be another on earth dearer to Me than he.

Nor, etc: There is none in the present generation. *He:* the man who hands down the sastra. *Shall be:* in future time. *On earth:* in the world.

अध्येष्यते च य इमं धर्म्यं संवादमावयोः ।
ज्ञानयज्ञेन तेनाहमिष्टः स्यामिति मे मतिः ॥ ७० ॥

70. And he who will study this sacred dialogue of ours, by him I shall have been worshipped by the sacrifice of wisdom, I deem.

Dialogue: this work which is in the form of a dialogue. Of the four kinds of sacrifice such as *vidhi* or ritual, *japa* or a loud prayer, *upamsu* or a prayer uttered in a low voice, *manasa* or a prayer offered with the mind, the *jnana-yajna* or wisdom-sacrifice comes under the head of *manasa* and is therefore the highest. Thus the Gita-sastra is extolled as a jnana-yajna.

Or, we may regard this passage as revealing what the real effect (of the act enjoined here) is, *viz.*, that the act will produce an effect equal to that of wisdom-sacrifice, of the contemplation of a Devata or the like.

The merit of hearing the Doctrine.

The benefit accruing to the hearer is stated as follows:

श्रद्धावाननसूयश्च शृणुयादपि यो नरः ।
सोऽपि मुक्तः शुभाँल्लोकान्प्राप्नुयात्पुण्यकर्मणाम् ॥ ७१ ॥

71. And the man also who hears, full of faith and free from malice even he, liberated, shall attain to the happy worlds of the righteous.

Even he: much more so he who understands the doctrine. *Liberated*: from sin. *The righteous*: those who have performed Agnihotra or such other sacrifices.

The Lord assured by Arjuna of his grasp of the Teaching.

The Lord now asks with a desire to know whether the pupil has understood or not the teaching of the sastra, the object of the question being that He might make the pupil understand the teaching by some other means, if the latter be found to have not understood it. And this is to show that it is the duty of the teacher to try again to make the pupil understand the teaching and enable him to attain his object,

कच्चिदेतच्छ्रुतं पार्थ त्वयैकाग्रेण चेतसा ।
कच्चिदज्ञानसम्मोहः प्रणष्टस्ते धनञ्जय ॥ ७२ ॥

72. Has it been heard by thee, O Partha, with an attentive mind? Has the delusion of ignorance been destroyed, O Dhananjaya?

It : what I have told thee. *Heard* : have you heard it without distraction and understood ? *Delusion of ignorance* : that absence of discrimination which is caused by ignorance and which is natural. Has your delusion been destroyed ? Its destruction is the object of all this exertion on your part to hear the *s*astra and of the exertion on my part as the teacher.

अर्जुन उवाच—

नष्टो मोहः स्मृतिर्लब्धा त्वत्प्रसादान्मयाऽच्युत ।
स्थितोऽस्मि गतसन्देहः करिष्ये वचनं तव ॥ ७३ ॥

Arjuna said :

73. Destroyed is delusion, and I have gained recognition through Thy Grace, O Achyuta. I am firm, with doubts gone. I will do Thy word.

Delusion : born of ajnana or ignorance, the cause of the whole evil of sa*m*sara, hard to cross like the ocean, *I* ; who have sought Thy Grace. *Recognition* : of the true nature of the Self. When this recognition is obtained, then will all the ties of the heart be loosened.—This questioning and answering about the destruction of delusion shows conclusively, what the purpose of the knowledge of the teaching of the whole Sastra is, namely, the destruction of delusion and the attainment of a recognition of the Self. So the *s*ruti (Chha. Up. 7-1-3, 26-2) begins with the words. " Not knowing the Self, I grieve " and then speaks of the loosening of all ties by means to Self-knowledge. There are also scriptural passages such as " The tie of the heart is broken " (Mu*n*d. Up. 2-2-8) and " To him who sees unity, what delusion is there, what grief ?" (Isa. Up. 7), *I am firm* : in Thy command. *Do thy word* : Arjuna means to say " Through Thy Grace I have achieved the end of life : I have naught to do."

Sanjaya extols the Lord and His teaching.

The teaching of the sastra is over. Now in order to connect it with the main narrative, Sanjaya goes on:

सञ्जय उवाच—

इत्यहं वासुदेवस्य पार्थस्य च महात्मनः ।
संवादमिममश्रौषमद्भुतं रोमहर्षणम् ॥ ७४ ॥

Sanjaya said:

74. Thus have I heard this wonderful dialogue between Vasudeva and the high-souled Partha, which makes the hair stand on end.

व्यासप्रसादाच्छ्रुतवानेतद् गुह्यमहं परम् ।
योगं योगेश्वरात्कृष्णात्साक्षात्कथयतः स्वयम् ॥ ७५ ॥

75. Through the grace of Vyasa have I heard this Supreme and most secret Yoga direct from Krishna, the Lord of Yoga, Himself declaring it.

Through the grace of Vyasa: by obtaining from him the *divya-chakshus* or divine vision. *Yoga*: this dialogue; the work is called Yoga because it leads to Yoga. Or, the word may mean Yoga itself. *Himself:* it is not through mere tradition that I have heard it.

राजन्संस्मृत्य संस्मृत्य संवादमिममद्भुतम् ।
केशवार्जुनयोः पुण्यं हृष्यामि च मुहुर्मुहुः ॥ ७६ ॥

76. O king, remembering every moment this wonderful and holy dialogue between Kesava and Arjuna, I rejoice again and again.

King: Dhritarashtra. *Holy:* as the mere hearing of it destroys sin.

तच्च संस्मृत्य संस्मृत्य रूपमत्यद्भुतं हरेः ।
विस्मयो मे महान् राजन् हृष्यामि च पुनः पुनः ॥ ७७ ॥

77. And remembering every moment the most wonderful Form of Hari, great is my wonder, O king; and I rejoice again and again.

Form: Visvarupa, the Universal Form.

Not to dilate much.

यत्र योगेश्वरः कृष्णो यत्र पार्थो धनुर्धरः ।
तत्र श्रीर्विजयो भूतिर्ध्रुवा नीतिर्मतिर्मम ॥ ७८ ॥

78. Wherever is Kṛishṇa, the Lord of Yoga, wherever is Arjuna, the archer, there fortune, victory, prosperity and polity are established, I deem.

Wherever: on that side on which. *The Lord of Yoga*: He is the Lord of Yogas, since the seed of all Yoga comes forth from Him. *Archer*: wielding the bow called the Gandiva. *There*: on the side of the Paṇḍavas. *Prosperity*: increase of fortune.

इति श्रीमद्भगवद्गीतासूपनिषत्सु ब्रह्मविद्यायां योगशास्त्रे
श्रीकृष्णार्जुनसंवादे मोक्षसन्यासयोगो नाम
अष्टादशोऽध्यायः ॥